edited by **KJELD ERIK BRØDSGAARD &**

ZHENG YONGNIAN

BRINGING
THE
PARTY
BACK IN

How China
is Governed

EAI
EAST ASIAN INSTITUTE
NATIONAL UNIVERSITY OF SINGAPORE

EASTERN UNIVERSITIES PRESS
by Marshall Cavendish

© 2004 Marshall Cavendish International
(Singapore) Private Limited

Published 2004 by Eastern Universities Press
An imprint of Marshall Cavendish International
(Singapore) Private Limited
A member of Times Publishing Limited

Times Centre, 1 New Industrial Road,
Singapore 536196
Tel:(65) 6213 9288
Fax: (65) 6284 9772
E-mail: mca@sg.marshallcavendish.com
Online Book Store:
http://www.timesacademic.com

ISBN: 981-210-252-3

A CIP catalogue record for this book is available
from the National Library Board (Singapore).

Printed by Times Graphics Pte Ltd, Singapore
on non-acidic paper

London • New York • Beijing • Shanghai
• Bangkok • Kuala Lumpur • Singapore

Contents

Acknowledgements

Earlier versions of Chapters 1, 3, 8, 9, 10 were published in *The Copenhagen Journal of Asian Studies*, 16 (2002); and Chapters 4, 5 in *The Copenhagen Journal of Asian Studies*, 17 (2003); Chapter 6 and 7 were originally published in *China: An International Journal*, 1:1 (2003) and 1:2 (2003) respectively. The editors are grateful to the two journals for their permission to publish these articles.

Introduction: Bringing the Party Back In

KJELD ERIK BRØDSGAARD AND ZHENG YONGNIAN

With its 66 million members, the Chinese Communist Party (CCP) is the largest ruling party in this world. Despite radical changes to other communist parties in other parts of the world, the CCP continues to dominate both China's domestic development and external affairs. The latest version of the Party Constitution states that the CCP is the vanguard of not only the working class, but also the Chinese people and the Chinese nation. For better or worse, the impact of any major changes over the CCP will go beyond China's national boundary. However, for two decades, the CCP has been marginalized in the field of China studies. The party is often deemed as obsolete, if not dead.

In this volume, we try to bring the CCP back in our understanding of China's development.[1] We attempt to place the party in the center of our analysis. The marginalization of the CCP in understanding China's development and governance is a reflection of general changes in western social sciences, especially in political science. It is worth discussing how paradigmatic shifts in social sciences have affected the field of China studies. While the CCP begins to engage in transition to maintain its dominant role in Chinese politics, it is also the time for us to "bring the party back in," – to paraphrase the famous "Bringing the State Back In" call by Evans, Rueschemeyer and Skocpol in their book on the role of the state almost two decades ago.[2]

THE PARTY IN CHINA STUDIES

Political parties, Montero and Gunther pointed out, "were among the first subjects of analysis at the very birth of modern political science."[3]

1

In the 1950s and 1960s, the political party was a major research subject in social sciences, especially in political science. An enormous amount of research work was generated on political parties in the West enabling an understanding of how political parties evolved in the process of political development and how they were linked to democratic practice. It is especially worthwhile to mention that in the 1960s, many scholars of comparative political development also studied political parties in developing countries.[4] These studies were also heavily influenced by the concepts developed out of the Western context, and scholars largely regarded the party as being responsive to various crises occurring in the processes of political development, such as legitimacy, integration, and participation. In other words, scholars treated political parties in the developing world in the same way as they did in the West. Nevertheless, attempts were also made to differentiate the parties in the West and those in the developing world and some scholars have tried to show how political parties in developing countries played a role unique from their counterparts in the West.[5] Scholars of political parties in the West often perceived them in terms of their representative functions. The situation was different among scholars on political parties in developing countries since they tended to focus more on their adaptive capabilities and their stabilizing rules. For example, Huntington placed political parties in the context of political stability. To a great degree, Huntington did not apply concepts originating from Western experience of political development to political parties in the developing world. Instead, he studied them as they actually behaved.[6]

Unfortunately, all these efforts did not lead to the formation of a theory capable of explaining political parties in developing countries like China. Most scholars still studied political parties in the developing world under the shadow of the concepts that originated from Western experience. Since they unduly searched for linkages between parties and democracy, they tended to regard the party as a means of political participation for social groups, and as a tool for the ruling groups to cope with rapidly expanding demands for mass political participation. In some sense, parties were nothing else but interest groups writ large. Parties, according to Sartori, "are the central intermediate and intermediary structure between society and government."[7]

Since the 1970s, studies of political parties have been marginalized. In the 1980s, an upsurge of interest in "the state" took place in comparative politics pushing research of the party and social movements out of the ruling paradigm. Dissatisfied with a society-centered approach, scholars such as Peter Evans and Theda Skocpol brought the state back into their research agendas.[8] The emphasis of the state-centered approach was on the state and its different components such as administration, bureaucracy and technocratic personnel. This is especially true in studies on East Asian development processes, where scholars such as Chalmers Johnson and Robert Wade were mostly interested in the emergence and functioning of the so-called "developmental state" based on an effective bureaucratic rule.[9] It is not difficult to find that in the state-oriented literature, the role of the party was neglected. Even when political parties were mentioned, their role was marginal and complementary.

Implicit in the state-centered approach was a notional separation between state and society. Though such a notional separation is theoretically useful, it raises as many questions as it answers. The state is autonomous from society and particular interests (including political parties) to a greater or lesser degree, and therefore is able to formulate and impose policies upon them. But how does this happen? What mechanisms are used to implement policies? On what basis are the policies formed, and by whom? And how does a state so separate, so autonomous, from society, obtain adequate information and get society to conform to its policies?

Such questions and reflections have led Migdal, Kohli and Shue to propose a "state-in-society" approach, which recognizes that states are embedded in societies and interact with them constantly in a process of mutual transformation.[10] They argued that state structures themselves are social organizations, which need to be disaggregated and analyzed at different levels.[11] By developing such an approach, these state-oriented scholars seem to be ready to recognize the role of the surrounding social structure and social forces in political development.[12] Nevertheless, the "state-in-society" approach so far has not brought political parties back in. A group of scholars recently noted, due to the shadow of interest group theories, "an emphasis on political parties is not uncontroversial in the study of contemporary democracies."[13] Although scholars have begun to realize that political parties matter in explaining democratic transition in the developing world and that they are major actors in shaping democratic politics, recent intellectual efforts still continue to study political parties in the narrow context of elections.[14] This intellectual bias is also prevalent in the study of post-communist party systems.[15]

To confound the bias, when globalization accelerated in recent decades, some scholars further shifted their foci from the state to NGOs and different forms of social forces as their basis of analysis. Others argued that global markets are reducing the powers and functions of the state.[16] For these scholars, the nation-state *per se*, in an age of globalization, is no longer important, let alone political parties. For many scholars, the decline of the study of political parties is natural since political parties are becoming increasingly irrelevant. Political Parties have failed to respond successfully to a series of challenges, and many of their functions can be now performed better by less formally organized social movements, by direct contact between politicians and citizens through the broadcast media or the Internet, or by innovations in direct democracy.[17]

Even though in recent years, a few scholars have "rediscovered" the role of political parties in maintaining a functioning democracy and in promoting democracy in the developing world,[18] the age of the centrality of political parties in political science has disappeared, and it will take considerable efforts to bring back political parties in political science research.

These paradigmatic shifts were also reflected in China studies. In the 1950s, 1960s and early 1970s, the CCP used to occupy the focal point of China studies. This was due to the fact that the CCP was the only actor in charge of nation-state building and socio-economic transformation at that time. The importance of the CCP was captured by American scholar Franz Schurmann. In his classic study of the CCP, Schurmann described the role of the CCP played as follows:

> Chinese Communism came to power and created the present People's Republic of China through revolutionary means...They have rebuilt a great country, disciplined its people, improved the conditions of life, and laid the foundations for growth...Communist China is like a vast building made of different kinds of brick and stone. However it was put together, it stands. What holds it together is ideology and organization.[19]

Schurmann's book reflected his belief in the central role of the CCP in building a new China. As mentioned, for more than two decades following the establishment of the People's Republic, the CCP was given tremendous space in Western scholarly works on China. Research themes included power struggles among top party leaders, party membership and organization, party cadres and bureaucracy, the penetration of party power into society and so on.[20] Indeed, during such a long period, to speak about the party was to speak about Chinese politics.

In the late 1970s and continuing into the 1980s, Western China studies shifted focus and new approaches to the study of Chinese politics emerged. Most of these stemmed from an interest in analyzing structural factors such as patterns of interest group politics or the role of bureaucratic agencies in the decision-making process. There were also a number of studies concerned with the implementation of state and government policies. A common denominator was an interest in state and bureaucracy and the factors influencing the formation and implementation of state policies. In this sense, there was a clear affinity to the state-dominated, preoccupation of the social science discipline.

Events surrounding and following the Tiananmen debacle in 1989 caused a redirection of the China field to focus on civil society, new social strata and groups and Chinese non-governmental developments. In short, Western research in the field of Chinese political and social developments directed its attention to the societal side of the state-society relationship, stimulating a plethora of studies on civil society and Chinese non-governmental developments.[21] This emphasis on society and social phenomena had the effect of pushing research of the state and party out of the ruling paradigm. Although it seems that the state as a focus of enquiry has been brought back in in recent years, the role of the party is still unduly neglected.[22]

Lack of attention to the role of the party seems to be related to the widespread belief that the Chinese Communist Party (CCP) is a thing of the past,[23] which has difficulties surviving in the modern globalized world. Adherents of this view point to the party's absence in the growing private sector. They argue that new social groups and strata have emerged with considerable economic power, which is bound to turn into political power, thereby challenging the dominant role of the party. They also argue that the young Chinese do not see party membership as a prerequisite to their career advancement, because the most interesting and well-paid jobs (in both the private and the joint venture sectors) are not dependent on party membership. A logical consequence of this line of thought is that the CCP is doomed and will ultimately suffer the same fate as the Soviet and East European Communist Parties and collapse, resulting in a new political order characterized by democratization and power-sharing among different social forces and groups.[24]

In contrast, we believe that although the reform and open-door policy have given rise to other political actors, the party remains the most important actor in Chinese politics. By bringing the party back in, we shall be able to show why and how the party should continue to be the focal point for our scholarly research.

SOCIO-ECONOMIC TRANSFORMATION AND PARTY GOVERNANCE

Like many other political parties in East Asia, the CCP has played an important role in promoting socio-economic transformation in post-Mao China. Among many questions related to the CCP, two stand out in our discussion on the party as a continuously important actor in governing China: How has the CCP survived and accommodated to rapid socio-economic transformation? How has it engaged in a transition in order to continue to lead China's socio-economic transformation? These are two questions that the chapters in this collection attempt to answer.

As discussed above, the CCP can be understood from two perspectives, i.e., ideology and organization. All authors in this collection have followed this tradition in their understanding of the CCP, its transition and the problems it has encountered in the process of that transition.

Ideology first. The post-Mao communist regime was characterized by pragmatism. Ideology was downplayed to carry out different socio-economic experiments. Ideological decline can be regarded as a necessary consequence of pragmatism. In his contribution, Børge Bakken discusses how the CCP has coped with ideological changes during the reform period. Bakken argues that the CCP once was based on an ideology that was fundamentally linked to social norms and values. But this is no longer the case. The original charisma of the party and its leaders seems to have gone in the direction predicted by Max Weber, that is, charisma cannot stand the test of everyday routines; it will eventually be rationalized and bureaucratized.

This theme of rationalization and bureaucratization is consistent with the technocratic argument presented by Brødsgaard and Zheng in later chapters. But it is important to note that in the West, rationalization and bureaucratization were often accompanied by democratization. This is not the case in China. While democratization did not take place, rationalization and bureaucratization often isolated the party from the masses, and thus rendered the legitimacy of the party problematic.

The party leadership has attempted different ways to justify its rule. One way is to justify its legitimacy externally, and another way is to do so internally. Externally, the party leadership has built a scenario of breakdown (e.g., the former Soviet Union and Eastern European countries) to justify its continuous rule. As Bakken points out, the party has utilized this breakdown scenario in its propaganda, trying to convince people that the CCP is China. Seen from this perspective, if the party collapses, the whole nation will surely disintegrate and break up. This warning has been one of the party's strongest arguments of legitimacy over the last decade and more.

Internally, the party has justified its legitimacy by adjusting itself to rapidly changing socio-economic conditions. The party has tried to reach out to the new social strata, allowing entry to those who become rich first, i.e., private entrepreneurs. Such efforts are embedded in the latest theory of "Three Representations" proposed by Jiang Zemin, the party general secretary from 1989 to 2002. The party leadership believes that constant change and renewal and pragmatic readjustments to the realities of a rapidly changing China will save the party and keep it in power.

But all these measures only work to a limited degree. With rapid modernization and industrialization, the Marxist paradigm continues to be relevant to China. Chinese workers still live in a condition of exploitation akin to those in England at the time of the Industrial Revolution. What the party leadership has done is to mix all kinds of ideological elements to serve different purposes, be it nationalism, socialism or capitalism. Bakken calls it a "heterogeneous mixture." As long as the party monopolizes the explanatory power of its mixed ideology, no one can cast serious doubts on it. Anyway, with the prevalence of materialism, no one takes ideology seriously in today's China.

Another important point in Bakken's paper is that rationalization and bureaucratization do not necessarily push China towards a reason-based political system. Bakken observes that with the decline of communist ideology, personal relations, or *guanxi*, between party leaders become even more important for the daily functioning of the organization. Ideology is often used to justify and glorify individual party leaders. For instance, the "Three Representations" theory aims to revitalize past charisma by elevating Jiang Zemin to a higher level in order to enter the hall of fame together with Mao and Deng.

While Bakken discusses the ideological side of the party, Brødsgaard deals with the other side of the party, i.e., organization. From the ideological side, the CCP has lost its uniqueness. As Bakken observed, in order to survive and stay relevant, the party seems to have embraced different sorts of ideological elements. Also, ideology now plays a less important role in governing the country. So, the question is how the CCP governs China. Brødsgaard points to the organization of the CCP, and argues that the party continues to play a dominant role in Chinese society and it is too early to pronounce it obsolete, if not dead.

Since party cadres constitute the core of the party's organizational machine, Brødsgaard attempts to understand how the Chinese political system works by looking at the composition and functioning of the cadre corps. Students of contemporary China have established the technocracy thesis for quite a while, but most scholars have looked at the issue in a narrow sense. Brødsgaard tries to redirect the technocracy thesis by placing it into broader social and political categories. The CCP has enhanced the cadre management system by introducing various modern forms of management. For example, political loyalty no longer is the most important credential for career mobility among Chinese cadres. For years, the party leadership has increasingly put emphasis on educational qualifications and occupational competence of cadres. The introduction of all these measures has transformed the Chinese state from a revolutionary one to a technocratic one.

But it is important to note that such a transformation has significance not only for China's governance, but also for students of contemporary China. By engaging in such a transformation, the CCP leadership aimed to build a more modern state to cope with a rapidly changing socio-economic environment. While the leadership is reluctant to initiate democratization, it is believed that a better governance system can be built through introducing changes to the cadre management system. Furthermore, the strengthening of the party's rule in China runs counter to the ruling paradigm in contemporary China studies. As discussed above, contemporary China studies through the 1990s have focused on the societal aspect of party/state-society relations, resulting in a plethora of studies on civil society, social organizations, private entrepreneurs and other forms of non-governmental development. By highlighting changes in the cadre management system and their relevance to China's socio-economic transformation, the author attempts to direct scholarly attention to the

Chinese Communist Party, the most important political organization in directing and managing China's rapid socio-economic transformation.

David Shambaugh discusses another important aspect of the CCP, i.e., the changing relationship between the party and the People's Liberation Army (PLA). The CCP is managing not only socio-economic transformation, but also its relationship with the military. Conventional scholarship argued that there exists an essential symbiosis between the army and the CCP. But Shambaugh finds that the issue is not so simple. He argues that while the PLA remains politically loyal to the CCP, there is evidence of important changes in the institutional relationship between the two institutions. The party-army relationship is no longer as intertwined and symbiotic as it has historically been; rather, there is evidence of a bifurcation between the two. The catalysts for this change have been the professionalization and relative de-politicization of the military, as well as the leadership transition in the CCP.

More importantly, Shambaugh introduces a third actor in the Chinese political system, namely the state, and its relationship with the army. One indicator of whether China is a modern state is whether PLA can transform itself from a party-army to a state army. When the party-army relationship is no longer symbiotic, the state has to come in to replace the party in commanding the army. Shambaugh observes that since the mid-1990s, a "subterranean struggle" over the jurisdictional control of the army has been played out between the army, party and government in China. While the army has sought greater autonomy from the party, the government has tried to increase its jurisdictional control over the army. Nevertheless, Shambaugh warns that an "essential symbiosis" between the ruling party and the army continues to exist. Indeed, before the party-state relationship is transformed, the PLA will continue to be a party-army rather than a national army.

The party-state relationship is the theme of the paper by Chao Chien-Min. Chao focuses on People's Congresses (PCs), which is theoretically the highest organ of state power. Previously, the PCs had been known for functioning as rubber-stamp institutions. By looking at changes over the PCs at different levels, one can see a changing relationship between the party and the state. While most studies of the PCs have focused on the national level, i.e., National People's Congress, Chao directs our attention to the PCs at local levels.

Chao first identifies major sources that have led to changes of the PCs. Economic reforms and urbanization caused major structural and institutional changes in the past two decades. The old system is not able to accommodate such drastic changes and a tremendous number of irregularities followed. In order to address the malfeasance, the CCP leadership decentralized a great amount of political power to local state organizations, and the PCs at local levels gained authority and space in leading political reforms. Furthermore, some internal changes in the PCs such as specialization and centralization of leadership have led to an augmentation of legislative oversight. Measures developed by the legislative institutions, such as *pingyi* (evaluation) and *zhifa jiancha* (inspection of implementation of laws), have enlivened a lethargic local political scene and given rise to the committee autonomy.

According to Chao, these political reforms have transformed local politics. Local political changes in turn pushed the CCP to change its power relations with the PCs, as Chao argues that the urgent need for institutional mechanisms to counter the vices associated with socialist market reform has prompted the Party to turn its attention to the PCs. As a result, a Leninist party-state system has been transformed into a new system in which the Party is allied simultaneously with the executive and the legislative branches. It is indeed a significant political change. Even though the party continues to stand above all state organizations, a preliminary and limited balance of power is now emerging in which the party is not totally immune. The newly accrued legislative powers have not only redefined the tenets of party leadership, but also rewritten its relations with the executive branch. Although power for vital decision-making is still in the hands of the party, changes over the PCs often force local party cadres and government officials to have second thoughts before straying too far from legal boundaries. In this sense, the PCs have been regarded as a rising third power center in China's political system. Such changes of the party-state relationship mean that the CCP has also made efforts to adjust its power relations with the state, especially with the PCs. While the party is still reluctant to give up power to the state, the party leadership has certainly attempted to search for a more effective governance structure to cope with socio-economic transformation.

The above four papers deal with overall institutional changes that are related to the CCP in the post-Mao era. Given its size and local diversity, many scholars have been suspicious whether one can understand China's political system by looking at what has happened at the national level. As an old Chinese saying "*Tian gao huangdi yuan*" (sky is high and the emperor is far away) indicates, policies made by the central government will not necessarily reach localities. In order to confirm our theme of party relevance, our next four papers discuss how the party has managed local affairs in the country.

In his contribution, Pierre Landry examines how the CCP maintains political control over municipal elites in the post-Deng era. Since the reform and open door policy, the center of gravity of the Chinese political economy has tilted towards cities. As Landry noted, cities now control a far greater share of the country's resources than at any point in the history of the PRC. Also important is that such a decentralization of economic resources has been accompanied by the decentralization of the personnel management system. So, the question is: Has the dual processes of economic and personnel management decentralization led to a decline of the CCP's capacity to enforce its key organizational norms at the city level?

To answer this question, Landry uses an ordered probit model of cadre promotion to examine the impact of the dual processes of economic and political decentralization, and finds that the CCP has retained its capacity to shape political outcomes at the city level, and its organizational system remains firmly in control of cadre careers, a conclusion that was also drawn by Brødsgaard in his contribution to this book.

Two other important findings by Landry are worth noting. First, party institutions so far have been powerful, but they are not necessarily efficient. According to Landry, the party has not been able to develop incentive mechanisms that reward officials who perform, and penalize those who do not. Without such mechanisms, the CCP will have difficulty in building an effective local governance system. As Landry points out, the CCP may want to govern effectively, but other political motivations - such as the need to distribute political rewards to a greater share of secondary officials - shape the political careers of local elites much more powerfully than the regime's stated goals of improving local governance. A second finding is even more interesting since it is unique to the CCP, as Landry suggests. Since the 1980s, the CCP has been proactive in rejuvenating the cadre corps, imposing strict retirement rules, and combating the entrenchment of local elites by keeping terms of office relatively short. Landry notices that such achievements are rare among communist systems, or even authoritarian ones. Such a proactive policy may help explain the durability of the Chinese political system.

Maria Edin, in her contribution, reaches a similar conclusion in her study of lower levels, i.e., county and township. She employs a local approach to see the transformation of the CCP. She notes that while the CCP has made efforts to restructure its governing institutions, the party is also reinventing itself during the same process. Looking at the issue, Edin focuses on the cadre responsibility system at the county and township levels. She finds that contrary to the conventional view that localism often prevails in terms of policy implementation, part of the radical reform proposals by the center in the 1980s have in fact been carried out at the local level.

Another important finding by Edin is that neither decentralization nor recentralization is a linear process. She points out that reforms which aim to change the way the state is functioning do not necessarily lead to a reduced state involvement as commonly assumed. The state is reasserting itself in a different manner that may result in a strengthening of the party-state. In post-Mao China, the nature of control has shifted from micro to macro-level: the state is no longer directly involved in implementation but instead prefers to provide strategic guidance. Since the early 1990s, there have been measures of political recentralization, aiming at strengthening the party. Meanwhile, the central government has also reclaimed macro economic control. But that does not necessarily mean the old style of centralization. Edin notes that the CCP is shifting the way it governs - withdrawing from some areas while reasserting itself in others. For instance, market forces have been used to make the old cadre management system more effective. The cadre responsibility system embodies both the retreat of the party-state in cadre management at one level and strengthening of party-state control at another.

While Edin deals with the CCP at the county and township level in rural areas, in their contribution, Kazuko Kojima and Ryosei Kokubun shift the focus to the role of the party in urban areas. Rural economic reforms led to the collapse of the old commune system, and thus pushed the CCP to reconstruct its rural governance. Village elections have been introduced since 1987, and villagers now can elect their own "governor," i.e., the village committee. A parallel development has occurred in urban areas. Market reforms and labor mobility have seriously undermined the *danwei* system. Instead, the role of the local residential community has been strengthened. In many cities, several Residents' Committees have been combined to form new *shequ* Residents' Committees, which often consist of an area (*shequ*) with 1,000-2,000 families. The party has realized the importance of strengthening its presence in these new local organizations in order to be able to counter 'unhealthy practices' at grassroots level, such as the Falun Gong, and it has attempted to organize the local party members under the local party organization.

However, the role of the CCP in "*shequ* construction" has not yet been defined. Kojima and Kokubun identify two mainstream views in China regarding the party's relationship with the *shequ*. One direction is to aim for coalescence with the *shequ* residents' committee, while the other is to differentiate the party from the *shequ* residents' committee. Kojima and Kokubun point out that this debate is actually similar to the debate on the separation of party and government that has repeatedly emerged in the political reform discourse. They also find that many CCP members have taken little interest in local community activities and as the *shequ* performs government activities, there is a widespread feeling that the party should not become too involved. In line with the general slogan of the separation of party and government, the view is that the party should just set the overall guidelines and function simply as the "directive core." Indeed, the separation is constantly taking place, and the *shequ* residents' committees and social associations are gradually losing their characteristics as the proxies of the government and strengthening their function as representatives of social forces.

Despite such a progress, the issue has not been settled. In rural villages, the CCP branch still exists along with the elected village committee, and power conflicts often take place between the village committee and the party branch. How the party branch will institutionalize its relationship with the village committee is still a question. Such a situation is also likely to appear in the urban *shequ*. As Kojima and Kokubun question: When the separation of party and government is accomplished, can the party really provide society with direction and guidance effectively? The party does not want to lose its power to the state and society, but it is searching for a more effective way to deal with state and society. Before the power relationship between the party, state and society can be rationally reconfigured, the party is unlikely to go away from the *shequ*.

Stig Thøgersen addresses the important issue concerning CCP's basis of legitimacy in the townships and villages. As mentioned in Bakken's paper, with the decline of the CCP's ideology, the party is searching for new sources to justify its legitimacy. At the national level, the party has appealed to nationalism, political stability and national unification for new sources of legitimacy. Such appeals might work for urban residents and intellectuals, but not every one. There is still a big question at the local level. As Thøgersen asks: How can the CCP legitimize its rule among farmers in inland areas with stagnating incomes and massive economic and social problems, and among the cadres who are confronted daily with their complaints and resistance? Obviously, nationalism plays a very limited role in party ideology and legitimacy in China's rural areas. So does national unification.

Based on his field study in Yunnan, Thøgersen attempts to answer this question. According to him, party legitimacy in rural areas can be defined in two ways. First, there is external legitimacy which relates to the viewpoint of the masses: why peasants should accept party rule when the party does not deliver the goods and only comes to them to collect taxes and check on population control program. A second aspect of legitimacy is internal to the party's own organization: how can basic level cadres in poor areas be given a sense of purpose and direction which will constrain their tendency towards corruption and abuse of power and make them work loyally for the party's agenda?

The CCP in rural areas is trying to redefine itself as an elite party whose cadres are better educated, more cultured and civilized, and have better organizational abilities than the rest of the rural population. The party initiative, i.e., Jiang's "Three Representations," is an attempt to redefine the CCP as an elite party. According to Thøgersen, top-level cadres in poor rural areas to a large extent share Jiang's vision of an elite party. Their claim to legitimacy is based on the perception that they represent a higher level of learning, information, and civilization than the population in the rural communities they rule. They also believe that the party they embody stands for modernity and progress and has the historical mission of leading the peasants to higher levels of economic development and social organization.

Nevertheless, as Thøgersen points out, these views are being seriously challenged by the peasants. How to justify its legitimacy at local levels continues to be an important agenda for the CCP leadership. We can add here the latest party initiative by the Hu Jintao-Wen Jiabao new leadership. Since it came into power in 2002, the new leadership has made efforts to shift the party's policy priority to lower classes such as workers and peasants. While the leadership continues to justify its legitimacy in rural areas, it also has realized that without delivering

14

economic benefits to these lower classes, the CCP's rule could be destabilized. Added to Thøgersen's argument, one can call it the materialist justification of the CCP legitimacy, i.e., legitimacy by delivering economic benefits.

The last two papers in this book deal with the relationship between the CCP and social classes. As discussed above, Thøgersen's paper has touched such a relationship, i.e., the party's relations with rural peasants, but Holbig's and Zheng's go one step further to discuss how the party copes with rising new social classes.

At the recently held 16th Party Congress, the "Three Representations" was written into the party constitution alongside "Marxism-Leninism, Mao Zedong Thought and Deng Xiaoping Theory," thereby giving the formal green light for admitting private entrepreneurs into the party. "Private entrepreneurs" or "private businessmen" were hitherto publicly barred from the Party. Traditionally, the CCP was supposed to represent the interests of only five major groups, i.e., workers, peasants, intellectuals, members of the PLA (People's Liberation Army), and government officials and cadres. The majority of the original rank and file of the Party was basically drawn from the "proletariat" background. The theory of the "Three Representations" justifies the existence not only of China's capitalist economy, but also party membership for capitalists.

The issue has been "hot" among intellectuals, business circles and policy makers, and many observers believe that it is a clear signal that the CCP was turning capitalist. But as Holbig points out, things become less clear when one looks not so much at ideologies but at actual facts. In her paper, Holbig makes an effort to collect and critically assess the information available on current developments of the private economy, and on the proportion of entrepreneurs who are already CCP members. Moreover, based on her analytical "deconstruction" of statistical data and categories, Holbig delineates motives and strategies that might lie behind the new policy of formally admitting private entrepreneurs into the party. She argues that one important reason could be that the CCP, by co-opting entrepreneurs, attempts to (re)gain access to the ever larger labor force employed in the growing non-public sector of the economy and thus strengthen its organizational presence at the grassroots level. In other words, admitting capitalists can be regarded as an important effort of the party leadership to rebuild the party in accordance with changing socio-economic conditions.

In his contribution, Zheng Yongnian addresses the issue of CCP transition. His main concern is whether the CCP will transform itself into a more democratic party by admitting capitalists into the party. Like Holbig, Zheng also recognizes that by admitting capitalists, the CCP was not to weaken, but to strengthen itself. Reform and development has bourgeoisified and benefited many party members and cadres. It has given rise to new social classes like private entrepreneurs. The party's decision is rational, since it is not going against the tide but is a recognition of reality. Apparently, to continue to grow and expand, the party must embrace the better educated and the most enterprising in society.

But will the capitalists within the party be catalysts to quicken the transformation of the party? This is not a simple issue. On the one hand, by admitting capitalists, the CCP has let in the Trojan horse. Capitalists will hopefully bring great dynamics into the party and push the party's transformation. This does not mean that the party will necessarily be able to represent the interests of different social classes, as indicated in the "Three Representations" theory. Zheng points out that China's political system does not have effective mechanisms for different social classes to articulate and aggregate their interests. Moreover, social interests are unequally represented in today's China. While rich social classes are more politically influential, workers and peasants do not have their own representatives in politics. If interest representation is to be materialized, democracy becomes important. Zheng argues that although the CCP has begun to consider the interests of newly rising classes and social groups, the primary aim is not to initiate a democratization process, but to bolster a one-party domination. But Zheng also cautiously suggests that by admitting capitalists, there is a possibility for the CCP to transform itself into a social democratic party in the long run. Capitalism and capitalists, by their nature, tend to be constructively destructive.

DEMOCRATIC TRANSITION?

In a recent article, Minxin Pei has argued that China is facing a crisis of governance. The country is ruled by a Leninist Party-state and therefore effective governance hinges on the strength of the Chinese Communist Party (CCP).[25] However, according to Minxin Pei, the power and strength of the CCP has declined in recent years. The decline of the CCP is evidenced in three areas: (1) the shrinkage of its organizational penetration; (2) the erosion of its authority; and (3) the breakdown of its internal discipline.

Minxin Pei is in fact only the latest in a long row of scholars and analysts who has maintained that the CCP is in serious decline and will wither away. David Shambaugh argues that one is likely to see a "slow, methodical and continued decay" of the CCP's capacity and legitimacy to rule.[26] Bruce Dickson also maintains that the party's authority and organization is experiencing steady decay and that two decades of reform have weakened its capacity to control the behaviour of not only the vast majority of Chinese, but also its own officials.[27]

As shown above, this volume is based on the premises that the party continues to play a dominant role in Chinese society and that rather than loosing its grip, the party has gradually strengthened its control over Chinese society in recent years. This is certainly the case in terms of personnel management, where the party's central organization department has taken back some of the powers it handed over to the personnel departments of the government in the late 1980s. The ideological campaign of the "Three Representations" also aims to strengthen the role of the party by co-opting important new social groups such as private businessmen. At the local level the party is also searching for more effective ways of governance. Other examples can be given. They all seem to show a slow but growing reassertion of party control. In sum, rather than "throwing in the towel", the party has reacted by attempting to streamline and bring to perfection its machine for governing an increasingly complex Chinese society

The views that the CCP is doomed and will eventually be abolished or wither away operate within the so-called transition paradigm which posits that once a country moves away from dictatorial rule, there is a linear process towards pluralism and democracy.

According to Thomas Carothers, five core assumptions define the transition paradigm. The first is that any country moving away from dictatorial rule is a country in transition towards democracy.[28] The second assumption is that the transition towards democracy (democratization) unfolds in a sequence of stages. First, there is the "opening", a period in which cracks appear in the ruling dictatorial regime, with the most prominent crack being a cleavage between hardliners and softliners. Second, there follows a "breakthrough" with the collapse of the regime and the emergence of a new democratic system and the establishment of new democratic institutional structures (e.g. a new constitution). Third comes "consolidation", a slow process of transforming democratic forms into democratic substance through elections, the reform of state institutions and the strengthening of civil society.[29]

The third assumption is a belief in the crucial importance of elections in the sense that elections will serve to broaden and deepen political participation. The fourth assumption is that basic and underlying conditions in the transitional countries – i.e. political traditions, institutional legacies, ethnic make-up, religious beliefs, and cultural background – will not be major factors in determining the outcome of the transition process. The fifth assumption is that democratic transitions are being built on coherent, functioning states whereby it is overlooked that often state-building is an integral part of the transition process.[30]

Carothers maintains that most transitional countries do not conform to these assumptions.[31] They instead enter a gray zone where they are neither clearly dictatorial nor clearly headed towards democracy. They get stuck in the transition process, so to speak. Two broad political syndromes seem to be common in the gray zone. The first is "feckless pluralism", where political participation extends little beyond voting and democracy remains shallow and shaky. The other is "dominant-power politics". In dominant-power countries, there is a blurring of the line between the state and the ruling party and the state's assets (jobs, public funding, information, coercive power, etc.) are at the service of the ruling party.[32]

On the surface, China fits the transition paradigm. There seems to have been cracks in the system and it is not difficult to discern hardliners and softliners in the political discourse as it unfolds in the state media and among intellectuals; direct elections for the position as village head have been instituted at the local level in the countryside etc..

To be sure, there have been political reform, but the process has not been linear, rather it has formed a zigzag pattern or a pattern of two steps forward and one step back. Moreover, China is clearly a country where a dominant party controls the state and its main assets. In sum, the Chinese experience actually challenges the transition paradigm in the sense that China seems to be fixed in a zone of dominant-power politics rather than in a continuous and linear process of democratization.

CONCLUSION

The strengthening of the party's role in China runs counter to the ruling paradigm in contemporary China studies, which through the 1990s, focused on the society aspect of party/state-society relations, resulting in a plethora of studies on civil society, social organizations, private entrepreneurs and other forms of non-governmental development. In fact, this focus on society and social movements was founded on the basic assumptions of the transition paradigm and therefore envisioned the decay and withering away of the party in a linear process of democratization.

This has clearly not happened. Instead of regime breakdown, we see regime resilience. The recent leadership change is a case in point. Here the regime carried out a peaceful and orderly transition to the fourth generation of leaders headed by Hu Jintao. Few authoritarian regimes have managed to conduct orderly and peaceful successions on schedule. Instead, the power transition has usually been a moment of crisis, involving factional strife and sometimes military intervention. That China was able to avoid such political turbulence is due to the fact that the major social and political force in Chinese society, the CCP, has been able to revitalize itself by reaching out to new social forces and by strengthening its organizational machine. It is high time to bring the party back in when conceptualizing the Chinese development process.

ENDNOTES

1   The papers in this volume are revised versions of papers presented at the conference "Bringing the Party Back In: How China is Governed," held in Copenhagen in June 2002 at the Asia Research Centre, Copenhagen Business School.

2   Peter B. Evans, Dietrich Rueschemeyer, and Theda Skocpol, *Bringing the State Back In* (Cambridge: Cambridge University Press, 1985).

3   Jose Ramon Montero and Richard Gunther, "Introduction: Reviewing and Reassessing Parties," in Richard Gunther, Jose Ramon Montero, and Juan J. Linz, eds., *Political Parties: Old Concepts and New Challenges* (New York: Oxford University Press, 2002), p. 2.

4   Joseph LaPalombara and Myron Weiner, eds., *Political Parties and Political Development* (Princeton, NJ: Princeton University Press, 1969).

5   Ibid.

6   Samuel P. Huntington, *Political Order in Changing Societies* (New Haven: Yale University Press, 1968), Chapter 7.

7   Giovanni Sartori, *Parties and Party System* (New York: Cambridge University Press, 1976), ix.

8   Together with Dietrich Rueschemeyer they published a by now classic work on the need to focus on the role of the state. See Evans, Rueschemeyer, and Skocpol, *Bringing the State Back In* .

9   Chalmers Johnson, *MITI and the Japanese Miracle: The Growth of Industrial Policy, 1925-75* (Stanford: Stanford University Press, 1982); Robert Wade, *Governing the Market: Economic Theory and the Role of the Government in East Asian Industrialization* (Princeton, NJ: Princeton University Press, 1990).

10   Joel S. Migdal, Atul Kohli and Vivienne Shue, eds., *State Power and Social Forces: Domination and Transformation in the Third World* (New York: Cambridge University Press, 1994). See also Joel S. Migdal, *State in Society: Studying How States and Societies Transform and Constitute One Another* (New York: Cambridge University Press, 2001).

11   Ibid.

12   Peter Evans, for example, has advanced the notion of "embedded autonomy" to describe that the effectiveness of the bureaucracy is dependent on the state's linkages and interaction with society. See Peter Evans, *Embedded Autonomy: States and Industrial Transformation* (Princeton, NJ: Princeton University Press, 1995)

13   Herbert Kitschelt, Denka Mansfeldova, Radoslaw Markowski and Gabor Toka, *Post-Communist Party Systems: Competition, Representation, and Inter-Party Cooperation* (New York: Cambridge University Press, 1999), p. 5.

14   Scott Mainwaring and Timothy R. Scully, eds., *Building Democratic Institutions: Party Systems in Latin America* (Stanford, CA: Stanford University Press, 1995).

15   Herbert Kitschelt, Denka Mansfeldova, Radoslaw Markowski and Gabor Toka, *Post-Communist Party Systems: Competition, Representation, and Inter-Party Cooperation* (New York: Cambridge University Press, 1999).

16   Susan Strange, *The Retreat of the State: The Diffusion of Power in the World Economy* (Cambridge: Cambridge University Press, 1996).

17   For this point, see, Montero and Gunther, "Introduction: Reviewing and Reassessing Parties," p. 1.

18   For example, Richard Gunther, Jose Ramon Montero, and Juan J. Linz, eds., *Political Parties: Old Concepts and New Challenges* (New York: Oxford University Press, 2002); Larry Diamond and Richard Gunther, eds., *Political Parties and Democracy* (Baltimore and London: The Johns Hopkins University Press, 2001).

19   Franz Schurmann, *Ideology and Organization in Communist China* (Berkeley, CA: University of California Press, 1968). The book remains one of the best works on the organization and ideology of the CCP.

20   Important works include John Lewis, *Leadership in Communist China* (Ithaca: Cornell University Press, 1963); A. Doak Barnett, *Cadres, Bureaucracy, and Political Power in Communist China* (New York: Columbia University Press, 1987); A. Doak Barnett (ed.), *Chinese Communist Politics in Action* (Seattle: University of Washington Press, 1969); Jacques Guillermaz, *The Chinese Communist Party in Power, 1949-76* (Boulder, CO: Westview Press, 1976).

21   See, for example, He Baogang, *The Democratization of China* (New York: Routledge, 1996); Brian Hook (ed.), *The Individual and the State in China* (Oxford: Clarendon Press, 1996); Tony Saich, 'Negotiating the State: The Development of Social Organizations in China,' *The China Quarterly*, no. 161 (March 2000), pp. 124-41; and Gordon White, et al., *In Search of Civil Society: Market Reform and Social Change in Contemporary China* (Oxford: Clarendon Press, 1996).

22   See, for example, Kjeld Erik Brødsgaard and Susan Young (eds.), *State Capacity in East Asia: Japan, Taiwan, China and Vietnam* (Oxford: Oxford University Press, 2000); Yongnian Zheng, *Globalization and State Transformation in China* (Cambridge: Cambridge University Press, 2004).

23   There are of course a few exceptions such as Shiping Zheng, *Party vs. State in Post-1949 China: the Institutional Dilemma* (New York: Cambridge University Press, 1997); and Bruce J. Dickson, *Red Capitalists in China: the Party, Private Entrepreneurs, and Prospects for Political Change* (New York: Cambridge University Press, 2003).

24   See Minxin Pei, "China's Governance Crisis," *China Review*, Autumn-Winter 2002", pp. 7-10. On the withering away or decaying of the CCP, see also David Shambaugh, "The Chinese Leadership: Cracks in the Façade?, in David Shambaugh (ed.), *Is China Unstable? Assessing the Factors* (Armonk, NY: M.E. Sharpe, 2000), pp. 26-39 and Bruce Dickson, "Political Instability at the Middle and Lower Levels: Signs of Decaying CCP, Corruption, and Political Dissent," in ibid., pp. 41-56.

25   See Minxin Pei, "China's Governance Crisis."

26   David Shambaugh, "The Chinese Leadership: Cracks in the Façade?, in David Shambaugh (ed.), *Is China Unstable? Assessing the Factors* (Armonk, NY: M.E. Sharpe, 2000), pp. 26-39 at p. 36.

27   Bruce Dickson, "Political Instability at the Middle and Lower Levels: Signs of Decaying CCP, Corruption, and Political Dissent," in ibid., pp. 41-56.

28   See Thomas Carothers, "The End of the Transition Paradigm," *Journal of Democracy*, Vol. 13, No. 1 (January 2002), pp. 5-21. This section is based on Kjeld Erik Brødsgaard "Party Rule in China: Some Empirical Evidence and Theoretical Inferences," Paper presented at the 6th Biennial Nordic Conference of Chinese Studies (NACS), June 17-19, 2003, Oslo.

29   Carothers criticism of "transitology" is primarily directed at O'Donnell and Schmitters seminal work on democratic transitions, especially their *Transitions from Authoritarian Rule: Tentative Conclusions About Uncertain Democracies* (Baltimore: Johns Hopkins University, 1986). Other works within the transition paradigm includes Samuel P. Huntington, *The Third Wave: Democratization in Late Twentieth Century* (Norman: University of Oklahoma Press, 1991); and Larry Diamond, Marc F. Plattner, Yun-han Chu and Hung-mao Tien (eds), *Consolidating the Third Wave Democracies* (Baltimore: The John Hopkins Press, 1997).

30   Carothers, "The End of the Transition Paradigm," pp. 6-9.

31   Ibid., p. 12.

CHAPTER 1

Norms, Values and Cynical Games with Party Ideology

BØRGE BAKKEN

LOSING THE MANDATE OF HISTORY

It has been argued that the 'mandate of Heaven' that represented legitimacy for the imperial dynasties was superseded by the Chinese Communist Party's 'mandate of history.' It is further posited that the CCP is vulnerable in the event that popular perception should deem that they have lost this authority.[1] This chapter will look at the ideology of the party, and raise the question whether the CCP is about to lose its mandate. It is possible that a bureaucratized party founded on an ideology that lacks any firm linkage to social norms and values, and divorced from any social movement, could be moving towards breakdown. The party is trying to renew and modernize itself, seeking new social moorings and support. It might succeed in reconstructing its 'mandate of history,' but there is a clear danger that it might lose its grip on the hearts and minds of the people.

Ideology is to a great extent linked to the image-making capacity of a power structure; indeed, it is a means of defending the prestige structure of a regime. Such a prestige structure depends on the creation and maintenance of an image that will inspire the admiration, fear, hopes and fortunes of its adherents. People must feel that the organization or party that carries this mandate is necessary for their own lives and fortunes. As pointed out by Mark Elvin: 'Once the image begins to suffer damage, little will happen for a while, but then a process of negative feedback develops, leading to a startlingly sudden collapse.'[2] The rituals of ideology gain in significance when viewed from this perspective. They bolster the facade of the party, and this is the key to its success and survival, and its capacity to stay in power. However, there are both ideological and structural processes that have the potential to erode the power of the party. Subversive elements might threaten the party from the outside, but there is also a structural threat which comes from within.

The generation that grew up with the Chinese Communist Party, those who were young and malleable in the 1950s and 1960s, were fired by a communist ideology that enjoyed a moral power in some ways similar to that of the great religions of Christianity, Islam or Buddhism. We should bear this in mind when we examine the state of ideology and the much commented upon moral decline in contemporary China. I shall argue that the power of ideology is to a great extent, although not exclusively, built on moral beliefs, social norms and values, and that its effectiveness is linked to the ethos of the society in which it operates. Consequently, when the social fabric starts to erode, so too does the power of ideology. I shall argue that the party's links to social norms and values have fractured in two crucial places. First, in terms of its being anchored to general social norms and values, unconnected with any social movement as such. Second, it is broken in terms of what Weber called charisma. The party, or its representation through the Ultimate Leader, has been emptied of heroic charisma. What Mao Zedong had in abundance, and Deng Xiaoping had to a lesser extent, does not apply to a Jiang Zemin. Jiang's popular nickname, Qiang Toucao, is a reference to the grass blowing in the wind, connoting opportunism and unprincipled pragmatism or bureaucratism. Jiang does not possess the charisma won through armed struggle in war and revolution, nor is his name linked to the grand narratives of heroism in any way. Both these 'broken links' point in the direction of a waning normative power. Ideology has lost its social and charismatic moorings.

I have elsewhere written on the uses of the norm as the basic element of a control system, pointing out the recurring patterns of Chinese 'exemplary norms' of Confucian as well as communist heroism and self-sacrifice.[3] These have always been ideal norms orchestrated from above and used for ideological purposes. However, despite the many examples of resistance against such 'exemplary norms,' the ethos of collectivism and the hopes of communism did find support and resonance among the general public to a much greater degree during earlier periods in the history of the People's Republic of China. It is hardly a controversial standpoint to claim that we have seen an erosion of this ethos during the reforms.

In the latest important ideological campaign (the 'Three Representations' [*san ge daibiao*]) leading up to the 16ᵗʰ Party Congress, Jiang Zemin addressed the role of the Chinese Communist Party, stating that: 'It is essential to have the strong leadership of the Communist Party of China. Otherwise, the country will fall into disunity and break up.'[4] I have gone back to Franz Schurmann's now classical *Ideology and Organization in Communist China* to see whether his description can give us clues about the present state of the party, and its future direction. Schurmann questions whether the complex structures of organization in a socialist society could continue to function without the Communist Party:

> [I]s the Communist party the keystone to the whole structure, so that its disappearance would mean the collapse of the structure? The weight of evidence, in my opinion, is that it is so; given Communist-type organization of state power, a Communist party would have to be created if it did not exist.[5]

It is the scenario of breakdown which haunts as well as legitimizes the leadership of the CCP. The party has utilized this breakdown scenario in their propaganda, trying to convince people that the CCP *is* China. From this perspective, if the party collapses, the whole nation will surely disintegrate and break up. This warning, together with the frequent references to the disintegration of the Soviet Union, has clearly been one of the party's strongest arguments of legitimacy over the last decade and more. The regime is constantly reminded of the possible breakdown in everything from the nation's own dynastic history to the more recent events of Cultural Revolution, via the breakdown of the Soviet Union, to their own experiences of mounting social unrest and disorder.

Li Tieying, Politburo member and leader of the Chinese Academy of Social Sciences (CASS), addresses the question by describing the disintegration and final breakdown of the Soviet Union as the 'most painful lesson of socialism' ever, and urges the party to avoid such an experience in China. Li sees a need to prepare and renew the party for the road ahead and the dangers to come, and advocates purely pragmatic 'constant change and renewal' as the way out for the party.[6] Li Tieying's position recognizes that the charisma of the Great Leader is gone, and that ideology is the medium through which a routinized party can regain unity and achieve renewal.

This utilitarian scenario claims that 'constant change and renewal' and pragmatic readjustments to the realities of a rapidly changing China will save the party and keep it in power. In this sense, reaching out to new groups becomes a rational way forward for the party. Ideology may have been downplayed since the time of the great campaigns, but it has not lost its validity as a unifying and renewing force. Ideology is played out, however, against the backdrop of an alternative breakdown scenario. In such a development, the very processes and techniques implemented to uphold power will instead contribute to its demise, paradoxically leaving the party 'like the sorcerer, who is no longer able to control the powers of the nether world whom it has called up by its spells.'[7]

Schurmann defined ideology not as a thinking characteristic of a class or individual, but as a manner of thinking characteristic of an organization.[8] As we shall see, the definition fits well with the present situation, and we therefore need to look at the party's organizational rationality and techniques of management. The transforming effect of ideology is an important issue. Any party or organization must eventually face the moment of routinization, Schurmann argued, pointing out that communist parties had always resisted routinization; 'sometimes by purges, more often by renewed outbursts of ideological activity.' This is the case, he claimed, both with younger revolutionary parties as well as the more bureaucratized ones: '[I]deology remains a latent instrument which can be reactivated if the leaders and the external situation call for it.'[9] In other words, ideology does have the rational function of renewal, and in addition, a potential unifying function countering the dangers of growing routinization and stagnation. Ideological change stands out as the preferred solution if we think of the alternative massive purges that plagued the party for so many years. They may have renewed the party, but in the end wore out both the organization and the people. The purges made people cynical and destabilized China as a result.

Cynicism is, however, an aspect of ideology too, and this fact should not be overlooked. Schurmann maintained that legitimacy flows from the leadership's ability to link decisions to the broad and accepted values and norms in society at large. In organizations based on powerful values and norms, consciousness is important. Values can only be held consciously, and norms can only be acted on, if people understand them, Schurmann contends.[10] Consequently he warns that: 'Cynical playing with ideology has often had disastrous results for those who saw it simply as a useful tool.'[11] We shall argue that such cynicism originates in the lack of social moorings of the new ideology and in the manipulation of social norms and values that follows. While reaching out to new elites, the party keeps its original legitimizing norm of being the 'vanguard of the working class.' One important aspect of the current ideological campaigns, however, is that they are linked to norms of an order other than the social - these can be termed *exemplary* norms. Such exemplary norms may prove to be a rather unstable substitute for the real thing. We shall later look more closely at how ideology is reactivated - and how it could possibly backfire - through the campaign of the 'Three Representations.'

PARTY IDEOLOGY, EXEMPLARITY AND THE SOCIAL NORM

One need not look for an internally consistent ideology in post-Mao China, because the socialist rhetoric is no longer promulgated as a credible ideology. The principal tenet is rather to uphold the party's prestige structure. While the party is reaching out to include new economic elites, it still utilizes its former social values of serving the people. According to the latest definitions of ideological correctness, the party represents 'the people's democratic dictatorship' (*renmin minzhu zhuanzheng*) led by the working class and based on the worker-peasant alliance.[12]

The party is fast developing into a self-proclaimed national and socialist party, with an emphasis on the 'national,' but a strengthening in the rhetoric of the 'socialist' element. Ideology has increasingly become a heterogeneous mixture of nationalist, socialist and capitalist strands, played to the tune of outworn socialist soundbites. The focus is not on internalizing specific social norms and values, but more about defining a set of 'standards' of correct behaviour, or rather, correct ways of defining the world. One observer has seen in this development a transformation of the party 'from a principle-oriented party to a utilitarian party' and goes on to define it as a corporate party.[13] While this may be an oversimplification (the party was always pragmatic and utilitarian), it does say something about the relative strength of its approaches. Perhaps one could argue that the cloak of ideology is threadbare and that the utilitarian undergarments are becoming more and more visible. At least the idea of a corporate party or a managerial party serves as a good description of the present situation.

The party has realized it must change, but is unwilling to let go of some of its socialist verbal baggage. There is a striking contrast between the realities of reform and the continuing invocation of communist ideals. Maintaining control and upholding power have always been important aspects of the ideology, but ideological campaigns now seem to be played out without striking any deeper resonance with the basic norms and values of society. Maoism became increasingly ritualized after the Cultural Revolution, and people, as well as the state and party bureaucracy, increasingly came to doubt official ideology. The political demobilization experienced after the Cultural Revolution may have effectively curtailed the penetration of ideology into the everyday lives of the people, but it could not stop the general disillusionment about the party ideology as such. People are now merely going through the movements, and for the party it has been particularly important to control those movements.

The party battle cry to 'become rich first' was crucial in kick-starting the economic reforms, but at the same time increased the opportunity for corrupt operations. Cynicism about ideology and increased opportunities for private enrichment gradually enhanced private rationalities both within and outside the party. The game of ideology led to a 'moral order' full of disillusion and simulation. Possessing the correct definitions of the present order seems to be the stuff of which power and careers are made. Few Chinese sincerely believe they are developing a socialist society fundamentally different from and superior to capitalism. For the party and its ideology, it is just a matter of defining any development as a renewed and advanced form of socialism. At the same time, the party still bases its legitimacy and power on its traditionalist communist identity. Consequently, to 'let someone get rich first' must be defined as a valuable contribution to socialist collectivism and solidarity, while the market has to be redefined as a socialist invention of 'market socialism,' and the good capitalist must become a 'model worker.' According to official Chinese propaganda, it is 'spiritual civilization' that makes the system different from and superior to the capitalist West. This is in reality not so much about moral superiority as it is about the ways to uphold social order. Legitimacy flows from the dual ability of the regime to uphold order and sustain growth.

The present ideology is full of nationalist hints about the advanced state of Chinese history and culture. Socialist rhetoric and exemplary models are formed into new legitimizing narratives of growth and order to defend the fading grand narratives of a once orderly socialist past. In both the memories of past greatness and the dreams of greatness to come, there are integrative elements - and in both there are dangers. According to official Chinese thinking, the best way to cope with such danger lies in the 'exemplary norm.'

It is one of the fundamental assumptions in the Chinese theory of learning that people are innately capable of learning from models. In addition, rule by morality was more widespread in traditional China than rule by law. Chinese society is undoubtedly a disciplinary society in many senses, but it is also an educative society. A combination of the disciplinary and the educational constitutes what could be termed an 'exemplary society.'[14] A discipline based on social norms and values is more durable than one based on outer force only, because it seeks to bind people to society with their own ideas. This is also reflected in the power of the party. It remains strong only as long as its *élan vital* derives from the values of the grassroots of society. It is linked to power in a way less likely to manifest force or violence. Regulation through the norm is based more on willed consent, and functions as a positive restraint. One should not forget that the Communist Party was once based on strong mass movements and popular support, and that its initial success originated from such social moorings. When ideology and the social norms are closely linked, one may refer to ideology as something one *is*, in the sense of being part of one's identity. This is a rare phenomenon, perhaps one resembling religion. More generally, ideology would normally be defined as something one *has* or as something one *uses*.

When the norm is not allowed to fluctuate naturally like a social norm, or when a norm prescribed from above no longer has a basis in social practice, then it turns into an exemplary or 'super-social norm.' This norm is prescribed from above and, in the case of today's China, it merely represents the party's power to define reality. The party no longer represents the social norm, but defines and stands above the norms of society. The enforced exemplary norm might be crucial in upholding order and maintaining the rule of the party for a shorter or longer period. At the same time, the inflexibility and the lack of social moorings represented by the 'super-social' norm can lead to a general erosion of order. In terms of the party's power, we might talk of an *eggshell theory*. On the outside the egg looks nice and fresh, but inside it could be rotten. The shell becomes more and more brittle, but this may be hard to detect on the surface. Change may come suddenly and dramatically. Indeed, as soon as the eggshell cracks, the party Humpty-Dumpty will be impossible to put together again because there is no longer a cohesive social normative basis, nor an economic incentive for upholding its leadership.

Of course, the party's power is not solely predicated on the normative social fundamentals of that organization. The party apparatus has a string of organizational and structural power bases that allow it to stay in power and uphold order by coercive means for a long period without recourse to any normative mass base. The point here, however, is to focus on the importance of such a base, and show how the lack of social moorings could weaken and challenge the entire organizational structure. Like Schurmann, I want to stress this fundamental social aspect of party power without harbouring any illusions that there exists a one-to-one relationship between this base and the actual power of the party.

COUNTERING THE BUREAUCRATIZATION OF CHARISMA

The exemplary norm is about guaranteeing order and stability in a society through the prediction of people's behaviour. The quest for order and predictability is the very core of the 'spiritual civilization' presented in party propaganda. The ideological campaign is about how to bind people to new definitions of exemplary norms. These definitions represent a means to counter the effects of bureaucratization as well as oiling the rusty machinery of the party, updating it and making it more effective in carrying out sweeping economic reforms.

At this juncture, we need to make a detour to educational theory to look at some of the basic tenets of party ideology and how it is supposed to function. Our focus will be on how model images are administered, which is a central theme in the three spheres of education, ideology and propaganda. Models can be seen as a way of ordering a society. They may be part of a culture and be based on commonly held social norms; however, models can also be imposed from above. While cultural heroes may endure for centuries, others come and go virtually unnoticed. The ideal of Chinese modelling theory, however, is still that models should emerge from below and not from above.[15] Models

29

emanating from below have social and cultural moorings that render them extremely stable and effective in holding society together. The imposed model, by contrast, lacks such moorings: it is a figure constructed 'outside' society itself. In China, we can find examples of both these types of models and modelling, but the new models increasingly resemble constructed images, considerably reducing their importance. According to worried Chinese educators, 'a devaluation (*bianzhi*) of models has taken place' as models become further and further removed from people's own daily experiences.[16]

The most important function of ideology and its exemplary models has been to represent an alternative to bureaucratic authority. Modelling in itself is a technique for achieving authority based upon the charismatic character of the model or the hero. Models represent charismatic authority in Chinese society, and can take the place of charismatic leaders in their absence. What is happening in China today is an example of what Weber characterized as the 'routinization of charisma.' In his description, Max Weber applies the term charisma to a personality 'regarded as of divine origin' or as 'exemplary' (*vorbildlich*) or as one possessing mythical and therapeutic wisdom.[17]

Cultural heroes, leaders and organizations all initially possess elements of charisma, but as time drags on and bureaucracies expand, this process is subject to the erosive effects of daily life and reality. Weber described the general routinization process that befalls charismatic authority thus:

> In its pure form, charismatic authority has a character specifically foreign to everyday routine structures. The social relationships directly involved are strictly personal, based on the validity and practice of charismatic personal qualities ... Indeed, in its pure form, charismatic authority may be said to exist only in the process of originating. It cannot remain stable, but becomes either traditionalized, rationalized, or a combination of both.[18]

The last sentence here is particularly important. Neither the charisma of the 'great leader' nor the exemplary model has proven stable in today's China. As in Weber's description of charisma, Chinese propaganda circles are now grappling with the problem that charismatic authority only seems to exist in the process of originating. Traditionalized charisma comes back as nostalgia of past greatness, and nationalism can sometimes be seen as an attempt to regain that type of charismatic power with all its rhetoric about the great Chinese past, the more than 5,000 years of Chinese civilization, etc.[19] As for the present, there is the problem of routinization and rationalization, and the attempts at renewal and unity through ideology do not possess the stability inherent in original charisma.

There is another trait of the Chinese past, not mentioned in the exemplary accounts of ideology and great harmony - namely, that of rebellion. Chinese historian Jin Guantao observed that Chinese feudal society was repeatedly shaken by social upheavals.[20] Violent and apparently successful rebellions repeatedly made old dynasties collapse and new ones appear. The typical historical scenario described by Jin is that, after an initial period of rest and popular support, the bureaucratic apparatus is gradually blown up. Corruption, disintegration and finally great chaos set in, leading to rebellion and a collapse of the dynasty. A new emperor then ascends the throne, and the crisis is met by a reform. The bureaucracy is simplified, and a restoration of the authority of the dynasty takes place as the new emperor apparently reinstates the basic social values of the past. The peasant uprisings had a cleansing effect as they got rid of bureaucracy and its power plays, but then started to restore the same structure, trying to build the new with the old.

We cannot here discuss Jin's work in detail, but one point he implicitly underlines is the effects of the routinization or rationalization of charisma. His work was thoroughly condemned in China in the late 1980s, and it was read into the present as a comment on the moribund state of the party during the 'Deng dynasty.' As a Chinese intellectual, Jin found no hope in mass rebellion, which he saw in the picture of endless repetitive cycles of feudal reproductive ultra-stability, but his work nevertheless centred on the feared scenario of breakdown, a still lingering source of anxiety during the present 'Jiang dynasty.'

THE 'THREE REPRESENTATIONS' AND THE IMPORTANCE OF THE PARTY

Jiang Zemin's campaign on the 'Three Representations' (*sange daibiao*), was first presented in February 2000, and was consolidated in his 1st July speech at the CCP's 80th anniversary in 2001. This central campaign has been presented as 'a new development of the Marxist theory of party building' and as a campaign for 'strengthening the party in the new period.'[21] Jiang's speech was acclaimed for 'creatively enriching and developing Marxism,' and the same party commentary has focused on its intent to counter 'Western hostile forces' in their attempt to 'Westernize and break up our country.'[22] The central tenet is about the Communist Party modernizing the nation by representing the 'development of advanced productive forces,' 'China's advanced culture,' and the 'fundamental interest of the overwhelming majority of the people.' The 'Three Representations' can be seen as an extension of the theory of 'two civilizations' applied to the party. The 'two civilizations' campaign is addressed in Jiang's speech. The outline of that campaign was originally formulated as early as in 1982, and presented by Hu Yaobang at the 12th Party Congress. In that campaign, material civilization (*wuzhi wenming*) stood for the productive forces or economic growth, while spiritual civilization (*jingshen wenming*) referred to China's advanced culture, in effect social order and stability.[23] The task of serving the people follows from the successful implementation of the two civilizations.[24] The theme of culture, morality and the 'spiritual' remains a central motif within the party. Ideology is still viewed as the cohesive element of the party, although we sometimes find economistic interpretations of spiritual culture along the lines of the Dengist emphasis on the productive forces.

Li Tieying gives such an interpretation of the present campaigns when he defines 'advanced culture' first and foremost as 'enterprise culture,' in particular, the 'advanced cultural achievements of foreign enterprises,' emphasizing how much the party can learn from such an approach.[25] Li's point is interesting, and we are well advised to follow his line of thinking and regard the party ideology as some sort of enterprise culture linked to the efficiency of the corporate party. We have already quoted Li's emphasis on 'constant change and renewal'; indeed, 'adapting to the situation' has become the watchword in the 'Three Representations' campaign. The major reason why the party has been able to maintain its power up to this point is that it 'retains its advanced nature,' according to one *Xinhua* report. The description of its advanced nature is very pragmatic and businesslike: '[T]he party is able to judge the times and seize upon situations, advance with the times ... [and] make efforts to suit the needs of the times.'[26] The campaign is about streamlining the party to face the challenges of a modernizing China.

The 'mass line' gets a pragmatic interpretation of order in the 'Three Representations' campaign. If corruption is not effectively punished, so

32

goes the argument, the party will lose the confidence and support of the masses. This might upset order, and in turn destroy the party and the country.[27] The party's theoretical journal *Qiushi* focuses on the chaotic public order, particularly in the rural areas, reminding us again of the importance of social order and fear of rebellion.[28] The 'Three Representations' have further links to the anti-crime campaigns, and are said to be effective in cracking down on criminal syndicates and 'evil forces' as well as guaranteeing rural stability.[29]

A crucial theme of the campaign is the criterion for party admission. The CCP used to be seen as the organized expression of the will of the proletariat. In Jiang Zemin's 1st July speech, there was due reference to the old slogans of the party being the 'vanguard of the working class' (*jieji xianfengdui*). At the same time, there are many references to the 'new social strata' (*xin de shehui jieceng*), who have 'contributed to the development of the productive forces'; most notably consisting of 'entrepreneurs and technical personnel employed by scientific and technical enterprises in the non-public sector (*minying keji qiye de chuangye renyuan he jishu renyuan*), managerial and technical staff employed by foreign-funded enterprises, the self-employed (*getihu*), private entrepreneurs (*siying qiyezhu*), and freelance professionals.'[30] With a twist of its original meaning, we might say with Lasch that the party has indeed seen a 'revolt of the elites.'[31] While the ideological facade still describes the working class as the 'masters' of Chinese society, a more realistic picture was presented in a book issued by the Academy of Social Sciences in January 2002.[32] The book operated with five categories, from the upper social strata (*shehui shangzeng*) to the lower strata (*dizeng*) and placing the working class in the two lowest categories, the middle-lower (*zhongxiazeng*) and lower (*dizeng*) strata. The book was first sold on the open market, but was soon withdrawn and circulated for 'internal distribution' only. Rumours in Beijing tell us it had a potentially destabilizing content.

Perhaps even more important than the formalized entry of entrepreneurs into the party (they have to some extent already been admitted since the 13th Party Congress), could be the announced revision of the Marxist theory of labour and labour value. In the old party statutes, it was explicitly stressed that members should 'not exploit the labour of others.' The conditions facing the Chinese leaders of today is, according to Jiang:

Quite different from those the founders of Marxism were faced with and studied. In light of the new conditions, we should make a thorough study of the theory on labour and labour value in a socialist society with a view to achieving a better understanding of this theory.[33]

The party's wielded power over theory, together with the lack of censorship by an absent international Marxist movement, allows it to impose any exemplary organizational norm on its members without resistance. The party can no longer be accused of being dogmatic or even Marxist, but should rather be seen as a managerial or utilitarian party where 'practical ideology' may even lead to the revision of its 'pure' Marxist basis. Many would welcome such a utilitarian approach to pure ideology, and the Chinese leadership sees in this renewal the basis for upholding and enhancing its power. These congratulatory statements should, however, be subject to further analysis. The labour theory of value lies at the very core of Marxism and its theory of surplus value and exploitation. Jiang's 'better understanding' of the theory is clearly in line with admitting capitalists into the party, and is aimed at accommodating the paradox of exploitation within an allegedly socialist China. On the one hand, this can be conceived as a realistic approach to the changing realities and class relations in today's China. On the other hand, it will be a massive task to legitimize the party as a communist party if the basic theories of exploitation are eliminated.

The economic reforms have created a new type of factory worker as millions of migrants pour in from the rural areas and as workers in the state-owned enterprises lose their jobs. In the rural areas, between 150-200 million peasants have failed to be absorbed into agriculture and rural industries, thus creating a vast tide of labourers streaming into the cities. Unlike the *zhigong zhi*, who enjoyed lifetime employment provided through the work unit, the new workforce is often made up of people who have travelled long distances to work on a temporary basis 'for a boss.' The new type of workers are referred to as *dagong zhi*, or for lack of a better word in English, as 'migrant workers.' There has been severe discrimination against such migrant workers. They suffer the abusive consequences of the invisible hand of the free market as well as the all too visible hand of disciplinary control, and experience something akin to urban apartheid. Accounts of the living conditions of these workers reveal shocking details of abuse and exploitation reminiscent of the primary stage of capitalism described by Marx in the footnotes to *Das Kapital*, or in Charles Dickens' novels and stories dating back to the Industrial Revolution.[34]

The unemployment rate in urban China in the late 1990s was 7.5 percent.[35] Some senior Chinese economists have estimated joblessness rates as high as 20 percent in urban China in the near future, and massive regional imbalances exist.[36] At the same time, the differences between classes as well as between urban and rural areas have increased dramatically. Depending on the source of income data, the Gini coefficient in China has just reached 0.50, moving the country rapidly towards the category of countries with the level of most unequal income distribution.[37] Social inequality has become a public concern, and a recent survey showed that more than 80 percent were 'dissatisfied with the general mood of society,' and the 'widening gap between the rich and the poor.' The same high percentage, in particular workers and women, had felt 'increasing pressures in their lives' over the last year.[38]

The legitimate rule of the party seems to reside in its ability to deliver in terms of economic growth and social order. Signs of an incipient economic crisis are however alarming. Premier Zhu Rongji recently claimed that the Chinese economy would have collapsed in 1998 without the state-initiated spending that is currently taking Beijing's government debt to record levels. Not all economic analysts concur with the mainstream view that the Chinese economy is a success story. Like Professor Krugman, who saw the warning signals before the Asian crisis, Professor Thomas Rawski has argued that China's economy may actually have been *contracting* since 1998.[39] The high official growth rates seem strangely out of touch with certain evident trends in Chinese society. The migrant population camp out under bridges and at railway stations, many of them already suffering the effects of long-term unemployment. Block after block of abandoned construction projects in cities strongly suggest that the money is drying up. Moreover, how can it be the case, Rawski argues, that energy use is falling in a booming economy? This phenomenon is unprecedented in economic history. Numerous reports of protests and violent clashes between police and civilians also attest to an emerging breakdown in social stability.[40]

Stability and exploitation are interlinked phenomena. It will take a massive amount of 'spin doctoring' to eradicate the issue of exploitation in line with Marxist theory. Here, we encounter the core of the problem.

The power to define what Marxism is about is much more important in terms of ideological 'ordering' and party power, than are the real issues of factual exploitation. The real problem of exploitation will certainly not disappear through an ideological revision of Marxism, and after all, the Communist Party is still legitimized by the 'support of the labouring masses.' One obvious alternative for the party would be to rid itself of Marxism altogether and create a *minzu dang*, a 'people's party.'[41] The gains would not be substantial, however, since the party will never cease to be a 'Marxist party' as long as Marxism continues to be defined according to the realities formulated by the party itself. In this sense, it does not really matter that politics is losing its links with orthodox Marxist ideology. The 'Three Representations' is not about the problems of exploitation and about 'serving the people' at all, it is simply about keeping the 'corporate party' with its prestige structures in power. Some who believe the party is moving towards greater openness and pluralism may be disappointed. According to one analysis of the 'Three Representations,' in solving the more complicated inherent contradictions among the people, 'the ideology absolutely should not become pluralistic.'[42]

One might argue that the party now represents the interests of capital, insofar as party membership is used as an important instrument to develop capital. Such membership is now sold as a commodity, and paid by exemplary obedience to the party statutes. The party has swelled its ranks at an impressive pace over the last decade: from 50 million members in 1990 to 66 million in 2002. This figure constitutes nearly 5 percent of the entire Chinese population.[43]

THE COMMUNIST ETHIC AND THE SPIRIT OF CAPITALISM

Jiang Zemin is not interested in the concept of class as such. He is letting the capitalists into the CCP while upholding the party slogan of being the vanguard of the working class. However, the main admission criteria are becoming more and more technical and pragmatic:

> The main criteria to admit a person into the party are whether he or she works hard wholeheartedly for the implementation of the party's line and programme and meets the requirements for the party leadership.[44]

This person should be judged 'mainly by his or her political awareness, moral integrity and performance.'[45] These are routinized technical and organizational criteria that reward exemplary loyalty rather than emphasizing the class line. We have, of course, always seen such criteria for admission to the party, but now they seem to be standing alone without any reference to class or class consciousness. An article in *Qiushi* stresses technical as well as managerial skills, and emphasizes the behaviour-oriented criteria for party admission:

> The two basic requirements of "conscientiously struggling for the party's line and guidelines" and of "meeting the criteria for party membership" should be handled as one single criterion: observation of actual performance (*xianshi biaoxian*).[46]

In addition, entrepreneurs who pay their taxes according to regulations and reinvest in production should be admitted. The will to reinvest for the good of the nation seems to represent for the entrepreneur class some sort of Weberian predestination - not in heaven, but as success inside the party. According to the new admission criteria, a Benjamin Franklin would surely be admitted although his Protestant ethic would have been redefined as a communist one. The stress on exemplary conduct is also made clear by Jiang's remark that governing the country by the rule of law (*fazhi*) should be combined with the rule of virtue (*dezhi*).[47] 'Evil' seems to be a very useful political concept in contemporary politics, not only in the simplified worldview of the Bush administration. People with 'evil minds and unhealthy conduct' should be kept out of the party, according to a political commentary in the *People's Daily*. The article goes on to claim that the party 'must ensure that good defeats evil, good never brokers a compromise with evil, and that good cannot be defeated by evil.'[48]

Since exploitation is soon to be abolished with one stroke of the brush, then the good cadre and the good party member are the only 'guarantees' left to secure the well-being of workers and peasants. The many references to high ethical standards, moral integrity, and high political ideological consciousness (*sixiang zhengzhi juewu*) are replacing the social basis of the party.[49] Class consciousness has become a no-word, and exemplarity has become the important factor of management control.

The stress on morality has of course a long tradition in China, and Confucian as well as communist morality have continuously been important elements of social control. The phenomenon now reappears in new forms. Jiang's new ideology means the final abolition of the class line while upholding its rhetoric. The heavy doses of morality that characterize the recent campaigns are supposed to bridge or harmonize the increasing distance between reality and ideology. It remains to be seen whether this gap can still be bridged.

RITUALS OF IDEOLOGY AND THE MANTRA OF 'SERVING THE PEOPLE'

It would be tempting to see the ideological campaigns of the party through the satirical eyes of an Aleksander Zinoviev, as the techniques of a machine recycling its own absurdities, and just look at the emptiness of their rhetoric. However, to confine the analysis to that level is to underestimate the serious game of ideology.[50] One fruitful approach to analyse the mechanisms and contents of ideological campaigns is to use the language of games, theatre and simulation. It is necessary to look at the empty forms of the campaign, and to distinguish its vacuous and bombastic presentation from what remains valid and important in its content. Ideology has become a vital power game of using the right words to describe things of importance. Perhaps there is a parallel here to the Confucian term *zhengming*. The *zheng*, however, in this case no longer refers to the correlation between the name and the object, but that between the name and what is in the more powerful listener's head.[51]

To uphold the facade of the party, there is a pressure to make public statements that express what *should be* rather than what is.[52] An inflated use of superlatives and ritualistic optimism about the present and the future situation of the party and the country have come to characterize the language of an ideological campaign. The campaign language has its own rules and internal logic, and at times may sound repetitive and even comical to an outsider. It is a language of power, and the script needs to be read between the lines. First of all, there are always realities to be identified and described. After all, without stating the problem to be rectified, there is no need for an ideological campaign. The existing problem is presented in a somewhat modified form, indicating the real problems without taking the description to excess. The gravity of the problem is always formulated in the hypothetical question of what would occur if the problems were not to be addressed in the right manner.

Through the party's presentation of the 'Three Representations,' we get a faint glimpse of the lack of enthusiasm and the absence of charisma in a bureaucratized organization. To justify rectification, the party admits that ideological and political work is hard to do in the new situation, and that the campaign has run into problems leading it to become a mere formality.[53] They also admit that 'some comrades have weakened their communist ideals,' and that they have started doubting whether Marxism and socialism work at all. It touches on the bureaucratic arrogance of leading party cadres, pointing to the phenomenon that 'the worse their temper, the higher their posts.'[54] It is also admitted that the party's ideological work is facing challenges from Western values and the diversification of economic factors and interests as well as from the internet.[55] Lastly, it admits that: 'The task of educating and administering party members and cadres is harder than at any time in the past,' owing to the fact that 'many party members and cadres are substantially inferior to the older generation.'[56] The situation has been deteriorating for many years already, and even people in charge of ideological education have developed cynical attitudes towards such education. According to one survey, only 8 percent of them bother at all about ideological education.[57]

Let us here return to the empty rhetoric, and what could be called the 'game of the always excellent situation.' Despite the described gravity of the situation, the severe difficulties are as a rule summed up by pointing to 'the extremely favourable conditions for properly carrying out ideological and political work.'[58] This game is followed up by another ritualistic way of staging the campaign: the game of successful implementation. Ideological campaigns are nearly always summed up in ritualized notions of success and enthusiasm. In a typical example, the participants of one recent campaign on party member conduct, the 'Three Stresses' (*san jiang*), (stressing politics, studies and healthy trends) had 'improved their spiritual status, become more enthusiastic, made new progress in their work,' etc.[59] The florid descriptions of success and 'ground-breaking improvements' are well known, and few believe that such reports mean anything other than that the educated participants can now breathe more freely again. The message has been disseminated, and the things of importance have been made clear for everyone to obey and to use.

There is a lot of ritualized talk in Jiang Zemin's speech on the 'Three Representations' about the importance of 'sharing the common faith with the masses' and 'taking the fundamental interests of the people as the starting point and purpose.'[60] Ideology is said to represent an important contribution in facilitating China's development and stability, and the methods reveal a fundamental belief in the power of example. The *People's Daily* urges leaders to set the example in showing good conduct, and urges the party to 'improve the party's construction of conduct.'[61] Emulating and admiring advanced models, and striving to become advanced models persist as fundamental tenets of ideological campaigns. During the *sange daibiao*, special efforts were to be made to carry out such political work among laid-off workers to help them solve difficulties.[62] In line with the new practice of assimilating capitalists and entrepreneurs into the party, they are even included in the working class. It was recently suggested that representatives from these groups be awarded the title of model workers. Han Xiya from the official All-China Federation of Trade Unions argues that this is a bad idea, and suggests that praise should perhaps be given in a different form, and the entrepreneurs be awarded another title of honour.[63] It should not be difficult to imagine that the enthusiasm involved in emulating your boss as a model worker for sacking you in order to strengthen the nation might prove of limited value for a recently laid-off worker. A commentator in Hong Kong sums up the situation for workers and peasants in China by stating that 'in Jiang Zemin's "new age", workers have been reduced to real "proletarians" and peasants to "hoodlum proletarians"... Workers and peasants have been reduced to a weak group in Chinese society, to whom the least attention has been given.'[64]

Continued failure on the part of the Chinese administration to confront the problems of laid-off workers and reduced peasants' livelihood has led many from these labouring classes into desperate circumstances not easily remedied through ideological campaigns.

RATIONALIZATION OR TRADITIONALIZATION

In less routinized organizations, the charisma of the 'great leader' can have immense importance, as history has shown us with devastating clarity. At this 'moment of origin,' however, it is still the values and norms of revolutionary movements or organizations which are powerful enough to make people act in strict compliance. Will the fading of revolutionary fervour and mounting routinization and bureaucratization lead to a stronger, legally based and less person-centred rationality? Will the utilitarian state simply be drawn towards rational solutions and legal reason? Not necessarily. Schurmann argued that in a bureaucratized and highly routinized organization, it is not so much charismatic personalities or revolutionary values but human *relationships* of a non-charismatic kind that provide the dynamics which the organization needs to function.

> [S]uch organizations often continue to function precisely because of the particular individuals in it who play the leading roles - if they are transferred, it usually has significant consequences for the functioning of the organization; men are more important than the roles they are required to perform.[65]

Personal relations between party leaders, their *guanxi*, subsequently do not become less important, but rather more important for the daily functioning of the organization. Schurmann goes on to explain that: 'routinization of such an organization would simply make the party into an elite club in which the political leaders meet to renew their solidarity.'[66] We see a traditionalization of charisma here. Weber seems right in his claim that charisma cannot remain stable, but becomes either traditionalized, rationalized, or a combination of both.

We see the attempts of the campaign to revitalize past charisma by elevating Jiang Zemin to a higher level in order to enter the hall of fame together with Mao and Deng, but there is also talk of a united leadership. The repeated references to safeguarding the core of the party has much to do with the particular individuals' relevance for the perceived stability of the nation and the party.[67] Jiang Zemin is now constantly referred to as being at the core (*wei hexin*) of the party, as were Deng and Mao before him. Still, however, only Marxism-Leninism represent an 'ism' (*zhuyi*), Mao holds the position of Mao Zedong 'Thought' (*sixiang*), and Deng's ideas are referred to as Deng Xiaoping 'Theory' (*lilun*). Jiang might be at the core, but he is merely 'holding the banner of Deng Xiaoping Theory.'[68]

In drafting *The Selected Works of Comrade Jiang Zemin*, the drafting group has drawn up a document listing Jiang's 'ten major achievements,' and the 'Three Representations' campaign is being elevated into a 'development of Marxism and Deng Xiaoping Theory.' In the army, we have recently seen a faint resemblance to Mao's Little Red Book, namely the 'selected important exposition of Mao Zedong, Deng Xiaoping and Jiang Zemin on strengthening ideals and convictions.'[69] There is apparently opposition to Jiang Zemin's newest campaign, and the attempts to strengthen Jiang's position.[70] In particular, the opposition against these developments comes from the old guard of elder statesmen (perhaps belonging to an earlier status quo that Jiang already has left behind) like Wan Li, Bo Yibo, Yang Baibing, Wang Enmao and Wang Hanbin who are claimed to be 'extremely disgusted with the lavish praises of Jiang Zemin.' The criticism here seems to be concentrated against the person of Jiang Zemin more than against any particular ideological or political issue. The opposition has used extremely harsh words to describe the campaign, but the critique is phrased in very general and sweeping statements. It is claimed that it has been implemented without the test of practice, that it is confusing and not easy to grasp, and worst of all, that the whole campaign is aimed at developing a feudal personality cult around Jiang Zemin.

More principled and less person-oriented criticism has been heard. Recent warnings against de-Maofication should be seen as a reaction against Jiang's ideological campaign straying too far away from the old ideology.[71] Jiang Zemin took action and suspended the leftist journals *Zhenli de zhuiqiu* [Seeking Truth] and *Zhongliu* [Midstream] which propagated such ideas and generally opposed Jiang's definition of the truth. Yu Quanyu, the editor-in-chief of *Zhenli de zhuiqiu* said in the final issue before suspension that a 'faction of capitalist roaders' inside the party would lead to its disintegration.[72]

PRIVATE RATIONALITIES AND CYNICAL GAMES OF 'ACTUAL PERFORMANCE'

Let us go back to the techniques of ideology in the former Soviet Union, and look at the Chinese ideological inventions of the capitalist model worker and the dawning eradication of exploitation in the light of those techniques. Mikhail Epstein, based on experiences from the former Soviet Union, has defined the concept of ideology in terms of the tactics involved in obtaining or enhancing political power, claiming that the only value left in the language games of ideology is that of power. The recent game of Chinese party ideology seems close to what Epstein identifies as '*ideologemes*.' The term describes the use of ideological expressions containing contradictory elements from both left and right, black and white, expressing the definitions of the present situational truth, a form of Orwellian 'new speak.' Could this be termed Marxism? In Epstein's view, Soviet ideology developed beyond any particular rational or irrational system, and became reality itself.[73] Soviet Marxism lost its specificity as a particular ideology and became instead 'an all-encompassing system of ideological signs that could acquire any significance desired.'[74]

It has been observed that in China too, ideology has survived only by absorbing a mixture of communist and capitalist ideals. In addition, such ideologemes have expanded to shape and pollute debates both inside and outside the party.[75] The ideology of ideologemes no longer depends on particular views and ideas as such, but turns into a power game of how to say things in a correct way at the correct time. The power to be able to define becomes the ultimate power, and at the level of ideology, evaluations based on personal judgements, desires or preferences seldom enter into the process of communication. A cadre can truly say with Wittgenstein, 'The limits of my language mean the limits of my world.' Mastering the language of ideology - the language of the party - becomes the way through which power is gained and careers are shaped. In other words, ideology becomes a form of social or ideological capital or a moral economy where 'correctness' or 'exemplarity' can be shored up and used for all kinds of political transactions. This is not a language to be believed or a truth to be internalized, nor a value or a social ideal to be cherished, it is merely an exemplary language to be obeyed and to be used. It is a pure instrument of power.

Let us go back to the party admission criteria, and the remarks on actual performance mentioned earlier in connection with the management character of such criteria. The actual performance (*xianshi biaoxian*), says Jiang Zemin, is what defines the quality of the cadre, not his class background, nor his material wealth or lack of such, nor his ability or lack of ability to exploit the working classes.[76] Performed exemplary conduct thus becomes the main qualification for a party member regardless of class background. The concept of *biaoxian* is central here. Jiang deliberately refers to a concept that stands at the centre of Chinese ideological-political discourse (a point that does not survive in the English translation of the speech) as it connotes a person's moral-political manifestations or outer conduct. *Biaoxian* is a controllable entity too, and that type of behaviour is even measurable on a point scale.[77] *Biaoxian* can also mean to 'show off.' Good *biaoxian* involves showing off virtue manifesting exemplary views or values, and thus describes a behaviour that contributes to the overall spectacle of virtue. Bad *biaoxian* is showing off self, disregarding the rules and norms of exemplarity or personal authority. In *biaoxian*, we find the cell of the disciplinary system. Through *biaoxian*, all kinds of 'little things' come under the surveillance of the exemplary norm, and discipline can be exercised over all types of behaviour. A regime of disciplinary power is established, and the issues of reward and punishment spread into the banalities of everyday life. *Biaoxian* comes very close to what Foucault has termed the 'micro-penalty' of power.[78] Within such a system, the slightest departures from the exemplary norm are open to surveillance because it threatens the prestige structure of the party. It serves as effective organizational cement when spiritual civilization (read exemplarity) is linked to material civilization (read economic management) in a powerful control system. The power of discipline turns productive, so one point about this system is that human energies are channelled in more productive directions, making people calculable and useful at the same time. This is what the corporate view of party admission criteria and the utilization of party cadres is about. It is the usefulness in terms of organizational exemplary and super-social norms that counts, not any social value or norm that might originate in some ideal conception of society. It is attachment to the ideologemes rather than the social norm that matters. The party needs ideology to constantly 'change with the times,' not because it is advanced, but in order to maintain its power.

People in China recognize the falseness and cynicism produced by the *biaoxian* approach. In a survey asking people to give their opinion about why people applied for party membership, only 4 percent answered: 'They believe in Communism and want to make a contribution.' In total, 59 percent said: 'In reality they want a "party card" which they can use as capital to receive future benefits.'[79] In other words, it is a truism in China that the 'exemplary' way bears a price tag - that of simulation. Even Premier Zhu Rongji admits the problems of bureaucratism and the emerging traits of a culture of deception in his speech at the 9th National People's Congress: 'Formalism and bureaucracy run rife and deception, extravagance and waste are serious in some localities... and with some leading cadres.' He urges officials 'to check bad practices, such as false reports to deceive one's superiors or subordinates.' [80] Zhu, however, simply moralizes over the problem, and urges everyone 'to speak the truth,' failing to see that there is a more structural problem here, that of private rationalities within the organization.

We may talk of structural 'ways of lying' inherent in an exemplary society that force people to behave in prescribed ways, prone to simulating exemplary objective standards. This type of control is different from a control based on shared social norms and values, and represents a counterproductive consequence of exemplarity. *Biaoxian* is about guaranteeing predictability and smooth running for the party machinery. The possibility for rational calculation and planning on a larger scale runs, however, the risk of being destroyed in the process. The rationality of the system has a tendency to be reduced to the private calculations of benefit that the system has to offer. The process described serves as a signal of disintegration, a pointer to the internal contradictions of the system and the limits of exemplary control. Outwardly, this simulated behaviour might give the impression of a society resting on unity and stability. An order based on simulation, however, is a superficial one, and the art of ruling loses its power by leaning too heavily on the mechanisms to elicit formal overt obedience.

Underneath the veneer of formal obedience and apparent harmony, we discern eruptive conflicts that may suddenly break through the surface in surprisingly violent ways. We have seen recurring peasant uprisings throughout Chinese history. In addition, the Cultural Revolution conjures up images of recent disorder still experienced as an ultimate trauma for the present party leadership. At the same time, the many clashes between police and people all over China are seen as a potential and very real threat to the power of the CCP. Waves of conflict are always close at hand in the apparent sea of tranquillity that is China's surface, and there is no reason to think that China's membership in the WTO will lessen that problem.

Jiang's '*xianshi biaoxian*' represents a situationalist form of behaviour where the situation defines an individual's action more than inner values do.[81] Sociologists talk about a 'situated identity' where strict social definitions and forms of conduct make it easier to enhance one's own influence and decide what to do or what to expect another person to do, be it inside or outside an organization.[82] Situated identity might thus be seen as social maps according to which an individual can orient himself, closely linked to, in our example, the all-embracing ideological 'standards' of conduct. In this sense, the 'standards' are not moral standards, but instrumental standards or standards of situational definition. This might represent a streamlining of the organization and the managerial culture, but again represents the danger of cynicism. It might seem an effective disciplinary and ordering technology, but that technology bites back through its lack of social moorings in a value system. There is another word - *biaoyan* - that actually describes the process of *biaoxian* better. *Biaoyan* means to perform or to act and can stand for performance and exhibition.[83]

IDEOLOGICAL WAYS OF LYING
AND EROSION FROM WITHIN

It is important to emphasize that the exemplary society, and thereby the party, is attacked from within. In fact, exemplary control and order produce their own non-exemplary uncontrollability and disorder. The emergence of private rationalities and lack of predictability is a true paradox of exemplary order. Exemplary control produces the seeds of its own breakdown rather than describing a form of total control. Exemplary society can be regarded as a thin veneer of order only, formalized and paraded to 'hold' a populace that is actually in constant movement, and which does not really see the party as the vanguard of their interests. The party slogan of 'moving with the times' becomes hollow seen in this perspective, as people and party move in different directions.

Organizational simulation suggests a structural lie - and has been described as a situation where one is forced to lie, to survive or cope with society or any other type of social or organizational setting for that sake.[84] This is a defensive type of lying. Religious dissimulation was found among the Reformation Protestants who, far from openly committing themselves to the new faith, dissembled their beliefs by a feigned conformity to Catholicism - a phenomenon called Nicodemism.[85] In China, the practice of *feng pai* (wind style) is illustrative of simulative action. After the purge of the Gang of Four in 1976, it had already become a rule that one should always lean in the direction of the present political wind whether it was blowing eastward or westward. Far from coping with that problem, Jiang Zemin's managerial party has just continued that tradition.

The *biaoxian* and simulation of party operators, however, is more about using power than hiding from it. There is a difference between hiding for survival and hiding for opportunity, but both hiding and attacking are part of the daily strategies of the party. The party might be accused of being Orwellian; it probably describes the situation better to call it Machiavellian. In the European tradition, Machiavelli's book *The Prince* is of course the work on simulation and dissimulation *par excellence*.[86] In Chinese culture, there is an even richer literature on strategy and deception.[87] Sunzi's work on the art of war is well known, Han Fei's less

46

so, but more recent books like Li Zongwu's *Thick Black Theory* [*Houheixue*], written in 1911, are probably even more important. The book applies well to the existing climate in the party, and it should come as no surprise that this deeply cynical book, banned until 1989, had the Central Party School in Beijing as its leading publisher. Li's theme is: 'When you conceal your will from others, that is *thick*. When you impose your will on others, that is *black*.'[88] This is the actual performance of the party that fits reality more than the alleged exemplary deeds.

To understand the logic of actual performance, and its inclination towards private rationality within the organization, we need to look briefly at the ideological campaign. The well-organized and well-rehearsed political campaign, the *yundong*, is the medium through which ideology is propagated. The participants of a campaign can be divided into instigators (*shandong*) and spectators (*kanke*), and this categorization might help us understand the internal logic of the campaign.[89] Some calculate that by playing the role of the instigator they can obtain personal advantage, and perhaps attain prominent political positions as well as economic benefits. These strategists might not be so dominant in numbers, but they form a core of key participants. The spectator is not necessarily a passive onlooker to campaign events, but his or her activities tend to be less calculated and have less of a strategy to them. Enthusiasm for a campaign project is again linked to real existing norms and values. Even if less enthusiasm has been shown for recent campaigns, it is wrong to state that enthusiasm has always been absent from political campaigns. On the contrary, enthusiasm has led to one 'craze' after another. The history of the People's Republic is full of frenzied activities related to ideological campaigns. Somewhat broadly, we might say that a campaign lies between a craze and a career, and the career system was always linked to the 'enthusiasm of the masses.' The career ladder and the party's reward system combined with the cynical attitude towards ideology in itself represents the new opportunity structure of corrupt activities inside the party. The organization and the campaigns are increasingly utilized for private gain. The ideological campaign has brought change, but was always a ladder for career-minded instigators. A campaign represents the time to move up in the organization, and increases the opportunity structure for deception, power and private gain.

Since morality and loyalty lie in the doing, the logic for the instigator to follow is that of any effective bureaucrat. The instigators are the ceremonial masters of overtly correct behaviour - the models of super-social norms. Instead of stopping a campaign that does not prove effective, instigators escalate it to reach their own aims. Such inner logic of course may prove highly counterproductive for the organization as a whole. Simulation is thus embedded in a structure of bureaucratic careerism where the parts become more important than the whole, and private rationalities gradually replace the organizational rationality. Without a viable value system at the base, soaring cynicism has replaced the occasional enthusiasm for ideological campaigns. The element of craze is gone in terms of support for campaign ideas, and party instigators are more and more 'going at it alone' without the cheers of campaign spectators. The number of enthusiastic spectators might shrink even further as the new social strata enter the gates of the party, since the new admission criteria are as much about leaving someone out as letting someone in. Opening up to the new social strata in practice means closing the door to groups further down in the social hierarchy.

Rebellion from down below is the dangerous scenario of ideological cynicism. If the party does not deliver in terms of social stability and economic growth, the brittle shell of the organization might instantly snap and break into pieces. The party would probably no longer survive a disaster along the lines of a 1950s Great Leap Forward. Even far smaller steps backwards might be devastating in the present situation, as the party is no longer crisis resistant. It is at the same time immensely powerful and immensely vulnerable. The very mechanisms used to forge and renew the party machine produce its own slag products, and utility might paradoxically turn to breakdown.

Cynicism at the top level produces cynicism throughout the organizational system. One problem is the lack of predictability linked to the party's exemplary norm and the career structure attached to it. This dilemma describes the problematic order of exemplary *xianshi biaoxian*. You cannot make good decisions unless you can continually monitor their effects. For this, you need people who can inform you about the real problems, in particular about the errors of the organization. Such negative feedback, however, is the last thing the leadership is likely to hear about. The bureaucrat or the lay party member will always be afraid of the judgement of higher levels, and whole careers are built on denying error. Lower levels, not being stupid, will routinely sugar-coat the information or just plain lie, delay the truth, or play all kinds of other games with the information.[90] If people cannot participate directly in making decisions and have no responsibility for them, it is the best strategy to tell the leaders what they want to hear. Every planner needs internal devil's advocates, critics and 'nay-sayers' who have nothing to lose by talking back and opposing the leader. Without such mechanisms, the leader runs the obvious risk of ending up in isolation, in a world of lies, illusions and anachronisms.

Not only do such games prevent predictability, they provide at the same time an ideal climate for corruption. Jiang and his people are aware of the destabilizing effect of corruption within the party, and the control aspect of the theory of the 'Three Representations' is therefore linked to the 'Three Stresses' (san jiang) campaign, typically focusing more directly on the conduct and the morality of party members. There are explicit warnings here against 'criminals' and 'evil forces' protected by 'connection networks' (guanxiwang) and 'protective umbrellas' (baohu san), linking the problem of corruption to more structural and cultural issues.[91] There is, however, an overall unwillingness or inability to see the solution to corruption in a more systematic structural and organizational manner. When addressing the problem of private rationalities and corruption, the suggested solutions do not themselves exceed the logic of exemplarity. Everything seems to rest with Jiang's rule of virtue and the morality of the cadres' so-called official virtue (guande). In particular, leading party cadres should possess such official virtue and become exemplary models (biaoshuai) for the masses.[92] The answer is once more to cultivate the socialist 'new man' in order to prevent evil from happening.[93]

This is of course not addressing the main problem of new opportunity structures and private rationalities which have become new realities of everyday life in the party. The new opportunity structures for corrupt activities are logically enhanced with higher placement in the party hierarchy. The higher the position, the better the opportunity for deception and corruption. The People's Daily, like Premier Zhu, simply prescribes new doses of morality, repeating over and over again the mantra that leaders should set the example and be models in exhibiting good conduct.[94] The party journal Qiushi, however, stumbles over the real issue. Noting that people in leadership posts have proven to be the most corrupt, the journal correctly blames leading party cadres for the culture of corruption.[95] Again, no effective checks and balances are suggested, except for urging lower levels to be on the alert and exercise their duties of moral supervision.

CONCLUDING REMARKS

With the memories of their own culture and history in mind, today's ruling elites gradually seem to be losing faith in their own exemplary control system, resorting to more open means of policing the populace. On the surface, everything may look calm and stable, but underneath, eruptive resistance and potential breakdown are building up. That the exemplary society is fading and that it produces resistance, however, does not necessarily mean that it will bring about its own demise; that is just one scenario among others. Even if an order built on exemplary norms with increasingly weak social moorings might be a potential time-bomb, resistance and rebellion can be halted. Jin Guantao's picture of armed insurrections overthrowing dynasty after dynasty is not likely to repeat itself, says Liu Binyan, suggesting a scenario of disorder where the peasants make use of the weapons of the weak to pillage and sabotage the regime and the cities.[96] In some ways, the Chinese system is highly effective in bringing about order overall. The 'dangerous' fragmentation represented by the modern can be halted by another, 'ordering' fragmentation. Andrew Walder has noted that factionalism and private vendettas were striking features of worker involvement in the Cultural Revolution. He found such personalized struggles to be highly unusual among workers' movements in industrial societies where collective demands are usually made to institutions and groups. Walder looked at the phenomenon from an organizational point of view, stating that 'this personalization of conflict was a direct outgrowth of the system of officially-organized patronage that personalized social control and rewards to an extent unusual in other industrial settings.'[97]

Even if the exemplary order is in many ways an inflexible order, the simulation strategies fostered by the system provide flexibility within inflexibility. Private rationalities might destroy the party from within, but private solutions to social problems among the masses might be sought without the mobilization of collective support. Instead of the scenario of breakdown, we witness a scenario of overall order on a background of local conflicts. The system might prove effective, not in keeping exemplary order, but in preventing collective action, easily wiping out local disorder wherever it occurs. In this scenario, we see neither the successful utilitarian solution of realistic pragmatism, increased democracy and impartial rule by law, nor the scenarios of total breakdown. Instead, we see the continuing power of the party based not on broad social support, but on a repressive system bolstered by social fragmentation. What we might see in China is not so much an exemplary elite serving the people, but rather the strengthening of a lawless elite, looting China in the interests of its members.

ENDNOTES

1   Mark Elvin, 'How Did the Cracks Open? The Origins of the Subversion of China's Late-Traditional Culture by the West,' *Thesis Eleven*, no. 57 (May 1999), pp. 1-16.

2   *Ibid.*, p. 3.

3   Børge Bakken, *The Exemplary Society. Human Improvement, Social Control, and the Dangers of Modernity in China* (Oxford: Oxford University Press, 2000).

4   Jiang Zemin, 'Speech at the Meeting Celebrating the 80th Anniversary of the Founding of CPC,' 1 July 2001, *Beijing Review*, no. 29 (Documents, part two) (19 July 2001), p. i. Hereafter referred to as Jiang Zemin, Speech (part two).

5   Franz Schurmann, *Ideology and Organization in Communist China* (Berkeley, CA: University of California Press, 1966), p. 105.

6   Li Tieying, 'Makesi zhuyi yao suizhe shidai de fazhan yu er fazhan' [Marxism Should Develop Along With the Times], *Qiushi website*, www.cass.net.cn/chinese/y/cn.html, 8 February 2002.

7   Karl Marx, *Manifesto of the Communist Party*, in Samuel Moore's classic translation from 1888, authorized and edited by Friedrich Engels.

8   Schurmann, *Ideology and Organization*, p. 18.

9   *Ibid.*, pp. 107-8.

10   *Ibid.*, p. 107.

11   *Ibid.*, pp. 108-9.

12   Jiang Zemin, 'Speech at the Meeting Celebrating the 80th Anniversary of the Founding of CPC,' 1 July 2001, *Beijing Review*, no. 28 (Documents, part one) (12 July 2001), p. xii. Hereafter referred to as Jiang Zemin, Speech (part one).

13   He Baogang, 'In Search of the Mixed Regime: Regime Change and Regime Maintenance in China.' Invited paper presented at the workshop on 'Regime Change and Regime Maintenance in Asia and the Pacific,' the Australian National University, Canberra, 12-13 February 2002, p. 11.

14   For a more thorough discussion on the exemplary society and its norms, see Bakken, *The Exemplary Society*.

15   Sun Xiting, Jin Xibin and Chen Xiaobin, *Jianming jiaoyu xue* [Concise Pedagogy] (Beijing: Beijing shifan daxue chubanshe, 1985), p. 231.

16   Qian Mingfang, 'Bangyang jiaoyu xiaoying ruohua de yuanyin yu duice' [The Weakening of the Model Education Effect and Its Countermeasures], *Pujiao yanjiu*, no. 3 (1990), p. 13.

17   Max Weber, *Grundriss der Sozial_konomik, III. Abteilung. Wirtschaft und Gesellschaft*, 3. Auflage, (Tübingen: Verlag von J. C. B. Mohr, 1947), p. 140. Translation taken from Weber, *The Theory of Social and Economic Organization*, trans. A. M. Henderson and Talcott Parsons (New York: Free Press, 1964), pp. 358-59.

18   *Ibid.*, pp. 142-43. English edition, pp. 363-64.

19   Jiang Zemin, Speech (part 1), p. iv. One of China's most distinguished archeologists, Su Bingqi, even claims that 'China's culture is an indigenous one with a tradition of nearly two million years.' See W. J. F. Jenner, 'Race and History in China,' *New Left Review*, no. 11 (September/October 2001), p. 56.

20   Jin Guantao, *Zai lishi de biaoxiang beihou: dui Zhongguo fengjian shehui zhao wending de tansuo* [Behind the Phenomenon of History: a Discussion of the Ultrastable Structure of the Chinese Feudal Society], (Chengdu: Sichuan renmin chubanshe, 1983).

21   Journal's commentator, 'Yixiang zhongyao de jichu jianshe' [Build an Important Foundation], *Qiushi*, no. 3 (1 February 2001), pp. 49-51.

22   Zhong Xuan, 'Zhengque renshi 'san ge daibiao' de kexue neihan' [Correctly Understand the Scientific Intensions of the 'Three Representations'], *Renmin Ribao*, 11 September 2001, pp. 1, 2.

23   See Hu Yaobang, 'Create a New Situation in all Fields of Socialist Modernization: Report to the 12th National Congress of the Communist Party of China, 1 September 1982,' *Beijing Review*, vol. 25, no. 37 (13 September 1982).

24   Jiang Zemin, Speech (part one), pp. viii-ix, xii. Xinhua report, 19 July 2000, quoted in *SWB-FE/3898*, 21 July 2000, p. G/7.

25   Xinhua report, 20 June 2000, quoted in *SWB-FE/3881*, 1 July 2000, pp. G/8-10.

26   Xinhua report, 11 July 2001, in *BBC Monitoring*, 24 July 2001.

27   Xinhua report, 19 July 2000, quoted in *SWB-FE/3898*, 21 July 2000, p. G/7.

28   Journal's commentator, *Qiushi*, no. 3 (1 February 2001), pp. 49-51.

29   Xinhua report, 21 August 2000, quoted in *SWB-FE/3927*, 24 August 2000, pp. G/4-6 and Xinhua report, 4 December 2000, quoted in *SWB-FE/4021*, 21 July 2000, pp. G/3-6.

30   Jiang Zemin, Speech (part two), p. v.

31   Christopher Lasch, *The Revolt of the Elites and the Betrayal of Democracy* (New York: W. W. Norton, 1995).

32   Lu Xueyi (ed.) *Dangdai Zhongguo shehui jiezeng yanjiu baogao* [Research report on the social stratification in today's China], (Beijing: Shehui kexue wenxian chubanshe, 2002). See figure on p. 9 for an overview of the stratification data.

33   Jiang Zemin, Speech (part one), pp. v-vi.

34   See Anita Chan, *China's Workers under Assault. The Exploitation of Labor in a Globalizing Economy*. (Armonk, NY/ London: M. E. Sharpe, 2001).

35 *Renmin ribao*, 16 February 2001, p. 5.

36 X. L. Ding, 'From Big Social Problems to Explosive Political Troubles? The Challenges of Managing a Huge Society under Rapid Transformation at a Politically Difficult Time,' in John Wong and Yongnian Zheng (eds.), *China's Post-Jiang Leadership Succession* (Singapore: Singapore University Press, 2002).

37 Data given by *China Center for Economic Research*, Beijing University in invitation document for the international symposium 'Equity and Social Justice in Transitional China,' Beijing, 11-12 July 2002. For a more detailed discussion on inequality in China and the use of the Gini-coefficient, see the discussion by Chris Bramall, 'The Quality of China's Household Income Surveys,' *The China Quarterly*, no. 167 (September 2000), pp. 689-705, and Carl Riskin, Zhao Renwei and Li She (eds.), *China's Retreat from Equality, Income Distribution and Economic Transition* (Armonk, NY/London: M. E. Sharpe, 2001).

38 *Zhongguo qingnianbao*, 23 December 1999, p. 1.

39 Thomas Rawski, 'What's Happening to China's GDP Statistics?,' *China Economic Review*, vol. 12, no. 4 (2001), pp. 347-54. See also Arthur Waldron, 'China's Economic Facade,' *Washington Post*, 21 March 2002, p. A35.

40 A scan through the *BBC Summary of World Broadcast* for just over a year from 2000-2001 revealed violent clashes between civilians and police and military forces involving all kinds of groups, often including thousands of protestors. See *SWB-FE*/3734, 3738, 3837, 3842, 3896, 3903, 3908, 4017, 4026, 4031, 4077, 4099, 4102. Some of the reports commented on several incidents.

41 Some observers tend to see Jiang's admission of broader social strata into the party as an attempt to rebuild the party precisely as a 'national party,' comparing the approach to Sun Ping's earlier call in 1990 for nationalizing the CCP into an 'all people's party' (*quanmin dang*). See He Baogang, *In Search of the Mixed Regime: Regime Change and Regime Maintenance in China*, p. 11.

42 Xinhua report, 2 April 2000, quoted in *SWB-FE*/3814, 4 April 2000, p. G/8.

43 Already in 1990 there were 700,000 party branches in China. The mere size of the organization makes it vulnerable to bureaucratization. See *Zhongguo nongye nianjian* [China Agricultural Yearbook] (Beijing: Nongye chubanshe, 1991), p. 141. See also He Baogang, *In Search of the Mixed Regime*,' p. 8.

44 Jiang Zemin, Speech (part 2), p. v.

45 *Ibid.*, pp. v-vi.

46 Qiushi website, www.qsjournal.com.cn, in Chinese, 16 November 2001. See also: Chinese journal on criteria for new party members, *BBC Monitoring*, 6 December 2001.

47 Jiang Zemin, Speech (part one), pp. xiii-xiv.

48 *Renmin Ribao* website, 11 October 2001, 'China: Party Daily Commentary Urges Leaders to "Set the Example",' *BBC Monitoring*, 15 October 2001.

49 Jiang Zemin, Speech (part two), p. v.

50 Aleksander Zinoviev, *The Yawning Heights* [*Ziiaiushchie vysoty*], trans. by Gordon Clough (London: Bodley Head, 1979).

51 Thanks to James Greenbaum for pointing out the connection to me.

52 See Mark Elvin, 'How Did the Cracks Open?,' p. 3.

53 The 'Three Stresses' campaign is closely linked to the 'Three Representations,' but focuses more directly on the conduct of the party members. See Xinhua reports 8 November 1999, quoted in *SWB-FE/3688*, and 10 November 1999, pp. G/9-10.

54 Zheng Hongfan and Chen Yan in a Xinhua report 9 January 2000, quoted in *SWB-FE/3734*, 11 January 2000, pp. G/4-7.

55 Xinhua report 3 April 2000, quoted in *SWB-FE/3814*, 4 April 2000, p. G/7.

56 Zhong Xuan, 'Zhengque renshi 'san ge daibiao' de kexue neihan,' *Renmin Ribao*, 11 September 2001, pp. 1, 2.

57 While only 8 percent of teachers in charge of ideological education cared about political education at all, 27 percent said they had no interest in such education. More than 50 percent paid ritual heed to such education. Li Shuli, 'Cong chongyang diaocha kan wo sheng zhengzhi jiaoshi duiwu' [A Sample Survey Look at the Province's Political Teachers], *Zhengzhi jiaoyu*, no. 10 (1986), pp. 33-35.

58 These are the very words used to describe the climate in which the recent 'Three Representations' campaign took place. See Xinhua report 2 April 2000, quoted in *SWB-FE/ 3814*, 4 April 2000, p. G/8.

59 Xinhua report in *SWB-FE/3614* 16 August 1999, pp. G/8-9.

60 Jiang Zemin, Speech (part one), pp. xiii-xiv.

61 *Renmin ribao* website 11 October 2001, 'China: Party Daily Commentary Urges Leaders to "Set the Example",' *BBC Monitoring*, 15 October 2001.

62 Xinhua report in *SWB-FE/3688*, 10 November 1999, pp. G/7-8

63 *Zhenli de zhuiqiu*, 11 December 2000, quoted from *SWB-FE/4063*, 6 February 2001, p. G/6.

64 *Xin Bao*, Hong Kong, 22 March 2001, p. 27, quoted in *SWB-FE/4103*, 24 March 2001, pp. G/6-9.

65 Schurmann, *Ideology and Organization*, pp. 106-7.

66 *Ibid.*, p. 107.

67 See for instance the speech by Defence Minister Chi Haotian, quoted by Xinhua, 20 August 2001: 'Chinese Defence Chief Tells Army to Study Jiang's 1 July Speech,' in *BBC Monitoring* 20 August 2001.

68 See for instance Jiang Zemin, Speech (part 1), p. vii, and Zhu Rongji, website of People's Daily, 6 March 2002, www.english.people.com.cn/ 200203/05/eng20020305 _91438.shtml

69 Xinhua report, 27 February 2001, quoted in *SWB-FE/4081*, 23 February 2001, p. G/7.

70 *Cheng Ming*, Hong Kong, 1 July 2000, pp. 14/16, quoted in *SWB-FE/ 3918*, 14 August 2000, pp. G/3-5.

71   See *Zhenli de zhuiqiu*, 11 June 2000, quoted in *SWB-FE/*3925, 22 August 2000, pp. G/8-9.

72   See 'Analysis: Chinese Media in Party Ideology Split,' BBC monitoring research, 30 August 2001, *BBC Monitoring*, 30 August 2001.

73   Mikhail N. Epstein, *After the Future: The Paradoxes of Postmodernism and Contemporary Russian Culture*, trans. by Anesa Miller-Pogacar (Amherst: University of Massachusetts Press, 1995), pp. 6, 153-61.

74   *Ibid.*, p. 155.

75   Geremie Barmé has shown how the techniques have spilled over to the opposition, in describing the language and the techniques of debate found among the student leaders at Tienanmen in 1989, most notably that of Chai Ling and her supporters. Geremie R. Barmé, *In the Red. On Contemporary Chinese Culture* (New York, Columbia University Press, 1999), pp. 326-33.

76   Jiang Zemin, Speech (part two), pp. v-vi.

77   Børge Bakken, *The Exemplary Society*, particularly pp. 255-68.

78   Michel Foucault, *Discipline and Punish: The Birth of the Prison* (New York, Vintage Books, 1979), p. 178.

79   Stanley Rosen, 'Political Education and Student Response: Some Background Factors Behind the 1989 Beijing Demonstrations,' *Issues and Studies*, no. 10 (1989), p. 19.

80   Website of *People's Daily*, 6 March 2002, www.english.people.com.cn/200203/05/eng20020305_91438.shtml

81   Francis K. Hsu regards the Chinese as 'situation-centred' in his analysis. From a sociological standpoint, not only Chinese but also Japanese culture can be considered as manifesting a situational ethic as opposed to the more universal ethic built around moral absolutes found in Western Christian thought. See George DeVos, 'The Relation of Guilt towards Parents to Achievement and Arranged Marriage among Japanese,' *Psychiatry*, vol. 23, no. 2 (1960), p. 288. Of course, one might argue that 'maintaining power at all costs' represent an 'inner value' as well, complicating the text's assumption.

82   Norman C. Alexander and Pat Lauderdale, 'Situated Identities and Social Influence,' *Sociometry*, vol. 40, no. 3 (1977), pp. 225-33.

83   He Xin, 'Gudu yu tiaozhan: zai hei shehui de bianyuan qu' [Loneliness and Challenge: on the Edge of Black Society], *Zixue*, no. 3 (1989), p. 16.

84   Perez Zagorin, *Ways of Lying* (Cambridge, MA: Harvard University Press, 1990).

85   *Ibid.*

86   Niccol— Machiavelli, *The Prince* (Toronto: Bantham Books, 1981).

87   See Alastair Iain Johnston, *Cultural Realism. Strategic Culture and Grand Strategy in Chinese History* (Princeton, NJ, Princeton University Press, 1995).

88   Li Zongwu, *Houheixue* [Thick Black Theory] Qiushi houheixue, (Hong Kong: Baicheng chubanshe, n.d.), and *Houheixue xubian* [Thick Black

Theory Continued] (Beijing: Tuanjie chubanshe, 1990). For excerpts from the book, see Geremie Barmé and Linda Jaivin (eds.), *New Ghosts, Old Dreams* (New York: Times Books, 1992) pp. 448-50, and Barmé, *In the Red.*

89 He Xin, *Dongfang de fuxing* [The revival of the East], (Heilongjiang jiaoyu chubanshe, Heilongjiang renmin chubanshe, Harbin 1991), pp. 285-86. Barmé, *In the Red*, p. 106, quotes He's first approach towards explaining the campaign mentality in He Xin, 'Zhongguo dangdai beiwanglu. Wode kunhuo yu youlü' [A Contemporary Chinese Cultural Aidem_moire. My Perplexities and Concerns], *Jingjixue zhoubao*, 8 January 1989, p. 5.

90 See Alvin Toffler, *Previews and Premises* (London: Pan Books, 1984), p. 97.

91 Xinhua report, 13 December 2000, quoted in *SWB-FE/4024*, 15 December 2000, pp. G/4-5.

92 Luo Suying, 'Yi dezhi guo zhong zai 'guande' ['Official Virtue' is the Key Link to Ruling the Country by Virtue], *Qiushi*, no. 12 (16 June 2001), pp. 43-44.

93 Yang Zhonghua, 'Zuo hao 'san jiang' gongzuo peiyu yi dai xinren' [Carry out Work on 'Three Stresses' Well, and foster a Generation of New Men], *Qiushi*, no. 19 (1 October 2000), pp. 45-47.

94 *Renmin ribao*, website, 11 October 2001.

95 According to *Qiushi*; 'Most corruption such as graft and bribery occurs among party-member cadres holding leadership posts; it is not at all easy to get them to supervise themselves, and this requires that the lower-level organizations and party members exercise their duties of supervision as equals within the party,' *Qiushi* website, Beijing, in Chinese, *BBC Monitoring*, 16 January 2002.

96 Liu Binyan, 'Another "Rural Encirclement of the Cities" Campaign?,' *China Focus*, no. 1 (1994), p. 4.

97 Andrew G. Walder, 'Communist Social Structure and Workers' Politics in China,' in Victor C. Falkenheim (ed.), *Citizens and Groups in Contemporary China*, Michigan monographs in Chinese Studies, no. 56, (Ann Arbor, University of Michigan Press, 1986), p. 84.

CHAPTER **2**

Management of Party Cadres in China

KJELD ERIK BRØDSGAARD

For more than a decade, Western studies of Chinese politics have focussed more on centrifugal forces in Chinese society rather than on what holds it together. Thus there have been only a few works on the role of the party and its organisation in governing China. The field has focussed on the societal aspect of state-society relations, stimulating a plethora of studies on civil society and non-governmental developments.[1] This focus on society and social phenomena has pushed research of the state and party out of the ruling paradigm.

Contrary to the ruling paradigm, this paper is informed by the belief that the party continues to play a dominant role in Chinese society and that it is too early to pronounce it obsolete, if not dead. In reality, in recent years the party has gradually strengthened its grip over Chinese society. In personnel management, the party has taken back some of the powers it handed over to the personnel departments of the government in the late 1980s and in the ideological sphere, the campaign of the "Three Representatives" clearly is about strengthening the role of the party. Other examples can be given. They all indicate a slow but growing reassertion of party control and that the party is rebuilding its machine for governing an increasingly complex Chinese society.

Party cadres constitute the core of the party's organisational machine. Therefore an understanding of the composition and functioning of the cadre corps is important in trying to conceptualise how the Chinese political system works. However, only a few studies discuss in detail the number, composition and role of the cadre force.[2] Those available are based on information gathered from a variety of scattered sources rather than a consistent set of data.

This paper is also concerned with patterns of career mobility. It will be argued that political loyalty no longer is the most important credential for career mobility among Chinese cadres. In recent years, increasing emphasis has been put on educational qualifications and occupational competence.[3] In fact, one could argue that China's leadership has turned into a technocratic leadership and that China has developed into a technocratic state.[4]

This argument is not new and has been developed by a number of scholars in relation to the top leadership organs in China such as the Politburo, the Politburo Standing Committee and the Central Committee. I substantiate and deepen the underpinnings of the "technocracy thesis" by redirecting attention to broader social and political categories, namely the 40.5 million party and state cadres in China. They form the recruitment basis for future leaders and therefore a detailed study of the cadre corps not only gives us important information on the current situation, but also allows for speculations as to the future of the Chinese Party-state.

The paper is structured in the following way. First, the concept of cadre will be discussed. Second, the number and composition of the cadre corps in terms of regional, ethnic and gender distribution as well as age and educational level will be addressed. Third, the category of leading cadre will be analysed and it will be shown that leading cadres in general have a higher educational background than ordinary cadres, and that the CCP increasingly allocates career opportunities according to educational credentials and age qualifications. Fourth, the issue of cadre management will be addressed both in terms of institutions involved as well as in terms of current regulations passed by the Central Committee of the CCP. Fifth, other measures of party control of the cadres will be discussed including cadre transfer and personnel rotation. Sixth, some concluding remarks will be offered.[5]

THE CONCEPT OF CADRE

The term "cadre" was first developed during the Russian revolution and then translated into Chinese as *ganbu*. In this original sense, the cadres are the leaders of the revolution and the masses the followers. They are the vanguard of the revolutionary class that Lenin, in his important "organisational manual" *What is to Be Done*, said should be created and trained to lead the revolution.[6] Lenin made it quite clear that the Party should create a veritable class of professional revolutionaries, who would act as the central nucleus of the Party and would "devote to the revolution not their free evenings but their whole life."[7]

After the 1949 revolution in China, cadres usually referred to persons in responsible or leading positions within an organisation or people who assumed responsibility for specific political tasks. Accordingly, a person's status as cadre did not necessarily involve membership of the CCP although in practice this would often be the case, especially for leading cadres (i.e., cadres above the county-level).

During the 1950s, there was a regularisation of the cadre corps. A full-fledged wage system was set up and a more detailed ranking system was introduced. According to a handbook published in 1958, cadres included the following personnel: (1) employees from clerical personnel and above; (2) industrial technicians; (3) agro-technicians; (4) maritime technicians; (5) public health technicians of middle level and above; (6) scientific technicians; (7) news and publishing personnel; (8) teaching personnel; (9) personnel in culture and the arts; (10) and translators.[8] In short, cadres were defined by simple bureaucratic distinctions according to their education and whether or not they were employed by the state.

Since then, there has been no fundamental changes in this categorisation. However, all along an undercurrent of doubt has existed as to whether such a purely bureaucratic distinction would suffice and therefore regular ideological campaigns have been conducted to ensure the continuous political and ideological education and training of the cadres.

COMPOSITION OF THE CADRE CORPS

There are currently 40.5 million cadres in China (see Table 1).[9] Except in 1957 and 1962, the number of cadres has risen steadily since 1949. The most significant increases occurred in the 1950s when the Party was expanding its grip on Chinese society. Since 1978, the number of cadres has grown every year without exception and now constitutes 3.3 percent of the total Chinese population.

TABLE 1   THE GROWTH OF CADRES IN CHINA, 1949-1998

Year	Number of Cadres	Growth in %
1950	908,000	n.a.
1955	7,170,500	8.1
1956	9,768,000	36.2
1957	9,535,600	-2.4
1958	9,550,800	0.2
1958	10,470,900	9.6
1960	11,326,500	8.2
1961	11,551,500	2.0
1962	10,606,600	-8.2
1963	11,031,400	4.0
1964	11,512,900	4.4
1965	11,923,400	3.6
1971	12,928,300	n.a
1972	13,766,300	5.4
1973	14,510,900	4.4
1974	15,148,200	4.4
1975	15,617,000	3.1
1977	16,158,100	2.6
1978	17,402,000	4.9
1979	18,138,700	4.2
1980	18,951,000	4.5
1981	19,771,600	4.3
1982	21,010,500	6.3
1983	21,954,600	4.5
1984	25,082,500	14.3
1985	26,553,600	5.9
1986	27,674,200	4.2
1987	29,032,000	4.9
1988	30,454,700	4.9
1989	32,056,900	5.3
1990	33,180,600	3.5
1991	34,971,700	5.4
1992	35,891,100	2.6
1993	36,996,500	3.1
1994	37,961,800	2.6
1995	38,316,900	0.9
1996	39,322,000	2.6

TABLE 1   THE GROWTH OF CADRES IN CHINA, 1949-1998 (cont'd)

Year	Number of Cadres	Growth in %
1997	40,191,100	2.2
1998	40,488,600	0.7

Source: Zhonggong zhongyang zuzhibu, Zhonggong dangshi yanjiushi, and Zhongyang dang'an guan, *Zhongguo gongchandang zuzhishi ziliao, 1921-1997, fujuan 1* (Material on the Organizational History of China's Communist Party, 1921-1997. Appendix Volume 1) (Beijing: Zhongyang dangxiao chubanshe), pp. 1329-1330.

Of the total number, 47.5 percent or 19.2 million cadres work in the so-called *shiye danwei* (service or non-profit organisations), 35.2 percent or 14.3 million in production enterprises and 17.2 percent or 7.0 million in government and Party organs. The percentage of cadres in government organs has not changed much since the onset of the reform period. But the share of cadres in *shiye danwei* has grown from 40.1 percent in 1984 to 47.5 percent in 1998, whereas the category of cadres in production enterprises has fallen from 41.8 percent in 1984 to 35.2 percent during the same period (see Table 2). The falling number of cadres in enterprises seems to reflect the decreasing importance of the state sector in the Chinese economy.

TABLE 2   SECTORAL DISTRIBUTION OF CADRES IN CHINA

Year	Total	Govt. organs		Service Units		Enterprises	
	(Mill.)	Number	%	Number	%	Number	%
1981	19.8	3.5	17.9	8.5	43.0	7.7	39.0
1982	21.0	3.9	18.5	9.1	43.5	8.0	37.8
1983	22.0	4.1	18.5	9.4	42.7	8.5	38.8
1984	25.1	4.6	18.2	10.1	40.1	10.5	41.8
1985	26.5	5.0	18.8	11.4	42.8	10.2	38.4
1986	27.7	5.3	19.2	12.0	43.2	10.4	37.5
1987	29.1	5.5	19.0	12.7	43.9	10.8	37.1
1988	30.5	5.7	18.8	12.8	42.0	12.0	39.3

TABLE 2   SECTORAL DISTRIBUTION OF
CADRES IN CHINA (cont'd)

Year	Total	Govt. organs		Service Units		Enterprises	
	(Mill.)	Number	%	Number	%	Number	%
1989	32.1	5.9	18.4	13.3	41.7	12.8	39.9
1990	33.2	6.1	18.5	13.8	41.4	13.3	40.1
1991	35.0	6.5	18.7	14.2	40.5	14.3	40.8
1992	35.9	6.6	18.5	14.6	40.7	14.7	40.8
1993	37.0	6.7	18.0	15.3	41.2	15.1	40.8
1994	38.0	6.8	17.9	15.8	41.6	15.4	40.6
1995	38.3	6.8	17.8	16.4	42.9	15.1	39.4
1996	39.3	6.9	17.3	17.5	44.4	15.0	38.3
1997	40.2	7.0	17.2	18.4	45.9	14.8	36.9
1998	40.5	7.0	17.2	19.2	47.5	14.3	35.2

Source: Zhonggong zhongyang zuzhibu, Zhonggong dangshi yanjiushi, and Zhongyang dang'an guan, *Zhongguo gongchandang zuzhishi ziliao, 1921-1997, fujuan 1* (Material on the Organizational History of China's Communist Party, 1921-1997. Appendix Volume 1) (Beijing: Zhongyang dangxiao chubanshe), p. 1332.

The regional distribution of cadres varies considerably. In Beijing, the cadre force accounts for about 11.8 percent of the population (see Table 3). The proportion of cadres is also relatively high in Tianjin (7.5 percent) and in Shanghai (6.9 percent). Beijing's case can be explained by its special status as the capital. Tianjin and Shanghai are important political and educational centers, and so clearly will have a larger proportion of cadres.

The provinces of Liaoning, Jilin and Heilongjiang are also over represented in terms of cadres. A plausible explanation is that these provinces are traditionally the locations of large state-owned enterprises, especially in the heavy-industry sector. This usually entails a considerable number of cadres subordinated to central ministries and organs in Beijing and national party organisations. Conversely, the comparatively lower proportion of cadres in Jiangsu, Zhejiang and Anhui seems to be related to the stronger focus of these provinces on foreign-funded enterprises and a growing private sector. In these economically less centralised sectors, the Party and its cadres play only a minor role and in many instances are not present at all.

TABLE 3   THE REGIONAL DISTRIBUTION OF CADRES IN CHINA

Province	Population (millions)	Cadres (thousands)	Proportion of population (%)
National	**1,248.10**	**40,488.60**	**3.25**
Beijing	12.46	1,474.10	11.83
Tianjin	9.57	724.70	7.57
Hebei	65.69	1,826.00	2.77
Shanxi	31.72	1,194.40	3.76
Inner Mongolia	23.62	893.20	3.78
Liaoning	41.57	2,152.20	5.18
Jilin	26.44	1,308.30	4.95
Heilongjiang	37.73	1,736.20	4.61
Shanghai	14.64	1,027.80	6.97
Jiangsu	71.82	2,304.20	3.20
Zhejiang	44.56	1,274.80	2.86
Anhui	61.84	1,297.50	2.09
Fujian	32.99	955.80	2.89
Jiangxi	41.91	1,114.20	2.72
Shandong	88.38	2,238.80	3.21
Henan	93.15	2,135.80	2.29
Hubei	59.07	2,167.70	3.67
Hunan	65.02	1,725.40	2.65
Guangdong	71.43	2,341.20	3.28
Guangxi	46.75	1,225.00	2.62
Hainan	7.53	223.50	2.96
Chongqing	30.60	1,036.90	3.39
Sichuan	84.93	1,934.50	2.27
Guizhou	36.58	903.70	2.47
Yunnan	41.44	1,182.40	2.85
Tibet	2.52	79.20	3.14
Shaanxi	35.96	1,225.30	3.41
Gansu	25.19	773.30	3.06
Qinghai	5.03	212.40	4.22
Ningxia	5.36	219.70	4.09
Xinjiang	17.47	973.10	5.57

Sources: Zhonggong zhongyang zuzhibu, Zhonggong dangshi yanjiushi, and Zhongyang dang'an guan, *Zhongguo gongchandang zuzhishi ziliao, 1921-1997*, *fujuan 1* (Material on the Organizational History of China's Communist Party, 1921-1997. Appendix Volume 1) (Beijing: Zhonggong dangshi chubanshe, 2000) p. 1344-1347; *Zhongguo tongji nianjian 1999* (China Statistical Yearbook 1999), p. 113.

EDUCATIONAL LEVEL

The educational level of cadres has improved dramatically during the reform period. While the share of cadres with Junior Middle School education and below was almost 49 percent in 1979, it nose-dived to 8 percent in 1998. Now 46.5 percent of the cadre force has a university degree compared to only 17.9 percent in 1979 and 6.9 percent in 1950 (Table 4). In addition to becoming more professionally qualified, the cadre corps has undergone a process of rejuvenation. In 1979, only 29 percent of the cadres were younger than 35 years of age. Now the proportion has increased to 49 percent (see Table 5). The share of the age cohort from 36 to 54 has fallen from 65 percent in 1979 to 45 percent in 1998, whereas the percentage of cadres at 55 years of age and above has remained almost unchanged.

TABLE 4 EDUCATIONAL BACKGROUND OF CADRES IN CHINA, 1979-1998

Year	Total Number	University degree		Senior High		Junior High and Below	
		Number	%	Number	%	Number	%
1979	18,138,700	3,250,200	17.9	6,052,200	33.4	8,836,300	48.7
1980	18,951,000	3,527,800	18.6	7,050,900	37.2	8,372,300	44.2
1981	19,771,600	3,725,100	18.8	7,884,400	39.9	8,162,100	41.3
1982	21,010,500	4,202,800	20.0	8,573,600	40.8	8,234,100	39.2
1983	21,954,600	4,646,500	21.2	9,235,200	42.1	8,072,900	36.7
1984	25,082,500	5,200,500	20.7	11,045,000	44.1	8,837,000	35.2
1985	26,533,600	5,802,100	21.9	12,115,500	45.6	8,636,000	32.5
1986	27,674,200	6,519,900	23.6	12,858,500	46.4	8,295,800	30.0
1987	29,032,000	7,316,100	25.2	13,819,200	47.6	7,896,700	27.2
1988	30,454,700	8,614,300	28.3	14,431,800	47.4	7,408,600	24.3
1989	35,056,900	9,675,700	30.2	15,195,000	47.4	7,186,200	22.4
1990	33,180,600	10,613,000	32.0	15,776,500	47.6	6,791,100	20.4
1991	34,971,700	11,617,200	33.2	16,668,800	47.7	6,685,700	19.1
1992	35,891,100	12,519,300	34.9	17,184,000	47.9	6,187,800	17.2
1993	36,996,500	13,399,900	36.2	17,945,000	48.5	5,651,600	15.3
1994	37,961,800	14,267,400	37.6	18,482,300	48.7	5,212,100	13.7

TABLE 4 EDUCATIONAL BACKGROUND OF CADRES IN
CHINA, 1979-1998 (cont'd)

Year	Total Number	University degree		Senior High		Junior High and Below	
		Number	%	Number	%	Number	%
1995	38,316,900	15,196,700	39.7	18,544,200	48.4	4,577,800	11.9
1996	39,322,000	16,492,100	41.9	18,711,600	46.6	4,118,300	10.5
1997	40,191,100	17,736,200	44.1	18,420,500	46.6	3,714,000	9.3
1998	40,488,600	18,744,900	46.5	18,433,400	45.5	3,220,300	8.0

Sources: Zhonggong zhongyang zuzhibu, Zhonggong dangshi yanjiushi, and Zhongyang dang'an guan, *Zhongguo gongchandang zuzhishi ziliao, 1921-1997, fujuan 1* (Material on the Organizational History of China's Communist Party, 1921-1997. Appendix Volume 1) (Beijing: Zhonggong dangshi chubanshe, 2000) p. 1344-1347; *Zhongguo tongji nianjian 1999* (China Statistical Yearbook 1999), pp. 1350-1352.

Women account for 35 percent of the total number of cadres. This is an increase compared to 1979, when only 26 percent of the cadres were women. The proportion of women among cadres at the county level and above is only 14.4 percent. National minorities account for 6.8 percent of the cadre corps, up from 4.9 percent in 1979.

It is often assumed that most cadres are party members. However, statistics seem to indicate that only 38.2 percent of the cadres are party members. This proportion is only slightly higher than in 1950 (37.2 percent). The relative share of party members topped during the readjustment phase in 1960-63, when the reformist faction led by Liu Shaoqi and Deng Xiaoping tried to consolidate the economy after the turbulence of the Great Leap Forward. Again in 1987 during the heyday of Zhao Ziyang, the proportion of cadres with party membership was relatively high (44 percent).

LEADING CADRES

In the Chinese political terminology, leading cadres (*lingdao ganbu*) are defined as cadres at the county (division) level and above. In political-administrative terms, the most important of these are the cadres working

TABLE 5 AGE DISTRIBUTION OF CADRES IN CHINA, 1979-1998

Year	Total Number	Below 35		36 to 45		46 to 54		55 and Above	
		Number	%	Number	%	Number	%	Number	%
1979	18,138,700	5,202,300	28.6	6,799,700	37.5	5,075,000	27.9	1,061,700	5.8
1985	26,533,600	10,419,100	29.2	7,663,800	28.9	6,991,300	26.3	1,479,400	5.6
1990	33,180,600	14,359,000	33.3	8,841,000	26.6	7,879,900	23.7	2,100,700	6.3
1991	34,971,700	15,357,400	43.9	9,423,000	26.9	7,482,600	21.4	2,708,700	7.8
1992	35,891,100	16,053,600	44.7	9,666,400	26.9	7,436,100	20.7	2,735,100	7.6
1993	36,996,500	16,841,800	45.5	10,073,800	27.3	7,376,900	19.9	2,704,000	7.3
1994	37,961,800	17,528,100	46.2	10,377,800	27.3	7,405,800	19.5	2,650,100	6.9
1995	38,316,900	18,181,800	47.4	10,247,200	26.7	7,326,700	19.1	2,561,200	6.7
1996	39,322,000	18,913,500	48.1	10,432,200	26.5	7,438,300	18.9	2,538,000	6.3
1997	40,191,100	19,872,800	49.4	10,543,100	26.2	7,356,400	18.2	2,418,800	6.0
1998	40,488,600	20,048,400	49.5	10,953,500	27.1	7,316,300	18.1	2,170,400	5.3

Sources: Zhonggong zhongyang zuzhibu, Zhonggong dangshi yanjiushi, and Zhongyang dang'an guan, *Zhongguo gongchandang zuzhishi ziliao, 1921-1997, fujuan 1* (Material on the Organizational History of China's Communist Party, 1921-1997. Appendix Volume 1) (Beijing: Zhonggong dangshi chubanshe, 2000) p. 1344-1347; *Zhongguo tongji nianjian 1999* (China Statistical Yearbook 1999), pp. 1355-1356.

in political and administrative agencies/organs (*jiguan*), such as party and government bodies. They form the core of the political system. Whereas less than half of the rank and file cadre corps are party members, about 95.3 percent of all leading cadres have a party membership. This clearly indicates the key role played by this segment of the cadre corps. In many ways, these cadres function as the revolutionary vanguard as old cadres did, whereas lower level cadres are often just referred to as state-salaried people. Consequently, changes in the composition and function of this group have profound implications for the way the Chinese party-system works.

Leading cadres in this sense of the definition number 508,025 and constitute only about 8 percent of the cadre corps in government organs. 92 percent of or 466,355 leading cadres work at the provincial level and below such as local city and county party secretaries (see Table 6). Only 34,221 of them work in the central organs in Beijing.[10]

The most important of leading cadres are those at the ministerial (provincial) level and above. Since central ministers and provincial governors and first party secretaries are at the same administrative rank, this level includes present as well as former cabinet ministers and provincial governors and party secretaries (see Table 7). There are only 2,562 of these (see Table 6), of which 888 work at the Center in Beijing. They all belong to the Central Committee's nomenklatura.

There are 39,108 cadres at the departmental level (= prefectural level in the provincial set-up), of which 6,580 work at the Center (Table 6). For the ministerial level cadres, the number has been relative stable over the years, whereas departmental level cadres at the center increased by 1,966 or 42 percent from 1979 to 1986. In the same period, the number of division level cadres at the Center increased even more, with an increase of 13,296 or 130 percent. Except for a few years at the end of the 1980s, the number has grown steadily ever since and there are now about 3.5 times as many division level cadres as in the 1979. This indicates that the bloating of the cadre corps has mainly taken place at the middle management level.

As mentioned above, women account for about a third of the cadre corp. However, they only account for 14.4 percent of the number of cadres above the county level. This indicates that the higher the level, the fewer the number of women. In fact, there is only one woman in the politburo and a total absence of female representation in the Politbureau Standing Committee. The proportion of national minority

TABLE 6   CADRES ABOVE COUNTY-LEVEL IN GOVERNMENT AGENCIES IN CHINA, 1979-1998

Year	Total	Of Which in the Center	Minist. Level and Above	Of Which in the Center	Dept. Level	Of Which in Center	Div. Level	Of Which in Center
1979	159,065	15,707	1,646	784	22,450	4,697	134,969	10,222
1980	167,650	17,498	1,882	916	23,483	4,984	142,285	11,598
1981	183,927	18,878	1,791	830	23,875	5,074	158,261	12,974
1982	198,229	21,282	1,849	856	25,123	5,737	171,257	14,689
1983	199,826	22,088	2,179	968	26,058	5,065	171,589	16,055
1984	230,776	26,982	2,143	978	26,294	6,142	202,339	19,862
1985	259,596	30,056	2,150	972	27,906	6,682	229,540	22,402
1986	287,809	31,165	2,197	984	28,899	6,663	256,713	23,518
1987	305,646	31,599	2,156	958	29,623	6,641	273,867	24,000
1988	317,123	29,557	2,316	898	30,322	6,307	284,485	22,352
1989	335,018	28,878	2,280	849	30,699	6,165	302,039	21,873
1990	344,785	29,274	2,261	868	30,259	6,138	312,265	22,268
1991	361,512	32,735	2,285	916	31,881	6,826	327,346	24,993
1992	376,773	34,766	2,258	930	33,148	7,093	341,367	26,743
1993	398,189	32,015	2,590	972	34,498	6,568	361,101	24,475
1994	406,119	37,728	2,465	935	33,451	6,645	370,203	30,148
1995	445,286	43,322	2,459	887	35,620	7,101	407,207	35,334
1996	468,274	44,950	2,317	818	37,011	7,181	428,946	36,951
1997	492,328	49,411	2,406	828	39,181	7,687	450,741	40,896
1998	508,025	41,689	2,562	888	39,108	6,580	466,355	34,221

Source: Zhonggong zhongyang zuzhibu, Zhonggong dangshi yanjiushi, and Zhongyang dang'an guan, Zhongguo gongchandang zuzhishi ziliao, 1921-1997, fujian 1 (Material on the Organizational History of China's Communist Party, 1921-1997. Appendix Volume 1) (Beijing: Zhonggong dangshi chubanshe, 2000), p. 1357.

representation among leading cadres (7.5 percent) is only slightly smaller than that of national minority representation among the total cadre force (6.8 percent).

TABLE 7   ORDER OF LEADING POSITIONS AND CORRESPONDING RELATIONSHIPS

Center	Provincial level	Prefectural level	County (city) township level
Premier			
Vice Premier			
State Councillor			
Minister	Governor, Mayor		
Vice Minister	Vice Governor, Vice Mayor		
Director of Dept. (*ju, si*)	Director of Dept. (*ju, ting*)	Mayor, Prefect-ural Head	
Vice Director of Dept.	Vice Director of Dept.	Vice Mayor, Vice Prefect-ural Head	
Head of Division (*chu*)	Head of Division (*chu*)	Head of Dept. (*ju*)	Head of County, Mayor
Vice Head of Division	Vice Head of Division	Vice Head of Dept.	Vice Head of County, Vice Mayor
	Head of Section (*ke*)	Head of Section (*ke*)	Head of Dept. (*ju*), Head of Township
	Vice Head of Section	Vice Head of Section	Vice Head of Dept., Vice Head of Township

69

In terms of educational background, the category of leading cadres are not surprisingly better educated than that of ordinary cadres. Thus 80.5 percent of leading cadres have received a college education compared to 46.5 percent for the total cadre corp.[11] For cadres at the departmental level, the figure is 88.7 percent. In 1981, 57.8 percent of leading cadres only had Junior Middle School education and below. The percentage had dropped to only 4.4 percent in 1998. For the total cadre corps, the figures for these years are 41.3 and 8.0 percent (Table 4).

According to findings by Li Cheng and Lynn White, the increasing educational qualifications of the cadres are also reflected in the composition of the Central Committee and the Politburo. 55.4 percent of the membership of the 12th CC elected in 1982 had a college degree.[12] The percentage rose to 92.4 percent in 1997 when the 15th CC was elected.[13] As to the educational level of members of the Politburo, Li and White found that the number of members with college degrees increased from 32 percent in 1982 to 83.8 percent in 1997.[14] They conclude that cadre recruitment in the reform era is based on education and technical training rather than class background and political attitudes.[15]

In short, since the early 1980s, the educational background and qualifications of Chinese leading cadres have dramatically improved. It is important to note, that this pattern is not only found at the very top of the power pyramid. In fact, the whole layer of the 500,000 plus leading cadres has educational qualifications that are equal to those we find among members of the Politburo. This means that there now exists a vast pool of highly educated cadres from which to recruit future leaders.

The technocracy thesis suggests that not only are members of the administrative and political elite better educated than in the past, they also have an educational background in primarily engineering and other fields of science and technology. My data do not provide information on this aspect. But they do inform on another aspect related to technocratic leadership, namely the ongoing trend of rejuvenation.

AGE BACKGROUND OF LEADING CADRES

Almost half of the total cadre force is below 35 years of age. However, only 5.8 percent of the leading cadres are below 35 (Table 8). At the departmental level, there are only 254 cadres (0.7 percent) below 35 and at the ministerial level and above there are none.[16] 38.9 percent

TABLE 8 AGE DISTRIBUTION OF CADRES IN CHINA, 1981–1998

Year	Total Number	Below 35		36 to 45		46 to 54		55 and Above	
		Number	%	Number	%	Number	%	Number	%
1981	158,261	1,983	1.3	16,761	10.6	95,979	60.7	43,358	27.4
1982	171,257	2,050	1.2	17,164	10.0	100,929	58.9	51,114	29.9
1985	229,540	9,930	4.3	51,178	22.3	118,811	51.8	49,621	21.6
1990	312,265	12,302	3.9	79,907	24.7	131,362	42.1	88,694	28.0
1995	407,207	18,364	4.5	131,006	32.2	164,682	40.5	93,155	22.9
1996	428,946	23,193	5.4	141,058	32.9	173,932	40.5	90,763	21.2
1997	450,741	27,956	6.2	148,810	33.0	180,376	40.0	93,599	20.8
1998	466,355	27,256	5.8	158,824	33.1	190,004	40.8	90,271	19.4

Sources: Zhonggong zhongyang zuzhibu, Zhonggong dangshi yanjiushi, and Zhongyang dang'an guan, *Zhongguo gongchandang zuzhishi ziliao, 1921–1997, fujuan 1* (Material on the Organizational History of China's Communist Party, 1921–1997. Appendix Volume 1) (Beijing: Zhonggong dangshi chubanshe, 2000) p. 1344–1347; *Zhongguo tongji nianjian 1999* (China Statistical Yearbook 1999), pp. 1363–1364.

of all leading cadres are below 45 years of age, but only 2.2 percent of the cadres are at ministerial level and above. As will be discussed below, the recent "development programme" of the Central Organisation Department stipulates that in the future, and no later than 2003, in leading bodies at the provincial and central ministerial level there should be more leaders around 50 and some "no more than 45 years old".

As indicated above in terms of party membership, the difference between the vast body of ordinary cadres and the layer of leading cadres is significant. Thus, only 15.5 million or 38 percent of the total cadre force are members of the CCP (see Table 9), while 95.3 of the leading cadres are members. The percentage has declined from 96.9 percent in 1981, reflecting recent attempt to bring in non-party representation in leading organs. Thus the percentage of members of the democratic parties among the leading cadres has increased from 0.5 percent to almost 1 percent (see Table 9).

TABLE 9   CADRES AND PARTY MEMBERSHIP IN CHINA, 1979-1998

Year	Total	Membership of CCP		Membership of Democratic Parties	
		Number	%	Number	%
1979	18,138,700	7,728,700	42.61	22,600	0.13
1980	18,951,000	8,231,200	43.43	25,400	0.13
1981	19,771,600	8,192,100	41.43	29,800	0.15
1982	21,010,500	8,566,600	40.77	38,200	0.18
1983	21,954,600	8,741,100	39.81	52,900	0.24
1984	25,082,500	9,906,700	39.50	63,300	0.25
1985	26,553,600	11,002,000	41.43	76,600	0.29
1986	27,674,200	11,837,400	42.77	95,200	0.34
1987	29,032,000	12,774,100	44.00	116,100	0.40
1988	30,454,700	13,023,500	42.76	139,500	0.46
1989	32,056,900	13,707,200	41.31	156,800	0.49
1990	33,180,600	13,767,200	41.49	167,900	0.51

TABLE 9   CADRES AND PARTY MEMBERSHIP
IN CHINA, 1979-1998 (cont'd)

Year	Total	Membership of CCP		Membership of Democratic Parties	
		Number	%	Number	%
1991	34,971,700	14,095,800	40.31	167,700	0.48
1992	35,891,100	14,231,000	39.65	165,500	0.46
1993	36,996,500	14,459,600	39.08	165,600	0.45
1994	37,961,800	14,701,200	38.73	165,000	0.43
1995	38,316,900	14,663,500	38.27	172,600	0.45
1996	39,322,000	14,945,900	38.01	227,800	0.58
1997	40,191,100	15,272,600	38.00	223,800	0.56
1998	40,488,600	15,450,500	38.16	232.900	0.58

Source: Source: Zhonggong zhongyang zuzhibu, Zhonggong zhongyang dangshi yanjiushi, Zhonggong zhongyang dang'an guan (eds.), *Zhongguo gongchandang zuzhi ziliao, 1921-1997, fujuan 1* (Material on the Organizational History of China's Communist Party, 1921-1997. Appendix Volume 1) (Beijing: Zhonggong dangshi chubanshe, 2000), p. 1358

These figures show that contrary to what is widely assumed, most party members are not cadres and most cadres are not party members. Consequently, there is no correlation between the number of cadres and the number of party members. The figures also show that almost all leading cadres hold a party membership. In this way, the party is able to maintain its control of the cadre corps. Additional control is maintained through the nomenklatura system.

In short, the cadre corps has changed its profile compared to the Maoist period. It no longer resembles the "proletarian" worker and peasant elite as it was in Mao's day. Present day cadres are much better educated and significantly younger. This is especially the case for cadres at the county level and above. It seems that in order to move up the career ladder and reach the departmental level, it is necessary to have at least a college degree. Middle school or vocational school education will no longer suffice. In terms of age, it also seems clear that promotion to the crucial departmental level will have to take place no later than the age of 45. In sum, the CCP increasingly allocates career opportunities according to educational credentials and age qualifications rather then political criteria.

THE ORGANISATION DEPARTMENT AND THE NOMENKLATURA

Organisationally, the cadres are managed by the Organisation Department of the Party Committees at central and local levels. The work of the organisation departments at these levels is supplemented by the personnel departments that are established at all levels of government and which belong to the *xitong* of the Ministry of Personnel. However in 1998, the Ministry of Personnel had to shift most of its management functions to the party, which now is in exclusive control of the cadre corps.[17]

The Organisation Department of the Central Committee has always been an important department in the Communist political system. Before 1949, Chen Duxiu, Mao Zedong, and Chen Yun had headed this department.[18] Since 1949, important leaders such as Peng Zhen, Deng Xiaoping, Hu Yaobang, Qiao Shi, and Song Ping have all served as heads of the department (see Table 10). In March 1999, Jiang Zemin's right-hand man Zeng Qinghong was appointed to this important position. During his two years in office, he has managed to turn the Department into a major platform for strengthening the role of the Party in organisational as well as ideological work.

The Organisation Department's principal instrument of power is its management of the nomenklatura system. This system consists of a list of positions over which the party committees has the authority to make appointments and a list of reserves for these positions.[19] The most important part of the nomenklatura is the list of 5,000 posts to be filled and managed by the Central Committee.[20] As the Chinese governing structure applies a system according to which the higher level takes charge of the lower, the Central Committee and its Organisation Department also control the nomenklatura of ministerial-level and provincial-level leading cadres. In the 1970s and early 1980s, the Organisation Department actually managed two levels down, which meant that in addition to the ministerial level, it also had control over the important *ju*-level in the Chinese administrative hierarchy.

TABLE 10 HEADS OF THE ORGANIZATION DEPARTMENT OF THE CCP, 1921-2002

Name	Tenure	Home Province
Zhang Guotao	1921-24	Jiangxi
Mao Zedong	1924-25	Hunan
Chen Duxiu	1925-27	Anhui
Zhang Guotao	1927 (May-June)	Jiangxi
Li Weihan	1927 (June-November)	Hunan
Luo Yinong	1927-1928	Hunan
Zhou Enlai	1928-31	Jiangsu
Kang Sheng	1931-33	Shandong
Ren Bishi	1933 (January-April)	Hunan
Li Weihan	1933-36	Hunan
Qin Bangxian	1936-37	Jiangsu
Chen Yun	1937-44	Shanghai
Peng Zhen	1944-53	Shanxi
Rao Shushi	1953-54	Jiangxi
Deng Xiaoping	1954-56	Sichuan
An Ziwen	1956-66	Shaanxi
Zhu Guang/	1967 (May-August)	n.a.
Guo Yufeng	1967-1969	Hebei
Guo Yufeng/Zheng Bingnian/Che Zhiying	1969-75	
Guo Yufeng	1975-77	Hebei
Hu Yaobang	1977-78	Hunan
Song Renqiong	1978-83	Hunan
Chen Yeping	1983-84	Sichuan
Qiao Shi	1984-85	Zhejiang
Wei Jianxing	1985-87	Zhejiang
Song Ping	1987-89	Shandong
Lü Feng	1989-94	Hebei
Zhang Quanjing	1994-99	n.a.
Zeng Qinghong	1999-	Jiangxi

Source: Zhonggong zhongyang zuzhibu, Zhonggong zhongyang dangshi yanjiushi, Zhonggong zhongyang dang'an guan (eds.), *Zhongguo gongchandang zuzhi ziliao, 1921-1997* (Beijing: Zhonggong dangshi chubanshe, 2000), Vol. 10, p. 71 and Vol. 11, pp. 228-229; Thomas Kampen, "The CCP's Central Committee Departments (1921-1991): A Study of Their Evolution," *China Report*, Vol. 29, No. 3 (1993), pp. 299-317.

From 1984, the Organisation Department's direct management power was limited to one level down. This move seems to be related to Deng Xiaoping's attempts to give more power to the provinces.[21] It also conformed to Zhao Ziyang's attempt to limit the reach of the Organisation Department and to upgrade the State Council's Ministry of Personnel. Thus in September 1988, Zhao transferred management of 54 enterprises and *shiye danwei* from the Organisation Department's control to the State Council.[22] Zhao Ziyang saw this as part of his plans to create a merit-based civil service system.[23]

According to these plans put forward at the 13th Party Congress in 1987, in the future, state and party cadres should be classified into two categories, a political-administrative category (*zhengwu gongwuyuan*) and a professional work category (*yewu gongwuyuan*).[24] Only the former category comprising some 500,000 of the 6 million-strong cadre corps was to be managed by the Party. The rest were to be managed by the newly formed Ministry of Personnel.

The new Ministry of Personnel was set up to meet the needs rising from Zhao Ziyang's attempts at administrative reform, in particular the separation of party and government and personnel reform. Thus the new government body was supposed to promote the introduction of a state "civil service system" and facilitate the government's involvement in personnel management. It was given responsibility for managing the state administrative leaders at the department (*ju*) – level. From the perspective of the party's Central Organisation Department, these moves signified an encroachment by the State Council on traditional party territory.[25]

The Organisation Department led by Song Ping fought back by refusing to transfer the cadre files to the Ministry of Personnel, a necessary first step for implementing Zhao Ziyang's personnel reform. The Department also tried to block the move to abolish Party core groups (*dangzu*) in government offices and departments.

The Organisation Department was further weakened when Song Ping in 1989 was appointed to the Standing Committee of the Politburo and Lu Feng, a deputy director since 1983, became head without belonging to the Central Committee. Lu Feng only became a member of the Central Committee at the 14th Party Congress in 1992. In 1994, a deputy director Zhang Quanjing replaced Lu Feng and headed the Organisation Department until 1999. At the time of appointment, Zhang

Quanjing was also not even a Central Committee member. None of the two made it to the Politburo.

In short, during the 1990s the Organisation Department was headed by relatively junior political figures who did not belong to the top policy-making bodies of the Party. This is a pattern quite unlike the 1970s and 1980s when the leaders of the Department were usually Politburo members with considerable political clout. This seems to indicate that although Zhao Ziyang was toppled in 1989, his personnel reform continued to exercise influence. The new civil service reform of 1993 is another indication of the weakening of the Organisation Department's role in personnel management and a continued strong role for the Ministry of Personnel.

However, from 1998, the process was reversed and the Organisation Department took back its appointment and management authority at the important *ju*-level in ministries and commissions at the central level;[26] a move clearly signifying that the government's role in cadre personnel work was being re-evaluated. This happened in connection with Zhu Rongji's 1998 institutional reforms which took away important functions from the Ministry of Personnel and cut its *bianzhi* by almost a half. Giving back to the Organisation Department the authority to manage leading personnel at the *ju*-level was part of a process of strengthening the role of the party in personnel management. The appointment of Jiang Zemin's close aide and confidant Zeng Qinghong as Director of the Department in March 1999 further signalled that the Organisation Department would increase its influence.

Currently, the civil service system which was implemented from 1993 onwards is in reality controlled by the Organisation Department. The Department regards all civil servants from the level of *ke* (section) and above as cadres. On this basis, it seems difficult to establish an independent civil service system. In fact, the very notion of the civil servants serving the state and not the party, runs counter fundamentally to the very idea of the leading role of the party.

Throughout the 1990s, especially from 1993 onwards, most Party documents issued to guide the work of leading personnel referred to civil servants (*gongwuyuan*) rather than cadres (*ganbu*). From 1999, the usage of the term "cadre" again gained prominence, indicating the shift in emphasis mentioned above.

APPOINTING AND SELECTING CADRES

Cadres are managed by the Party according to detailed regulations comprising recruitment, appointment, performance evaluation, training, etc.. The objective of cadre management is to make sure that professionally competent people are recruited and promoted and that these remain loyal to the Party's ideological and political line.

It is especially important to keep control over the leading cadres, who form the backbone of the system. Formally, the leading cadres in China at and above the county level are managed according to the "Interim Regulations on Selection and Appointment of Party and Government Leading Cadres" issued in February 1995.[27]

The General Provisions of these regulations emphasise that when selecting and appointing leading cadres in China, it is important to follow a number of basic principles. These include openness, equality, competition, and the selection of the best. Although the cadre corp should be based on meritocratic principles, it is also stressed that cadres should have both political integrity and ability (*de cai jianbei*) and that the Party should manage the cadres.

The chapter on Selection and Appointment Conditions stipulates that candidates to be promoted to leading party and government posts higher than the county (division) level must have held at least two posts at lower level organs and that candidates who are promoted from deputy post to a head post (*zheng zhi*) generally must have worked at the deputy post for more than two years. Also party and government cadres should be promoted one grade at a time. These stipulations have apparently been included to avoid the kind of "helicoptoring" which some cadres experienced during the Cultural Revolution. Finally, the chapter also stipulates that an educational level higher than vocational school is generally required and leading cadres at the ministerial or provincial leader level should have a college education or the equivalent.

Candidates to be considered for selection and appointment to leading posts should be proposed by so-called democratic recommendation procedures by the party committee at the same level or by the higher level organization or personnel department. At the time of an official's change of term, various people and personnel are consulted such as party committee members, leading members of government organs, leading members of the discipline inspection commissions and people's courts, and leading members of lower-level party committees and governments. Members of democratic parties and representatives of people without party affiliation should also be consulted.

Candidates that have been nominated will have to undergo evaluation according to elaborate procedures, which may include interviews for a number of leading offices or when an official is nominated to a new position in his or her own department. Evaluation is not confined to the end of the term of office. Leading members of party committees and government departments are also evaluated in the middle of their term. Any promotion or dismissal arising from the evaluations must undergo a process of deliberation (*yunniang*) and be reported to the party committee at the higher level.

The interim regulations also carry intricate provisions concerning how to make decisions through discussion in party committees and party core groups (*dangzu*). It, for example, requires a two-third quorum of the members of a given committee when appointment and dismissal of cadres are being discussed.

Chapter 7 of the interim regulations clearly underlines the power of the Party in appointing leading officials in state and government organs. Much of this power rests in the right to recommend candidates for leading positions. However, in certain circumstances, the Party has to take into account dissenting views on its recommendation of candidates. If for example a recommended candidate twice fails to get the approval of the standing committee of the people's congress for a government position, he shall not be recommended for the same post in the same locality again.

Chapter 8 deals with job exchange/transfer and avoidance (*huibi*). As a general rule, any leading member of a local party committee or government who has served in the same post for more than 10 years must be transferred to a new post. Normally, the principal party leader and the principal government leader of a locality or department should not be transferred simultaneously. As to avoidance, a system of job avoidance should be implemented among leading cadres of party and government organisations and their relatives such as spouses, lineal relatives by blood, and close relatives by marriage. People who are related in these ways may not work in the same office under the same superior or in jobs of a superior-subordinate relationship. Moreover, during discussion of cadre appointment held by a party committee or the organisation department an attendee must leave the room if it concerns his or her relatives. Finally, it is stipulated that under normal circumstances no individual must serve as party or government head in his native town.

These stipulations concerning post avoidance resemble the "avoidance" system of imperial China which forbade officials to serve in leading positions in their home provinces and also adopted measures to prevent civil servants with kinship relations to work in the same administrative office. The reactivation of the avoidance system seems to be related to attempts to break up powerful and sometimes corrupt networks which had developed in many localities and offices during the 1980s.[28]

Recently, the final version of the "Interim Regulations" was adopted and circulated. The revised regulations include references to "*sange daibiao*" in the preamble. More importantly, it is for the first time officially stipulated that leading cadres will need to have a college education to be promoted, and that *ju*-level cadres at least what equals a BA (*daxue benke*).[29]

In 1998, the "Interim Regulations" were supplemented by a development programme for establishing a national party and government leadership for 1998-2003, which among other things stressed the necessity to develop a reserve contingent for leading positions.

THE CADRE DEVELOPMENT PROGRAMME

According to the "development programme" of the Central Organisation Department, by the year 2003, every administrative level from the central down to the county and town (*zhen*) level should have a leadership line-up consisting of different age groups, ranging from leaders in their 60s to young cadres in their 40s.[30] This is to ensure a flexible cadre corp with a so-called rational age composition in the leadership bodies (*lingdao banzi*).

The formal requirement at the central ministerial (*bu, wei*) level is that in addition to leaders in their 60s, there should be "a number of" leaders around 50 and "at least" one member of this leadership group should be of no more than 45 years of age. It is stipulated that there must be "a number of" formal leaders of ministries and commissions (*zheng zhi*) who are in their 50s.

At the provincial level, there must also be a leadership body composed of different age groups. Requirements related to party leadership at this level include that there should be at least three leaders below the age of 50, whereas two cadres below this age would suffice for state organs at a similar level. For both party and state organs, at least one member of the leadership group should be no more than 45 years old. "A number of" formal party and government leaders should be no more than 50 years of age.

At bureau-level (*ju*, *si*, *ting*), the next lower level in the administrative hierarchy, similar rules established by the Organisation Department apply, but general age requirements are lowered by an additional 5 years in each category. For example, there must be "a number of" bureau directors and department leaders who are around 45 years of age and at the division level the requirement is 40 years of age.

As a general rule, the development plan emphasises that there should be at least one female member in the party and state leadership groups from the provincial down to the county level. This appears to be a very minimalist solution to the problem of under-representation of women in leading organs; and in general, one cannot escape the impression that the organisational department is more concerned with rejuvenating the leading organs rather than tackling the question of gender representation.

Minorities and people from non-CCP groups should be represented in leading organs according to the development plan. Thus party and government organs above the county level should be allocated cadres of national minority origin who possess both ability and political integrity. Government organs from the provincial level and below should include non-CCP cadres, and plans for the inclusion of such cadres in leadership organs at central levels should be worked out. At lower levels, province, city and county should at least have 10, 15 or 20 percent representation respectively of non-CCP cadres. This has paved the way for non-CCP cadres to make careers in the civil service. However, in general, these cadres will not assume the very top post (*zheng zhi*) in the administrative organs, but only the deputy position.

According to the development plan, it is necessary to establish a group of reserve cadres (*houbei ganbu*). These are the people who should be groomed to take over leadership positions. At the county level and above, there should be two persons listed on the reserve list for every head and one for every vice-head of a ministry, bureau or department. Non-CCP cadres should be represented on the list, with shares of 10, 15 and 20 percent respectively at the province, city and county level. The reserve list is important as the future leaders will be selected from this group. Therefore the list will be part of the nomenklatura system at the different levels of the power pyramid.

Finally, the development plan stresses the need to constantly upgrade the cadres through education and training. This has been restated recently in a major party document concerning cadre education and training for 2001-2005.[31] The document stipulates that all cadres at the county (division) level and above must attend at least three months of training in a Party school during the period. In addition, cadres should also attend at least 12 days of collective study a year organised by the Party committee.

At the ministerial (*bu*) and provincial (*sheng*) level, 400 cadres each year will receive training and refreshment courses on a rotational basis, so that altogether 2,000 cadres at this level will have undergone further study and training in the Central Party School, the Central School of Administration or in the National Defence University at the end of the period. The same number of party secretaries at the county level will receive further training in the planning period. The new training programme also acknowledges the need to expose leading cadres to the outside world in order to broaden their horizon and make them more qualified to lead. About 200 ministerial (*bu*) and department (*ting*) level cadres will be sent abroad on a yearly basis to conduct studies and inspection.

CADRE TRANSFER

The 1998-2003 development plan reinforces the sense of stronger Party control, which was already evident in the 1995 regulations. An instrument of further control which is often used in order to prevent "local fiefdoms" from developing is the so-called cadre transfer system. For lower level cadres, the rules are that leading cadres have to be transferred after their second term, i.e., after a maximum period of ten years. For top-level cadres, this rule is perhaps even more important and often takes place at the discretion of the ultimate power-holders in Beijing.[32]

Transfers can occur in two principal ways. One is inter-provincial transfer where cadres are transferred from one province to another. Examples include the transfers of party secretaries Wu Guangzheng of Jiangxi to Shandong in 1997 and Li Changchun of Henan to Guangdong in 1998 to replace local party leaders.

A second way of transfer is from provinces to the center or from the center to the provinces. In some cases, the transfer indicates promotion, as when Zhu Rongji was transferred from Shanghai to Beijing in 1991 or when provincial party secretary Jiang Chunyun was transferred from Shandong to the center in 1995 to serve as member of the central Party Secretariat; but in other cases transfer to Beijing could mean a demotion, as was true in the case of former Hainan provincial leaders Liu Jianfeng and Deng Hongxun in 1993. Transfer from the center to the provinces can also indicate attempts to reassert central control, as when politburo standing committee member Wei Jianxing replaced Chen Xitong as head of the Party in Beijing in 1997 or when Minister of Labour Ruan Chongwu replaced both Liu Jianfeng and Deng Hongxun in Hainan in 1993. Finally, transfer from center to province can take place in order to further someone's political career, as was probably the case when Song Defu in 2000 was transferred to Fujian to serve as party secretary of the province. Song Defu, a confidant of Hu Jintao, has important leadership experience from working in Beijing, e.g. as Minister of Personnel, but lacks provincial experience in order to seriously contend for national-level leadership.[33]

In fact, there is much more mobility and flexibility in the provinces than these examples would indicate. The legally specified term of office for a governor is five years. In reality, since 1979 the average tenure length for governors is only 2.85 years and 3.44 years for party secretaries.[34] Thus tenure patterns for top provincial officials do not seem to indicate considerable administrative localism in China in the reform era, as has been argued by some scholars.[35]

At lower levels, there are also considerable rotations. In 1996, the Ministry of Personnel disseminated the "Provisional Measures of Position Change Among Civil Servants." Following the decision to adopt these measures, in the 1996-1998 period, 400,000 civil servants were rotated.[36] The measures stipulate that normally rotations should affect no less than 30 percent of the civil servants from the section level and above. The mechanism is considered an important instrument to prevent localism and corruption.[37]

IDEOLOGICAL WORK

An additional mechanism for ensuring control over the cadres is ideological work. The ideological dimension of cadre behaviour appears again and again in the post-1949 period. It is epitomised in the concepts of "red" and "virtue" (*de*). At times, this dimension took over so that the cadres' political and moral credentials became more important than their professional and technical abilities. This was especially evident during the Great Leap Forward (1958-1960) and during the Cultural Revolution (1966-1976).

During Deng's era, one notes a certain de-ideologization. Deng favoured pragmatism and empirical work and downgraded lofty ideological debates and campaigns. The result was a weakening of the Party's legitimacy.

In tandem with the strengthening of cadre work and the Organisation Department's role in cadre management, Jiang Zemin has focussed on developing a stronger ideological orientation for the Party and its cadres. Thus Jiang introduced the "Three Talks" (san jiang) campaign in 1999 and in February 2000 a campaign called the "Three Representatives" (sange daibiao). This campaign has assumed major proportions and now forms the core of the CCP's current propaganda work. Recently, Jiang has introduced the notion of "rule by virtue" (yide zhiguo) in an attempt to bolster the Party's authority.[38]

For the cadres, this chain of events means a re-emphasis on "red" and "virtue" in the "red-expert" and "virtue-ability" dichotomies. For the Party, it is a way of ensuring that its instrument of power, the cadres, do not transform into purely civil servants who only care about their work in a bureaucratic sense and forget their larger mission of ensuring the legitimacy of the Party and its continued rule.

In fact, Party documents are increasingly stressing that cadres are supposed to possess both virtue (de) and ability (cai). In general, virtue is viewed as the fervour with which a cadre carries out the ideological line of the Party. Ability is generally interpreted as professional competence and performance in one's job. "Virtue and ability" represents a view of the role of the cadres which is also found in the concept of "red and expert". It implies that cadre management is not just a question of personnel management, it is also a question of upholding the correct ideological line.[39] Whereas Mao stressed redness (de), Deng tended to stress expertness (cai). Jiang Zemin's "Three Representatives" campaign can be seen as an attempt to close the distance between the two polar views of the role of the cadres. However, he is increasingly fighting a difficult battle and most cadres focus on developing their educational credentials and professional competence rather than deepening their ideological commitment.

DEEPENING CADRE WORK

Recently, cadre management has received new attention. This is related to the leadership change that is scheduled to take place as the third generation of Chinese leaders prepares to leave the scene at the next Party Congress in 2002. This change of guard will necessitate that new cadres be trained at lower levels so that there will be a pool of young leaders (fifth or sixth generation) to move up, when the time is ripe.

The recently published "Programme to Deepen the Cadre Personnel System" outlines the actions that will be taken in order to create a competent and more professional cadre corps.[40] In recruiting cadres, key measures include open appointment and selection. Within the next three to five years, all positions below the provincial *ting*-level will be filled according to a public notification system (*gongshi zhi*) and there will be experiments with multi-candidate elections for leading government and party posts. In supervising the cadres, clear measures for evaluation (*kaohe*) are to be introduced and combined with a public feedback on the quality of the work done, which involves soliciting public opinion on the performance of the cadres.

The Programme also envisages a further strengthening of the principle of work exchange between different departments and regions, so that cadres from the Eastern provinces would work for a while in Western provinces and vice versa. The programme also introduces other measures to ensure the flexibility and mobility of the cadre corps such as flexible remuneration based on performance and clear guidelines for removing incompetent leaders. Finally, a number of other measures will be adopted to strengthen the supervision and monitoring of the cadre personnel system, including pecuniary rewards for good job performance.

To be sure, many of these measures are already in effect and have been discussed through the 1990s and even earlier.[41] But it has a certain significance that they are now restated in a comprehensive form and discussed in a number of important editorials in the press. The programme has been worked out by the Organisation Department under Zeng Qinghong rather than the Ministry of Personnel, implying that the "deepening cadre personnel system" is the responsibility of the Party. The measures taken by the Party are expected to run parallel to Zhu Rongji's institutional reform as worked out by the State Council. This common long-term goal is a more efficient use of cadres and civil servants in the Chinese political system.

CONCLUSION

Cadres are the most important socio-political group in China. They staff the bureaucracy and form the backbone of the system. By controlling the cadres, the Chinese Communist Party ensures its control over Chinese society at all levels. To be sure, not all cadres are party members and not all party members are cadres. However, almost all leading cadres are members of the party.

As a result of modernisation and reform, the public sector in China is confronted with new and complex tasks. Therefore, it is necessary to create a more competent and professional cadre corps. New guidelines and regulations have been adopted with stipulations concerning open appointment and selection of cadres and filling of official positions and examination. These include a public notification system for filling positions below the *ting*-level and experiments with multi-candidate elections for leading government and party posts; regular job rotation from the section level and above; strengthening the supervision of cadres by introducing clear measures for performance evaluations combined with public feedback on the quality of work done. There will also be flexible remuneration and pecuniary rewards to high performers.

Cadres in China have become better educated and are younger of age than was the case in Mao's time. About 80 percent of leading cadres (defined as cadres at the county level and above) have some kind of college education, and as for *ju*-level cadres, the proportion is 88 percent. These trends are so significant that some scholars posit the emergence of technocratic leadership and a technocratic state in China.

Clearly, age and education play a key role in selecting new leaders at the various level of the system. However, the nomenklatura system is still in place and in recent years, the party has actually strengthened its role in managing the cadre force. This has meant that the Ministry of Personnel has lost a significant part of its authority to appoint and manage leading personnel. Most significantly, the ministry has had to hand over to the Central Organisation Department the authority to appoint leaders at the *ju*-level which it had acquired in 1988. Moreover, in recent years, the Organisation Department has been involved in drawing up and circulating all major guidelines for cadre management at the central as well as at local levels. The Organisation Department is even closely involved in holding the examinations for future civil servants which have taken places recently in Beijing and in many other provinces. The massive "*sange daibiao*" campaign is further proof of current attempts to bolster the party's authority.

The strengthening of the party's role in China runs counter to the ruling paradigm in contemporary China studies, which through the 1990s, have focussed on the societal aspect of party/state-society relations, resulting in a plethora of studies on civil society, social organisations, private entrepreneurs and other forms of non-governmental development. In fact, this focus on society and social movements has pushed the party out to the ruling paradigm. It is high time to bring the party back in.

ENDNOTES

1   See, for example, Kjeld Erik Brødsgaard and David Strand, *Reconstructing Twentieth Century China: State Control, Civil Society, and National Identity* (Oxford: Clarendon Press, 1998); He Baogang, *The Democratic Implications of Civil Society in China* (New York: St. Martin's Press, 1997); Tony Saich, "Negotiating the State: The Development of Social Organizations in China," *The China Quarterly*, No. 161 (March 2000), pp. 124-141; Gordon White et al., *In Search of Civil Society* (Oxford: Clarendon Press, 1996).

2   The standard work on the Chinese cadre system in the era of Deng Xiaoping is Hong Yung Lee, *From Revolutionary Cadres to Party Technocrats in Socialist China* (Berkeley: University of California Press, 1991). See also Melanie Manion, "The Cadre Management System, Post-Mao," *The China Quarterly*, No. 102 (June 1985), pp. 203-233 and John P. Burns, "Strengthening Central CCP Control of Leadership Selection: The 1990 Nomenklatura," *The China Quarterly*, No. 138 (June 1994), pp. 458-491. Newer work include Shiping Zheng, *Party vs. State in Post-1949 China* (Cambridge: Cambridge University Press, 1997); Maria Edin, *Market Forces and Communist Power* (Uppsala: University Printers, 2000); and David S.G. Goodman, "The Localism of Local Leadership Cadres in Reform Shanxi," *Journal of Contemporary China*, Vol. 9, No. 24 (2000), pp. 159-183. For the Maoist period see especially A. Doak Barnett, *Cadres, Bureaucracy, and Political Power in Communist China* (New York: Columbia University Press, 1967); John Lewis, *Leadership in Communist China* (Ithaca: Cornell University Press, 1963); and Michel Oksenberg, "Local Leaders in Rural China, 1962-65: Individual Attributes, Bureaucratic Positions, and Political Recruitment," in A. Doak Barnett (ed.), *Chinese Communist Politics in Action* (Seattle: University of Washington Press, 1969).

3   For a discussion of the role of political and educational credentials in career mobility, see Andrew G. Walder, "Career Mobility and the Communist Political Order," *American Sociological Review*, Vol. 60, Number 3 (June 1995), pp. 309-328.

4   Pertinent literature on technocratic leadership and technocratic development in China include Hong Yong Lee, *From Revolutionary Cadres to Party Technocrats in Socialist China* (Berkeley: University of California Press, 1991); Li Cheng and Lynn White, "Elite Transformation and Modern Change in Mainland China: Empirical Data and the Theory of Technocracy," *The China Quarterly*, No. 121 (March 1990), pp. 1-35; Li Cheng and Lin White, "The Fifteenth Central Committee of the Chinese Communist Party: Full-Fledged Technocratic Leadership with Partial Control by Jiang Zemin," *Asian Survey*, Vol. 38, No. 3 (March 1998), pp. 231-264; and Zheng Yongnian, "Technocratic Leadership, Private Entrepreneurship and Party Transformation in Post-Deng China" (Paper presented to the Annual Meeting of the Association for Asian Studies, Washington, April 2-4, 2002).

5   The paper is mainly based on recently published material on the organisational history of the Chinese Communist Party (CCP), which also contains statistics on the evolution and composition of Chinese cadres in the 1949 to 1998 period. See Zhonggong zhongyang zuzhibu, Zhonggong zhongyang dangshi yanjiushi, Zhonggong zhongyang dang'an guan (eds.), *Zhongguo gongchandang zuzhi ziliao, 1921-1997* (Beijing: Zhonggong dangshi chubanshe, 2000), Vol. 1-19. Another important collection of materials consists of 22 volumes of party documents covering the period from 1980 to 2000. Renshibu zhengce fagui (ed.), *Renshi gongzuo wenjian xuanbian* (Selection of Documents Concerning Personnel Work) (Beijing: Zhongguo renshi chubanshe, 1991), Vol. 1-22. These documents contain unique details concerning cadre recruitment and management.

6   See Lenin, *What is to be Done?: Burning Questions of Our Movement* (Beijing: Foreign Languages Press, 1973, originally published 1902).

7   Ibid., p. 225.

8   See Ezra F. Vogel, "From Revolutionary to Semi-Bureaucrat: The 'Regularisation' of Cadres," *The China Quarterly*, No. 29 (January-March 1967), pp. 36-60.

9   A substantial part of my research on Chinese cadres and the CCP was conducted during a one-year research stay at the East Asian Institute, National University of Singapore (2000-2001). This and the following sections on the Organisation Department and on the formal regulations concerning cadre appointment are drawn from Kjeld Erik Brødsgaard, "China's Cadres: Professional Revolutionaries or State Bureaucrats", *EAI Background Brief No. 94* (July 2001); and id., China's Efforts at Cadre Management," *EAI Background Brief No. 95* (July 2001).

10   See Zhonggong zhongyang zuzhibu, Zhonggong dangshi yanjiushi, and Zhongyang dang'an guan, *Zhongguo gongchandang zuzhishi ziliao, 1921-1997, fujuan 1* (Material on the Organisational History of China's Communist Party, 1921-1997. Appendix Volume 1) (Beijing: Zhonggong dangshi chubanshe, 2000) p. 1357.

11   Ibid., p. 1359.

12   Li and White, "The Fifteenth Central Committee of the Chinese Communist Party: Full-Fledged Technocratic Leadership with Partial Control by Jiang Zemin."

13 The percentage almost reached 98 percent when in November 2002, a new CC (the 16th CC) was elected. See Kjeld Erik Brødsgaard, "The 16th Party Congress in China: A Note on Personnel Changes," *The Copenhagen Journal of Asian Studies*, No. 16 (December 2002), pp. 138-149.

14 At first glance it is surprising that the member of the Politburo in general have a lower education than members of the Central Committee. However, it can be explained by the fact there are still a number of veteran party leaders, born and raised before 1949, who have only received rudimentary education.

15 Li Cheng and Lynn White, "The Thirteenth Central Committee of the Chinese Communist Party: From Mobilizers to Managers," *Asian Survey*, Vo. 28, No. 4 (April 1988), pp. 371-399; and id., "Elite Transformation and Modern Change in Mainland China and Taiwan: Empirical Data and the Theory of Technocracy". For a different perception, see Xiaowei Zang who claims that "it would be a sweeping generalization to argue that college education is a precondition for promotion" in China. See Xiaowei Zang, "Provincial Elite Recruitment: Education and Experience," *Provincial China*, No. 4 (October 1997), pp. 50-55. My data shows that a high eduational level is a *sine qua non* for rising in the cadre system. This also applies to provincial elite recruitment which is the topic of Zang's article.

16 Ibid., p. 1372.

17 See "Liao Wang" zhoukan bianjibu, bian, *Guowuyuan jigou gaige gailan* (General Survey of the Institutional Reform of the State Council) (Beijing: Xinhua renmin chubanshe, 1998), 85-92.

18 See Thomas Kampen, "The CCP's Central Committee Departments (1921-1991): A Study of Their Evolution," *China Report*, Vol. 29, No. 3 (1993), pp. 299-317.

19 On the nomenklatura system in China, see, for example, John P. Burns (ed.), *The Chinese Communist Party's Nomenklatura System* (New York: M.E. Sharpe, 1989); Manion, "The Cadre Management System, Post-Mao: The Appointment, Promotion, Transfer and Removal of Party and State Leaders."

20 There is also a secondary list, the "List of Cadre Positions to be reported to the Center", which actually extends the party's control into many of the organisations mentioned in the first list and also covers economic enterprises and *shiye danwei*. See "Zhongyang zuzhibu guanyu xiuding 'zhonggong zhongyang guanlide ganbu zhiwu mingchengbiao' de tongzhi" (Notice of the CCP Organisation Department on Revision of the "Job Title List for Cadres Managed Centrally by the Chinese Communist Party"), May 10, 1990, in Renshibu zhengce fagui, bian, *Renshi gongzuo wenjian xuanbian* (Selection of Documents Concerning Personnel Work) (Beijing: Zhongguo renshi chubanshe, 1991), Vol. 13, pp. 35-53. See also John Burns, "Strengthening CCP Control of Leadership Selection: The 1990 Nomenklatura," *The China Quarterly*, No. 138 (June 1994), pp. 458-491.

21 Ibid., p. 464.

22 "Zhongyang zuzhibu guanyu biandong wushiwuge qishiye danwei lingdao ganbu zhiwu guanli quanxiande tongzhi" (Notice of the Central

Organisation Department on Changing the Management Jurisdiction for Leading Cadre Positions of 55 Enterprises and Service Units), September 24, 1988, in Renshibu zhengce fagui, bian, *Renshi gongzuo wenjian xuanbian* (Selection of Documents Concerning Personnel Work) (Beijing: Xuefan chubanshe, 1989), Vol. 11, pp. 6-9.

23   Works on the Chinese civil service system include John P. Burns, "Chinese Civil Service Reform: the 13th Party Congress Proposals," *The China Quarterly*, No. 120 (December 1989), pp. 739-770; Jean-Pierre Cabestan, "The Reform of the Civil Service," *China News Analysis*, No. 1437 (15 June 1991), pp. 1-8; King K. Tsao, "Civil Service Reform," in *China Review 1993* (Hong Kong: The Chinese University Press, 1993), pp. 5.1-5.23; King W. Chou, "The Politics of Performance Appraisal," in Miriam K. Mills and Stuart S. Nagel (eds.), *Public Administration in China* (Westport, Connecticutt: Greenwood Press, 1993), pp. 105-122); Tao-chiu Lam and Hon S. Chan, "Reforming China's Cadre Management System," Asian Survey, Vol. XXXVI, No. 8 (August 1996), pp. 773-786.

24   See Zhao Ziyang, "Yanzhe you Zhongguo tese de shehuizhuyi daolu qianjin" (Advance Along the Road of Socialism with Chinese Characteristics), *Renmin Ribao*, November 4, 1987.

25   Kjeld Erik Brødsgaard, "Institutional Reform and the *Bianzhi* System in China," *The China Quarterly*, No. 170 (June 2002), pp. 79-104.

26   On the importance of bureau-level cadres, see also Yasheng Huang, *Inflation and Investment Controls in China: The Political Economy of Central-Local Relations During the Reform Era* (Cambridge: Cambridge University Press, 1996).

27   "Zhonggong zhongyang guanyu yinfa 'dang zhengfu lingdao ganbu xuanba renyong gongzuo zanxing tiaoli' de tongzhi (Notice of the Central Central Committee of the CCP Concerning "Interim Regulations on Selection and Appointment of Party and Government Leading Cadres"), February 9, 1995, in *Renshi gongzuo wenjian xuanbian* (Selection of Documents Concerning Personnel Work), Vol. 18 (Beijing: Zhongguo renshi chubanshe, 1996), pp. 13-26.

28   For a discussion of the role of the avoidance system in cadre management in China, see also Jean-Pierre Cabestan, "The Reform of the Civil Service," *China News Analysis* (June 15, 1991), pp. 1-9. In April 1999, the General Office of the CC issued a notice on work exchange among leading cadres. It emphasized once more that county and municipal heads should not be appointed to their home regions and that those who had headed a county or city for more than ten years should be transferred. The notice also called for more frequent transfer of provincial leaders, either to another province or to the national level. See Zhonggong zhongyang bangongting guanyu yinfa 'dangzheng lingdao ganbu jiaoliu gongzuo zanxing guiding' de tongzhi (Notice of the General Office of the Central Committee of the CCP Concerning "Interim Regulations on the Job Exchange of Leading Government and Party Cadres"), April 22, in *Renshi gongzuo wenjian xuanbian*, Vol. 22, pp. 27-32

29   See "Dang zhengfu lingdao ganbu xuanba renyong gongzuo tiaoli" (Regulations on Selection and Appointment of Party and Government Leading Cadres), *Renmin Ribao*, July 23, 2002

30   Zhongyang zuzhibu (Organization Department of the CCP), "1998-2003 nian quanguo dang zheng lingdao banzi jianshe guihua gangyao" (Development Programme Concerning the Establishment of a National Party and State Leadership for 1998-2003), June 24, 1998, in *Renshi gongzuo wenjian xuanbian*, Vol. 21, pp. 90-100.

31   "2001-2005 nian quanguo ganbu jiaoyu peixun guihua" (The 2001-2005 Education and Training Plan for All Cadres), *Renmin Ribao*, May 11, 2001.

32   See also "Zhongong zhongyang guanyu yinfa 'dang zhengfu lingdao ganbu xuanba renyong gongzuo zanxing tiaoli' de zongzhi" (Notice of the Central Central Committee of the CCP Concerning "Interim regulations on Selection and Appointment of Party and Government Leading Cadres"), February 9, 1995, pp. 13-26.

33   For information on elite politics and elite transfer, see various issues of the monthly journal *China aktuell* which carries updated information on elite appointmnents and transfers at central and provincial level. See also Cheng Li, "After Hu, Who? – China's Provincial Leaders Await Promotion," *China Leadership Monitor*, Issue One (Winter 2001), pp. 1-14 and Tables 1-5; Joseph Fewsmith, *Elite Politics in Contemporary China* (Armonk, N.Y.: M.E. Sharpe, 2000); and Zheng Yongnian, "China's Incremental Political Reform: Lessons and Experiences," in Wang Gungwu and John Wong, eds., *China: Two Decades of Reform and Change* (Singapore: Singapore University Press, 1999), pp. 11-40.

34   Huang Yasheng, *Inflation and Investment Controls in China*, p. 115.

35   See, for example, Li Cheng and David Bachman, "Localism, Elitism, and Immobilism: Elite Formation and Social Change in Post-Mao China," *World Politics*, Vol 42 (October 1989), pp. 64-94.

36   See *People's Daily Online*, August 16, 2000.

37   For a discussion of these measures in relation to the issue of corruption in China, see Zou Keyuan, "Why China's Rampant Corruption Cannot be Checked by Laws Alone," *EAI Background Brief* No. 74 (2 November 2000). On Chinese cadres and the issue of corruption see also Xiaobo Lü, *Cadres and Corruption: The Organizational Involution of the Chinese Communist Party* (Stanford: Stanford University Press, 2000).

38   See Zheng Yongnian and Lai Hongyi, "Rule by Virtue: Jiang Zemin's New Moral Order for the Party", *EAI Background Brief* No. 83 (March 2001).

39   For a discussion of this aspect of cadre management, see also Franz Schurmann, *Ideology and Organization in Communist China*, pp. 162-172.

40   "Shenhua ganbu renshidu gaige gangyao" (The Programme to Deepen the Cadre Personnel System), *Renmin Ribao*, August 21, 2000.

41   See Thiagarajan Manoharan, "Basic Party Units and Decentralised Development," *Copenhagen Papers in East and Southeast Asian Studies*, No. 5 (1990), pp. 137-146.

CHAPTER 3

Civil-Military Relations in China: Party-Army or National Military?

DAVID SHAMBAUGH

INTRODUCTION

As the Chinese Communist Party (CCP) has had to adapt to changes in Chinese society during the reform period and in the wake of the collapse of communist party-states elsewhere,[1] it has also had to adjust and renegotiate its relationship with other key organs of state power.[2] Among these has been the party's relationship with the People's Liberation Army (PLA). Yet the renegotiated relationship has occurred not just between party and army, but also between both and a third party: the state. Since the mid-1990s there has been an evident, if subterranean, three-way struggle over the jurisdictional control of the military being played out among the army, party and government in China. The army has sought greater autonomy from party control so as to better pursue its redefined professional missions, which has forced the party to redefine and adjust its instruments of control over the army, while the government (state) has tried to increase its own jurisdictional control over the armed forces while continuing to delineate its sphere of responsibilities distinct from the party (*dang-zheng fenkai*).

While this subterranean struggle has been evident to careful observers, because of their inherently political and highly sensitive nature, these changes have been only incremental and subliminal. They rarely spill over into the public domain. No explicit and radical restructuring of party-army relations has been undertaken. To do so would call into question the very legitimacy of the CCP as a ruling party. The longstanding Maoist paradigm that the 'party controls the gun' remains standard mantra (*tifa*) and is, in fact, still the case. We certainly cannot claim that the army has gained its 'independence' from party control. The army would certainly follow orders from the party leadership to use force against external threats and most likely against internal ones as well. The army does remain loyal to the party. There is no danger of a military *coup d'état* of the army against the party, as is often the case in other one-party authoritarian states. Nonetheless, as this paper argues, there do exist growing signs of 'bifurcation' between these two institutions - which cumulatively add up to a significant, and ongoing, redefinition of the institutional and jurisdictional relationship between the CCP and PLA.

FROM PARTY-ARMY TO CIVIL-MILITARY RELATIONS

Western analysts of the PLA have long considered it more appropriate to use the term 'party-army relations' rather than the more generic term 'civil-military relations,' as commonly used elsewhere in the world. This was so because of a number of important historical considerations that set the PLA's relationship to the ruling Chinese Communist Party apart from its counterparts in other countries. It was recognized that militaries in communist political systems are intrinsically and inherently different from other one-party authoritarian systems, to say nothing of militaries in democratic polities.

In communist party-led political systems (the People's Republic of China included), the military is an institutional and armed instrument of the party. Communist militaries do not exhibit the degree of 'corporate' identity and political autonomy characteristic of Western militaries. This is so for a number of reasons. The first is that the act of seizing - and maintaining - power is usually a violent one, in which armed force is used for political ends. This fact intrinsically places the military (and other coercive security services) in the position of being an armed adjunct of the party rather than as an autonomous force charged with defending the nation against external threat.[3] As such, a communist military's national security mission is a dual one - to be used against both internal and external enemies. Moreover, communist militaries (including the PLA) are institutionally penetrated by the ruling communist party - particularly through a network of political commissars, party committees and other mechanisms. This is the essence of Leninist parties - to penetrate institutionally all key organs of state and society. Yet it is not simply an issue of zero-sum penetration, but also a positive sum relationship whereby the army is given an important stake in the ruling party. One way this is done is to co-opt the military elite into the party elite. In the PLA, all officers above the rank of Senior Colonel are party members. This is even more evident at the top of the political system through the 'interlocking directorate,' where there is usually a high percentage of senior serving military officers on the party's elite organs (the Central Committee and Political Bureau), with many more senior party officials having previously served in the armed forces (trading their uniforms for civilian garb but maintaining close factional ties with military elites). In such communist militaries, 'political work' and ideological indoctrination of the officer corps and the rank and file are prominent and occupy considerable time (net time not spent in training).

In short, in communist militaries (including the PLA), there exists an essential *symbiosis* between the army and ruling communist party. Sometimes this symbiosis is reflected in party attempts to assert greater *control* over the military, while at other times communist militaries have become more politically assertive vis-à-vis the ruling party – although in such systems, because of the essential symbiosis, militaries do not engineer *coups d'état* against their ruling parties (although they may become involved in intra-party factional manoeuvring).

Such a model of party-army relations was wholly applicable to China until the second half of the 1990s, although I argue in this paper that it has been only partially applicable since that time. For a variety of reasons and judged by a variety of indicators, the relationship between the PLA and the CCP is evolving significantly and possibly transforming fundamentally. To be sure, it is still a party-army in important respects, but a number of the criteria noted above no longer characterizes the CCP-PLA relationship. The military's mission today is almost exclusively external, to protect national security rather than internal security (the People's Armed Police has been created to take primary responsibility for this mission). Importantly, the 'interlocking directorate' has been completely broken by generational succession, whereby not a single senior party leader today possesses a single day of military experience and, currently, only two senior PLA officers in the High Command (Generals Chi Haotian and Wang Ruilin) have any significant experience in high-level politics - a trend that will become more pronounced with the transition to the 'fourth generation' CCP leadership. The party-army elite has clearly become 'bifurcated' from each other.

Another change is that the criteria for career advancement in the PLA are no longer as dependent on political factors. Senior PLA officers from the Central Military Commission down to Group Army commands are now promoted on meritocratic and professional criteria, while political consciousness and activism count for very little. The officer corps is becoming increasingly professional in classic Huntingtonian terms. Indeed, recruitment into the PLA is now based almost exclusively on technical criteria. The role of the ideology is virtually nil and political work has declined substantially; concomitantly the General Political Department's mission has become more oriented to providing welfare for soldiers and their families than to indoctrinating them. Time formally spent in political study (approximately 30 percent in the past) is now spent in training. Political work (*zhengzhi gongzuo*) itself is now much more oriented towards welfare, morale and living issues than to ideological indoctrination. This is also true of curriculum content in institutions of professional military education (PME), now mandatory for all officers above the division level. Officers spend time learning the intricacies of doctrine, strategy and tactics rather than communist doctrine. With commercial divestiture, time formerly spent in business is now also spent increasingly in training, as PLA units have been ordered to divest themselves of their commercial holdings. The military is also now subject to control by a large number of formal laws and regulations, instead of the informality and personalization of command and control. The State Council and Ministry of Finance are now exerting much stronger control over the PLA budgeting process, and at least on paper (the National Defence Law) the President and National People's Congress possess command and oversight responsibilities over the PLA.

Accordingly, for these reasons, it is now more analytically appropriate to consider *civil-military* rather than *party-army* relations in the PRC. The driving catalyst for all of these changes has been the professionalization of the armed forces.[4] To be sure, as is argued below, this evolution is ongoing and incomplete. The former model has not, and is not likely to, replace completely the latter model. Yet, along a number of criteria, it does seem clear that the PLA is moving away from its traditional communist institutional ethos into a new stage of limited autonomy from the ruling party.

Theoretically, in terms of the comparative study of civil-military systems, this new stage may also be viewed as the intermediate stage in a transition from a party-army to a 'national army'. China and the PLA are clearly not there yet, and it is very questionable whether a national army can exist within the context of a political system dominated by a single, ruling communist party. Yet there have been, and continue to be, subterranean discussions in China and the PLA about greater state control of the military, a military that serves the nation and not just the ruling party, and a military controlled by civilian rule and governed by legislative oversight. As if to put a fine point on the sensitivity of such considerations, there has been a series of ongoing condemnations of such 'bourgeois' concepts in the party and military media from time to time. It is clearly a sensitive issue that cuts right to the core of PLA identity and CCP legitimacy, if not the efficacy of the PRC itself.

Is it feasible to have a national army in a Leninist system? Or can such a military only exist in a democratic system? Given the evidence of economic and educational reforms in China, to take but two issue areas, it is not inconceivable that a hybrid relationship of a professional national military could co-exist with a ruling communist party, but within a framework of state and legislative control. Yet, on the other hand, many of the elements necessary to proclaim the PLA a 'national army' seem anathema to the CCP and its rule. For example, it would require at least the following: a 'real' Ministry of National Defence (not the hollow shell of the MND at present); a civilian Minister of Defence; presidential chairmanship of the Central Military Commission; thorough control of military by the state President, National People's Congress, and State Council; a series of established laws and procedures governing the use of force and mobilization of the military; strong legislative oversight of the armed forces; complete budgetary control over the military by the legislature and no extra-budgetary revenue; and no political content in professional military education. Judged on these criteria, it is clear that the PLA and China are a long way from becoming a national army, yet there are discussions and tendencies in this direction taking place in China and the PLA today.

To understand how the PLA and the CCP got to this stage, it is appropriate to understand some historical context, before considering the implications of recent changes that have occurred in civil-military relations.

HISTORICAL AND COMPARATIVE CONSIDERATIONS

Any consideration of civil-military relations in China as it enters the twenty-first century must proceed from clear cognizance of the past. Over the last century, individual military actors and the military as an institution have played key and active roles in the Chinese regime and nation. This has taken a variety of forms over time, but the military has never been fully isolated from the political arena. Both military and party elites have viewed military involvement in politics, domestic security, society and even commerce as legitimate. While the political involvement of the Chinese military is distinct from the Western tradition of military corporatism and separation from the political arena (based on the Ottoman, European and American experiences[5]), it is hardly unique among developing or socialist countries. Many post-colonial and developing nations have experienced sustained military rule and praetorian intervention,[6] while most former communist party-states were based on the 'interlocking directorate' of party and military elites and the penetration of the military and security services by party control mechanisms.[7] More recently, scholarly attention has been paid to the military's withdrawal from politics and subordination to civilian control in the process of the transition to democracy across the developing and industrializing world.[8] An interesting literature has also begun to address civil-military relations in the Chinese context of a democratizing Taiwan.[9] Scholars specializing in post-1949 Chinese military politics would do well to tap into all of these studies, as the PLA shares many commonalities with these other cases. As professionalism and corporate identity rise in the PLA, and greater efforts are made to subject the military to state control, comparing other national experiences will be increasingly pertinent to understanding the future evolution of the PLA.[10]

Understanding the interrelationship among party, state and army in the PRC today must also recognize several long-standing and unique features of civil-military relations in China historically. Throughout the past century, from the late imperial to the post-Deng era, the Chinese military has played an active role in the political and economic life of the nation (even if soldiers, along with merchants, were at the bottom of the Confucian social order). Key late-Qing reformers, such as Li Hongzhang, were military men who believed that the path to 'wealth and power' (*fu-*

97

qiang, the cardinal tenet of all subsequent Chinese elites) lay in mastering military technologies and building a strong self-defence capability in order to rebuff foreign encroachment and regain China's unity and lost greatness. Li's policy of 'building shipyards and arsenals' and dispatching students to Europe and America to study in defence colleges and scientific institutes bespoke this bias. To be sure, heated debate existed among Qing elites over the wisdom of this policy - some argued that it was a distorted path to development which disproportionately emphasized military modernization over the need for a more comprehensive technological base; others opposed the inherent 'Westernization' and cultural contamination implicit in the strategy; while still others believed that the 'sources of wealth and power' were less technological and more civic, political and intellectual in nature. These debates have resonated over the past century, and echoes of them are still present today.

After the republican revolution of 1911, military elites remained prominent in the new government (not the least of which was General Yuan Shikai, who became the first President of the republic) and an emphasis on building a modern military remained a high priority. With Yuan's death in 1916, the ensuing constitutional crisis and failure of the new regime to consolidate national power, China slipped into a prolonged period of territorial division, national fratricide and rule by an ever-shifting variety of military warlords. This blood-thirsty period was halted only when force was met with force during Generalissimo Chiang Kai-shek's 1928 Northern Expedition, which united the country under the civil-military rule of the Nationalist party and army (Kuomintang and Kuominjun). The new KMT elite during the 'Nanjing decade' (1927-37) contained a large proportion of military officers, secret police and intelligence operatives - many trained under Chiang at the Whampoa Military Academy and in military and paramilitary institutions in Germany and the Soviet Union. This regime would only become more militarized following the outbreak of the Sino-Japanese War in 1937.[11]

Meanwhile, in the communist-controlled base areas of China's interior, a similar militarily dominant political regime was also taking shape. The Red Army was born not only of necessity, out of the need literally to fight for survival against Japanese and KMT forces, but also as a result of the strong Soviet and German influences on the politicization of the military and militarization of the party. Throughout the revolutionary period, an essential symbiosis existed between party and army in pursuit of state power.[12] The Chinese Communists' ultimate victory in 1949 was at least as much a military as political one - as the Red Army fought the Japanese invaders and defeated Kuomintang forces on the battlefield, pacified the countryside, and occupied the cities.[13] So closely intertwined were the institutions of party and army historically, that one must recognize the unique and often dominant roles that the military has played, as a normative and institutional actor, in the life of the nation. As Chairman Mao astutely observed, 'Political power grows out of the barrel of a gun!' Yet, as early as 1929, Mao also warned that, 'Our principle is that the party commands the gun, and the gun must never be allowed to command the party.'[14] Mao's edict actually obscured the organic party-army symbiosis - a condition that obtained until the 1980s when Deng Xiaoping and Yang Shangkun began to implement reforms that had the net effect of incrementally increasing the corporate autonomy and separate identity of the armed forces vis-à-vis the CCP. As a result of this symbiosis, the military came to the party's aid in suppressing civil unrest at several key junctures after 1949 (not the least of which during the Cultural Revolution). The CCP may have been born in the Shanghai underground and Jiangxi Soviet, but it had militarist parentage and was reared on the battlefield. Its formative years were spent at war, and it matured in a society with a strong militaristic tradition.

It was precisely because of this symbiotic relationship that the military never balked when instructed to maintain social order, suppress 'counter-revolutionaries,' arrest the Gang of Four, or perform other internal security duties. In other words, *involvement* by the army in 'political' affairs and domestic security was considered normal and legitimate, rather than a matter of *intervention*. This perspective also goes a long way towards explaining the PLA's role in the 1989 suppression of pro-democracy demonstrators and other citizens of Beijing, although the questioning by some senior military elites of this action and insubordination in the ranks at the time suggests the previous predominant identity of symbiosis had begun to give way to one of greater 'autonomy' of the armed forces vis-à-vis the Communist Party. Following the Tiananmen crackdown, there was a renewed attempt by the party (and its constituent organs inside the PLA) substantially to increase control over, and ensure the loyalty of, the military. But this only lasted a year or two, and subsequently disparate signs of increased PLA 'autonomy' became apparent. As is discussed below, one dimension of this increased autonomy has been the tentative moves to increase *state* (i.e. government and legislative) control over the military, as distinct from party control. On the one hand, this does not mean that the longstanding party-army symbiosis is inert; nor, on the other hand, does it mean that a new era of a 'national army' (*guomin jundui*) or 'state army' (*guojia jundui*) has dawned. But recent changes do indicate that the interrelationship of party, army and state are in flux, and that the demands of 'professionalism' are redefining civil-military relations in China in directions more familiar in other modernizing nations.

THE IMPACT OF THE PAST ON THE PRESENT

This background has profound implications for understanding Chinese communist civil-military relations after the CCP came to power and in the present period. Scholars in PLA studies have devoted substantial analysis, and have had a lively discourse on this issue in recent years. Unfortunately, this discussion has taken place almost entirely among PLA specialists, and has been largely sidelined to the periphery in the field of Chinese political studies. In this discourse, Ellis Joffe has noted three schools of thought and lines of argument that have emerged over time: *symbiosis*, *party control* and *professionalism*.[15] Too often, analysts have juxtaposed these approaches whereas, as Joffe astutely notes, they should be viewed as complementary. These are not mutually exclusive categories of analysis. Professionalism has been an ongoing process since the 1950s and Marshall Peng Dehuai's tenure as Minister of Defence. Even under Marshall Lin Biao in the 1960s, and contrary to conventional wisdom, the military continued to professionalize and modernize in several dimensions. If there has been a tension, it has been between *party control* and *limited military autonomy*. While the norm of a symbiotic party-army relationship has been sustained over time, in different periods over the last 50 years (notably 1959-62, 1971-82 and 1989-92) the CCP has taken extra efforts to exert control over the armed forces, while at other junctures the military has sought to increase its corporate autonomy from the CCP. On several occasions, the military sought to exert its role in the high-level party affairs (notably 1967, 1976, 1989 and to a certain extent in 1996), but it can be plausibly argued that this had more do with certain elites 'pulling' the military into politics during periods of social unrest and party weakness.[16] In other periods (1954-59, 1974-75, 1982-89), the armed forces have sought to increase their autonomy from the party, but this must be carefully distinguished as *limited autonomy*, as at no time has the PLA ever sought fully to separate itself from the CCP (or vice versa).

The military has simply sought greater autonomy over affairs it considers to be fully in its corporate domain - training, doctrine, force structure, personnel appointments, military education and protection of national security. Meanwhile, professional tendencies have been more or less persistent over time, although with a particular emphasis in the late-1950s, mid-1980s and late-1990s. The PLA has been, in Joffe's apt phrase, a 'party-army with professional characteristics'.[17] Thus, the army's relationship with the party-state has evolved and fluctuated over time. Harry Harding has astutely noted that this fluctuation as a function of the strength or weakness of the party-state.[18] That is, during periods when the party-state was strong and the society stable, the military tended to act as a corporate bureaucratic lobby. When the party-state was weakened, the military tended to act either as a political arbiter between competing factions, support one faction against another, or intervene more broadly to stabilize society.

Joffe's characterization remains partially apt today, although since the mid-1990s we may have witnessed increasing military autonomy from the party in general, as well as nascent signs of increased state (i.e. government) control of the armed forces.[19] This would suggest a slight variation on his typology: a more linear evolution from *symbiosis* to *control* to *limited autonomy*. This is discussed at greater length above and below, but suffice to note here that increased state control need not imply, ipso facto, the zero-sum displacement of the party's relationship with the army. From one perspective, the relationship of the military to the state and party can be seen as complementary. That is, the state may be increasing its mechanisms of control and lines of authority over the armed forces, while the party withdraws to a more 'elevated' position. This has certainly been the case during the last decade in terms of the party-state relationship with respect to economic management, whereby the CCP sets forth the broader policy direction (*fangzhen*) while the state formulates more concretely the policy line (*luxian*) and implements specific policies (*zhengce*). The issue here is really one of *relative autonomy* and jurisdictional distinctions between institutional hierarchies and within functional policy spheres (which some political scientists refer to as the 'zoning of authority'). As the party has increasingly 'withdrawn' from its former totalistic and monopolistic influence over society and economy, greater 'space' and relative autonomy have been created for institutional and civic actors in China. While the tight symbiosis of party and army was forged early on, it is necessarily one of the last bonds to be broken in the reform process.

THE CHANGING RULES OF CIVIL-MILITARY RELATIONS

Since the 1990s the 'rules of the game' in civil-military relations in China have changed as a result of several developments:

- The institutional narrowing of the arenas of interaction (to the CMC);
- The more limited range of issues on which PLA leaders have a legitimate right to voice opinions, and their increasing reluctance to do so;
- Increased professionalism in the senior officer corps and a concomitant decline in the promotion rates of officers with backgrounds as political commissars;
- A PLA desire to concentrate solely on issues of 'army building' and a generally non-interventionist approach to non-military issues;
- The creation of the PAP and concomitant disengagement of the PLA from internal security functions;
- An implicit bargain struck between Jiang Zemin and the PLA High Command that as long as he supports PLA budgets and professional goals, they will defer to his leadership status.

The 'rules of the game' have also been changed fundamentally as, for the first time, there now exist rules that define the military's functions and roles. These have been codified in several laws, documents and regulations in recent years. Their promulgation has been instrumental in advancing the twin goals of regularization (*zhengguihua*) and professionalization (*zhiyehua*) of the armed forces. The NPC has passed 12 laws and regulations, including: the National Defence Law, Military Service Law, Military Facilities Protection Law, Civil Air Defence Law, Reserve Officers Law, Hong Kong Special Administrative Region Garrison Law, Military Service Regulations, and Military Officers Ranks and Regulations.[20] The State Council and CMC have jointly adopted 40-odd administrative laws and regulations, and the CMC has implemented 70-odd on its own, while individual PLA departments, service arms and military regions have formulated more than one thousand military rules and regulations.[21] Taken together, the roles and functions of the PLA are now specified as never before.

The National Defence Law (NDL) has significant implications for civil-military relations. Adopted as law by the Fifth Session of the 8th National People's Congress in March 1997 and authorized by Presidential Decree No. 84, the National Defence Law is important for a number of reasons.[22] The law went through five years of drafting and revision prior to its promulgation. This drafting process took place entirely within military legal circles, as co-ordinated by the Military Legal Office of the CMC.[23]

The NDL provides an overall framework for 'administering the army according to law' (yifa zhijun). The NDL elaborates in some detail various aspects of the armed forces organization, duties, 'construction' and legal responsibilities. It contains specific information about mobilization for war, maintenance of the armed forces during peacetime, leadership over the armed forces, the defence industrial and scientific establishment, military education and training, and many other aspects. These details are set forth in a lengthy document of 12 chapters and 70 articles. Associated publications interpret and spell out in further detail the content and meaning of the provisions of the NDL.[24]

Among these areas of importance, the NDL is particularly striking for one notable fact: the subordination of the military to the state. In Chinese, the clear connotation of the term for state (guojia) is government, as distinct from the party. In China, this is operationalized to mean the State Council and its constituent ministries and commissions, the PRC President, as well as the National People's Congress (NPC). Beginning in the 1980s, there was a conscious and deliberate attempt more clearly to demarcate the jurisdictional responsibilities of the CCP, State Council and NPC - particularly the policy of 'separating party from government' (dang-zheng fenkai) in economic policy-making and commercial management. Of course, this general process required the promulgation of numerous laws and regulations which had the cumulative effect of strengthening the NPC as a fourth institutional pillar of the PRC, along with the party, army and government. In the process, the NPC itself gained increased oversight functions vis-à-vis the government. State Council policies, budgets and appointments became at least nominally subjected to legislative review by the NPC. However, the Communist

103

Party as an institution has always insisted that it should police itself and its own membership, and this remains unchanged. This has included party members in the armed forces, who are subject to the CCP's Discipline Inspection Commission system. The CCP accordingly has its own constitution and its own 'election' procedures for its leadership. The party is clearly separated from the state. Its relationship to the armed forces has always been one of symbiosis and/or control. Certainly, the party has institutionally penetrated the military to ensure this relationship.

However, the 1997 National Defence Law suggests some fundamental departures in the relationship of the military to the party and state. In a number of its articles, and in several significant respects, the NDL clearly subordinates the 'armed forces' (which is defined as including the People's Armed Police, militia, and reserves) to *the state*. The term 'state' (*guojia*) is mentioned no fewer than 39 times in the law. Lest there be any ambiguity about the implications of this term, and the institutional subordination of the armed forces to state control, it is specified in some detail. Only in a single clause is the relationship of the army to the party mentioned (Article 19): 'The armed forces of the People's Republic of China are subject to leadership by the Communist Party, and CCP organizations in the armed forces shall conduct activities in accordance with the CCP constitution' (i.e. presumably with regard to party committees and discipline inspection work). Everywhere else in the NDL, the military's subordination to the state is made abundantly clear, e.g.:

- (Article 5): 'The state shall exercise unified leadership over national defence activities.'
- (Article 7): 'The Chinese People's Liberation Army and the Chinese People's Armed Police shall carry out activities to support the government....'
- (Article 10): 'The Standing Committee of the National People's Congress shall decide on the proclamation of a state of war and on general mobilization or partial mobilization in accordance with provisions of the constitution, and shall exercise other functions and powers in national defence as prescribed by the constitution.'
- (Article 11): 'The President of the People's Republic of China shall proclaim a state of war and issue mobilization orders in pursuance with the decisions of the National People's Congress and its Standing Committee....'

- (Article 12): 'The State Council shall direct and administer the building of national defence and exercise the following functions and powers' (nine categories of responsibilities, including fiscal appropriation).
- (Article 13): 'The Central Military Commission shall direct the armed forces of the country and exercise the following functions and powers' (ten categories).
- (Article 14): 'The State Council and Central Military Commission may call co-ordination meetings according to circumstances to solve problems concerning national defence.'

In numerous other articles, the NDL stipulates responsibilities of the state for national defence matters. The absence of mention of the CCP is striking in this important law, which signals an important shift in civil-military relations.

The shift signalled in the NDL was explicated further in the 1998 National Defence White Paper. While the White Paper includes the single clause that 'Given the new historical conditions, the Chinese army upholds the absolute leadership of the CCP...,' greater emphasis is placed on the NPC, State Council and CMC as the institutions controlling the PLA, e.g.:

> In accordance with the Constitution, the National Defence Law and other relevant laws, China has established and improved its national defence system. *The state exercises unified leadership over defence-related activities.* The NPC of the PRC is the highest organ of state power. It decides on questions of war and peace, and exercises other defence-related functions and powers provided for in the Constitution ... *The State Council directs and administrates national defence work*, and the CMC directs and assumes unified command of the nation's armed forces ... *The active components of the PLA comprise the state's standing army ... The state exercises unified leadership and planned control over defence research and production. The State Council leads and administrates defence research and production, as well as defence expenditure and assets.* The CMC *approves* the military equipment system of the armed forces and military equipment development plans and programs ... in co-ordination with the State Council, and manages defence outlays and assets jointly with the State Council. *The state* practises a *state* military supplies order system to guarantee the acquisition of weapons and other war materials. *The state* practises a financial

allocations system for defence spending. It decides the size, structure and location of defence assets and the adjustment and disposal of these assets in accordance with the needs of national defence and economic construction. The State Council and CMC jointly lead mobilization preparation and implementation work.[25] [*emphasis added by author*]

The adoption of the NDL provides evidence that the PLA is being placed increasingly under state control with the concomitant removal of party controls. To be sure, ambiguities remain. For example, it is unclear if references to the Central Military Commission mean the state or party CMC. This may be a moot point given that the membership composition of these two bodies is currently identical, although the language describing the CMC strongly suggests that its relationship to the armed forces is either one of joint administration with the State Council or merely 'line authority' to implement decisions, whereas broad decision-making authority seems to rest ultimately with the State Council, NPC Standing Committee and President of the republic. But, here, ambiguity exists insofar as Jiang Zemin concurrently holds the offices of President, CCP General Secretary, and CMC Chairman. Only when the President no longer heads the party but directs the CMC (as may occur in 2002 at the 16th Party Congress) will we know for sure that the party-army link has been fully severed. Another sign would be if the CMC were to become a body solely composed of military officers (similar to the Joint Chiefs of Staff) and the Minister of Defence were a civilian.

While one should have little doubt that the Chinese Communist Party and its leadership remain the ultimate source of political power and authority in China, it does seem clear that these steps taken in 1997-98 and subsequently, are efforts to disentangle the military from party control. While the 1975 and 1978 national constitutions both explicitly subordinated the armed forces to the command of the CCP and its Chairman, that is no longer the case. Even much of the ambiguity of the early 1990s is being clarified.[26] Of course, it is difficult to determine the extent to which these reforms are taking root normatively and psychologically in the army, state and society. Interviews with PLA officers in the late-1990s still suggest substantial ambiguity over the issue of state versus party control. In fact, to many it remains a non-issue. When asked whether the armed forces are subordinate to the state or party, some officers have a puzzled look and respond, 'What do you mean? Of course, the PLA is loyal to the party! The party rules the country and the PLA defends it!'[27] For many in the PLA, as this officer's response illustrates, the issue is precisely one of loyalty rather than constitutional control, and many still see the CCP as synonymous with the state and country! If orders came to defend the nation against an external opponent or enforce internal security, few officers or soldiers would question whether the order ultimately came from the CMC, State Council, NPC Standing Committee, PRC President or CCP General Secretary. While there have clearly been attempts to demarcate the parameters of authority between party, army and state by law, there still exists an essential fusion of the three - with ultimate party control - in the minds of most Chinese citizens. After 70 years of party control and symbiotic fusion between the three, it is not easy to redefine these interrelationships.

The continued ambiguity is also reflected in PLA publications and materials used by the General Political Department (GPD). Authoritative materials published to explain the new National Defence Law tend to emphasize the state's control over the armed forces, while GPD materials tend to take the opposite tack and emphasize party leadership.

The standard textbook used for 'political work' in the armed forces, published *after* the promulgation of the National Defence Law, is quite explicit about the CCP's relationship to the PLA.[28] It states unambiguously:

> The party's absolute leadership over the army is a fundamental feature of army building ... The CCP should be our army's only and independent leader and commander ... At no time can the CCP share authority over the military with other parties or organizations ... If the Communist Party loses its military authority, it will have no status ... Our army is an armed group to carry out the party's political tasks.[29]

The GPD volume is also explicit that the PLA is organizationally subordinate to the CCP Central Committee and *Party's* CMC.[30] This runs in direct contradiction to the NDL and line of authority discussed above. Nowhere does the volume mention the role of state President, NPC, State Council, or state more generally. Perhaps most interesting is the extent to which the 'bourgeois' notion of state control of the armed forces is sharply criticized:

Bourgeois liberal elements' advocacy of the military's "non-party-fication" (*jundui feidanghua*) is nonsense. In modern society there is no army that is not involved in politics and, essentially, there is no army not controlled by a ruling party. In Western capitalist countries, which practise the multi-party system, armies superficially do not belong to the party but to the state. But, in essence, it is a military that is led by the capitalist class and its ruling agents, the party ... Therefore, behind the state there are always capitalist parties that lead and command armies, and carry out capitalist dictatorship. Capitalist parties are never neutral in politics ... The basic content of this involvement is to oppress the proletariat and people's revolutions internally, and carry out invasion and expansion externally ... We must never allow ourselves to copy the Western capitalist countries' model, and never allow the excuse of the state's leadership over the army to deny the party's leadership over the army. Political work in our armed forces should criticize the absurd theory of a "non-party-fied army", and should emphasize and consistently insist on the absolute leadership over the army and ensure that our army is under the party's absolute leadership forever.[31]

In contrast, PLA materials used to explain the National Defence Law to troops take a very different approach by emphasizing state control.[32] Unlike the GPD source above, this volume states unambiguously, 'National defence is one of the state's functions, and therefore the leadership and management of national defence is an important expression for state organs to realize their state functions.'[33] This volume explicates in 550 pages the various ways and justifications for state control over the military in China. It states that the head of state exercises 'commanding power over the armed forces,' but subsequently states that this 'commanding power' is 'exercised by the CMC Chairman'.[34] This is not a problem at present as Jiang Zemin occupies both positions, but this has not historically always been the case (perhaps it is to indicate that the CMC Chairman and state President will henceforth be one and the same individual). It states clearly that the NPC Standing Committee is the 'highest organ of state power' and that the 'CMC is subordinate to the highest organ of state power,' but then confuses matters by stating that 'it is *also* subordinate to the CCP Central Committee.'[35] In a telling paragraph (that should not be surprising but makes mockery of efforts to separate and strengthen state power), the volume explains: 'Insisting on the party's leadership over the army is important in realizing *the party's leadership over the state ... Due to historical reasons, the army is actually led by the Party's CMC.'*[36] The volume then goes on to define and justify various mechanisms that have been put into place to increase state supervision over various aspects of the military matters.

Discussions in the Chinese military media, such as the army newspaper *Liberation Army Daily*, also continue to indicate that the debate over party vs. state control of the armed forces remains alive. A sharp unsigned article in April 2001 attacked 'Western hostile forces that vigorously advocate the armed forces should be "separated from the party" (*fei dang hua*), "depoliticized" (*fei zhengzhi hua*) and "placed under the state" (*guojia hua*).' The article went on to add that, 'This is a corrosive agent that vainly attempts to weaken and do away with the CCP leadership and tries to disintegrate the soul of our armed forces, and is the great enemy of our party, state, and armed forces.'[37]

PROSPECTS FOR THE FUTURE

Despite efforts to legislate and codify increased state/government authority over the PLA, the essential control by the CCP remains apparent (even if the symbiosis has become attenuated). If anything, there appears to be an ongoing struggle between the party and the state, but the winner is likely to be the military as it exerts increased autonomy from both.

Changes in the interrelationship of party, army and state in contemporary China must also be viewed in the context of emerging patterns of civil-military relations across Asia. With few exceptions (North Korea, Vietnam), civil-military relations in East, Southeast and South Asia have been fundamentally redefined in recent years in the process of democratization. In a number of countries that have known harsh authoritarian and military rule (South Korea, Taiwan, the Philippines, Indonesia, Thailand, Bangladesh and Pakistan), the armed forces have been removed from political power and influence, made accountable to sovereign legislatures, and returned to the barracks. Militaries in mufti have been replaced by democratically elected civilians. In all of these countries, the emasculation of political power and praetorian tendencies of the militaries has been a crucial element in establishing democratic institutions and rule. The trend in Asia follows that of Latin America and Africa.

The experiences of these countries, but particularly Taiwan, are suggestive for future civil-military relations in China. Thus far, the emerging literature on the process of democratic transition in Asia has paid relatively little attention to the civil-military dimension,[38] although it is viewed as an important variable in the comparative literature.[39] More comparative research needs to be done on Asian militaries and civil-military relations.[40] Scholars of the PLA and Chinese politics need to place the recent changes in civil-military relations in the PRC outlined above in this broader regional context, while comparativists need to look more closely at the Chinese case. The current state of politics in the PRC certainly does not suggest that a creeping transition to democracy is silently taking place,[41] as the CCP retains its grip on power. But, at the same time, we must not mistake the potential significance of the legislative efforts to subordinate the PLA to state control.

The Chinese case must also be placed in the comparative context of former socialist states led by communist parties.[42] Broadly speaking, the experiences of the former Soviet and East European militaries suggest that professionalization and party control are by no means mutually exclusive, but in not a single case were these militaries consciously placed under state control via legislative means. Indeed, in many cases, they fought (unsuccessfully) to save their ruling communist parties.[43] The problem for the Chinese military has never been to subordinate itself to civilian authority, but rather to state control. Also, unlike the Soviet and East European experiences, the PLA has exhibited a long-standing tension between professionalization and attempts of politicization by the CCP.[44]

In these respects, the Chinese military is moving - or rather is being moved - into an entirely new era of civil-military relations and corporate professionalism. As such, one would surmise that the PLA will not shirk from the task of defending national security against external enemies – but will it do so again against internal enemies that may threaten the rule of the Communist Party? This will be the ultimate test of the redefined relationship of the army to the party and state in China.

ENDNOTES

*   This paper draws and expands upon a chapter in my forthcoming book *Modernizing China's Military: Progress, Problems & Prospects* (Berkeley and London: University of California Press, forthcoming 2002)

1   For further explorations on this topic see my 'Remaining Relevant: the Challenges for the Party in Late-Leninist China,' in David Finkelstein (ed.), *China's New Leadership* (Armonk, NY: M. E. Sharpe, forthcoming 2002).

2   This will be the subject of my forthcoming book *Hanging On: the Chinese Communist Party since the Collapse of Global Communism.*

3   For further elaboration of this concept see my 'Building the Party-State in China, 1949-1965: Bringing the Soldier back in,' in Timothy Cheek and Tony Saich (eds.), *New Perspectives on State Socialism in China, 1949-65* (Armonk, NY: M. E. Sharpe, 1997).

4   This is also recognized by You Ji in his 'China: From Revolutionary Tool to Professional Military,' in Muthiah Alagappa (ed.), *Military Professionalism in Asia: Conceptual and EmpiricalPerspectives* (Honolulu: East-West Center, 2001), pp. 111-36.

5   The classic typology is, of course, Samuel P. Huntington, *The Soldier and the State: The Theory and Politics of Civil-Military Relations* (Cambridge, MA: Harvard University Press, 1957). Also see Morris Janowitz, *The Professional Soldier* (New York: The Free Press, 1960).

6   The pertinent literature here is extensive. See, for example, Timothy Colton and Thane Gustafson (eds.), *Soldiers and the State* (Princeton: Princeton University Press, 1990); Abraham F. Lowenthal and Samuel J. Fitch (eds.), *Armies and Politics in Latin America* (New York: Holmes & Meier, 1986); Alfred Stepan, *Rethinking Military Politics* (Princeton, NJ: Princeton University Press, 1988); Viberto Selochan, *The Military, the State, and Development in Asia and the* Pacific (Boulder, CO: Westview Press, 1991); Amos Perlmutter, *The Military and Politics in Modern Times* (New Haven, CT: Yale University Press, 1977); Eric A. Nordlinger, *Soldiers in Politics* (Englewood Cliffs, NJ: Prentice-Hall, 1977); Catherine M. Kelleher (ed.), *Political-Military Systems* (Beverly Hills, CA: Sage Publications, 1974).

7   This sub-field has also generated a substantial, if somewhat dated, literature. See, for example, Dale Herspring and Ivan Volges (eds.), *Civil-Military Relations in Communist Systems* (Boulder, CO: Westview Press, 1978); Jonathan Adelman (ed.), *Communist Armies in Politics* (Boulder, CO: Westview Press, 1982); Dale R. Herspring, *Russian Civil-Military Relations* (Bloomington: Indiana University Press, 1996); Kenneth M. Currie, *Soviet Military Politics* (New York: Paragon Press, 1991).

8   See Larry Diamond and Marc F. Plattner (eds.), *Civil-Military Relations and Democracy* Baltimore: The Johns Hopkins University Press, 1996).

9   Monte Bullard, *The Soldier and the Citizen: The Role of the Military in Taiwan's Development* (Armonk, NY: M. E. Sharpe, 1997); Cheng Hsiao-shih, *Party-Military Relations in the PRC and Taiwan* (Boulder, CO: Westview Press, 1990); Bruce J. Dickson, *Democratization in China and Taiwan: The Adaptability of Leninist Parties* (Oxford: Clarendon Press, 1998); David Shambaugh,

111

'Taiwan's Security: Maintaining Deterrence amidst Political Accountability,' in David Shambaugh (ed.), *Contemporary Taiwan* (Oxford: Clarendon Press, 1998); Lu-Hsun Hung, 'Observations on Civilian Control of the ROC Armed Forces Following the Passage of Two Laws Concerning National Defense,' *Taiwan Defense Affairs*, vol. 1, no. 2 (Winter 2000/01), pp. 7-38; and Chin-chiang Su and Ming-shih Shen, 'Taiwan's Political Warfare System and Civil-Military Relations,' *Taiwan Defense Affairs*, vol. 1, no. 2 (Winter 2000/01), pp. 39-64.

10   Recent efforts to do this are Thomas Bickford, 'A Retrospective on the Study of Chinese Civil-Military Relations since 1979: What Have We Learned, Where Do We Go?;' and David Shambaugh, 'Commentary on Civil-Military Relations in China: The Search for New Paradigms,' in James C. Mulvenon and Andrew N. D. Yang (eds.), *Seeking Truth from Facts: A Retrospective on Chinese Military Studies in the Post-Mao Era* (Santa Monica, CA: The Rand Corporation, 2001).

11   Hans van de Ven, 'The Military in the Republic,' *The China Quarterly*, no. 150 (June 1997).

12   David Shambaugh, 'The Soldier and the State in China: The Political Work System in the People's Liberation Army,' in Brian Hook (ed.), *The Individual and the State in China* (Oxford: Clarendon Press, 1997); Harlan Jencks, *From Muskets to Missiles: Politics and Professionalism in the Chinese Army, 1945-1981* (Boulder, CO: Westview Press, 1982), chapters 1-3.

13   This assertion does not obviate the important roles played by land reform and nationalism.

14   Mao Zedong, 'Problems of War and Strategy,' *Selected Works of Mao Zedong*, vol. II (Beijing: Foreign Languages Press, 1975), p. 224.

15   Ellis Joffe, 'Party-Army Relations in China: Retrospect and Prospect,' in David Shambaugh (ed.), *China's Military in Transition* (Oxford: Clarendon Press, 1997). Interestingly, this typology mirrors the debates among scholars of civil-military relations in the former Soviet Union. Albeit in a different context, Timothy Colton articulated the symbiosis thesis, Roman Kolkowitz the control thesis, and William Odom the autonomy thesis.

16   See Ellis Joffe, *The Military and China's New Politics: Trends and Counter-Trends* (Taipei: Chinese Council on Advanced Policy Studies, CAPS Papers, no. 19, 1997).

17   *Ibid.* In his landmark study, Harlan Jencks tends to juxtapose the two as he argues that, 'Chinese officers, especially those below corps level, are strongly disinclined toward political involvement.' See Jencks, *From Muskets to Missiles*, p. 255.

18   See Harry Harding, 'The Role of the Military in Chinese Politics,' in Victor Falkenheim (ed.), *Citizens and Groups in Contemporary China* (Ann Arbor: University of Michigan Center for Chinese Studies, 1987), pp. 213-56.

19   Many analysts are dubious that this process is underway, and some - such as Jeremy Paltiel - believe it to be a false dichotomy. Paltiel asserts that 'the Chinese armed forces have never faced a choice between loyalty to the state and obedience to the party.' See Jeremy Paltiel, 'PLA Allegiance

on Parade: Civil-Military Relations in Transition,' *The China Quarterly*, no. 143, September 1995. Paltiel is correct in this observation, but I would argue that increasing state authority and control over the armed forces does not ipso facto imply a zero-sum displacement of the party's relationship with the army. They may be seen as complementary.

20   See Thomas A. Bickford, 'Regularization and the Chinese People's Liberation Army: An Assessment of Change,' *Asian Survey* (May/June 2000), pp. 456-74.

21   *China's National Defence* (Defence White Paper), issued by the Information Office of the State Council, (July 1998).

22   For an excellent evaluation of the National Defence Law, see Samantha Blum, 'The National Defence Law of China - the Dragon's head of Military Law,' unpublished paper (May 2001).

23   Interview with Sr. Col. Zhu Jianye and Sr. Col. Shen Qiuchao of this office (April 1999).

24   The most important of these is Xu Jiangrui and Fang Ning, *Guofangfa Gailun* [Survey of the National Defense Law] (Beijing: Junshi kexue chubanshe, 1998).

25   *Ibid*, pp. 15-17 (English edition).

26   For excellent and learned discussions of the legalities during this period see Jeremy Paltiel, 'PLA Allegiance on Parade' and 'Civil-Military Relations in China: An Obstacle to Constitutionalism?,' *The Journal of Chinese Law*, (September 1995), pp. 35-65.

27   Interview with Academy of Military Sciences officer, (September 1998).

28   National Defence University Party History and Party Building Research Office (ed.), *Zhongguo Renmin Jiefangjun zhengzhi gongzuoxue* [A Study of Political Work in the Chinese People's Liberation Army] (Beijing: National Defence University Press, 1998).

29   *Ibid*, pp. 197-98.

30   *Ibid*, pp. 198-200.

31   *Ibid*, pp. 203-04.

32   Xu Jiangrui and Fang Ning, *Guofangfa Gailan*.

33   *Ibid*, p. 114.

34   *Ibid*, pp. 122-23.

35   *Ibid*, p. 118.

36   *Ibid*.

37   No author, 'Clearly Understanding the Essence of "Separating the Armed Forces from the Party", "Depoliticizing Them", and "Placing Them under the State",' *Jiefangjun bao*, 18 April 2001, in FBIS-CHI, 18 April 2001.

38   See Larry Diamond and Marc F. Plattner (eds.), *Democracy in East Asia* (Baltimore: Johns Hopkins University Press, 1998); and Diamond, Plattner, Yun-han Chu and Hung-mao Tien (eds.), *Consolidating the Third Wave Democracies* (Baltimore: Johns Hopkins University Press, 1997).

39   See Diamond and Plattner , *Civil-Military Relations and Democracy*.

40   For a significant effort in this direction see Muthiah Alagappa (ed.), *Coercion and Governance: The Declining Role of the Military in Asia* (Stanford, CA: Stanford University Press, 2001).

41   For one view to the contrary see Minxin Pei, ' "Creeping Democratization" in China,' in Diamond, Plattner, Chu and Tien (eds.), *Consolidating the Third Wave Democracies*, pp. 213-27.

42   To be sure, there is no small literature in this field. See the sources noted in footnote 13.

43   See Gerald Segal and John Phipps, 'Why Communist Armies Defend Their Parties,' in Richard H. Yang (ed.), *China's Military: The PLA in 1990/91* (Kaohsiung: National Sun Yatsen University, 1991), pp. 133-44.

44   In the large literature on this subject, see in particular Harlan Jencks, *From Muskets to Missiles*.

4

The National People's Congress Oversight: Power and the Role of the CCP

CHAO CHIEN-MIN

INTRODUCTION

How to gain more autonomy by insulating itself from executive branch interference while at the same time representing the interests of the constituency - this have been the central issue of Western legislative governments, which have a strong tradition of checks and balances. However, these two goals are constantly at odds, as is demonstrated by the United States Congress. As Kenneth A. Shepsle (1988) observed, before the 1970s, House Standing Committee members focused on insulating the House from the executive branch, rather than on representing constituents' interests. Similar trade-offs have been noted in other legislatures, too. While writing about the German Bundestag, for instance, Schuttemeyer (1994: 51) suggests that policy-making by an increasingly professionalized parliament has been stressed at the cost of ties between representatives and constituents. Studies of newly emerging legislatures have manifested an analogous trend in that legislators are devoting more attention to law making at the expense of their engagement with voters (Colton 1996).

Facing this dilemma, most scholars agree that institutionalization is a key indicator of legislative change, since institutionalization inevitably brings enhanced autonomy to a legislature (Canon 1989; Polsby 1968; Squire 1992). Whether a parliament can develop an identity of its own has long been a focus of legislative attention. Typically, scholars use measures such as membership turnover, competition, and difficulty of entry to leadership as a gauge of a legislature's autonomy and its success at 'boundary-maintenance'.

China's National People's Congress (NPC) is known for functioning as a rubber-stamp institution. This body has proved unable to create an autonomous niche for itself, in order that interventions from other power sources, such as the Communist Party, can be effectively reduced to the minimum. However, reforms have been undertaken since the 1980s to revitalize the institution's functions. Amid the raging wave of corruption and malfeasance caused by the decentralization of resources for the sake of developing the economy, the People's Congress is increasingly viewed as a formidable organ to combat the irregularities. How far has the NPC travelled down the road towards institutionalization? Can the NPC evolve into a representative body similar to its counterpart in the West? Has the relationship between the NPC and the CCP changed over the years as the economic reforms progress? This article will try to provide answers to these questions.

The article first examines the theory of legislative institutionalization as extrapolated from the US experience, and then goes on to examine China's National People's Congress. There can be no doubt that the autonomy of the National People's Congress has increased greatly since the 1980s. With regard to the issues of strengthening functions, institutionalizing organizational structures and supporting facilities of the NPC standing committees, here too one finds evidence of increased professionalization. The article concludes by reinforcing the observation that the legislature in China is more professionalized and therefore more autonomous. The traditional function of the NPC as a representative body of the People's Democratic Dictatorship is downplayed in the study.

FROM RUBBER STAMP TO THE 'THIRD POWER CENTRE'?

Contrary to the prevalent view that representative assemblies in communist countries are no more than rubber-stamp organizations, deprived of the real power of policy-making (Skilling 1973: 96), scholars generally agree that the People's Congress (PC) in China has begun to perform some concrete functions since the 1980s, when the country reversed its development course by adopting an open-door policy and

116

reforming its economy. One Hong Kong scholar even goes so far as to suggest that the PC has become 'a third power centre' in addition to the Communist Party and the executive branch of Government (Wu 1999: 327-38). Some recent studies on the PRC's legislative establishments concentrate on the PC's new autonomy and assertiveness (Nathan 1996; O'Brien 1994, 1998, 1990a, 1990b, 1988), especially in the area of lawmaking and the decrease in the Communist Party's control over the legislative organ (Tanner 1994, 1995). Other studies are attracted by PC's institutionalization (O'Brien 1990; McCormick and Unger 1996), or they discuss the opposition and contention that PCs have manifested while in session (Solinger 1982), or stress the importance of PC's representation (O'Brien 1998; McCormick and Unger 1996: 36-38). One topic conspicuously missing from the academic discourse has been the representative assembly's supervisory power.

Owing to the Communist Party's overwhelming dominance, the supervisory power has been considered either as being 'seldom exercised' (Nathan 1996: 49) or as having an uneven record unworthy of further study (O'Brien 1994: 97). This article argues that a new round of political reforms has quietly started at the provincial legislatures and that PCs, especially those at the provincial level, have managed to develop rights to check the executive administration and to some extent the Party itself. And these locally initiated reforms have often become part of the reformation drive at the central level after their effectiveness has been proven. This is not happening, moreover, at the expense of Party authority; on the contrary, this change has been underwritten by the Party itself and the Party has benefited accordingly, with its authority enlarged and bolstered.

With the mounting need for the rule of law and anti-corruption measures, and in view of the fact that PCs and People's Congress Standing Committees (PCSCs) have in the past been largely inactive for structural reasons, specialization in the legislature in the form of a differentiation in committees and subcommittees has become a political exigency. As a newly invigorated set of institutions still struggling to define their position, the PCs are nevertheless weak in the triad of power distribution vis-à-vis the other two institutions - the Communist Party and the executive branch of the government. What has been germinating in the legislative bodies is that both of the specialized committees are groping constantly for more responsibilities as well as a powerful and centralized leadership. The trends of specialization and centralization of leadership

117

have contributed not only to the rise of oversight in the previously insipid legislative assemblies, but also to a redistribution of power in the local political arena. In the end, the central government often is forced to adopt a bottom-up approach and continue reforms initiated and experimented with at the local level.

SPECIALIZATION, DIFFERENTIATION AND THE GROWTH OF COMMITTEES

It has been argued that control of the administration is one of the most important functions of legislative bodies in all modern democracies (Loewenberg *et al.* 1985). The value of legislative monitoring of the executive branch, many contend, is to ensure the triumph of representative government by lines of accountability running through the organ that embodies popular sovereignty. Therefore, representativeness rather than effectiveness is the irreducible core (ibid.: 546). The perceived goals of legislative oversight are to check dishonesty and waste, guard against harsh and callous administration, evaluate implementation in accordance with legislative objectives, and ensure administrative compliance with statutory intent (ibid.: 547).

In his seminal work on the US Congress, Samuel P. Huntington (1990) concluded that structurally this organ has become more specialized with less leadership since its creation. The tendency of the weakening of central leadership and the dispersion of power to the committees have shifted the function of the US Congress to that of oversight. Other studies confirm the theory that knowledgeable oversight is being promoted by committee and subcommittee layouts. It is further contended that members' aspirations tend to strengthen committee government at the expense of executive autonomy and, to some degree, of party discipline (Loewenberg *et al.*1985: 556)

Committees have existed intermittently in China's NPC since 1954, when the first constitution was promulgated, but without great effect. Committee members could not 'thoroughly, specifically, and rigorously' examine financial matters, nor did they take part in drafting legislation or oversight (O'Brien 1988: 364-65). The 1979 constitution used the term 'special committee' (*zhuanmen weiyuanhui*), for the first time, a phrase that was retained in the 1982 constitution. In February 1979, the NPC set up a Committee on Bills and Proposals and a Committee on Minorities with the authority of drafting and revising regulations.[1] The 1982 constitution further set up six permanent committees on Law; Nationalities; Finance and Economics; Education, Science, Culture, and Public Health; Foreign Affairs; and Overseas Chinese Affairs. These committees gained the rights to draft legislative proposals and to examine bills and inquiries referred by the NPC or NPCSC (O'Brien 1994: 365). In April 1988, one more committee - the Committee on Internal and Judicial Affairs - was created. In March 1993, the Committee on Environment Protection was set up at the Eighth NPC Congress.[2] Finally, at the Ninth NPC Congress in March 1998, the Committee on Agriculture and Villages came into existence. Since 1988, all NPC committees have enacted their own organic rules and in addition to the permanent (or special) committee, the NPC also has ad hoc committees and provisional committees. The Preparatory Committee for the Special Region of Hong Kong, set up by the NPCSC in January 1996 in accordance with authorization from the NPC, was designed to cope with the legal aspect of Hong Kong's reversion to China.

Though a late development, the committees have rapidly emerged as the core of the NPC. At the Sixth NPC meeting held in 1983, leaders decided that bills must be sent to the Law Committee or relevant committees for review after the first reading. This heralded the arrival of the legislative reading system and six committees were created as a result. The new development also effectively changed the old legislative process in which the NPCSC took the central seat. The year 1986 was pivotal in terms of specialization when Chen Bixian, an NPC vice chairman, announced that the six committees were to become a permanent part of the NPC institution. At the same time, it was decided that those NPCSC members residing in Beijing should, in principle, join committees. A reinforcement plan was executed when over 40 members of the NPC Standing Committee were assigned to committee responsibilities, constituting 63 percent of the entire NPCSC membership committee members. At the Seventh NPC meeting held five years later, the number rose to 80 percent. Ever since the Eighth NPC meeting, virtually all NPCSC members - save the chairman - have joined committees. This is a significant increase compared with the first three NPC Congresses held in the 1950s and 1960s, when the NPCSC members were a rarity in the two committees.[3]

Instead of ideologues, committee members are now almost exclusively former government functionaries, party secretaries, State

Council officials, researchers, provincial leaders, and representatives of the major mass organizations, including the Chinese Women's Federation, Workers' Federation, and Youth Corps.

Along with institutionalization, professionalization has been a conspicuous component of legislative development. Nelson Polsby stated that the internal complexity of the US Congress can be measured by growth in the autonomy and importance of committees, in the growth of specialized agencies of party leadership, and in the increase in the provision of various emoluments and auxiliary benefits to members in the form of office space, salaries, allowances, staff aid, and committee staffs (Polsby 1968: 153).

TABLE 1 MEMBERSHIP DEVELOPMENT OF THE NPC COMMITTEE

Committees	1st 1954	2nd Sept. 1954	3rd April 1959	4th Jan. 1965	5th Jan. 1975	6th June 1983	7th April 1988	8th March 1993	9th March 1998
Minorities	85	84	114	–	81	14	22	25	23
Law*	33	37	41	–	36	13	21	18	29
Internal and Judicial Affairs	–	–	–	–	–	–	20	19	20
Finance and Economics	–	–	–	–	–	14	28	29	21
Education, Science, Culture and Public Health	–	–	–	–	–	17	30	31	34
Foreign Affairs	–	–	–	–	–	10	18	15	15
Overseas Chines Affairs	–	–	–	–	–	9	17	21	16
Environment Protection	–	–	–	–	–	–	–	17	21
Agriculture and Villages	–	–	–	–	–	–	–	–	26

* The committee was named the Committee for Bills and Proposals for the 1st, 2nd, and 3rd NPC Congresses. The name was kept when the committee was resurrected in 1979. Since the 6th NPC Congress, it was renamed the Law Committee.
Sources: Quanguo renda changweihui bangongting yanjiushi (ed.) 1990; NPCSC Communiqué, 1991-98.

TABLE 2   THE CHANGING NATURE OF
THE NPC SPECIAL COMMITTEES

Congress	No. of Committees	% of NPCSC Membership	Newly-acquired powers
6th	6	63	Jurisdiction of committees delineated; legislative review; reading system; investigation; becomes permanent institution; NPCSC meeting rules enacted
7th	7	80	Auxiliary institution created; right to hear government reports; committee organic rules enacted; interpolation; legal inspection; subcommittees formed; NPC meeting rules enacted
8th	8	Nearly the entire membership	Joint legislative review; more legislation
9th	9	Nearly the entire membership	

Source: Chien-min Chao and Chang Chun-hsiang 2000: 195.

TABLE 3   EXPANDING POWERS OF THE NPC COMMITTEE

	Bills Reviewed		Government Work Reports Heard	Laws Passed and Amended
NPC	Committees	NPCSC	NPCSC	NPCSC
1		0	40	35
2		0	86	7
3		0	23	3
4		0	2	1
5		0	63	19
6		137	65	42
7		168	69	48
8	566	273	65	75

Sources: Liu, Yu and Cheng 1991; Yang 1997: 321-36.

In the case of China, not only has the number of standing committees increased steadily, but subcommittees have also been created to help with drafting and reviewing responsibilities assigned to the committees. Legislative hearings have been introduced in the process of legislative deliberation. New ad hoc institutions have been formed within the Party to help with the work of PCs.

It was decided in 1983 that a bill would have to be sent to the Law Committee or relevant committees for review after first reading. However, the NPCSC Meeting Rules passed in 1987 and NPC Meeting Rules in 1989 require that all bills in the NPC and NPCSC be reviewed by the Law Committee and relevant committee(s) simultaneously. In order to better understand the feasibility of bills, the Law Committee in June 1984 started an investigation into the reviewing of bills. Since then, legislative investigation has become an important and integral part of the committee's legislation.

TABLE 4   NPC COMMITTEE STRUCTURE

NPC	No. of Committees	Size	New Committee(s)
1	2	118	–
2	2	121	–
3	2	155	–
4	–	–	–
5	2	117	2
6	6	77	4
7	7	158	1
8	8	175	1
9	9	205	1

Sources: **Quanguo renda changweihui bangongting yanjiushi (ed.) 1990; NPCSC communiqué, 1991-98; Quanguo renda changweihui bangongting yanjiushi (ed.) 1998: 214-15.**

Legislative hearings or *lunzheng* (to discuss and substantiate) first begin as meetings and then seminars are held. Usually a bill is reviewed by the Law Committee and a relevant committee at the same time (Tanner 1995). Committees have the power to decide whether *lunzheng* is necessary. The procedure is as follows: after being briefed by the drafter at a plenary meeting at the NPCSC, a bill is sent to the Law Committee and a relevant special committee for review. The Law Committee then sends the draft bill, as a required step, to the Provincial People's Congress (PPC), the minorities' autonomous regions, concerned departments at the central government (National People's Consultative Conference, the Supreme Court, the Supreme Prosecutor's Office, relevant departments of the State Council, the Chinese Federation of Unions, Chinese Federation of Women, and the Youth Corps) for advice. The Law Committee also decides, according to the importance and contentiousness of the bill, if a hearing (*lunzheng*) is needed. For an ordinary standing committee, the first half of the legislative investigation is missing, but *lunzheng* is often exercised when bills are examined.

Although a bill is examined simultaneously by the Law Committee and a relevant committee, the effectiveness of the opinions expressed do differ. For ordinary committees, the opinions are given, in printed copies, to members of the NPC, NPCSC and the Law Committee for reference. It is the Law Committee that has the ultimate power of deciding whether to incorporate those opinions and bring them to the attention of the Praesidium of the NPC or the NPCSC plenary meeting. Without this procedure of *tongyi shenyi* (to examine indiscriminately),[4] a bill is not allowed to progress to the second reading. The role of the Law Committee is especially significant for the NPC owing to its large size and short meeting time (only a couple of weeks per annum). Because of the issue of duplication and redundancy (that is, a bill being reviewed by two committees at the same time), the Committee on Internal and Judicial Affairs started to work with the Law Committee in 1994, thereby ushering in a new era of joint hearings and deliberations.

Publication in the mass media is often required for major bills to seek responses from the masses. The opinions solicited are periodically printed in a newsletter *Fazhi gongzuo bao* [Newspaper for Legal Work], published by the Working Committee on Legal Affairs, a supporting institution under the NPCSC, and forwarded to the NPCSC and its leadership, members of the Law Committee, and relevant agencies of the central government. One case that stands out is the Contract Law passed at the Eighth NPC Congress. Altogether there were 12 universities and research institutes that took part in the drafting process. Another example is the Company Law, where 210 agencies or departments were consulted before the bill passed into law (Quanguo renda changweihui bangongting yanjiushi (ed.) 1998: 24).

Since the idea of a market economy was imported from overseas, foreign experience is often sought in the enactment of economic legislation. Outside influence can be detected in laws such as the Company Law, Accounting Law, Law for Commercial Notes and Checks, and Law to Prevent Improper Competition. In addition, the Litigation Law, the Law for Civil Administration, and the hearing system in the administrative punishment bear the hallmarks of a non-indigenous legalistic influence.

To cope with the increasing diversity of legislation, some localities have gone one step further by setting up advisory boards to help with drafting. The Law Committee of the Chongqing People's Congress has a panel of 29 legislative consultants, and most of these legislative assistants are professors at the Southwestern University of Politics and Law, among them four professional lawyers. When the Chongqing PC proceeded with the task of evaluating the 24 laws one year after enactment in 1999 (a practice started in 1986 when the Organic Law of the Local Government was amended), 12 of these legal advisors were asked for assistance.[5]

Structurally, NPC committees have been growing in number as well as in membership. In the first two NPC congresses, the two committees - the Committee on Minorities and the Committee on Bills & Proposals - had a joint membership of 118. The fact that racial equality was upheld as one of the founding tenets of the new republic had a lot to do with the impressive size. When the same two committees were resurrected in 1979 (as the Committee on Nationalities and the Law Committee), the tradition was basically kept. The large size warranted the symbolic status of the committees. When four additional committees were created in 1983, the size was drastically reduced with a combined membership of 77 for all six committees. With the addition of three new committees and enlarged functions, the number increased nearly threefold to a total of 205 at the Ninth NPC.

In yet another move of further differentiation, subcommittees have also been brought into existence. The increasing demand for legislation and the infrequent and short meeting times for the committees (once a month for a meeting that lasts no more than a couple of days) are two reasons behind the rise of the new organizations. There are two kinds of subcommittees at present: ad hoc and permanent. A subcommittee, or a *xiaozu* (small group), can be formed if deemed necessary by the committee. The organic rules of the Committee on Finance and Economics and the Committee on Education, Science, Culture, and Public Health allow such a formation (NPC Committee on Internal and Judicial Affairs 1992). Since 1989, two subcommittees - the Group on Women's and Children's Affairs and the Group on Adolescence - were created on a permanent basis under the jurisdiction of the Committee for Internal and Judicial Affairs. Ever since then, strengthening the functions of the subcommittees has been one of the central tasks of the NPC reforms.

The Group on Women's and Children's Affairs has a membership of 22 while the Group on Adolescence has 27. A close scrutiny of the structures of the two groups substantiates professionalization as the central principle of organization: only a paltry 18 percent of the aggregate membership are NPCSC members while the remaining 82 percent are outside recruits with expertise (Zhou 1998: 78). The subcommittees have the power to review bills and proposals, to propose motions and bills, and to research issues of concern and come up with solutions. Alternatively, a legislative group may also function solely as an advisory body to the special committees or as a frontline reviewer of bills and proposals, as is the case of the Committee on Finance and Economics.

CENTRALIZATION OF LEADERSHIP

The centralization of leadership in the legislature is also considered more appropriate to meet the needs of the modern environment. A centralized leadership can forge closer connections between the legislative institution and major external forces and groups. While dispersion of powers to the committees is definitely a new development in China's People's Congress system, the past Leninist tradition of party-state dictatorship has certainly helped in forging a strong leadership in the legislative assembly.

The head of the PCs is in many ways a powerful position. Li Peng was the Number Two man in the CCP hierarchy. Directors of LPCs most likely also hold the post of secretary of the local Party committee. The chairmanship group meeting is a very important forum in formulating the NPCSC agenda and in screening bills and proposals. In a typical directorate group meeting for an LPC, the agenda is basically set by the permanent committees - a sign of the importance of the committees. The chairmanship group meeting is composed of the NPCSC chairman and vice chairmen (up to 19 in number) and the secretary-general. Theoretically, decisions are reached collectively and the chairman refrains from making unilateral decisions. In reality, though, the power of the chairman/director is very much dependent on the stature of the individual. This is especially the case after a directive was passed down recently demanding that all the local party secretaries concurrently serve as LPC directors. As such, a dominant party secretary can almost single-handedly dictate the agenda.[6]

The chairman of the NPCSC and the directors of the LPCs wield tremendous statutory as well as hierarchical power within their organizations. They can revise the opinions expressed by the committees in their reviewing of bills and proposals. The chairman also wields a lot of influence in setting the committee agenda, by initiating an investigation into the process of legislative review, deciding if a proposal should be tabled, and determining if a bill should go to the Law Committee or other relevant committee. In addition to these statutory powers, the opinion of the chairman carries much weight in terms of personnel management for those associated with the PCSCs. The fact that only about one half of the LPCSC membership work full-time and the meetings of the PCSCs last no more than a few days have also rendered additional powers to the chairmanship.

According to the Organic Law, the NPCSC chairman is charged with coordinating the day-to-day work of the legislative body as well as its special committees. The same regulation is vague, however, as to what exactly constitutes the daily work, nor is the chairman held accountable to the NPCSC or otherwise under its supervision. In some provinces, the director alone is responsible for setting the entire agenda of the PCSC meetings and some directors are even granted power to permit the arrest or to detain deputies by law enforcement agencies, provided that the decision is later sent to the chamber for approval. The opaqueness of the stipulation evidently gives the chairman more liberty in this capacity. The fact that many of the LPCs directors are also the secretary or deputy secretary of Party committee has bolstered the chairmanship vis-à-vis that of the PCs as an institution. A case in point is Li Peng. Li was slighted in his capacity as premier in the State Council, but has been acclaimed as one of the most productive chairmen in NPC history. His past experience as premier and the fact that he outranked Zhu Rongji (former premier) in the CCP has definitely enhanced Li's credentials.[7]

Party-state political tradition and the institutional design have led some observers to the conclusion that the chairmanship group may become an 'authoritative and efficient organ of power' and a base for the chairman to expand his influence. Some even go so far as to suggest that the chairman may become a 'formidable political figure,' perhaps even one of the four pre-eminent leaders in an interlocking party-state directorate and that the NPCSC is a 'legislature-within-a-legislature.' (Cheng 1983; O'Brien 1988: 364; Weng 1982). It is common now to place the PC meetings, PCSC meetings, and the directorship group meetings on par and collectively address them as the three meetings of the LPCs (Zhang Yuankun 1997:1).

It was decided at the Sixth NPC meeting that to facilitate effective functioning, the committee chairmanship should be concurrently served by the vice chairmen of the NPCSC - the committee vice chairman would also have to be a member of the NPCSC. Since the Eighth NPC, however, NPCSC vice chairmen no longer serve as committee chairmen. When the committee is not in session, it is the committee chairmanship group - composed of the committee chairman and vice chairmen (numbered four to six) - that makes the decisions on behalf of the committee. The committee chairmanship group meets once every month and committee vice chairmen form the Committee Office Work Meeting (*weiyuanhui bangong hui*). The meeting is held once every two weeks to discuss day-to-day affairs. The work of subcommittees is also coordinated at the meeting. Committee chairmen and vice chairmen are forces to be reckoned with as they have the final word in the deliberations by the committee regarding a bill or proposal. The chairman is usually the agenda-setter for the committee and he can also participate in the NPCSC chairmanship group meeting and express opinions on behalf of the committee. Committee and vice chairmen are also the most important factors in the positioning and repositioning of personnel in the committee.

LEGISLATIVE OVERSIGHT

The legislative oversight of the NPC has been developed in line with its institutionalization and specialization, and again it is local legislatures that took the initiative. In 1984, in a law approved by its PCS - the Provisional Regulation on the PCSC's Work - the city of Tianjin first legalized the work of legislative oversight. Now almost all provinces have similar enactments (Zhang Wei 1996: 64). Although a draft of the supervisory law has been contemplated by the NPC for quite some time, its passage is still not in sight. Among the supervisory powers that the PCs have invented, the most effective have been the *pingyi*, a measure to evaluate and discuss the work of government agencies and officials, and *zhifa jiancha*, inspection on the implementation of laws.

Nanan Prefecture People's Congress of the city of Chongqing organized deputies in 1984 to review the work of officials approved by the Congress, however superficial, upon appointment. The system has quickly spread to other places and, in many cases, been made into law. In November 1991, marking acceptance of the excellent method developed from below, a meeting was convened by the NPC Committee on Internal and Judicial Affairs to summarize experiences of the *pingyi*. The new tool subsequently won acclaim by NPC Vice Chairmen Peng Chong in 1992 and Tian Jiyun in a work report to a NPC meeting in 1995 (Du 1998: 59-60).

Pingyi can be used to inspect the work of government departments (*gongzuo pingyi*) or officials whose appointments need PC approval (*shuzhi pingyi*). It can be aimed at a specific policy implemented by the government or at the work of a *xitong* (system).[8] It can be carried out at a single level of the bureaucratic hierarchy or at all levels of the government from the province down to the township (*xiang*). It can be implemented by PC delegations, or by the PCSCs, the committees, or the PCs.

A *pingyi* motion can be initiated by deputies, PC delegation, special committees, or the directorate group meeting. It can also be proposed by the masses. Once a motion is approved by the directorate group meeting and concrete proposals framed, a *pingyi* leading group is established, led usually by the director or a deputy director, composed of a few members selected from the PCSCs and PC deputies. Relevant committees are the driving force throughout the entire process. At the second stage, members of the investigation team have to engage themselves in an educational and self-learning session, where relevant laws and regulations are studied. At the third stage, an investigation is carried out. The *pingyi* group travels to the targeted department and holds a plenary meeting, attended by all employees as well as officials, and goals of the inspection are pronounced. Interviews are conducted with the employees of the targeted department, employees working at concerned agencies, and selected masses who had dealings with that particular department. Documents are reviewed and confession sessions held. At the fourth stage, a *pingyi* meeting is held to *ping* (to criticize) and *yi* (to opine) the targeted. Opinions organized by the inspection group are expressed at the plenary meeting in which employee attendance is required. At the fifth and final stage, the targeted department is required to come up with a written proposal of rectification within a month and report in writing the results to the PCSC within two to six months. The *pingyi* leading group then pays another visit to the targeted department to check up on the situation. If the results are less than satisfactory, then compulsory measures may be considered.

Over the years, the law enforcement agencies - the so-called *zhengfa xitong* (political-legal system) - have been the prime targets of *gongzuo pingyi*. The reason for the emphasis is simple - to fight corruption. Almost all provinces have launched *pingyi* inspections in the past few years to oversee the work of the police, the prosecutor's office, and the court system. The commerce and taxation departments also have become priorities. Because of the scale of people mobilized in the process, normally *gongzuo pingyi* is carried out once a year.

On the other hand, officials subject to *shuzhi pingyi*, usually in the form of being given a work report by the requested official, have been extended to include those whose appointments need approval from the PCs, including heads of the departments and agencies and sometimes deputy provincial governors. In addition to inquisitions, this group of officials may sometimes face a written examination, conducted by the Law Committee or Committee on Legal Work (a supporting institution working for the PCSCs rather than a special committee), before getting approval from the PCSCs.

PCs at different levels have enacted hundred of laws and regulations,[9] however, the implementation of those legal documents has been less than comprehensive. It is estimated that only 15 percent of the laws enacted have been faithfully implemented (Zhang Yuankun 1997: 39). Consequently, *zhifa jiancha* (inspection on the implementation of law) has emerged as one of the major elements of PCSC oversight in the past decade.

Heralding the much-touted new practice, the LPCs were given the power to supervise the implementation of the constitution as well as laws when the Organic Law of Local People's Congress and Local People's Government (hereafter Organic Law) was amended in 1986. NPCSC, collaborating with PCs down the line, carried out inspections of over 21 laws and relevant legal decisions made at the Eighth NPC session between 1993 and 1998, while its committees inspected twice as many in the same period (Quanguo renda changweihui bangongting yanjiushi 1998: 33-34).

129

According to the law 'Some Regulations on the Improvement of Inspections of the Implementation of Law', ratified by the NPCSC in 1993, *zhifa jiancha* seeks to tackle 'major problems engendered in the process of socialist modernization' and other 'issues strongly expressed by the masses.'[10] For the sake of specialization, legislative committees have once again become the backbone of newly acquired power.

Much like *pingyi*, *zhifa jiancha* was a local initiative, developed out of the need to combat vices brooked in the modernization of the socialist economy. As also is the case with *pingyi*, *zhifa jiancha* is not exempt from the strong tradition of mass mobilization inherited from a former 'movement regime'.[11] Once a law is targeted, a task force is formed. The inspection team is headed by one of the deputy chairmen/directors of the NPC/PCs, with members of the PCSCs constituting its bulk. An education session and then investigation soon follow, while masses are mobilized and meetings held. To underscore the importance of legality and broaden its effects, propaganda is emphasized. In an inspection organized to check the efficacy of the laws related to the work of the legal-political system, the Putien PC, in a small city located in the vicinity of Fuzhou, launched a 'big discussion' session to 'erect viewpoints of the masses and to enforce the laws rightfully and in a civilized way'. Telephone numbers were advertised in the press. A reception office was created to receive those who wanted to come and relay their stories. As it turned out, 221 letters along with 243 visitors were received with over 100 cases being raised. At the end, 56 cases were selected and relayed to corresponding agencies for reference (Zhang Yuankun 1997: 42). In what is known as a strategy of *shangxia liandong*, a vertical mobilization of PCs, targets are broadened to maximize effect.

As in the case of *pingyi*, the most critical phase of the *zhifa jiancha* lies in 'rectification and improvement' (*zhenggai*). Criticism and self-criticism are heavily involved. Interpolation, investigation and removal from duty are possible means at the sponsor's disposal. The Supervision Act passed by the Guangdong PPC in 1994 stipulated that a 'legal supervisory paper' with the signature of five PCSC members and approved by the directorate group meeting can be issued to an official guilty as charged. The official is obliged to report to the PCSC within a specified time span or must face punitive actions.[12] Here again, a political reform process starting from below and slowly working its way upward is discernible. After being introduced by local PCs in 1986, the Seventh

NPC (1988-93) and its Standing Committee incorporated and brought the practice to the central government. During that period, in cooperation with LPCs, the NPCSC and its committees organized 53 inspection tours with 31 laws and six legal decisions targeted for inspections (Zhang Wei 1996: 57).

NEW PARTY-EXECUTIVE-LEGISLATIVE RELATIONS

While many believe that there is an institutional decentralization of party control over law-making (Tanner 1994: 384-88) and a growing weakness of the Chinese apparatus of the state (Scalapino 1993), there is no academic discourse on the changed executive-legislative relations. The invigorated legislative oversight is bound to herald a new era for the bilateral relationship between the two branches of the government. Rather than being stymied in the party-state dyad, the new relations have begun featuring a limited accountability in the previously rigid political system. An institutionalized channel of communications has been established between the Party and the two branches of the government. Now it is routine for government officials to be present at meetings held by the PCSCs. To avoid superficiality, some PPCs even require heads of the government (rather than their deputies) to take part in these sessions and give the work report. A new development has been that the government work report, instead of being distributed and reviewed in its entirety, is broken into several reports in accordance with their nature and then reviewed by different groups of deputies organized by their spheres of interest and specialization. The new division of work is basically being drawn in line with the legislative committees such as Finance; Legal Affairs; Agriculture & Forestry; Municipal Construction; Education, Science & Culture, etc.

Since 1991, the PC of the city of Chengdu decided to request reports on those subjects most discussed by its citizens. A feedback system has also been established by many PCs so that the executive branch is forced to respond to decisions and resolutions adopted by the PCSCs and to opinions expressed after reviewing a bill. The Huchen County PC has come up with a tracking system, whereby the opinions expressed by its PCSC after reviewing a proposal are written in a *cuebanka* (a memorandum for action) and signed by the office director of the relevant legislative committee or by the committee vice chairman in charge of the investigation. The memorandum is then forwarded to the executive branch. The official who holds the ultimate responsibility for the case, the head of the government or his deputy, is required to give a progress report to the PCSC at the next session. Normally a case is allowed a three-month grace period with an additional three months for particularly difficult ones. In the end, the memorandum has to be co-signed by the responsible official and returned to the PCSC for conclusion (Zhang Yuankun 1997: 12).

Another innovation is that reshaping executive-legislative relations is the creation of liaison offices. In Dague County, Liaoning Province, a deputy county magistrate designated as the liaison officer meets every quarter with his counterpart (a deputy director at the PCSC) to discuss issues of mutual concern. Heads of the county's PC are invited to the magistrate's work meeting and the government work meeting. A resolution entitled 'Regarding the Serious Acceptance of PC Supervision' was passed by the county government to show deference to the PC work (Zhang Wei 1996: 66). It is now common practice after each LPC session for the executive branch to convene meetings to reflect motions and proposals previously raised at the legislature.

The country's economic performance over the last two decades has led some observers to conclude that China is capable of transforming its Leninist political system and discarding Marxism-Leninism in favour of a 'developmental nationalism.' (McCormick and Unger 1996: 2). While decisions over important matters are still made by the Party, the Party is said to involve itself less with the day-to-day administrative duties while the legislature is used as a proxy (O'Brien 1989: 62). Another observation is that the Party is decentralizing its control over law-making (Tanner 1994: 384-88). An interesting development is that the Party is actually gaining strength by delegating powers to the legislature.

The Party has been the most important supporting as well as inspiring force behind the new expansion of supervision, but ironically, it is also the biggest deterrent. As early as 1994, former NPC chairman Peng Zhen demanded that local party committees at all levels discuss the PC work on a regular basis. In a decree entitled 'The Party Must Resolutely Maintain Socialist Legality', released in July 1986, the Party asked all its cadres to recognize the importance of the legality and support the work of the PCs and their resolutions. On the other hand, an equal number of resolutions have been passed by the Party demanding stronger leadership over the PCs. The resolution entitled 'A Decision to Strengthen the Linkage between the Party and the Masses' which was adopted at the Sixth Central Committee Plenary Meeting of the Thirteenth Party Congress held on March 1990, is one example. Consequently, what has emerged is not a weaker party leadership in the legislature, as some have suggested (Tanner 1994: 384-88). On the contrary, while being involved less with day-to-day legislation, the Party has nonetheless strengthened its leadership at the legislative chamber level, with its communication network having been revitalized.

The new Party-legislative relations are as follows. First, local Party committees regularly convene meetings, with representatives from both the executive and legislative branches attending, to co-ordinate work in the sphere of the political-legal *xitong* and to mobilize support for the legislature. Before each *pingyi*, *zhifa jiancha*, and inspection mission is launched, the Party organization within the PCSC (the *dangzu*) - comprised of the PCSC director, deputy directors, and secretary-general who are also members of the Party - has to report the plan to the Party committee at the same level in detail and ask for approval and endorsement.

LIMITATIONS

The increasing specialization and the embryonic oversight function that the PCs possess have fundamentally changed Party-executive-legislative relations. Some even argue that this change may gradually lead to a system that would essentially render a mighty Communist Party to be checked and balanced to some extent by the legislature.[13] This argument seems valid at first glance. Despite the fact that the Party still enjoys overwhelming control over the nomination and management of cadres, those at the second tier of officialdom have to face interrogation before appointment and, sometimes, downright rejection.[14] These officials occasionally face scrutiny after assuming office as well. There is no doubt that the Party is gradually easing out of the day-to-day decision-making in the new political machinery, leaving the executive branch responsible for daily operations. The Party's retreat has also paved the way for the surge in legislative power. Through mechanisms (mostly newly-invented or resuscitated) including interpolation, *pingyi* and legal inspections, the LPCs are no longer powerless institutions.

As Anthony Dick observes, the legal system in China remains a tool of the CCP (Dick 1989: 542). The party-state conglomeration is still in place, and the closer one is to the bottom of the bureaucratic hierarchy, the worse the situation gets. What we have is a new party-state system in which the Party no longer makes all the decisions. Organizationally, the overwhelming overlap between the party and the state characterized by the old Leninist party-state system is now a thing of the past. It was not unusual previously for the Party organization to be staffed more than the administration of the organization. Today, the Party remains strong, but is much smaller in size relative to that of the state. Notwithstanding, the Party's dominance remains supreme. For example, nearly one-third of the PPC chairmen in 2000 were also concurrently secretaries of the Party committees (http://www.peopledaily.com.cn.).

The crux still lies in the Party and the issue is over the right of decision-making. The constitution and the Organic Law give the LPCs powers to decide on the 'vital issues' in areas including politics, economics, education, science, culture, hygiene, civil affairs and minorities. However, decades of Stalinist tradition have moulded the Party as the ultimate and uncompromising source of vital policy-making. It has been suggested that 'vital decisions' be further divided into 'issues with overall implications' and 'with limited implications'. For issues like major reforms, development strategies, and large-scale construction projects, it is urged that the tradition of Party command be sustained. As for such matters as regional planning, educational reforms and the protection of the minorities, it is suggested that the Party had better step aside and provide leadership by guidance (Won and Fu 1991: 52). Despite academic discussion, major decisions are still reached through the Party machine. It is not uncommon for the Party to make decisions unilaterally and then forward them to the executive branch for implementation, thereby bypassing the legislature. Joint decrees between the Party and the executive remain problematic, rendering legislative oversight impossible. A laughable case often cited is the one issued jointly by the State Council and the CCP a few years back resetting the summer clock. Which commands supremacy, law or superior? The case remains open.

The permanent committees at the NPC and many PPCs have undoubtedly become key players in their institutions, but specialization there is still a goal to be fully realized. The nine committees in the NPC, although this represents a major step towards differentiation and specialization, are far from sufficient to be a national legislature for a country the size of China. Furthermore, the committee system is still under development and efforts are being made to allow them to function better. Besides, all legislative acts are subject to examinations by the Law Committee before being tabled by the Chairman's Meeting for readings. This practice has also cut the effectiveness of other committees.

At the provincial level, the committee is an even weaker institution. Among the 31 provinces, autonomous regions and municipalities, there are a total of 164 committees, with an average of 5.4 committees per province.[15] Among them, nearly three-quarters are 'working committees,' a weaker institution compared to the 'committees' both in statute and in reality, subject to the PCSCs rather than the PCs, while PCs at the lower levels hardly have any committees (Zhang Wei 1996: 78-79). As for the *xiang* and township PCs, a lack of standing institutions has nullified the PC institution as a whole. Lately, a new development has been the creation of a standing chairman at the praesidium and a full-time staff to handle daily affairs.

Another major problem obstructing the legislative specialization has been a lack of professionalization. Two-thirds of the NPC committee members are newly recruited from its congress held once every five years. Usually those posted for the job at the PCs are cadres nearing retirement, as the average age for NPC committee membership is between 60 and 70. Some committees have less than half of their membership working full-time and many of them are living in places across the landmass of China. An institution staffed with a 'second line of cadres', which meets no more than a couple of days per month, is not going to be taken that seriously. At the provincial level, full-time PPCSC members usually constitute a little less than half of the entire membership. It is no wonder that a lot of important policies made by the Party or the administration are not brought to the PCs for approval. The rights of interpolation and acquisition, investigation and dismissal are also rarely utilized in many places. It is not uncommon for the officials who are required by law to be present at the PCSC meetings to refuse to show up. This recalcitrance has prompted some county PCs in Shandong and Hubei to adopt stringent measures by refusing substitution when writing their government work reports (Zhang Yuankun 1997: 15-16).

Pingyi is another case in point. It has remained a local initiative. Many PPCs have started to review the work of the administrative and the judicial branches of the government and sometimes local officials are 'tested' before appointment. However, these practices remain primitive and their results mixed. Consequently, praise rather than censure is often the outcome of these 'inspections'.

CONCLUSION

While the attention of China studies has focused on grassroots elections (a practice that has effectively remoulded the lives of many villages), less attention has been paid to developments in legislative transformation, especially at the provincial level. However, the urbanization and the structural and institutional changes undergone in China in the past two decades have been nothing short of spectacular. To redress the malfeasance brought by the new decentralization of economic resources, PPCs are taking the lead in another round of incremental political reforms. This paper confirms the theories that legislative specialization is indeed an institutional adaptation to the complex needs of a new environment cultivated by the industrialization started by the late paramount leader Deng Xiaoping.

Contrary to the experiences of many industrialized countries in the West, a centralized leadership has been retained in the Chinese legislature. The combination of specialization and centralization of leadership has led to an augmentation of legislative oversight. Measures developed by the legislative institutions, such as *pingyi* and *zhifa jiancha*, have enlivened the previously lethargic local political scene and given rise to the committee autonomy. These political reforms, though underpublicized, have transformed local politics, forcing the central government (the NPC) to follow suit. The urgent need for institutional mechanisms to counter the vices associated with the socialist market reform has prompted the Party to turn its attention to the PCs. Consequently, a Leninist party-state system - one in which the Party constantly overrode the executive branch of the government and one in which the legislature was totally stymied - has been transformed into a new system in which the Party is allied simultaneously with the executive and the legislative branches.

A preliminary and limited balance of power is now emerging in which the Party is not totally immune. The exclusive right to personnel management is challenged, though in a preliminary way, by the PCs in the name of legislative oversight. The newly acquired legislative powers have not only redefined the tenets of Party leadership, but have also rewritten its relations with the executive branch. Although the PCs are still often barred from vital decision-making, new devices such as *pingyi* and *zhifa jiancha* are forcing some local officials to have second thoughts before venturing too far from legal boundaries.

ABBREVIATIONS

CCP Communist Party of China
LPC Local People's Congress
LPCSC Local People's Congress Standing Committee
NPC National People's Congress
NPCSC National People's Congress Standing Committee
PPC Provincial People's Congress
PC People's Congress
PCSC People's Congress Standing Committee

ENDNOTES

1   The Committee on Bills and Proposals is one of the two committees (the other is Minorities) set up by the 1st, 2nd, and 3rd NPC. The NPC was destroyed during the Cultural Revolution period. When the committee system was revived in 1979, the name was kept, but it was renamed as the Law Committee in 1983.

2   The committee was renamed the Committee for the Protection of Environment and Resources in 1995.

3   There were 3, 4, and 15 NPCSC members that joined the two committees, Law and Minorities, at the three congresses (Zhou 1998: 34).

4   'Tongyi shenyi' is stipulated in Article 24 of the NPC Meeting Rules and Article 16 of the NPCSC Meeting Rules.

5   Author's interview with Chongqing PC's senior legislators in July 2000.

6   Author's interview with personnel working with the Zejiang PC.

7   This opinion is shared by almost all the scholars and local legislators whom the author has interviewed in many places across China over the past few years.

8   Chinese use the term 'system' to divide bureaucracies into different groupings (see Lieberthal 1995: 194-207). According to Lieberthal, there are six major *xitongs*. The six-*xitong* divide is basically confirmed by Yan Huai, but with slight differences (see Yan 1995: 39-50).

9   During the Eighth NPC session (1993-1998), 85 laws and 33 legal decisions were approved. In the same period, 4,200 local regulations were approved by the NPC also. See Quanguo renda changweihui bangongting yanjiushi 1998: 2-7.

10   The stipulation can be found in *A Handbook for the Work of PC Oversight* edited by NPC Committee on Internal and Judicial Affairs 1996.

11   Some scholars use the term 'movement regime' as a substitute for the totalitarian regimes, because of their inclination and love for mass mobilization and political movements (Tucker 1967: 343-58).

12   Article 13 of the Act (NPC Committee on Internal and Judicial Affairs 1996: 220-25)
13   Interviews with PC deputies from various parts of China.
14   Among the 573 cadres recommended for approval by the provincial Party committee in 1988, 94 or 16.4 percent of them were rejected by the PPCs (Won and Fu 1991: 51).
15   PPC committees are numbered between two to eight, with five and six the medium. (*Quanguo renmin daibiao dahui zhuanmen weiyuanhui gongzuo shouce* 1992: appendix).

REFERENCES

Canon, David T. 1989. 'The Institutionalization of Leadership in the U.S. Congress.' *Legislative Studies Quarterly* 14 (August): 415-43.

Cheng, Joseph Y. S. 1983. 'How to Strengthen the National People's Congress and Implement Constitutionalism.' *Chinese Law and Government* 16: 88-122.

Chao, Chien-Min 1999. 'Dangguo tizhi xia dang yu lifa jigou guanxi de ruogan sikao.' [A Few Reflections on the Relations between the Party and the Legislative Organs under the Party-State System] *Zhongguo dalu yanjiu* [Mainland China Studies]. Taipei (September): 13-25.

Chao, Chien-Min and Chang Chun-hsiang 2000. *Zhonghua renmin gongheguo lifa yu xianju zhidu* [Electoral and Legislative Systems in the PRC] Taipei: Guoli bianyi guan.

Colton, Timothy J. 1996. 'The Constituency Nexus in the Russian and Other Post-Soviet Parliaments.' In Jeffrey W. Hahn (ed.), *Democratization in Russia: The Development of Legislative Institutions.* Armonk, NY: M. E. Sharpe.

Dick, Anthony 1989. 'The Chinese Legal System: Reforms in the Balance.' *The China Quarterly* 119 (September): 540-76.

Du Gan (ed.) 1998. *Jinyibu wanshan difang renda zhidu ruogan wenti yanjiu* [Several Issues on Furthering Improvement on the LPC Institution]. Sichuan: Renmin chubanshe.

Hamrin, Carol Lee and Suisheng Zhao (eds) 1995. *Decision-making in Deng's China: Perspectives from Insiders.* Armonk, NY: M. E. Sharpe.

Huntington, Samuel P. 1990. 'Congressional Responses to the Twentieth Century'. In Pietro S. Nivola and David H. Rosenbloom (eds), *Classic Readings in American Politics.* New York: St Martin's Press.

Lieberthal, Kenneth 1995. *Governing China: From Revolution through Reform.* New York: W. W. Norton & Company.

Liu Zheng, Yu Youmin and Cheng Xiangqing (eds) 1991. *Renmin daibiao dahui gongzuo quanshu* [Handbook on the Work of People's Congress] Beijing: Zhongguo fazhi chubanshe.

Loewenberg, Gerhard, Samuel C. Patterson and Malcolm E. Jewell (eds) 1985. *Handbook of Legislative Research.* Cambridge, MA.: Harvard University Press.

McCormick, Barret L. and Jonathan Unger (eds) 1996. *China after Socialism: In the Footsteps of Eastern Europe or East Asia?* New York: M. E. Sharpe.

Nathan, Andrew 1996. 'China's Constitutionalist Option.' *Journal of Democracy* 7 (4): 43-57

NPC Committee on Internal and Judicial Affairs 1992. *Quanguo renmin daibiao dahui zhuanmen weiyuanhui gongzuo shouce* [Manual for the Work of NPC Special Committees]. Beijing: Zhongguo minzhu fazhi chubanshe.

NPC Committee on Internal and Judicial Affairs 1996. *Renda jiandu gongzuo shouce* [Handbook for the Work of PC Oversight]. Beijing: Zhongguo minzhu fazhi chubanshe.

O'Brien, Kevin 1988. 'China's National People's Congress: Reform and Its Limits.' *Legislative Studies Quarterly* 13 (August): 343-74.

—— 1989. 'Legislative Development and Chinese Political Change.' *Studies in Comparative Communism* (Spring).

—— 1990a. *Reform without Liberalization: China's National People's Congress and the Politics of Institutional Change.* Cambridge: Cambridge University Press .

—— 1990b. 'Is China's National People's Congress a "Conservative Legislature"?' *Asian Survey* 30 (8): 782-94.

—— 1994. 'Chinese People's Congresses and Legislative Embeddedness: Understanding Early Organizational Development.' *Comparative Political Studies* 27 (1): 80-107.

—— 1998. 'Institutionalizing Chinese Legislatures: Trade-offs between Autonomy and Capacity.' *Legislative Studies Quarterly* 23(1): 91-108.

Polsby, Nelson W. 1968. 'The Institutionalization of the U.S. House of Representatives.' *The American Political Science Review* 62: 144-68.

PRC National People's Congress, NPCSC communiqu_, 1991-98.

Quanguo renda changweihui bangongting yanjiushi (ed.) 1990. *Zhonghua renmin gongheguo renmin daibiao dahui wenxian ziliao huibian 1949-1990* [Compilation of Documents on the PRC's NPC]. Beijing: Zhongguo minzhu fazhi chubanshe.

Quanguo renda changweihui bangongting yanjiushi (ed.) 1998. *Zhongjie, tansuo, zhanwang* [Summarization, Exploration, and Future Prospects]. Beijing: Zhongguo minzhu fazhi chubanshe.

Scalapino, Robert 1993. 'China in the Late Leninist Era.' *The China Quarterly* 136 (December): 949-71.

Schuttemeyer, Suzanne S. 1994. 'Hierarchy and Efficiency in the Bundestag: The German Answer for Institutionalizing Parliament.' In Gary W. Copeland and Samuel C.

Patterson (eds), *Parliaments in the Modern World: Changing Institutions.* Ann Arbor, MI: University of Michigan Press.

Shepsle, Kenneth A.1988. 'Representation and Governance: The Great Legislative Tradeoff.' *Political Science Quarterly* 103: 461-84.

Skilling, Gordon H. 1973. 'Opposition in Communist East Europe. In Robert A. Dahl (ed.), *Regimes and Oppositions.* New Haven, CT: Yale University Press.

Solinger, Dorothy 1982. 'The Fifth National People's Congress and the Process of Policy Making: Reform, Readjustment, and the Opposition.' *Asian Survey* 22 (12): 1238-83.

Squire, Peverill 1992. 'The Theory of Legislative Institutionalization and the California Assembly.' *Journal of Politics* 54: 1026-54.

Tanner, Murray Scot 1994. 'The Erosion of Communist Party Control over Lawmaking in China,' *The China Quarterly* 138 (June): 381-403.

—— 1995. 'How a Bill Becomes a Law in China: Stages and Processes in Lawmaking.' *The China Quarterly* 141 (March): 39-64.

Tucker, Robert C. 1967. 'The Deradicalization of Marxist Movements.' *The American Political Science Review* 61 (2): 343-58.

Weng, Byron 1982. 'Some Key Aspects of the 1982 Draft Constitution of the PRC,' *The China Quarterly* 91: 492-50.

Won Wenzou and Fu Lunbe 1991. 'Shilun wanshan difang guojia quanli jiguan de juece zhineng.' [Ways to Improve the Decision-making Function of the Local People's Congress]. *Faxue* (August): 51.

Wu Guoguang 1999. 'Cong paixi jingzheng dao zhidu jingzheng.' [From Factional Competition to Systemic Competition]. In Lin Jialung (ed.), *Liangan dangguo tizhi yu minzhu fazhan* [The Party-state System across the Strait of Taiwan and Democratic Development]. Taipei: Yuedan Publishing Co.: 327-38.

Yan Huai 1995. 'Organizational Hierarchy and the Cadre Management System.' In Carol Lee Hamrin and Suisheng Zhao (eds), *Decision-making in Deng's China: Perspectives from Insiders.* New York: M. E. Sharpe: 39-50.

Yang Shengchun 1997. *Zhonghua renmin gongheguo guohui zhi bianqian* [Evolution of the PRC's Parliament]. Gaoxiung: Huwen tushu chubanshe.

Zhang Yuankun 1997. *Difang renda gongzuo gailun* [Introduction to the Work of Local People's Congress]. Beijing: Zhongguo minzhu fazhi chubanshe.

Zhang Wei 1996. *Renmin daibiao dahui jiandu zhineng yanjiu* [A Study on Oversight Functions of the People's Congresses]. Beijing: Zhongguo fazhi chubanshe.

Zhou Wei 1998. *Geguo lifa jiguan weiyuanhui zhidu bijiao yanjiu* [A Comparative Study on the System of Legislative Committees]. Dissertation, Wuhan University.

140

CHAPTER 5

The Political Management of Mayors in Post-Deng China

PIERRE F. LANDRY

INTRODUCTION

During the post-Maoist era, the centre of gravity of the Chinese political economy tilted decisively towards cities. The unprecedented pace of China's economic transformation favoured urban growth, which in turn increased the political relevance of municipalities and the officials who rule them. Cities now control a far greater share of the country's resources than at any point in the history of the People's Republic. In 2000, Chinese municipalities accounted for 51.8 percent of the country's GDP, 50.1 percent of its industrial output and 76 percent of the value of services (Jiang and Cui 2001). This increased economic might was largely deliberate. As early as 1979, the Centre[1] targeted some of its boldest policy initiatives at municipalities, symbolized by the early creation of Special Economic Zones (Crane 1990; Kleinberg 1990). After 1984, economic decentralization was generalized to other areas, but Premier Zhao Ziyang stressed that coastal cities would enjoy economic privileges that would not be extended to the less developed and more rural Chinese hinterland (Yang 1990). The leadership's favourable bias towards cities survived the transition of 1989. Until 2002, Jiang Zemin and Zhu Rongji - both former mayors and party secretaries in Shanghai - presided over further reform initiatives that benefited cities (Naughton 1995; Wang and Hu 1999).

In parallel with their rapid economic transformation, cities also enjoy greater formal institutional weight. Their number rose rapidly - from less than 200 in 1978 to over 660 today[2] - but more importantly their formal bureaucratic rank as well as those of the cadres who rule them has also increased. Many county seats have been elevated to the status of 'prefecture level municipalities' (*diji shi*), and 15 cities now have 'vice-provincial' rank (*fushengji shi*).[3]

Scholars who have examined China's decentralization often conclude that the economic power of the localities has eroded the political authority of the Centre.[4] This article examines how this authority is exercised with respect to city mayors. My choice of focus is not simply because cities are inherently important, but also because the terms of the debate on the political impact of China's economic decentralization rely excessively on *provincial* aggregate data. Critics of decentralization who focus on central-provincial fiscal relations (Hu and Wang 1996; Wang 1994, 1995, 1997) conclude that state capacity has weakened, while their detractors, who emphasize the role of institutional and political controls - particularly the power of appointment of central Party institutions (Brødsgaard 2002; Burns 1989; Harding 1981; Manion 1985), argue that the political authority of the Centre is still very much intact in high-priority areas (Bo 2002; Huang 1995, 1996; Lampton 1992).

As important as provinces are, they may not constitute the proper level of analysis to adjudicate the debate, because of their particular position in the Chinese political hierarchy. Both Huang (1996) and Bo (2002) find evidence that central control over provincial appointments facilitates policy enforcement, but that result is hardly surprising given that Beijing has always retained direct *nomenklatura* authority over provincial leaders. The institutional capacity of the Chinese state should instead be tested against a tougher standard, namely Beijing's capacity to impose its policy preferences when principal-agent relations are not as straightforward as those linking central and provincial leaders. It seems more fruitful to focus on *local* political actors over which Beijing only exercises *indirect* control - such as mayors.

The party control mechanisms differ vastly between provincial and municipal cadres. Although personnel management over city, county and township cadres has evolved over time, under the current system, top municipal leaders are appointed by the provinces, without direct central control (Burns 1989, 1994; Landry 2000).[5] Furthermore, focusing on municipal elites allows one to test hypotheses about regional differentiation that cannot be evaluated by looking at provinces alone. Specifically, one can learn whether the Party's organizational practice vis-à-vis local officials is consistent across provinces, and whether its personnel choices follow the logic of rewarding good governance in the localities. This article tests the hypothesis that municipal performance affects the political fate of mayors.

THE POLITICAL CONTROL OF CADRES

The CCP has mobilized considerable resources to enhance its political control over the local cadres. It sought to improve personnel management by gradually reshaping the institutions that collect information, monitor the performance of local governments, and sanction officials (Harding 1981; Huang 1995; Whiting 2001). These institutional reforms were designed to act as a counterpoise against the centrifugal forces of economic decentralization. The web of Party organization departments (*zuzhi bumen*), discipline inspection commissions (*jiwei*) and local CCP committees is expected to root out cadres who flaunt central policies, are guilty of 'localism', or who are shown to be corrupt.[6] This strategy of reform has allowed economic decentralization to proceed, but seeks to reduce the costs of devolution.

The political principals of the Chinese state recognize that effective governance is a necessary condition to maintain regime legitimacy among ordinary citizens (Tang and Parish 2000). They rely on the CCP's institutional dominance to enforce the norm among cadres that the goal of achieving a 'relatively wealthy society' (*xiaokang shehui*) is critical to the regime's strategy for long-term survival. They stress the need to recruit and promote officials who deliver good governance - defined, for the most part, in terms of economic growth (Wei 2002: 1733). Article 6-2 of the 'Regulations on the Work of Selecting and Appointing Leading Party and Government Cadres' specifies that 'cadres should . . . be determined to carry out the reform and opening-up policy, be devoted to the cause of modernization, and work hard for the building of socialism and the making of concrete achievements' (CCP Organization Department 2002). The Centre has devised various incentive mechanisms to reduce shirking and to improve the performance among local cadres.[7]

The question of how best to select and reward local officials has always vexed the CCP's 'organizational and personnel management system' (*zuzhi renshi xitong*), but the problem is especially acute when the cadre management system is decentralized (Zhang 1994). In his classic

143

analysis of the Maoist polity, Schurmann (1968) argued that reliance on ideology could effectively compensate for weakened state organizations during periods of decentralization. The decline of ideology in the reform era has revived the role of formal organizations as instruments of political control. The Centre's challenge of controlling cadres is dual: local officials not only have broad leeway to steer the local economy in a direction that they choose, but *leadership selection itself* is also decentralized. Since Beijing controls directly only a handful of posts below the provincial level, it must trust that appointed provincial leaders have both the will and the capacity to implement personnel selection policy in a fashion that does not undermine the Party's political authority at the sub-provincial level.

OPERATIONALIZATION AND DATA COLLECTION

Evaluation of the CCP's personnel management strategy is based on fairly systematic data about China's municipalities.[8] Mayors (*shizhang*) constitute a natural pool to study how Party committees allocate political power: they exercise broad responsibilities in economic management, but remain politically subordinate to *provincial* Party organizations. They do not rank so high that they stand no chance of further promotion if they perform well. In recent years, the composition of the top echelon of party leaders has reflected the importance of experience as mayors and municipal secretaries for promotion to higher political office.[9] Since mayors typically serve concurrently as (first) deputy secretary of municipal CCP committees (*shiwei fushuji*), promotion to the post of municipal secretary is a natural career move for analysis. Other types of promotions are also possible: mayors sometimes become provincial vice-governor, or are deployed in central ministries. Thus, the dependent variable of interest is promotion, within the same locality or elsewhere.

The collection of local political and economic data in the PRC is a challenging task. Data collection about provinces has improved (Bo 2002; Huang 1996), but this is decidedly *not* the case below the provincial level. Although basic socio-economic performance indicators have generally been available since the 1990s, systematic political data are much harder to collect. Until recently, even lists of local officials were typically not available below the provincial level, let alone detailed biographical information about the cadres in question. Thus, practical considerations have motivated the focus on mayors: They are the lowest level of local cadres for whom reasonably systematic biographical information is available. Since the late 1980s, the Chinese Urban Development Research Council (CUDRC) has been publishing biographical notices of mayors annually (Zhongguo chengshi fazhan yanjiuhui 1985-2001; Li and Bachman 1989). This information has been combined in the present study with a cross-section time-series dataset of municipal performance, supplemented with data gathered from a variety of sources that allow one to track, with reasonable confidence, cadre careers after their terms as mayor.[10]

MUNICIPAL GOVERNANCE IN THE ERA OF MARKETIZATION

Prima facie, performance standards are clearly spelled out and uniform across cities. The Zhongguo chengshi fazhan yanjiuhui (2001) lists 33 socio-economic indicators of municipal modernization (see Appendix at end of article) and rates cities accordingly. The linkage between performance and promotion is even highlighted visually, with the mayor's name, picture and short biography prominently displayed above the table.

Mayors have a broad mandate to 'govern well', but they must do so under market pressures that increasingly constrain the capacity of the local state to control local outcomes. In fact, many objectives of good governance tend to *reduce* bureaucratic control in favour of non-state actors. Several indicators measure the growing impact of market forces that are beyond the direct control of local officials. For example, the share of services in the GDP (Indicator 3) depends heavily on the size of the non-state sector in the local economy. Similarly, openness to international trade (Indicator 5, calculated as Import + Exports/GDP) is affected in part by global market conditions which local officials can hardly control. These indicators probably measure the pace of the localities' economic modernization, but it is harder to conclude that they accurately measure the leadership's contribution to the modernization of the local economy.

These indicators are powerfully biased towards GDP performance: the variables that seek to measure 'economic development' not only account for almost a third of the overall index, but other factors are also strongly correlated with output growth, either by construction (Indicator 9) or indirectly (Indicators 10, 11 and 12, *inter alia*). Simple co-linearity tests between the main components of the index confirm that the indicators are deceptively broad (see Table 1).

145

TABLE 1   TEST OF CO-LINEARITY BETWEEN
KEY COMPONENTS OF THE CUDC
MUNICIPAL PERFORMANCE INDEX

Dependent Variable:
Infrastructure Index: Regression with robust standard errors (N=104)

	F(1,102)	23.86	Prob > F	0.00
	R2	0.22	Root MSE	2.07
Variable		Coef.	Robust SE	
Environment Index		0.358	0.073	***
Constant		5.367	1.040	***

Dependent Variable:
Economic Performance Index, Regression with robust standard errors (N=104)

	F(1,102)	37.75	Prob > F	0.00
	R2	0.26	Root MSE	3.37
Variable		Coef.	Robust SE	
Environment Index		0.692	0.113	***
Constant		6.947	1.511	***

Note: The data are based on the subset of cities (N=104) for which
performance indicators are published. This does not represent a complete set
of all Chinese cities.
Source: Zhongguo chengshi fazhan yanjiuhui 2001.

Market forces also have the effect of exaggerating performance
gaps across localities. The rise of regional disparities has been well
documented across provinces (Wang and Hu 1999), but the differences
are even more pronounced among sub-provincial units. Table 6
illustrates the large inter-municipal disparities in contemporary China,
although the broad components of the overall performance exhibit some
co-linearity.[11]

Large inter- and intra-regional disparities have disturbing
implications for the Party authority. At worst, persistently poor
performance undermines the credibility of the regime's claimed
successful transition to a 'socialist market economy with Chinese

146

characteristics'. If the CCP is serious about penalizing poor governance and rewarding good governance, then career patterns among local cadres should reflect this heavily differentiated landscape. By this reasoning, officials posted in fast-growing cities ought to be promoted more frequently than their counterparts posted in regions in relative economic decline.

In summary, China's rapid economic transformation has aggravated the Party's adverse selection problem. Provincial CCP committees may have the power to appoint and dismiss mayors, but this institutional strength remains theoretical in the absence of accurate ways to measure the leadership abilities of local officials. As marketization deepens, it is increasingly difficult to map the economic performance of the localities to the specific action of officials.

WHO ARE CHINA'S MAYORS?

Chinese mayors are typically well-educated men in their fifties and overwhelmingly *Han*[12]. Although they share the broad characteristics of provincial officials (e.g. more than two-thirds have received some form of tertiary education), they are younger. Whereas Bo (2002) reports a mean age of 55.5 years, male mayors typically are just above 50 and their female counterparts just above 48. In contrast to provincial officials, ethnic minorities seem under-represented (under 5 percent) - a low number, but one that also reflects the concentration of municipalities in coastal *Han*-dominated provinces.

Formal personnel regulations (CCP Organization Department 1995, 2002) strongly suggest that the odds of promotion depend on a cadre's personal characteristics. The rule of retirement (60 for most cadres, 55 for women) constrains career prospects heavily. Age limits were initially introduced to rejuvenate the post-Cultural Revolution leadership (Manion 1993; Shen 1994). This policy not only led to the replacement of 'old revolutionaries' by 'career bureaucrats' (Harding 1981; Lee 1991), but was also conducive to a considerable improvement in the overall level of education among cadres, since newly appointed officials were typically better trained than their predecessors (Landry 2000; Shen 1994). (See Tables 2 and 3.)

TABLE 2   MAYORS: LEVEL OF EDUCATION (1990-2000)

Education Level	Male	Female	All Cases (as % of total)
Graduate Level	297	9	(12.3)
College	1,149	22	(47.1)
Vocational College (dazhuan)	419	13	(17.3)
High School*	68	0	(2.7)
Other**	504	2	(20.3)
Total	2,437	46	
(%)	(98.1)	(1.9)	

Source Database.
**Including vocational education (zhongzhuan); *including missing data.

TABLE 3   MAYORS' AGE, BY GENDER AND MINORITY STATUS (1990-2000)

Gender	Mean Age	No.	Std.Deviation
Male	50.50	1,979	4.97
Female	48.10	0,046	4.54
Total	50.44	2,025	4.97
Ethnicity			
Han	50.43	1,920	4.98
Minority	50.58	0,105	4.74
Total	50.58	2,025	4.97

Source: Database.

Enforcing the retirement age is no longer controversial: the mayors' average age has hovered around 50 since 1990, well within formal regulatory limits. The data indicate strongly that they are always removed from office by the age of 60, unless they serve in deputy-provincial-level cities or centrally administered municipalities (CAMs), where the formal retirement age is higher. Even in this group, no one has remained in office beyond the age of 64.[13] Mayors also tend to serve shorter terms: the 1990 average of 3.2 years that matched the regulatory standard of three-year appointments had declined to a mere 2.3 years by 2000. Since 1998, few mayors have served a full three-year term (see Table 4 and Figure 1).

TABLE 4   MAYORS: AGE DISTRIBUTION (1990-2000)

Year	No.	Mean	Std.Dev.	Min.	Max.
1990	197	50.5	5.4	35	63
1991	198	50.4	4.9	36	63
1992	196	50.6	5.3	36	64
1993	176	50.3	4.8	37	62
1994	175	50.9	4.7	38	62
1995	183	50.9	5.1	34	63
1996	162	50.7	5.1	35	64
1997	164	50.8	5.1	39	61
1998	175	50.0	4.8	37	61
1999	194	50.2	4.7	38	62
2000	205	49.6	4.6	38	63

Source Database.

The norm of retirement is a powerful way to guarantee that relatively young cadres - who are arguably better trained and more attuned to the workings of a market economy - reach leadership positions in the localities. However, its enforcement can also come at the expense of cadre accountability. O'Brien and Li's finding that cadre rotation among rural cadres weakens accountability (1999: 176) applies here as well. It is difficult to see how a mayor, no matter how effective he may be, can signal his contribution to local development if his expected tenure in office is barely above two years.

FIGURE 1   MAYORS' AVERAGE TENURE (1990-2000)

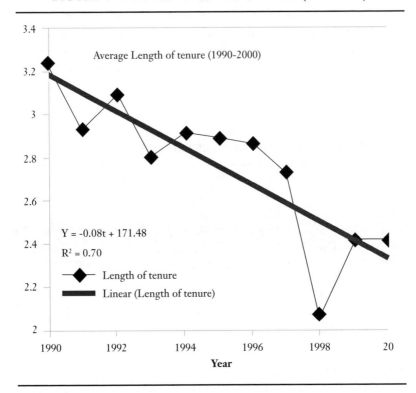

Note: Units are years of tenure at the time of observation.
Source: Database.

MODELLING THE RELATIONSHIP BETWEEN CADRE CHARACTERISTICS, MUNICIPAL PERFORMANCE AND POLITICAL OUTCOMES

Dependent Variable: Promotion

For the sake of tractability, a mayor's political fate is ordered along a single dimension and analysed as an ordered probability model: In a given year, he/she can 'exit'[14] (coded 0), 'continue' as mayor or be transferred to a position of identical rank (coded 1); or be 'promoted' to the rank of municipal party secretary (coded 2) in the same city or elsewhere.[15] Recall that ordered probit models make no scaling assumption of any kind: one need not assume that the difference between an exit and continuation is more or less desirable than the difference between 'continue' and 'promoted'. One need only be satisfied that:

Exit < Continue < Promoted

While the definitions of 'promotion' and 'transfer' are not particularly controversial, the reader may question the treatment of an 'exit' as less desirable than continuing as mayor. Mayors disappear from the dataset for various reasons. In some cases, they die in office or retire from public life. Alternatively, cadres may be eased into non-executive positions at the local People's Congress or the People's Political Consultative Conference. This ranking assumes that such posts are less desirable than the post of mayor. However, a third possibility is decidedly more threatening to statistical inference: exit may also reflect promotions to unobserved posts in provincial departments or central ministries. Since there is no comprehensive database of Chinese leaders above the prefectural level, there is no way to confirm that this third case is rare enough to ignore. However, every effort was made to verify that officials coded as 'exit' do not reappear in executive positions elsewhere.

A mayor's appointment marks the beginning of the last decade of his political career, barring exceptional circumstances. The dataset includes a handful of leaders who attained high office in the 1990s, including Jiang Zemin, Zhu Rongji, Li Ruihuan and Bo Xilai, but the presence of former mayors among China's top leaders should not mask the grimmer reality that promotions are relatively rare events.

Independent Variables

Mayors' Individual Characteristics

The model accounts for the salient individual attributes of cadre promotion regulations. These variables include age (in years), level of education, gender, as well as whether the cadre is *Han* Chinese or not. The effects of these variables are discussed in detail in the next section. In addition, two contrasts capture the length of tenure up to the year of observation: three to five years, which corresponds roughly to a second term in office, and six years or longer.[16]

Municipal Bureaucratic Rank

A second set of variables captures the bureaucratic rank of each municipality. 'Central Appointment' accounts for cities whose leadership is managed from Beijing. Furthermore, CAM party secretaries often sit as full or alternate members of the Central Committee, which enhances their visibility and access to core decision-makers. Their peculiar position in the Chinese political hierarchy is likely to increase their odds of promotion. In addition, an interaction term for 'Vice-Provincial Cities' accounts for instances of extensive autonomy over economic policy combined with partial central political control. Such is the economic status of provinces, but only their mayor and party secretary are centrally appointed. Deputy mayors and secretaries remain under provincial management, since they have the rank of prefecture-level cadres (*diji ganbu*).

Municipal Performance

At the current stage of the dataset development, it is necessary to restrict the set of municipal performance criteria to four indicators that are highly correlated with the municipal performance index published in 2001:

- the city size (population);
- the city's overall wealth (GDP per capita);
- the extent of the transition to a market economy - measured by the share of services to the local GDP; and
- openness to the world economy, measured by the magnitude of foreign direct investment (FDI) in the city.[17]

Provincial Contrasts

A set of dummy variables tests the hypothesis of systematic disparities in the way provincial party committees exercise political authority. Most of the published research on disparities refers to economic disparities (Hu and Wang 1996; Tan 1997; Wang 1995, 1997; Wang and Hu 1999). Here, provincial contrasts relate instead to a *political* logic. Assuming that economic disparities are reasonably accounted for by municipal performance indicators, provincial contrasts capture systematic differences across provincial party committees. Recall that apart from CAMs and vice-provincial cities, it is the provinces and not the Centre that exercise direct *nomenklatura* authority over municipal leaders.

Principles of organizational discipline suggest that personnel policy is implemented uniformly across provinces. If the hypothesis holds that cadre management practices are similar across provinces, these contrasts should be irrelevant in the multivariate model. Conversely, if systematic variations exist across provinces, these contrasts should exhibit both statistical significance and powerful substantive effects.

FIGURE 2   MAYORS: DISTRIBUTION OF POLITICAL FATE (1990-2000)

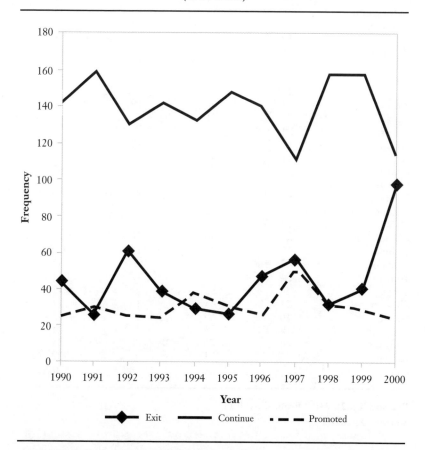

Note: In order to avoid 'right censoring', the analysis ends in 2000, a year when the fate of almost all mayors is known.
Source: Database.

TABLE 5   MAYORS: PROMOTIONS, EXIT, AND
CONTINUATION BY PROVINCE (1990-2000)

Province	Promotion Category (%)			
	Exit	Continue	Promoted	N(row)
Beijing	18	45	36	11
Tianjin	18	64	18	11
Hebei	21	62	18	120
Shanxi	33	54	13	61
Neimenggu	28	53	19	43
Liaoning	25	61	14	152
Jilin	19	60	21	84
Heilongjiang	27	59	14	21
Shanghai	9	73	18	11
Jiangsu	16	71	13	137
Zhejiang	28	62	11	104
Anhui	15	66	19	124
Fujian	23	71	6	78
Jiangxi	24	61	15	66
Shandong	17	64	19	151
Henan	21	62	17	153
Hubei	23	67	11	93
Hunan	24	66	10	131
Guangdong	18	63	19	186
Guangxi	22	68	10	87
Hainan	14	82	5	22
Chongqing	0	90	10	10
Sichuan	17	72	11	135
Guizhou	22	75	3	32
Yunnan	24	63	12	41
Tibet	9	82	9	11
Shaanxi	22	65	13	77
Gansu	16	69	15	55
Qinghai	18	73	9	11
Ningxia	24	76	0	25
Xinjiang	27	73	0	22
China	21	65	14	2,366

Pearson X^2(62): 73:18 Probability: 0.11
Source: Database.

At face value, differences in the political fate of mayors exist across provinces. In Xinjiang and Ningxia, mayors (who usually belong to ethnic minorities) *never* become party secretary, while in Beijing, Jilin, Shandong, Anhui and Guangdong, promotions occur in about 20 percent of cases, which is well above the national average of 14 percent. It remains to be seen whether these differences are statistically significant and reflect true behavioural differences across provincial party committees. I shall return to this point in my discussion of the ordered probit model.

Time Contrasts

Finally, annual dummy variables[18] account for two distinct processes. They control for time-specific shocks that are not specifically encapsulated in the model. Furthermore, annual dummy variables 'purge' the stochastic term of possible biases caused by omitted time-dependent variables and reduce autocorrelation among error terms, a major pitfall of cross-section time-series models.[19]

Results

I present three closely related versions of the multivariate model of mayor promotion. Model 1 estimates the odds of the ordered outcome (exit<continue<promotion) for the entire sample. Models 2 and 3 split the sample between cities located in coastal provinces and cities of interior provinces.

TABLE 6   ORDERED PROBABILITY ESTIMATES

		Model 1			Model 2			Model 3		
		All Provinces			Coastal Provinces			Inland Provinces		
		1780			874			941		
Log-Likelihood		-1453.9			-674.1			-761.6		
P>X2		0.000			0.000			0.000		
Independent variables	Type									
Mayor's Characteristics										
Tenure 3-5 years	d	-0.191	0.063	***	-0.183	0.062	***	-0.191	0.064	***
Tenure 6 years	d	-0.496	0.147	***	-0.483	0.143	***	-0.493	0.148	***
Year of birth, 1972-1965	c.	0.029	0.008	***	0.025	0.008	***	0.027	0.008	***
Gender, 1=Female	d.	-0.012	0.183		0.010	0.177		-0.013	0.181	

TABLE 6: ORDERED PROBABILITY ESTIMATES (cont.)

		Model 1			Model 2			Model 3		
		All Provinces			Coastal Provinces			Inland Provinces		
		1780			874			941		
Log-Likelihood		-1453.9			-674.1			-761.6		
P>X2		0.000			0.000			0.000		
Independent variables	Type									
Mayor's Characteristics										
Minority, 1=Minority	d.	0.026	0.198		-0.041	0.151		-0.016	0.152	
Graduate	d.	-0.060	0.163		-0.019	0.155		-0.016	0.158	
College Education	d.	0.010	0.130		0.036	0.122		0.018	0.125	
Voc.College Educ.	d.	-0.059	0.154		-0.064	0.145		-0.021	0.148	
City Characteristics										
Central Appointment	d.	0.492	0.270	*	0.331	0.213		—	—	
Deputy Provincial City	d.	-0.466	0.306		-0.268	0.278		-0.036	0.201	
Population (10,000 people)	c.	0.000	0.000		0.000	0.000		0.000	0.000	*
GDP per capital (RMB 1000)	c.	0.011	0.005	**	0.013	0.007	*	0.011	0.006	
Share of services (% GDP)	c.	-0.006	0.003	*	-0.007	0.003	**	-0.007	0.003	**
FD (US$1000)	c.	0.000	0.000		0.000	0.000		0.000	0.000	
Provincial Contrasts										
Chongqing	d.	—	—		—	—		-0.362	0.375	
Hebei	d.	0.162	0.184		0.031	0.100		—	—	
Shanxi	d.	-0.059	0.245		—	—		-0.210	0.196	
Neimenggu	d.	-0.030	0.161		—	—		-0.162	0.193	
Liaoning	d.	0.224	0.170		0.083	0.120		—	—	
Jilin	d.	0.370	0.238		—	—		0.228	0.189	
Heilongjiang	d.	-0.012	0.181		—	—		-0.162	0.134	
Jiangsu	d.	0.146	0.191		0.017	0.105		—	—	
Zhejiang	d.	-0.112	0.199		-0.235	0.127	*	—	—	
Anhui	d.	0.339	0.201	*	—	—		0.176	0.143	
Fujian	d.	-0.031	0.205		-0.162	0.140		—	—	

TABLE 6: ORDERED PROBABILITY ESTIMATES (cont.)

		Model 1			Model 2			Model 3		
		All Provinces			Coastal Provinces			Inland Provinces		
		1780			874			941		
Log-Likelihood		-1453.9			-674.1			-761.6		
P>X2		0.000			0.000			0.000		
Independent variables	Type									
Provincial Contrasts										
Jiangxi	d.	0.084	0.255		—	—		-0.055	0.202	
Shandong	d.	0.310	0.219		0.173	0.159		—	—	
Henan	d.	0.229	0.207		—	—		0.059	0.145	
Hubei	d.	-0.070	0.195		—	—		-0.233	0.130	*
Hunan	d.	-0.146	0.180		—	—		-0.309	0.100	**
Guangdong	d.	0.310	0.209		0.197	0.144		—	—	
Guangxi	d.	0.056	0.196		—	—		-0.096	0.148	
Hainan	d.	0.181	0.170		0.070	0.109		—	—	
Sichuan	d.	0.283	0.194		—	—		0.105	0.128	
Guizhou	d.	-0.085	0.170		—	—		-0.227	0.081	***
Yunnan	d.	-0.038	0.255		—	—		-0.198	0.206	
Shanxi	d.	0.347	0.266		—	—		0.189	0.227	
Gansu	d.	0.549	0.275	**	—	—		0.394	0.261	
Qinghai	d.	0.255	0.207		—	—		0.110	0.167	
Time Contrasts										
1999	d.	0.558	0.127	***	0.542	0.126	***	0.544	0.125	***
1998	d.	0.693	0.136	***	0.668	0.133	***	0.671	0.132	***
1997	d.	0.731	0.147	***	0.701	0.145	***	0.710	0.143	***
1996	d.	0.479	0.143	***	0.451	0.140	***	0.459	0.140	***
1995	d.	0.951	0.137	***	0.971	0.135	***	0.925	0.134	***
1994	d.	0.967	0.157	***	0.921	0.152	***	0.944	0.154	***
1993	d.	0.790	0.168	***	0.744	0.165	***	0.766	0.167	***
1992	d.	0.644	0.170	***	0.591	0.166	***	0.621	0.167	***
1991	d.	1.090	0.176	***	1.026	0.170	***	1.068	0.172	***
1990	d.	0.873	0.181	***	0.790	0.177	***	0.852	0.177	***

TABLE 6: ORDERED PROBABILITY ESTIMATES (cont.)

		Model 1	Model 2	Model 3
		All Provinces	Coastal Provinces	Inland Provinces
		1780	874	941
Log-Likelihood		-1453.9	-674.1	-761.6
P>X2		0.000	0.000	0.000
Independent variables	Type			
Ancillary Parameters				
Cut 1		56.366 15.65 ***	47.484 23.855 ***	51.276 15.184 ***
Cut 2		58.404 15.66 ***	49.534 23.873 ***	53.332 15.198 ***
Observed Distribution of the Dependent Variable				
Probability (Exit)		0.19	0.18	0.20
Probability (Continue)		0.67	0.67	0.66
Probability (Promotin)		0.14	0.16	0.13

Note: Observations are mayor-years. Some provincial are omitted due to missing data or for the purpose of ensuring model identification. The baseline of the time contrasts is 2000. 'C' denotes a continuous variable,'d' a dummy. All models use robust standard errors, adjusted for clustering by city.***:p<0.01 **:p<0.05 *: p<0.10

Municipal Performance

Does municipal performance matter? Municipal economic performance seems to have a positive but limited impact on the political fate of mayors. Figure 3 plots the fitted odds of promotion for a typical case.[20] It evaluates the impact of municipal performance by varying municipal GDP per capita within sample values, and does so in three cases: mayor whose 'tenure so far' is less than three years; three to six years; and more than six years. While all three models suggest that performance - in this relatively narrow sense - matters, they still point to the limited capacity of Chinese political institutions to reward 'good' governance. First, the odds of promotion remain low if we limit our measure to 'typical cities'. The observed maximum GDP of RMB 148,000 per person in Shenzhen in 2000 is a far cry from the sample mean of RMB 8,651. If we restrict our assessment to the effect of economic performance around the mean, the results are far less spectacular: our typical mayor overseeing a hypothetical trebling of the GDP from the sample mean to RMB 18,170 (namely, a one standard deviation improvement) would only see the odds of promotion shift from 0.11 to 0.13, a trivial gain.[21] Disturbingly, developing the service economy seems detrimental to one's political career, even if we restrict the analysis to interior provinces where such changes are arguably welcome.[22] Finally, the impact of economic openness (measured by the amount of FDI) is nil. These results hold when the sample is split between coastal and interior cities. Thus, it appears that the Party's stated preference for performance-based career advancement is hardly consistent with the revealed preferences of provincial party committees. In this sense, my findings are in accordance with Bo's conclusion that growth *per se* does not explain promotion patterns among provincial cadres (Bo 2002).[23] Overall, it is doubtful that municipal leaders are being rewarded for their economic performance while in office.

As discussed earlier, the decentralized and increasingly marketized nature of municipal economies may well be at the root of this weak principal-agent relationship. Regardless of the statements of the officials concerned, it is not altogether clear that mayors and government officials 'cause' or 'slow' economic development in the first place. To use Naughton's image (1995), as the economy 'grows out of the plan', the mapping of bureaucratic actions to specific outcomes is arduous, if not irrelevant.

The weak linkages between performance and political careers may also be rooted in other political considerations. Even though shortening tenure lengths tend to obfuscate personal accountability, appointers may still have a powerful incentive to do so, for two reasons. First, frequent turnover allows CCP committees to reward a larger proportion of secondary officials. Long tenures would increase competition for (rare) desirable posts and be demoralizing to competent cadres whose prospects for political advancement would be limited. These concerns motivated the push for cadre rejuvenation and orderly retirement in the first place. The pool of secondary officials is very large: typical cities have at least three deputy party secretaries and three vice-mayors. With shorter tenure at the helm, more officials can expect to reach the top executive positions.

Second, the fight against corruption provides the other incentive to shorten cadre tenure. Leaders who remain entrenched in their localities are more likely to develop extensive informal '*guanxi*' networks that undermine party authority. When cadres spend only a couple of years in executive positions, opportunities for 'corrupt' or 'localist' behaviour are less likely to arise.

FIGURE 3   FITTED IMPACT OF MUNICIPAL ECONOMIC PERFORMANCES ON THE PROBABILITY PROMOTION OF MAYORS, BY TENURE LENGTH

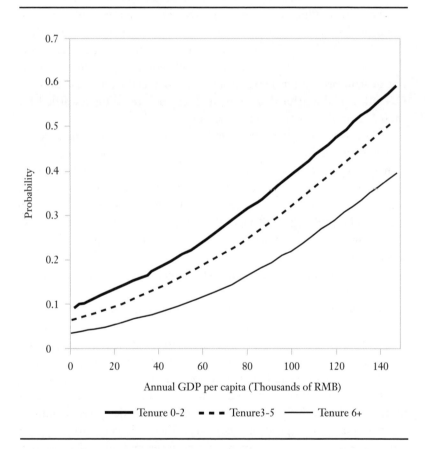

Note: Plots are based on model 1.

Municipal Bureaucratic Rank and Size

Model 1 also indicates an important political difference between mayors under direct central management and those whose careers are primarily handled by provincial party committees. All else being equal, the former are more likely to be promoted than the latter. The interaction term shows no difference between CAMs and deputy provincial cities. What matters is the existence of central political control, not whether a city has the full rank of a province or not.[24]

Cadre Characteristics

On the other hand, all three models highlight the importance of the cadres' individual characteristics and are highly consistent with the hypothesis that key organizational rules on cadre promotion prevail in the localities. Older mayors are less likely to be promoted than younger ones. The effect of age is particularly acute when length of tenure is also taken into account. At the beginning of his sixth year in office, the same hypothetical mayor in Jiangsu discussed above - but this time varying his age and holding GDP per capita at the sample mean - has a mere 1.2 percent chance of promotion if he were born in 1940, in contrast to a 20 percent chance for an otherwise identical mayor born in 1970, in his first term. Notice that the effect of tenure is not linear: the substantive effect is much greater among younger mayors than older ones.

Since provincial organizations departments take personnel regulations seriously and since cadres rarely become mayor before the age of 50, the logic of tying promotions to performance works as an incentive to keep tenure relatively short, lest competent cadres reach the age limit by the time they reveal themselves as leaders worthy of promotion. To some extent, this seems to be the case.

Gender and Ethnicity

In addition to a rule of earlier retirement than men, female cadres also suffer from significant institutional discrimination. Not surprisingly, the pool of Chinese women mayors is very small (16 since 1990; see Table 7) and promotions are exceedingly rare: only Xu Xiaoqing eventually became party secretary in Jingdezhen where she was mayor from 1995-97.[25] The promotion model suggests that discrimination affects female cadres at earlier stages of their career, not when they have already reached the rank of mayor. Uneven access to tertiary education and membership in

161

the Communist Party are likely act as powerful barriers to entry in the cadre corps. However, once selected into officialdom, some women do seem to suffer from unequal treatment, at least among mayors.

Similar results obtain with respect to ethnic minorities. Again, when we discount the issue of access to the cadre corps in the first place, there is scant evidence of discrimination against ethnic minority mayors. Consider Model 3, which encompasses all 'autonomous regions', as well as many inland provinces with a high proportion of ethnic minorities such as Sichuan, Yunnan, Qinghai and Gansu. *Ceteris paribus*, mayors in autonomous regions are not promoted to party posts less often than their counterparts in ordinary provinces, despite the conventional wisdom that high positions for minority leaders are restricted to government jobs, while *Han* officials hold key Party posts. These results hold when the

TABLE 7   FEMALE MAYORS, 1990-2000

Name	Year of Birth	Education	Comment
An Li	1948	College	Mayor of Liaoyuan (Jilin), 1992-94
Huang Yanrong	1955	Vocational College	Mayor of Ya'an (Sischuan), 2000.
Li Kang	1957	College	Mayor of Qingzhou (Guangxi), 2000-. Zhuang Nationality
Li Yumei	1956	Graduate	Mayor of Linyi (Shandong) 1997-
Ma Languo	1954	College	Mayor of Xingtai (Hebei), 1998
Ma Qiaozhen	1945	College	Mayor of Jincheng (Shanxi), 1996-98
Shi Lijun	1948	Vocational College	Mayor of Laiwa (Shandong), 1993-97
Shu Xiaoqin	1956	Vocational College	Mayor of Jingdezhen (Jiangxi), 1995-97 Promoted Party Secretary of Jingdezhen, 1998-
Song shu'ai	1944	College	Mayor of Chengde (Hebei), 1990-92
Xu Yan	1944	College	Mayor of Nantong (Jiangsu), 1990-94
Wang Xia	1954	M.A.	Mayor of Yan'an (Shaanxi) 1999-. Promoted Party Secretary of Yan'an, 2001-
Wang Jumei	1949	Unknown	Mayor of Nanyang (Henan) 1999-
Xuan Lin	1948	College	Mayor of Wuhu (Anhui), 2000-
Yuang Fenglan	1942	Vocational College	Mayor of Guilin (Guangxi), 1991-94
Yuan Shiwu	1936	College	Mayor of Huzhou (Zhejiang), 1992-94
Zhu Tong	1949	N.A.	Mayor of Baishan (Jilin), 1998-2000

Source: Database

minority status of individual cadres is included. In short, the Party does not discriminate (positively or negatively) between *Han* and other officials, measured spatially or individually. (See Table 8.)

Regional Differentiations

The regional contrasts do not reveal particularly severe disparities in the way provincial committees manage the political careers of mayors. The cleavage is instead institutional. The Centre seems somewhat keener to promote mayors under its purview than are the provinces, perhaps because it uses these large, prosperous and politically important cities as testing-grounds for officials earmarked for future critical appointments in the central bureaucracy. Lin Shusen's recent promotion in Guangdong is a case in point. After his long tenure as mayor of Guangzhou, he was promoted to party secretary in Guangzhou and obtained a seat as alternate member of the CC in November 2002. To be sure, a few provinces exhibit the usual behaviour: for example, in Hunan, Hubei and Guizhou, promotions seem to be rare. Yet, the overall results fall short of exhibiting rampant localism in the form of large and systematic differences in the behaviour across provincial Party committees.

TABLE 8   PERCENTAGE OF CASES OF MINORITY MAYORS, 1990-2000, BY PROVINCE

Province		%
Tibet	AR	93.3
Inner Mongolia	AR	51.5
Ningxia	AR	45.7
Xinjiang	AR	40.6
Guizhou		23.3
Jilin		5.1
Liaoning		4.5
Gansu		3.8
Guangxi	AR	2.8
Hebei		2.8
Heilongjiang		2.8
Jiangxi		2.0
China	3.5	

Notes: Units Of analysis are mayor-years AR= Autonomous Regions

FIGURE 4   FITTED IMPACT OF AGE ON THE PROBABILITY
PROMOTION OF MAYORS, BY TENURE LENGTH

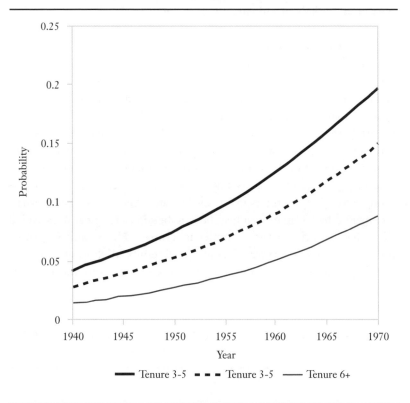

Note: Plots are based on Model 1.

CONCLUSIONS

The Chinese Communist Party has retained its capacity to shape political outcomes in the localities. Despite decentralization, the organizational system remains firmly in control of cadre careers. On the surface, provincial Party organizations are applying the broad policies laid out since the 1980s to rejuvenate the cadre corps, impose strict retirement rules, and combat the entrenchment of local elites by keeping terms of office relatively short. These achievements are rare among communist systems, or even authoritarian ones, and may help explain the durability of the Chinese political system. They are even more noteworthy when one considers the high degree of decentralization that characterizes contemporary Chinese institutions. Unlike so many studies of decentralization in other issue areas, I find little evidence of rampant localism with respect to cadre management: the rules seem to apply evenly across provinces.

Party institutions may be powerful, but they are not necessarily efficient. The CCP is proving less able to develop incentive mechanisms that reward officials who perform, and penalize those who do not. In its urge to rejuvenate the cadre corps and combat corruption, the CCP's institutional response is to accelerate turnover among mayors. This decision seems to have taken precedence over the need to allow officials who perform to remain in place. To be sure, there appears to be a slight positive bias in favour of cadres who oversee quantitative growth, but the political system is not designed to promote desired qualitative changes that take place in the long run. I concur with Huang (1995) and Edin's (2003) view that state capacity is not necessarily declining, but I question the conclusion that Beijing's core economic priorities take precedence over other political considerations. The CCP may want to govern effectively, but the preponderance of the evidence in this study suggests that other political motivations - such as the need to distribute political rewards to a greater share of secondary officials - shape the political careers of local elites much more powerfully than the regime's stated goals of improving local governance.

ENDNOTES

1   By 'Centre', I refer to the Chinese term *zhongyang* which implies the leadership and institutions of the Communist Party and the Central Government, in contrast to provincial and local party and government institutions.

2   In 1978, China had only 193 officially recognized cities, including 92 county-level cities (*xianji shi*). By 2000, the number had risen to 663: four centrally administered municipalities (CAMs); 15 'vice-provincial-level cities' (*fu shengji chengshi*); 244 ordinary municipalities (*diji shi*); and 400 county-level cities (*xianji shi*) (Dai 2000; Zhongguo guojia tongji ju 2001).

3   Dalian, Guangzhou, Xian, Shenyang, Wuhan, Ningbo, Hangzhou, Chengdu, Nanjing, Shenzhen, Qingdao, Harbin, Changchun, Xiamen and Jinan. Chonqing was upgraded to a CAM in 1997.

4   The literature of decentralization and central-local relations in the post-Mao era is vast. (See *inter alia*: Blecher and Shue 1996; Falkenheim 1980; Friedman 1993; Goodman 1986, 1992, 1994; Goodman and Segal 1994; Hao and Lin 1994; Huang 1996; Lampton 1992; Liu 1996; Oi 1992, 1995; Oksenberg and Tong 1991; Park *et al.* 1996; Shirk 1990; Solinger 1977,

1996; Walder 1995; Watson 1984; Whiting 2001; Wong 1997; Xie *et al.* 1995; Yang 1990, 1994, 1997).

5   However, the practice of 'reporting for information' (*bei'an*) confers on the Centre the right to overrule provincial decisions within a specified amount of time.

6   The latest personnel regulations explicitly stress the need to control deviant behaviour and root out corruption among the cadre corps (Cui 2002).

7   In 2000, Zhu Rongji introduced the 'cadre responsibility system' for local officials. Various types of 'responsibility systems' have been implemented in many issue areas, including family planning (Chu 1999), public health and the fight against SARS, as well as flood prevention and control (Zhang and Wang 2000). The system extends to county and township officials (O'Brien and Li 1999; Edin 2003).

8   County-level cities are not included in the analysis.

9   This group extends beyond the well-known 'Shanghai Faction' (Jiang Zemin, Zhu Rongji, Wu Bangguo and Chen Zhili), including among others: Li Ruihuan (former mayor of Tianjin); state councillor Wu Yi (former vice-mayor of Beijing); Yu Zhengsheng (minister of construction and former mayor and CCP secretary of both Yantai and Qingdao); and Chen Yaobang (minister of agriculture, and former deputy CCP secretary of Wuxi).

10   In addition to the biographical notices of the Zhongguo chengshi fazhan yanjiuhui [China Urban Development Research Committee], leadership information was compiled from local and provincial yearbooks, issues of the *Zhongguo chengshi fazhan baogao* [Chinese Urban Development Report], issues of *China Directory*, as well as municipal government websites. Refer to the data sources section of the bibliography for statistical sources on municipal performance. Special thanks to Julie Zeng, Yumin Sheng and Shiru Wang for their research assistance, and to the Universities Service Centre for China Studies at the Chinese University of Hong Kong.

11   This part of the analysis is limited to the set of 104 cities for which all 33 performance indicators are available. Unfortunately, indicators and related indices have only been by published by the CUDC since 2000. The remainder of the article is based on a much broader cross-section time-series political-economic dataset.

12   Namely, somebody who does not belong to any officially recognized ethnic minority.

13   Li Ziliu, mayor of Guangzhou, was 64 when he was replaced in 1996.

14   A mayor who is removed from office to the position of chairman of the Municipal People's Congress is treated as an exit because the post does not imply executive authority. This was the case of Jiang Jin, mayor of Jiangmen (in Guandong) from 1999-2001. Similarly, appointments to the Local Political Consultative Conference are treated as exits.

15   Transfers are coded 1 (continue) when cadres are deployed to a similarly ranked city. For instance, Li Jianchang was appointed mayor of Baoding (Hebei) in March 1998. He was subsequently sent to serve as mayor of

Kaifeng (Henan). The rule applies to transfers to provincial CCP or government bureaus. For instance, Huang Huahua, mayor of Meizhou in 1991, became secretary general of the Guangdong provincial committee in 1992. When a mayor becomes party secretary of a city or assumes a higher-ranking post in provincial or central governments, she is coded 2 (promotion). For instance, Xu Mingyang, mayor of Jiaozuo (Henan) until July 1995, was promoted to vice-chairman of the Tibet A.R., a clear promotion, even though he never served as CCP secretary in Jiaozuo.

16   I do not use the simple continuous measure of tenure length because it is unreasonable to assume a linear relationship. Instead, the relationship is J-shaped: cadres are not expected to be replaced immediately after their appointment, but the odds of reassignment/exit increase substantially as they enter their second term (three to five years) and should be even greater beyond the end of a second term (six years and more).

17   It would be preferable to rely on foreign trade, as listed in the performance indicators of the Zhongguo chengshi fazhan yanjiuhui. Unfortunately, municipal-level foreign trade data are too inconsistent for the early 1990s to be incorporated in the model.

18   The baseline (omitted) is the year 2000.

19   In addition, all models use the method of robust standard errors, adjusted for clustering by municipality.

20   The simulation assumes that the mayor is male, Han, was born in 1960, holds a college degree and is posted in an ordinary municipality in Jiangsu province.

21   The predicted probability of the highest ranked outcome (here, promotion) in ordered probit models is equal to $\_(k-X\_)$, where k is the last cut-point estimate, $X\_$ the linear effects and $\_$ the cumulative normal distribution (Long 1997: 114-47).

22   The coefficient is not only of the wrong sign, but it is also significant at the 0.1 level, or better!

23   However, I cannot confidently conclude that the fiscal element in career prospects can be ruled in or out as a predictor of promotion, as Bo does. Unlike provinces, municipal statistical data do not indicate the share of fiscal revenue that cities remit to the centre, whether directly (since 1994) or indirectly through the provincial tax collection bureaux (before 1994).

24   The result does not seem to hold when the sample is split between coast and interior provinces. The very small number of observations in each sub-sample is likely to explain the larger standard error estimates.

25   Wang Xia's promotion as party secretary of Yan'an in 2001 falls beyond the period of analysis.

REFERENCES

Blecher, M. and Vivien Shue 1996. *Tethered Deer: Government and Economy in a Chinese County.* Stanford: Stanford University Press.

Bo, Zhiyue 2002. *Chinese Provincial Leaders: Economic Performance and Political Stability since 1949.* Armonk, NY: M. E. Sharpe.

Brødsgaard, Kjeld Erik 2002. 'Institutional Reform and the *Bianzhi* System in China.' *The China Quarterly* 170: 361-86.

Burns, John P. (ed.) 1989. *The Chinese Communist Party's Nomenklatura System.* Armonk, NY: M.E. Sharpe.

—— 1994. 'Strengthening Central CCP Control of Leadership Selection: The 1990 *Nomenklatura.' The China Quarterly* 138: 458-91.

CCP Organization Department 2002. 'Regulations on the Work of Selecting and Appointing Leading Party and Government Cadres.' [http://www.china.org.cn/english/features/45399.htm accessed 18 May 2003].

Chu Junhong 1999. 'Quality Reorientation of the Family Planning Program in China: Some Conceptual Issues.' Harvard Center for Population and Development Studies: Working Paper 99.17.

Crane, George 1990. *The Political Economy of China's Special Economic Zones.* Armonk, NY: M. E. Sharpe.

Cui, Shixin 2002. 'New Rules and Regulations Governing the Selection of Leading Cadres Aim to Root out Corruption.' *Renmin wang,* 23 July 2002 [Translated in *FBIS Daily Report - China,* 24 July 2002].

Dai, Junliang 2000. *Zhongguo shizhi* [China's Urban System]. Beijing: China Map Publishing.

'Dangzheng lingdao ganbu xuanba zuoyong gongzuo zanxing tiaoli' 1995. [Temporary Regulations on the Work of Selecting and Appointing Leading Party and Government Cadres] In K. Zeng (ed.), *Xin shiqi dang de jiceng zuzhi (dangwei, dangzongzhi, dangzhibu) gongzuo shouce* [Handbook on the Party's Basic Organizations (Party Committees, Party General Branches and Party Branches) in the New Era]. Beijing: Hongqi chubanshe 2002: 946-54.

Edin, Maria. 2003. 'State Capacity and Local Agent Control in China: CCP Cadre Management from a Township Perspective.' *The China Quarterly* 173: 35-52.

Falkenheim, Victor C. 1980. 'Decentralization and Control in Chinese Local Administration.' In D. Nelson (ed.), *Local Politics in Communist Countries.* Lexington, KY: The University Press of Kentucky: 191-210.

Friedman, Edward 1993. 'China's North-South Split and the Forces of Disintegration.' *Current History* 575(September): 270-74.

Goodman, David 1986. *Centre and Province in the People's Republic of China: Sichuan and Guizhou, 1955-1965.* Cambridge: Cambridge University Press.

—— 1992. 'Provinces Confronting the State?' In H. C. Kuan et al., *China Review 1992,* Hong Kong: CUHK Press: 3.2-19.

—— 1994. 'The Politics of Regionalism: Economic Development, Conflict and Negotiation.' In D.G. S. Goodman and G. Segal (eds), *China Deconstructs: Politics, Trade and Regionalism.* London and New York: Routledge: 286-321.

—— and Gerald Segal (eds) 1994. *China Deconstructs: Politics, Trade and Regionalism*. London and New York: Routledge.

Hao, J. and Zhimin Lin 1994. *Changing Central-Local Relations in China: Reform and State Capacity*. Boulder, CO: Westview Press.

Harding, Harry 1981. *Organizing China: The Problem of Bureaucracy, 1949-1976*. Stanford, CA: Stanford University Press.

Hu, Angang and Shaoguang Wang 1996. 'Changes in China's Regional Disparities.' *Washington Center for China Studies (WCCS)* Papers: 6 (9).

Hu, Angang *et al*. 1995. *zhongguo diqu chaju baogao* [Regional Disparities in China], Shenyang: Liaoning renmin chubanshe.

Huang, Yasheng 1995. 'Administrative Monitoring in China.' *The China Quarterly* (143): 828-44.

—— 1996. *Inflation and Investment Controls in China. The Political Economy of Central-Local Relations during the Reform Era*. Cambridge: Cambridge University Press.

Jiang, M. and Ruchun Cui 2001. *2000 Nian woguo chengshi jingji shehui fazhan gaikuang* [Overview of the Economic and Social Developments of China's Cities in 2000]. In Zhongguo chengshi fazhan yanjiuhai (ed.), *zhongguo chengshi nianjian*. [China Urban Yearbook 2001] Beijing: China Urban Yearbook Publishing: 178-80.

Kleinberg, Robert 1990. *China's 'Opening' to the Outside World: The Experiment with Foreign Capitalism*. Boulder, CO: Westview Press.

Lampton, David 1992. 'A Plum for a Peach: Bargaining, Interest, and Bureaucratic Politics in China.' In K. G. Lieberthal et al. (eds), *Bureaucracy, Politics and Decision Making in Post-Mao China*. Berkeley, CA: University of California Press: 33-58.

Landry, Pierre F. 2000. *Controlling Decentralization: The Party and Local Elites in Post-Mao Jiangsu*. Ph.D. diss., The University of Michigan.

Lee, Hung-Yong 1991. *From Revolutionary Cadres to Party Technocrats in Socialist China*. Berkeley, CA: University of California Press.

Li, C. and D. Bachman 1989. 'Localism, Elitism, and Immobilism - Elite Formation and Social Change in Post-Mao China.' *World Politics* 42 (1): 64-94.

Liu Junde (ed.) 1996. *Zhongguo xingzheng quhua de lilun yu shijian* [Theory and Practice of China's Administrative Divisions]. Shanghai: Huadong shifan daxue chubanshe.

Long, J. Scott. 1997. *Regression Models for Categorical and Limited Dependent Variables*. Thousand Oaks, CA: Sage Publications.

Manion, Melanie 1985. 'The Cadre Management System, Post-Mao: the Appointment, Promotion, Transfer and Removal of Party and State Leaders.' *The China Quarterly* (102): 203-33.

—— 1993. *Retirement of Revolutionaries in China*. Princeton, NJ: Princeton University Press.

Naughton, Barry 1995. *Growing Out of the Plan: Chinese Economic Reform 1978-1993*. Cambridge: Cambridge University Press.

169

O'Brien, Kevin J and Lianjiang Li 1999. 'Selective Policy Implementation in Rural China.' *Comparative Politics* 31(2): 167-86.

Oi, Jean C. 1992. 'Fiscal Reforms and the Economic Foundations of Local State Corporatism in China.' *World Politics* 45(1): 99-126.

—— 1995. 'The Role of the Local State in China's Transitional Economy.' *The China Quarterly*, 144: 132-49.

Oksenberg, M. and James Tong 1991. 'The Evolution of Central-Provincial Fiscal Relations in China, 1971-1984: the Formal System.' *The China Quarterly* 125: 1-32.

Park, A. *et al.* 1996. 'Distributional Consequences of Reforming Local Public Finance in China.' *The China Quarterly* 147: 751-78.

Schurmann, Franz 1968 [1966]. *Ideology and Organization in Communist China.* Berkeley, CA: University of California Press.

Shen, Mingming 1994. *A Policy-driven Elite Transformation and its Outcomes: A Case Study of the New Local Elites of China.* Ph.D. diss., University of Michigan.

Shirk, Susan L. 1990. ' "Playing to the Provinces": Deng Xiaoping's Political Strategy of Economic Reform.' *Studies in Comparative Communism* 33 (3/4): 227-58.

Solinger, Dorothy J. 1977. *Regional Government and Political Integration in Southwest China, 1949-1954.* Berkeley, CA: University of California Press.

—— 1996. 'Despite Decentralization: Disadvantages, Dependence and Ongoing Central Power in the Inland - the Case of Wuhan.' *The China Quarterly* 145: 1-34.

Tan, Chenglin 1997. *Zhongguo quyu jingji chayi yanjiu.* [Research on China's Regional Economic Disparities]. Beijing: Zhongguo jingji chubanshe.

Tang, W. and William L. Parish 2000. *Chinese Urban Life under Reform: The Changing Social Contract.* Cambridge: Cambridge University Press.

Walder, Andrew 1995. 'Local Governments as Industrial Firms: An Organizational Analysis of China's Transitional Economy.' *American Journal of Sociology* 101(2): 263-301.

Wang, Shaoguang 1994. 'Central-Local Fiscal Politics in China.' In J. Hao et al. (eds), *Changing Central-Local Relations in China.* Boulder, CO: Westview Press: 92-112.

—— 1995. 'The Rise of the Regions: Fiscal Reform and the Decline of Central State Capacity in China'. In A. G. Walder (ed.), *The Waning of the Communist State. Economic Origins of Political Decline in China and Hungary.* Berkeley, CA: University of California Press: 87-113.

—— 1997. 'China's 1994 Reform: An Initial Assessment', *Asian Survey*, 37(9): 801-18.

—— and Angang Hu 1999. *The Political Economy of Uneven Development: The Case of China.* Armonk, NY: M. E. Sharpe.

Watson, Andrew 1984. 'New Structures in the Organization of Chinese Agriculture: a Variable Model.' *Pacific Affairs* 57: 621-45.

Wei, Y. Dennis 2002. 'Beyond the Sunan Model: Trajectory and Underlying Factors of Development in Kunshan, China.' *Environment and Planning'* 34 (10): 1725-47.

Whiting, Susan H. 2001. *Power and Wealth in Rural China: The Political Economy of Institutional Change*. Cambridge: Cambridge University Press.

Wong, Christine P. W. 1997. *Rural Public Finance: Financing Local Development in the People's Republic of China*. Hong Kong and Oxford: Asian Development Bank & Oxford University Press: 167-212.

Xie, Qingkui *et al.* 1995. *Zhongguo zhengfu tizhi fenxi* [An Analysis of China's Government Structure]. Beijing: Zhongguo guongbo chubanshe.

Yang, Dali 1990. 'Patterns of China's Regional Development Strategy.' *The China Quarterly*, 122 (June): 230-57.

—— 1994. 'Reform and Restructuring of Central-Local Relations'. In D. S. G. Goodman and Gerald Segal (eds), *China Deconstructs: Politics, Trade and Regionalism*. London and New York: Routledge.

—— 1997. *Beyond Beijing: Liberalization and the Regions in China*. London and New York: Routledge.

Zhang, X. and Ling Wang 2000. *The Role of Hydrological Information Collection Sub-System in China National Flood Control Decision System*. Paper presented at the International Conference on Hydro-Science and Engineering. Seoul, 2000.

Zhang, Zhijian. 1994. *Dangdai zhongguo de renshi guanli* [Personnel Management in Contemporary China]. Beijing: Jindai zhongguo chubanshe.

PRINCIPAL DATA SOURCES

Zhongguo guojia tongji ju 1985-2001. *Zhongguo chengshi tongji nianjian* [China Urban Statistical Yearbook]. Beijing: Zhongguo tongji chubanshe. [Multiple issues]

1999. *Xin zhongguo chengshi 50 nian* [Fifty Years of Chinese Cities]. Beijing: Xinhua chubanshe.

Zhongguo chengshi fazhan yanjiuhui 1993-2001. *Zhongguo chengshi nianjian* [China Urban Yearbook]. Beijing: Zhongguo chengshi nianjian chubanshe. [Multiple Issues]

Zhongguo chengshi jingjihui 1985-1992. *Zhongguo chengshi jingji shehui nianjian* [China Urban Social and Economic Yearbook]. Beijing: Zhengguo chengshi jinggi shehui nianjian chubanshe. [Multiple Issues]

Radiopress 1990-2001. *China Directory*. Tokyo, Japan: Radiopress, Inc. [Multiple Issues]

Wang, Daohan (ed.) 2000. *Zhongguo chengshi fazhan baogao* [China Urban Development Report] Beijing: Xindu chubanshe.

APPENDIX : MUNICIPAL PERFORMANCE
INDICATORS OF 104 CITIES (2000)

		Indicator	Goal	Weight	Mean	S.D	Min.	Max.
Economic Development (28 Points)	30	GDP per capita (US dollars)	5000 and over	8 points	2.59	1.66	0.46	8.00
	2	Share of non-agricultural sectors in GDP (%)	90 and over	4 points	3.74	0.43	2.15	4.00
	3	Share of services in GDP (%)	55 and over	4 points	2.97	0.68	1.13	4.00
	4	Contribution of technical progress to GDP (%)	50 and over	4 points	3.29	0.69	0.40	4.00
	5	Imports + exports / GDP	45 and over	4 points	1.43	1.30	0.00	4.00
	6	Degree of urbanization (%)	60 and over	4 points	2.81	1.15	0.46	4.00
Subtotal					16.10	3.89	5.86	27.06
Human Capital (17 points)	7	Literacy rate among people ages 15 and above (%)	95 and over	3 points	2.95	0.15	1.85	3.00
	8	Proportion of the population with vocational college education and above (%)	10 and over	3 points	2.06	0.94	0.01	3.00
	9	Educational expenditure as % of GDP	5 and over	3 points	1.09	0.69	0.01	3.00
	10	Average lie expectancy (Years)	75 and over	4 points	3.87	0.13	3.47	4.00
	11	Reduction in natural growth rate of the population (per thousand)	5 and below	2 points	1.63	0.44	0.52	2.00
	12	Death rate during delivery (per thousand)	10 and below	2 points	1.67	0.49	0.46	3.00
Subtotal					12.07	3.19	1.37	16.96

APPENDIX : MUNICIPAL PERFORMANCE
INDICATORS OF 104 CITIES (2000) (cont'd)

		Indicator	Goal	Weight	Mean	S.D	Min.	Max.
Quality of Life (22 points)	13	Engel's Index (%)	30 and below	4 points	3.13	0.42	1.71	4.00
	14	Available housing space per capita (m2)	18 and over	2 points	1.68	0.38	0.79	3.16
	15	Electricity use per capita (Kilowatts per hour)	600 and over	2 points	1.03	0.56	0.20	3.00
	16	Phone penetration per 100 peoples (units)	50 and over	2 points	1.33	0.58	0.18	2.00
	17	Home computer utilization ration (%)	20 and over	2 points	0.84	0.60	0.00	2.00
	18	Number of commercial points (per 10,000 people)	100 and over	2 points	1.78	0.42	0.44	2.00
	19	Number of financial points (per 10,000 people)	10 and over	2 points	0.94	0.49	0.09	2.00
	20	Number of libraries, museums and theatres (per 10,000 people)	1 and over	2 points	0.81	0.66	0.06	2.00
	21	Number of doctor's visits (per 10,000 people)	50 and below	2 points	1.24	0.57	0.01	2.52
	22	Number of criminal cases (per 10,000people)	15 and below	2 points	1.21	0.70	0.18	2.01
Subtotal					13.22	2.86	2.72	21.87
Environment-Al Protection (18 points)	23	Coverage of green areas	35 and over	3 points	2.38	0.75	0.09	3.00
	24	Availability of public green space per capita (m2)	10 and over	3 points	1.94	0.77	0.28	3.00
	25	Treatment of used industrial water (%)	90 and over	3 points	2.63	0.61	0.20	3.00
	26	Treatment of used household water (%)	60 and over	3 points	1.86	0.93	0.04	3.00
	27	Handling of garbage (%)	80 and over	3 points	2.54	0.79	0.13	3.00
	28	Air pollution level (Grade)	Second Grade and below	3 points	2.76	0.44	1.50	3.00
Subtotal					13.02	3.10	2.34	18.00

APPENDIX : MUNICIPAL PERFORMANCE
INDICATORS OF 104 CITIES (2000) (cont'd)

	Indicator	Goal	Weight	Mean	S.D	Min.	Max.
29	Availability of paved roads per cabin (m2)	10 and over	3 points	2.24	0.73	0.36	3.00
30	Utilization of motorized Vehicles (per 10,000 people)	1000 and over	3 points	1.66	0.97	0.02	3.00
31	Availability of running water (%)	100	3 points	2.82	0.46	0.81	3.00
32	Consumption rate of natural gas (%)	100	3 points	2.45	0.65	0.37	3.00
33	Number of domestic and international air routes (N)	30 and over	3 points	1.89	1.18	0.10	3.00
Subtotal				10.03	2.34	3.98	15.00
Total	100 points			64.45	11.16	27.5	90.33

Source: **Date compiled from Zhongguo chengshi nianjian (2001).**

6

Remaking the Communist Party-State: The Cadre Responsibility System at the Local Level in China

MARIA EDIN

The Chinese party-state is restructuring its governing institutions, and it is reinventing itself in the process. The state is withdrawing, market forces are given greater rein, and government functions are delegated while others are contracted out or privatised. Reforms which aim to change the way the state is functioning do not, however, necessarily lead to a reduced state involvement as commonly assumed. On the contrary, the state is reasserting itself in a different manner that may result in a strengthening of the party-state. The nature of control has shifted from micro to macro-level: the state is no longer directly involved in implementation but instead prefers to provide strategic guidance. The Chinese authorities have delegated many government functions to service organisations that perform administrative duties for them, relieving the financial burden of the centre.[1] In the public administration literature, this is described as ridding the state of some of its functions to enable it to concentrate on its core responsibilities. Freeing the state from daily operations may allow it to exercise more effective control of strategically important issues.[2] Thus, what is sometimes mistaken as a retreat of the state is often a shift in style of regulation and control. The lessening of regulation at one level may be accompanied by re-regulation at another.[3]

This article aims to highlight this shift in governance, as well as the attempts by the Chinese Communist Party (CCP) to reinvent itself. China is not only remaking its public management (as excellently described in the volume edited by Lee and Lo), but is also gradually transforming the internal functioning of the party-state.[4] The restructuring of the party-state organisation itself has been under-researched and deserves more attention. A study of the party-state organisation reveals that the same trend visible in public management is also present in the Communist party-state itself. The focus here is on the reform of the cadre management system of local leaders, and the introduction of the cadre responsibility system (*gangwei zerenzhi*) at the local level in China. Market forces have been used to make the old cadre management system more effective. The cadre responsibility system embodies both the retreat of the party-state in cadre management at one level, but also a strengthening of party-state control at another.

Three pairs of parallel developments are highlighted here. The first pair is the decentralisation of personnel management of ordinary cadres and the delegation of evaluation and monitoring functions to society. This is in combination with the strengthening of party organisation control over its leading cadres. The second concerns the replacement of old mandatory targets with guidance targets. How cadres implement guidance targets is linked to the bonuses they receive. At the same time, the centre's goal is to ensure that its priority policies are carried out by local leaders, and the implementation of priority targets is linked to promotion and demotion decisions. The final pair is the increasing autonomy given to localities generally but higher levels also increase their control over selected counties. In a way, this is similar to the approach used to control strategically important leaders. China is generally viewed to have carried out extensive economic reform but has stopped short of political reform. Political reform was on the agenda in the 1980s but is thought to have been abandoned after 1989. The radical proposals from the 1980s to establish a modern civil service and separate party and government were finally adopted in 1993, although what remained was believed to be a much watered-down version.[5] Despite such a view, it is proposed in this study that part of the radical plan - such as the plan to distinguish between politically appointed civil servants and career civil servants presented at the 13th Party Congress in 1987, and thought by many observers to have been abandoned - has in fact been carried out at the local level. Other parts, such as reforms to improve the efficiency of the bureaucracy, which were seen as less path-breaking at the time, have also been implemented at the local level and have proved more politically significant than initially understood. The Party's organisation department was to control only politically appointed cadres, while the civil service system regulated the personnel decisions of career civil servants.[6] It was noted at that time that less than 1% of about four million cadres working in the executive branch of government were designated political civil servants.[7] Today, at the local level, only the leading cadres (*lingdao ganbu*) are included in the cadre responsibility system and controlled by the party organisation department. In this paper, I argue that the leading cadres on the nomenclatura list controlled by the Party Organisation Department correspond to the designated political civil servants in the earlier proposals. In other words, although there is no formal separation between political and career civil servants, the distinction between the two is made within the Party. This particular reform has been executed in practice.

The cadre responsibility system is part of broader administrative reforms and aimed at improving the efficiency of the bureaucracy. Administrative reforms have until recently mainly focused on streamlining and downsizing government bodies and personnel. Various rounds of downsizing were introduced in 1982, 1988, 1993, and 1998. The 1998 round was the boldest attempt with the goal to reduce government personnel at all levels by half. Chan and Drewry and Yang all point to how administrative streamlining is intimately linked to reducing the government's role in the economy.[8] In this way, the objective of reforms is not only to reduce the number of personnel but also to change the role of government and its functions. The notion "small government, big society" illustrates that some government functions are given to society, and societal organisations perform administrative duties on behalf of the party-state. If there is no existing service organisation to carry out these duties, the state creates one. The state is withdrawing at the same time as it reasserts its influence on priority policies. As Chan and Drewry write, "the underlying aim of the organisational reform was not the creation of a 'small government' in the sense of giving up its powers to society or the market but the creation of a 'small government' in the sense of its being more unified and efficient."[9]

The picture of the CCP presented here thus differs from the common view of a communist party in decay, and only an empty shell that will eventually fall apart. The CCP is wrongly viewed as a remnant of an old past which will automatically fall from power as market reforms deepen.[10] On the contrary, the Party is using market forces to reinvent itself, and has proved to be much more innovative than it is usually given credit for. At the same time, the CCP under Jiang Zemin has re-centralised political power and attempted to rebuild party control in the 1990s. The dominating theoretical paradigm in studies on party-state and its cadres is the technocratic perspective which characterizes the party cadres as technocrats.[11] I maintain that the technocratic approach has become outdated to understand party transformation in China. Although advocates are right in pointing out that cadres are getting younger and better educated, they tell us very little about the way the party-state functions. Recent research also reveals that cadres with higher education are promoted more slowly, an indication that technocratic characteristics by themselves do not necessarily have an effect on governance institutions.[12] Previous studies have described the cadre responsibility system as a straightforward process in which cadres get rewarded for good performance - economically in the form of bonuses, and politically in the form of promotion.[13] This study analyses the cadre responsibility system as a governing institution and highlights the political control mechanisms of the system.

As a method to capture the dynamic changes taking place, I favour a local approach to study the transformation of the CCP. One important reason why a local approach is valid is that systemic changes can often be observed at the local level first. It is generally agreed in the literature that when policies, laws and regulations are adopted nationwide in China, they first emerged in the localities, as did the household responsibility system, the township enterprises, etc. This is not to say that the centre does not play a role; the central authorities are clearly decisive in allowing or promoting experimentation of policies, and in putting an end or adopting them nationwide. But a large number of policies are first tried out in local areas, whether initiated by the centre or by the localities themselves, and this is certainly true for the reform of the cadre management system. Organisational reforms were first experimented with at county testing sites.[14] Today some central authorities have begun experimenting with the system, even though among local governments it is widely practised.[15] The project draws on seven months of fieldwork conducted at the county and township level between 1996 and 1999. The field research was carried out in a number of different places (12 counties), all very developed areas, in Southern Jiangsu, Shandong and Zhejiang province. Two townships (the first in Suzhou prefecture in Jiangsu, and the second in Zibo prefecture in Shandong) served as base field sites, and other sites were added on to place the information in a comparative perspective. Some 150 interviews were carried out with local cadres and local entrepreneurs, involving personnel from the party organisation department and the personnel bureau at the county level as well as with leading cadres of townships.[16]

DECENTRALISING PERSONNEL MANAGEMENT BUT CONTROLLING LEADING CADRES

The basis of CCP control is the nomenclatura system. The nomenclatura, inherited from the Soviet model and still in use, is a list of leading positions over whose appointments the Party exercises full control. Party committees exercise authority over the appointment of senior personnel, their promotion, dismissal and transfer one step down the administrative hierarchy, and the lower level is accountable to the next level up.[17] Higher levels can conduct evaluation of lower levels because they are part of a hierarchical party-state organisation. Principal control is vested in the organisation department of the party committee, which maintains personal dossiers that contain information related to decisions regarding appointments. Before 1983, party organizations controlled personnel decisions two levels down but in 1983 they were decentralised to only one level down the administrative hierarchy. By decentralising cadre management, the authorities sought to reduce the number of cadres controlled centrally and by provincial party committees.[18] It is this system that confers the county party organisation department authority to make personnel decisions involving township leaders.

The nomenclatura is sometimes mistaken for the *bianzhi*. The term *bianzhi* refers to the authorised number of personnel (the number of established posts) in a party or government administrative organ, service organisation, or working unit. Brødsgaard has stressed the importance of making a clear distinction between the two: the *bianzhi* covers all employed in a given unit whereas the nomenclatura only lists the cadres in leadership positions. In other words, all members of staff on the state payroll are included in the *bianzhi* but only the top leaders at different levels are on the nomenclatura.[19] The civil service regulations, and the national regulations on evaluation of civil servants, were passed in 1993 in an attempt to improve government efficiency

179

and to allow the performance of public officials to play a greater role. One of the most important developments in the 1990s has been the separation between the leading cadres (*lingdao ganbu*) and the non-leading cadres (*feilingdao ganbu*), or ordinary cadres. Leading cadres on the nomenclatura are as we have seen, the responsibility of the organisation departments (*zuzhibu*). Ordinary cadres on the *bianzhi* are the responsibility of the personnel departments (*renshibu*) and fall under the civil service regulations.

Simply put, the Party has decentralised control of the ordinary cadres and recentralised control over the leading cadres. At the township level, these parallel developments are seen from the different ways ordinary cadres and leading cadres are managed: Ordinary cadres, including the vice party secretaries (with the exception of the township head) and the vice township leadership, evaluate all mayors. In contrast, depending on the status of the township, the county or higher levels evaluate the party secretary and township head. All state cadres at the local level are hence evaluated but it is only the leading cadres of the township government - the party secretary and government head - that are held accountable to higher levels. Today party secretaries and township heads literally sign performance contracts (*gangwei mubiao zerenshu*),[20] one of the novel features of the cadre responsibility system.[21] In these contracts, township leaders pledge and are personally held responsible to achieve certain targets laid down by higher levels. In all areas where I conducted field research, performance contracts were in use. There are different contracts for different fields, such as industrial development, agricultural development, tax collection, family planning, social order, etc. Collective contracts are drawn up between the county and township level, and are signed either by the party secretary or township head, depending on the content of the contract. Economic affairs formally fall under the responsibility of the government head while party affairs naturally fall under the responsibility of the party secretary. Ordinary cadres may also sign contracts, but these contracts are set up with their work unit or the township leaders.

In evaluating and monitoring the leading cadres, the party needs the help of the local community and has therefore delegated some of the evaluation and monitoring functions. Questionnaires and opinion polls are nowadays part of the annual evaluation by higher levels. Colleagues from the cadre's own work unit, and representatives from the subordinate units take part in a democratic appraisal meeting (*minzhu pingyi*). Typically, they fill in a questionnaire rating the work performance of township leaders on a scale from excellent to unqualified along four criteria: integrity, ability, diligence, and performance. The rating is conducted anonymously.[22] In the new regulations on leading cadres, an article has been added which stipulates that a cadre should normally be removed from his or her position if more than one-third of the pollers grade the cadre to be unqualified, and has been certified by the authority as being not up to standard.[23] These opinion polls are clearly not decisive. According to interviewees spoken to at the end of the 1990s, the party launches an investigation if many people are dissatisfied with a leader.[24] Even if the effect of opinion polls are limited, public input is given which provides the Party with crucial information.

Citizens submitting complaint letters to higher levels fulfil a similar function in the monitoring of local leaders. O'Brien and Li have highlighted how complaint letters affect the evaluation score of local leaders, who may be downgraded if too many complaints are filed or if complaints are not dealt with properly.[25] In one county in Zhejiang, two situations are considered to pose serious problems for the cadres: one is where complaint letters are not treated appropriately at the county level such that the complainant appeals to the next higher level (*yueji shangfang*) and the other is, in direct translation, "to assemble a mob in order to submit a letter of complaint" (*juzhong shangfang*).[26] Information from citizens plays a major role in uncovering cadre misbehaviour as it is an alternative channel of information, and intervention from the public also puts pressure on the Party to act. One study reports that 80% of the tipoffs about cadre misconduct and financial irregularities came from letters of complaint sent by the public.[27]

Both opinion polls and petitioning help higher levels to evaluate local leaders and obtain information they might not otherwise receive. It is also possible that the Party would prefer to have local leaders who are popular, as long as they implement the Party's priority policies. In this way, opinion polls and petitioning perform at least two functions. The effect of polls and letters is nonetheless limited in that the Party has the prerogative on how it chooses to act upon the information received and is under no obligation to the people to dismiss unpopular leaders. This raises the question whether the delegation of evaluation to the local community is related to democratic influence. The current system combining evaluation by higher-level authorities and popular elections at the village level seems to have substituted genuine democratic reform.[28] Village elections are in my view part of the same trend to delegate evaluation and monitoring functions to the local community. While local citizens can exercise more influence, the Party maintains the veto power on personnel decisions. In the case of village elections, the township government maintains the power to appoint the village party secretary. Client rating, part of the market management model, should clearly be distinguished from democratic rights. These are two separate matters: client rating is intended to improve governance and efficiency, while democratic rights are inherent rights that cannot be compromised to gain results. In other words, opinion polls and petitioning is part of a top-down approach to improve political governance institutions while at the same time to give citizens a greater say. The responsibility system with its client rating increases transparency and accountability, but not democracy.

The party-state has delegated evaluation and monitoring functions to society, and it has also delegated implementation of policies to local governments.

DELEGATING IMPLEMENTATION BUT ENFORCING PRIORITY POLICIES

In the old planning system, mandatory targets were issued to lower levels through the annual and five-year plans. Guidance targets have replaced mandatory targets in the reform era. Local cadres are given more autonomy choosing the means used to achieve the targets given them by higher levels, and economic incentives are provided to improve efficiency. But the difference today is that the CCP spells out its priority policies, and the implementation of these policies weighs much more heavily than other policies in the evaluation of local leaders.

Non-leading and leading cadres are assigned performance targets (*kaohe zhibiao*) which are internally ranked in importance: there are soft targets (*yiban zhibiao*), hard targets (*ying zhibiao*) and priority targets with veto power (*yipiao fojue*).[29] While non-leading cadres are usually held responsible for fulfilling the soft targets, leading cadres are ultimately held accountable to higher-level authorities for achieving the hard and priority targets with veto power. Soft targets are usually those difficult to measure and quantify, and policies that are not deemed important by higher levels, such as cultural and social development.

182

Hard targets are typically drawn from the economic and social development plan. Tax revenues submitted to the county, for example, were invariably defined as a hard target in all the areas I visited. Priority targets with veto power is an institutional tool exclusively used for key policies of the centre and sometimes also for key policies of local levels. There are two priority targets which are enforced nationwide, mirroring the importance which the CCP places on these policies: family planning and social order (*shehui zhi'an*).[30] In all the areas where I conducted field research, these two were made priority targets. All targets play an equal role in the evaluation in terms of bonus, but attainment of hard targets and priority targets are important for personnel decisions. Veto power implies that if township leaders fail to attain these priority targets, all the other work performance in the comprehensive evaluation, however successful, would be cancelled.

Performance targets are not static, but part of a very flexible governance institution that can quickly adjust to changing circumstances. If higher-level authorities wish to shift priority policy, they can upgrade or downgrade the status of a target. When the Party, for instance, wishes to integrate complaint letters in the evaluation, or simply to focus on social stability, limiting the number of complaint letters would be made a target in the annual evaluation. For example, in a Zhejiang county, keeping down the number of complaint letters was incorporated into the evaluation in 1999 after these letters gained the attention of higher authorities.[31] Targets also mirror local conditions to some extent. If localities experience serious problems, the problem may become a local priority target. Cremation of the dead, for example, was declared an additional priority target in order to reserve land for productive use in one area, thereby indicating that land waste was a particular problem in that county.[32] The current system endorses management by setting goals. However, the CCP seems to have started paying attention to the means used to achieve the goals. One example can be found in the implementation of family planning: in order to improve the responsibility system, new policies emphasise the revision of evaluation criteria to take into account how the policy is executed, whether it is done in accordance with the law and if clients are satisfied.[33]

From the ranking of targets, we can deduce that under normal circumstances, the CCP places economic development first, especially the submission of tax revenues to the centre. At the same time, it is evident that the bottom line is social stability and that the Party would not promote economic growth at the expense of large-scale social instability. If social unrest continues to increase in rural areas, the central authorities could be expected to deal with this through adjusting and adding new targets for leading cadres at the local level. In fact, the addition of limiting the number of complaint letters as a target in the evaluation in the example above is a case in point. The heavy burden faced by peasants is often cited as one important source of social unrest in rural areas.[34] If higher levels want to emphasise the importance of reducing the peasant burden, it could be made into a target in the evaluation to become a priority target with veto power that could cancel out successful work performance in other fields. What constitutes serious disturbance to social order varies between areas. Three situations have been defined as such disturbances in one county: economic crime (where more than 200,000 yuan are embezzled), violence (resulting in a person's death), and large-scale demonstrations (with more than 50 people gathered).[35]

The fulfilment of the different types of performance targets is used as a basis for the issuance of bonuses. Economic incentives are pegged to work performance. The use of bonuses has been well described in the literature.[36] Implementation of priority policies are however not only linked to bonuses, but more importantly, to personnel decisions, in particular promotion.

REASSERTING PARTY CONTROL SELECTIVELY

Reforms since 1978 have undoubtedly given localities more autonomy, not the least in the economic sector. Decentralisation and fiscal reforms have benefited local governments, and many observers have noted their increasing power. Parallel with this decentralisation, the party-state is reasserting control selectively through political appointments and promotion power. The political appointment of leading cadres is described above. In this section different types of promotion as a means to control selected leading cadres and local governments are described. Earlier accounts of the evaluation system have described it as a straightforward process where local cadres work towards fulfilling their performance targets and get rewarded economically as well as politically. The assumption is that local cadres work towards fulfilling higher-level goals to further their bureaucratic careers.[37] The question pivots upon whether or not there is a correlation between good performance and promotion. The only study of which I am aware that empirically examines this is done by Landry, who has made a survey testing the relationship between the work performance of municipal mayors and their promotion to the post of General Secretary (or transfer to a more important municipality). The performance criteria are 33 socio-economic indicators, which are powerfully biased towards GDP performance. Landry finds that high performance has no bearing on the probabilities of promotion of municipal mayors.[38] If Landry's findings hold, how do we explain them? Are there evidence that the evaluation system of cadres is an empty process and that "political reliability" still predominates? Or is the cadre responsibility system foremost a governance institution that is unrelated to performance and promotion? First, it should be noted that there might be a stronger relationship between economic performance and political promotion at the township level than at the municipal level. Second, Landry's list of 33 indicators does not take into account the varying importance of soft, hard and priority targets. As we have seen, the higher levels are more concerned about the hard and priority targets with veto power. Third, it is also possible that municipal mayors are promoted to positions other than the post of general secretary. Fourth, it is likely that economic performance is rewarded in many different forms besides regular promotion.

I interpret Landry's result by looking at the cadre responsibility system as a governance mechanism that integrates political incentives with political control. It is in this light that we ought to view the promotion process or, as I would like to emphasise, the various types of promotions. Higher levels of the party-state aim to control strategically important local leaders, especially those from economically successful areas. I want to draw attention in particular to the practice of promoting successful township leaders concurrently to posts at higher levels of the party and government.[39] The difference between regular promotion and appointment to concurrent posts at higher levels is that the township leader does not leave his post at the township, but still moves up one rank in the party hierarchy, usually from Section Chief to Vice Division Chief. In one county in southern Jiangsu, for example, the Township Party Secretary of the highest ranking township concurrently held the position of Vice Party Secretary of that county.[40] Successful township leaders might also be promoted to higher level posts in the party or government, such as members of the county party standing committee, standing committee of the county level People's Congress, or Vice Mayor of the county, while still continuing to perform their job at the township level. While this type of promotion is a positive incentive offered by the higher levels, the incorporation of successful township leaders into higher levels also strengthens the latter's political control over local leaders. One township party secretary called it a "political bonus," but at the same time it is also a means for higher levels to secure control over strategically important townships.[41] This combined method of reward and control is not generally applied, but is selectively used on the leaders which higher levels deem to be important.

We may look upon political representation to higher levels in a similar light. Bo has found that provinces with higher revenue contributions and faster economic growth have gained more representation in the central committees compared to other provinces.[42] Again, a combined method of reward and control is visible in representation to political bodies at higher levels. Also, successful local entrepreneurs are incorporated into the Party in the same fashion, i.e., they hold political positions which give them economic and political advantages, but their appointment also facilitates the Party's control over them. Almost all the successful entrepreneurs that I interviewed were members of either the People's Congress, or political consultative conference at higher levels, or held positions in the township economic committee. In the areas I visited, highly successful entrepreneurs at the village level also held the position of village party secretary. One chairman of the board of a conglomerate in Shandong, for example, was not only the party secretary of the village but also the Vice Party Secretary of the township, party committee member of the district level, and a member of the People's Congress at the provincial level.[43] This policy was widespread in the local areas during the 1990s, and was recently reaffirmed at the 16th Party Congress held in Nov. 2002 where a decision was made to invite private entrepreneurs into the Party.

Another form of promotion that works both as a political incentive and political control is the practice of promoting the status of the whole locality. Counties can be upgraded to county-level cities (*xianjishi*). Correspondingly, the bureaucratic rank of its cadres is also upgraded and the tangible benefits to both the county as well as to its cadres increase. Ordinary counties are under the leadership of the municipal governments as part of the decentralisation scheme and the principle "city in charge of the county" (*shi guan xian*). Counties upgraded to county-level cities, however, are part of a re-centralisation effort that places these counties under the direct authority of the province. The formation of county-level cities gives the province the right to appoint the mayor and party secretary of the new city. Again, the choice made by higher levels is very selective and the aim is to control strategically important counties, especially economically successful ones. Landry finds in Jiangsu province that Nanjing was anxious to gain control over appointment and resource allocation only in areas of critical importance to the province's economic development, whereas ordinary counties remained under firm municipal authority.[44] This seems to be the case also outside Jiangsu province. Many of the economically successful counties in which I carried out field work in southern Jiangsu, Shandong, and Zhejiang province had been upgraded to county level cities.

In sum, the evaluation process of local leaders is double-sided. It is an effort to improve efficiency of the bureaucracy by rewarding implementation of the centre's priority policies but is also a mechanism of party rule. The Party is reinventing itself - and it is selectively strengthening its control.

CONCLUDING REMARKS

The reform era brought decentralisation and delegation of both political decision-making and allocation of economic resources to lower levels of government and society. There is no doubt that local governments and social entities have benefited and been empowered by reform. At the same time, there has been a re-centralisation of political control in the 1990s, and the centre under Jiang Zemin has attempted to strengthen the Party. Also, in the economic sphere, the central government has reclaimed macro-control after delegating day-to-day management to lower authorities and enterprises. This paper suggests a way to understand these two parallel developments that do not necessarily contradict each other. The CCP is shifting the way it governs - withdrawing from some areas while reasserting itself in others. It is not a linear process. The nature of control and regulation has changed from a micro-level to a macro-level. The party-state is ridding itself from some of its functions to enable it to become more efficient in carrying out others. The case study of cadre management at the local level fits well into this broader picture of remaking public management and China's governing institutions.

ENDNOTES

1   Lam Tao-Chiu and James L. Perry, "Service Organizations in China: Reform and Its Limits," in *Remaking China's Public Management*, ed. Peter Nan-Shong Lee and Carlos Wing-Hung Lo (Westport, Connecticut: Quorom Books, 2001); and Kenneth W. Forster, "Administrative Restructuring and the Emergence of Sectoral Associations in China" (paper presented at the Association for Asian Studies Annual Meeting, Washington, DC, 7 Apr. 2002).

2   Jon Pierre and Guy B. Peters, *Governance, Politics and the State* (Houndsmill, Basingstoke: MacMillan, 2000), p. 68.

3   Christopher Hood, Colin Scott, Oliver James, George Jones, and Tony Travers, *Regulation inside Government: Waste-watchers, Quality Police and Sleaze-busters* (Oxford: Oxford University Press, 1999), p. 194.

4   Lee and Lo, *Remaking China's Public Management*.

5   John P. Burns and Jean-Pierre Cabestan, eds., "Provisional Chinese Civil Service Regulations," *Chinese Law and Government* 23, No. 4 (1990/91).

6   Chen Yizi, "The Decision Process Behind the 1986-1989 Political Reforms," in *Decision-Making in Deng's China: Perspectives from Insiders*, ed. Carol Lee Hamrin and Zhao Suisheng (Armonk, New York: M.E. Sharpe, 1995), p. 149.

7   John P. Burns, "Chinese Civil Service Reforms: The 13th Party Congress Proposals," *The China Quarterly* No. 120 (1989): 741; and Jean-Pierre Cabestan, "Civil Service Reform in China: The Draft "Provisional Order Concerning Civil Servants,"" *International Review of Administrative Sciences* 58 (1992): 423.

8   Chan Che-Po and Gavin Drewry, "The 1998 State Council Organizational Streamlining: Personnel Reduction and Change of Government Function," *Journal of Contemporary China* 10, No. 29 (2001): 553-72; and Yang Dali, "Rationalizing the Chinese State: The Political Economy of Government Reform," in *Remaking the Chinese State: Strategies, Society, and Security*, ed. Chao Chien-min and Bruce J. Dickson (London: Routledge, 2001).

9   Chan and Drewry, "The 1998 State Council Organizational Streamlining," p. 569.

10   For this view, see for example, Merle Goldman and Roderick MacFarquhar, "Dynamic Economy, Declining Party-State," in *The Paradox of China's Post-Mao Reforms*, ed. Merle Goldman and Roderick MacFarquhar (Cambridge: Harvard University Press, 1999); and David Shambaugh, "The Chinese State in the Post-Mao Era," in *The Modern Chinese State*, ed. David Shambaugh (Cambridge: Cambridge University Press, 2000).

11   One of the first studies to highlight the transformation from revolutionary cadres to technocrats was Hong Yung Lee, *From Revolutionary Cadres to Party Technocrats in Socialist China* (Berkeley: University of California Press, 1991). For recent studies, see for example David Shambaugh, "The CCP's Fifteenth Congress: Technocrats in Command," *Issues & Studies* 34, No. 1 (1998); and Li Cheng, *China's Leaders: The New Generation* (Lanham: Rowman and Littlefield, 2001).

12   Bo Zhiyue, *Chinese Provincial Leaders: Performance and Political Mobility Since 1949* (Armonk, New York: M.E. Sharpe, 2002).

13   Susan H. Whiting, "The Cadre Evaluation System at the Grassroots: The Paradox of Party Rule" (paper prepared for the workshop "Cadre Monitoring and Reward: Personnel Management and Policy Implementation in the PRC," University of California, San Diego, 6-7 Jun. 1998; revised in Sep. 1999); and *Power and Wealth in Rural China: The Political Economy of Institutional Change* (Cambridge: Cambridge University Press, 2001).

14   Joseph Yu-shek Cheng and Ting Wang, "Administrative Reforms in China in 1992: Streamlining, Decentralization and Changing Government Functions," in *China Review 1993*, ed. Joseph Cheng Yu-shek and Maurice Brosseau (Hong Kong: The Chinese University Press, 1993).

15   According to Han, the responsibility system had been practised by 65% of state institutions at the provincial level and by 90% at prefectural-municipal level and below. See Han Tian, ed., *Lingdao ganbu kaocha kaohe shiyong quanshu* (Practical Comprehensive Handbook of Reviewing and Evaluating Leading Cadres) (Beijing: China Personnel Press, 1999), pp. 100-1, as cited in Ma Shu-Yun and Chan Wai-Yin, "The Provision of Public Goods by a Local Entrepreneurial State: The Case of Preservation of the Nanyue Relics in China," *The Journal of Development Studies* (Nov. 2002).

16   For a more detailed discussion of the fieldwork, see Maria Edin, *Market Forces and Communist Power: Local Political Institutions and Economic Development in China* (Uppsala: University Printers, 2000).

17   Burns has written extensively on the nomenclatura system; see John P. Burns, "China's Nomenclatura System," *Problems of Communism* XXXVI, No. 5 (1987); *The Chinese Communist Party's Nomenclatura System: A Documentary Study of Party Control of Leadership Selection, 1979-1984* (Armonk: M.E. Sharpe, 1989); "Strengthening Central CCP Control of Leadership Selection: The 1990 Nomenclatura," *The China Quarterly* No. 138 (1994). See also Melanie Manion, "The Cadre Management System, Post- ao: The Appointment, Promotion, Transfer and Removal of Party and State Leaders," *The China Quarterly* No. 102 (1985).

18   After 1989, there was a wave of limited re-centralisation of cadre management. The 1990 nomenclatura added the positions of prefectural bureau chief and deputy chief to the central Organisation Department's scope of management, see Burns, "Strengthening Central CCP Control of Leadership Selection," p. 468.

19   Kjeld Erik Brødsgaard, "Institutional Reform and the *Bianzhi* System in China," *The China Quarterly* No. 170 (2002): 363.

20   Performance contracts have been described earlier in Kevin J. O'Brien and Li Lianjiang, "Selective Policy Implementation in Rural China," *Comparative Politics* 31, No. 2 (1999): 172. See also George P. Brown, "Budgets, Cadres and Local State Capacity in Rural Jiangsu," in *Village Inc. Chinese Rural Society in the 1990s*, ed. Flemming Christiansen and Zhang Junzuo (Richmond: Curzon Press, 1998), p. 32. Township leading cadres thus sign contracts of a similar fashion to those signed by collective-run enterprises and households.

21   For a more detailed description of the cadre responsibility system, see Maria Edin, "State Capacity and Local Agent Control in China: CCP Cadre Management from a Township Perspective," *The China Quarterly* No. 173 (forthcoming, Mar. 2003). The content of different performance contracts is described there.

22   The rating of local leading cadres in the appraisal meeting is from the text, Edin, "State Capacity and Local Agent Control in China" and the interview source referred to in fn. 24.

23   "Regulations on the Work of Selecting and Appointing Leading Party and Government Cadres," Article 55, Central Committee of the Communist Party of China, 9 Jul. 2002. <http://www.china.org.cn/english/features/45399.htm> [12 Nov. 2002].

24   Interview SCA1 with the village party secretary cum chairman of the board of the village corporation in Shandong village, 1998; and interview ZCa1 with the vice mayor cum director of the industrial office and the vice director of the industrial office in a Zhejiang township, 1998.

25   Kevin J. O'Brien and Li Lianjiang, "The Politics of Lodging Complaints in Rural China," *The China Quarterly* No. 138 (1995).

26   Interview ZC5 with the vice director in charge of evaluation in the party bureau of rural affairs in a Zhejiang county, 1998.

27   Lu Xiaobo and Thomas P. Bernstein, *Taxation Without Representation in Rural China: State Capacity, Peasant Resistance, and Democratization, 1985-2000* (Cambridge: Cambridge University Press, forthcoming).

28   Kevin J. O'Brien, "Implementing Political Reform in China's Villages," *The Australian Journal of Chinese Affairs* No. 32 (1994): 37.

29   The internal ranking of targets and examples of such targets can be found in Edin, "State Capacity and Local Agent Control in China."

30   The Chinese source Rong Jingben *et al.*, *Cong yalixing tizhi xiang minzhu hezuo tizhi de zhuanbian: xianxiang liangji zhengzhi tizhi gaige* (Transformation from the Pressurised System to a Democratic System of Cooperation: Reform of the Political System at the County and Township Levels) (Beijing: Zhongyang bianyi chubanshe, 1998), p. 271 mentions that the county party committee should accomplish the two compulsory tasks of imposing family planning and maintaining public order. Birth control is also referred to as a task to assume veto power in Kevin O'Brien and Li Lianjiang, "Selective Policy Implementation," p. 172.

31   Interview ZE3 with one section chief of the party committee and one section chief of the party committee organisation department in a Zhejiang county, 1999.

32   See fn. 31.

33   Edwin A. Winckler, "Chinese Birth Policy at the Turn of the Millennium: Stability and Change" (unpublished paper, East Asian Institute, Columbia University, 2002).

34   See, for example, Lu Xiaobo, "The Politics of Peasant Burden in Reform China," *The Journal of Peasant Studies* 25, No. 1 (1997).

35 Interview ZC5 with the vice director in charge of evaluation in the party bureau of rural affairs in a Zhejiang county, 1998.

36 See, for example, Jean C. Oi, *Rural China Takes Off: Institutional Foundations of Economic Reform* (Berkeley: University of California Press, 1999), pp. 49-50.

37 Whiting, *Power and Wealth in Rural China*, p. 18.

38 Pierre F. Landry, "Controlling Decentralization: The Party and Local Elites in Post-Mao Jiangsu" (PhD dissertation, University of Michigan, 2000). See also Landry, "Local Performance and the Political Fate of Chinese Mayors" (paper presented at the conference "Bringing the Party Back In: How China is Governed," Copenhagen Business School, Copenhagen, 7-9 Jun. 2002).

39 For a longer and more detailed discussion and analysis of how higher levels of the party-state aim to selectively control local leaders, see Edin, "State Capacity and Local Agent Control in China."

40 Interview JAb1 with the township party secretary cum vice party secretary of a southern Jiangsu county, 1996.

41 Interview SCa3 with the party secretary of a Shandong township, 1998.

42 Bo Zhiyue, "Provincial Power and Provincial Economic Resources in the PRC," *Issues & Studies* 34, No. 4 (1998); and Bo, *Chinese Provincial Leaders*.

43 Interview SCa1 with the chairman of the board of the village corporation cum party secretary of a Shandong village, 1998.

44 Landry, "Controlling Decentralization," p. 80.

CHAPTER 7

Parasites or Civilisers: The Legitimacy of the Chinese Communist Party in Rural Areas

STIG THØGERSEN

The Communist Party of China (CPC) is fighting an uphill struggle to redefine its basis of legitimacy and give village and township cadres and ordinary Party members a sense of purpose and direction. This paper examines the arguments and cultural resources that the Party draws upon in this process. The focus is on the economically less developed rural areas of the country, with particular consideration given to Xuanwei County, Yunnan Province.[1]

Questions of ideology generally receive little attention in studies of post-1989 China compared to "hard" issues such as economic performance and institutional change. However, one of the most provocative recent Chinese studies of rural affairs, *China Along the Yellow River*, by Cao Jinqing, highlights the crucial role of ideology and the closely related question of legitimacy in deciding the fate of the Party-state. In a characteristic conversation between Cao and four county and township level officials, the question of values and motivation is raised, not in the moralising way in which we often read it in Party propaganda, but as a genuine problem. The rural cadres are strongly pessimistic about the situation under the market economy:

> The social order is chaotic, and there is no longer any faith. As for the local basic level cadres, they are busy all day implementing tasks assigned to them from above, but inside their minds they feel deeply frustrated. They see no direction, they don't know the meaning of what they are busying themselves with all day.

They feel that if things continue in this fashion we may run into big trouble some day.[2]

This surprises Cao Jinqing. In the 1970s and 1980s, he recalls, it was fashionable among intellectuals and urbanites to talk about a crisis of faith, but in the 1990s this issue completely vanished from intellectual circles. It is now being raised by rural cadres instead, and if these people no longer have any common faith, writes Cao, what will keep them from being selfish and corrupt, caught as they are between the particularism of rural society and the merciless demands of the market economy?[3]

Cao's discussion reflects the growing problem of legitimacy facing the CPC in poor areas. After the demise of socialist ideology in China, most observers agree that the legitimacy of the Party rests mainly on three legs: its ability to promote economic development, maintain social order, and defend China's national unity and international status.[4] Arguments about economic development and social order, however, are bound to work better among the relatively privileged groups than in poor villages, where rising expectations rather than tangible improvements have characterised the last decade or so. Intellectuals and white-collar employees have now, at least to some extent, overcome their "crisis of faith" as they have experienced rising living standards and a more comfortable life. But how can the CPC legitimise its rule among farmers in inland areas with stagnating incomes and massive economic and social problems, and among the cadres who are daily confronted with their complaints and resistance? It is often claimed in the West that nationalism has filled the vacuum after socialism, but while I will in no way deny the role of nationalism as a legitimating factor for the regime among students and intellectuals, and maybe even among the urban population more generally, I think that nationalism plays a very limited role in Party ideology and legitimacy in China's rural areas.[5]

As indicated in the title of this paper, I suggest that the Party at the ideological level responds to the crisis of legitimacy by presenting itself and its cadres as civilising agents bringing prosperity, science, morality, and social organisation to the villages. This should be seen in contrast to the image of cadres as predators, or parasites on the social body, which one often finds among Chinese farmers and entrepreneurs, and which is also openly expressed in the Chinese public debate, for example in a remarkable best-seller titled *I will Tell the Truth to the*

193

Premier, by Li Changping, a former Township Party Secretary. When Li asked his old schoolmates what he should do in order to become a good official they presented him with their completely disillusioned view of rural China: "They [i.e., the cadres] are eating the peasants, and their sons and daughters are eating the peasants, the corps of peasant-eaters is growing in strength year by year." In the eyes of Li's friends, these peasant-eating cadres had their own interests which were incompatible with those of the peasants. Together with the commercial elite, they were turning the results of economic reforms into a system of "bandit capitalism", and a single township official could do little to change this trend.[6]

The Party is thus facing a vital ideological task: to change the public image *and* the self-perception of basic-level cadres from peasant-eating parasites to civilising agents.

THE CPC AND THE QUESTION OF LEGITIMACY

When even the system's own cadres begin to see themselves and the state as predatory, it is no exaggeration to say that the CPC is facing an ideological crisis. The question of legitimacy is important for the fate of the Party-state in China not so much because public opinion in itself can shake the Communist leadership, but because the Party-state can get things done only if its leadership is seen as legitimate.

There are two main aspects of Party legitimacy. What I shall call external legitimacy relates to the viewpoint of the "masses". In the poor rural areas, it boils down to the question of why peasants should accept Party rule when the Party does not deliver the goods and only comes to them to "demand money and lives" (*yao qian, yao ming*), i.e., collect taxes and check on population control programmes. External legitimacy is no doubt important to the Party's ability to implement its policies, but it can be substituted by force, because poor peasants have few resources and their acts of protest are usually uncoordinated and on a relatively small scale.[7]

There is, however, another aspect of legitimacy which is internal to the Party's own organisation, and which may prove to be more critical: how can basic level cadres in poor areas be given a sense of purpose and direction which will constrain their tendency towards corruption and abuse of power and make them work loyally for the Party's agenda? Since the 1980s, an elaborate system for monitoring cadre performance has been established, complete with discipline committees sent down from higher levels and an evaluation system which deducts points from a cadre if there are too many complaints about him from the public.[8] However, the effects of this system in poor areas are doubtful and its costs are high. According to the critics, the outcome is not much different from that under the planned economy: cadres do all they can to please their superiors by apparently reaching the targets laid out in their contracts and evaluation forms, even if they have to distort data, and even when their acts are detrimental to the peasants' interests.[9] This strongly indicates that the lack of clear vision of the Party's overall political mission cannot be neutralised by bureaucratic measures.

In the following sections, I discuss which arguments the Party is using in its fight for gaining legitimacy in China's villages. I first look at Jiang Zemin's writings on the "Three Represents", which I see primarily as an attempt to redefine the CPC as an elite Party. I then discuss the present situation of the Party and its cadres in one county in Yunnan province in the light of Jiang's ideas. My focus is mainly on internal legitimacy and the cadres' view of their own role, but I also discuss how the villagers relate to the Party, and particularly how they challenge the Party's claim to leadership.

JIANG ZEMIN'S "THREE REPRESENTS" AND THE MOVE TOWARDS AN ELITE PARTY

Jiang Zemin's speeches on the "Three Represents" is the most authoritative statement on how the Party's self-perception is presently being reshaped, and therefore also of its claim to legitimacy.[10] The term "Three Represents" refers to three factors, which the CPC, according to Jiang, has represented all through its history and should continue to represent in the future. These factors are not related to any particular social class, but are rather trends in the country's socioeconomic development: (1) the requirements of the development of China's advanced productive forces; (2) the orientation of the development of China's advanced culture; and (3) the fundamental interests of the overwhelming majority of the people in China.

Jiang repeatedly stresses the continuity of CPC ideology and places his own ideas in a chain of necessary adjustments of classic Marxism to Chinese realities. This cannot hide the fact, however, that he suggests major revisions of the Party's self-perception, and makes decisive moves towards an understanding of the CPC as an elite party rather than a vanguard party in the Leninist sense. A vanguard party is supposed to be present even at the humblest level of society and represent the working classes in pushing history forward towards socialism. It claims to have a superior knowledge about where society is moving through its grasp of Marxist theory. An elite party, on the other hand, will skim the cream of Chinese society by recruiting the most competent and successful members of different social groups and sectors. It will then channel their efforts into its own organisational framework and direct them towards the common goal of making China strong, prosperous and civilised. An elite party will profess to manage society more competently than any of the alternatives because its members are better educated and more capable than the population at large, and it claims to represent modernity and economic growth rather than any particular social class.

Jiang is most explicit about this transformation in his speech at the 80th anniversary of the CPC, where he argues that the Party should recruit "outstanding elements" (*youxiu fenzi*) among entrepreneurs and other members of the economic elite. He sees the Party as a "big smelting furnace" (*da ronglu*) which will raise the political consciousness of its members and thus guarantee social cohesion.[11] Through the smelting process, members of different social strata will be purified and liberated from the particular interests of their own social groups, and thus become ready to work for the "vast majority of the people". In a situation where the Party is alienating at least some of its traditional backbone members from the working classes, Jiang is here outlining a new potential social basis.[12]

According to Jiang, a huge developing multi-ethnic state like China would dissolve and sink down into the abyss of chaos without the firm leadership of the Party, and he repeatedly emphasises the cohesion of Chinese society as absolutely essential.[13] He also mentions the danger of the Party itself becoming a "plate of loose sand" if the members do not follow Party discipline.[14] In his view, the Party should thus be a centre of gravity in China's social order, a dense mass of ability and competence capable of keeping lighter and more drifting social elements in their right places. This raises the question of what will be the nature of the cement that will keep first the Party, and then society from dissolving. The Party members are not supposed to form an interest group as such, so what binds them together must be some sort of higher purpose or idea, a project with an identifiable end goal. This is what will lend legitimacy to Party rule, both internally by giving cadres and other Party members a sense of a mission, and externally by justifying to the population the Party's political monopoly. So we are, in fact, back to the problem raised by Cao Jinqing's cadres quoted in the beginning of this paper: what is the meaning of what we are doing, and what is the direction? Unfortunately, Jiang, like Cao, offers no real answer to this question.

The first step towards turning the CPC into an elite party was taken when Deng Xiaoping in one of his very first revisions of Maoist ideology, included the intellectuals in the working class. As a consequence, the Party has for two decades, systematically (but not without internal opposition) tried to recruit more people with higher education. The rising educational level of its members, and particularly of its cadres, is invariably reported as a positive accomplishment of post-Mao party building efforts. Among the almost 12 million new members recruited since the 15th Party Congress 79 per cent had at least a senior middle school degree, a clear sign of how the Party sees its target group.[15]

This is quite a normal development for a Leninist party. Ken Jowitt has described it as a phase of "inclusion", such as what took place in the Soviet Union and Eastern Europe during the 1960s following the two first phases of transformation of the old society and consolidation of the revolutionary regime.[16] To include the economic elite in the core force of the regime as well, however, is a bigger step both at the theoretical and emotional level. Under the planned economy, the Party was able to control economic decision-making by placing politically reliable members in management positions, but it lost much of this power as a consequence of the reforms. The new "bosses" (*laoban*) and "entrepreneurs" (*qiyejia*) are not under direct Party control, so the challenge is now to make members of the economic elite politically reliable and useful by enrolling them into the Party. This process has no obvious parallel in other Leninist regimes, and it has not been met with universal support inside the Party. In an interview in *Asiaweek*, Yan Shuhan of the Central Party School admitted that some "old cadres" were sceptical about Jiang's proposal to actively recruit successful entrepreneurs. Yan summed up the fronts in the debate quite clearly: "The old cadres see the new capitalists as the same as the old capitalists, and we believe that they are wrong."[17]

Jiang finds further arguments for his policy of including the elite in the CPC in global economic trends, because he believes that "the global competition at present and in the future is fundamentally a competition for qualified people (*rencai*)".[18] As economic success is essential for the Party's legitimacy, and competent managers and highly-skilled employees are the key to economic success, the fate of the Party is closely tied to its ability to be a rallying point for "qualified people" and "outstanding elements". It is therefore quite logical that the Party should recruit and purify them in the big ideological smelting furnace. From there they will emerge ready to work for the common good of the "vast majority of the Chinese people", whom they will lead to ever higher levels of civilisation.

This can be seen as an outline of a revised master narrative of the CPC, a new base of legitimacy combining the logic of the market with the technocratic and meritocratic trends of the post-Mao period, and with roots dating back to the pre-1949 elite's claims to civilisational and moral superiority. It is also, however, a trend which can be expected to weaken the Party's basis in the rural hinterlands where there are relatively few "outstanding elements" with high levels of education. The situation in rural China does not figure prominently in Jiang's speeches. He does acknowledge that the relation between peasants and basic level Party organs has changed fundamentally after the dissolution of the collectives and sees this as an "important problem which we must seriously study and solve", but the only solution he offers is apparently to strengthen the collective sector of the rural economy.[19] As rural China presently seems to be moving in the exact opposite direction with still more enterprises going from collective to private ownership, this policy may face a bleak future.[20]

AN ELITE PARTY IN THE MOULD?
THE CASE OF XUANWEI, YUNNAN

Does the notion of the CPC as an "elite party' make sense at the lower levels of Chinese rural society, and how can the CPC invest it with meaning? The following should be understood as a preliminary exploration of this issue inside one specific locality in China rather than as a general statement about "rural China". As the CPC has made economic growth the cornerstone of its political programme, it is obvious that the Party's position and legitimacy in a specific locality depend very much on how successful the local economy is, on the mix of private and collective enterprises, etc. One therefore has to be very careful with sweeping generalisations. I take my examples from Xuanwei in the northeastern part of Yunnan Province. Xuanwei is a "county-level municipality" (*xianji shi*) bordering on Guizhou with a population of 1.3 million, which is 94 per cent Han. It has some comparatively wealthy and industrialised areas around the county seat, but also some very poor townships in the mountains.

The CPC in Xuanwei has 49,720 members, or 3.8 per cent of the county's population, which is well below the national level average of 5.2 per cent.[21] The average educational level of the members is rising only moderately. In 1979, less than 3 per cent of all Xuanwei Party members held senior middle school degrees or higher, and this share had only grown to eight per cent by 1995, while the proportion of illiterate members dropped from 44 per cent to a still considerable 25 per cent.[22] If we turn to those organs where serious political and administrative power is exercised, however, we find a different picture. Party branches inside county level administrative organs (*zhishu jiguan*) recruited 83 new candidate members in year 2000 out of whom 47 per cent were college graduates and 42 per cent were graduates of senior middle schools.[23] This indicates a pattern where peasants maintain their status as rank and file in the village branches, while Party members in leading and influential posts are recruited among the better educated.

Within Xuanwei, we find townships and villages at very different levels of economic development. In the wealthier areas, leaders are emerging who come close to the notion of local "outstanding elements". In the year 2000 village elections, 160 enterprise managers were elected to village leadership posts.[24] The most prominent case, which received much media attention, was Su Wenfang of Hongqiao village in Banqiao township, one of the most economically successful localities in Xuanwei.

Village Leaders: The Ideal Type

Su Wenfang is a very wealthy entrepreneur who owns a large number of enterprises inside and outside of his village, and he was elected village head almost unanimously. It is particularly noteworthy, however, that Su the year before had already been elected village Party Secretary (PS). It is quite common, of course, that village PSs and other local leaders run enterprises and become rich, and there are also many cases where

PSs run for village head.[25] But to be successful in business first and then be elected as both PS and village head is still unusual. It is, however, exactly an example of what Jiang Zemin calls for: the local Party branch had recruited an "outstanding element" of local society. The county newspaper made very clear that Su's case pointed out the direction for the future, and it asked the villagers to elect more people like him: first, the new leaders should have political qualifications, which meant that they should be just and fair and not corrupt; second, they should be around 40 years old and hold at least a senior middle school diploma; and, third, voters should:

> ...pay attention to [the candidates'] actual ability to lead the masses towards prosperity, and make it a condition for the election of village cadres that they have a strong awareness of the market economy, and a strong ability to become rich. Here their personal ability to get rich should be of particular importance. If someone cannot find a way to make himself rich, how can he lead the masses towards prosperity?[26]

What we see here is Jiang Zemin's recruitment policy implemented locally without the veils of Marxist ideology: Su Wenfang's personal success as a businessman made him a natural community leader, so he was co-opted by the Party, which boosted its own legitimacy, first through Su's economic achievements, and then through the public mandate he received in the elections.

Leadership in Poor Villages

Unfortunately, few people of Su's type can be found in the poorer villages. Guoqiao township may serve as an example of the Party's problems in poor areas, where its legitimacy can be expected to be particularly low, because its economic goals, to some extent at least, have not been fulfilled.[27] Guoqiao is a predominantly agricultural township in a mountainous area. Tobacco is its principal source of income supplemented by pork. It has a population of 37,570 people divided into 10 administrative villages or villagers' committees, each of which has a number of villagers' small groups corresponding approximately to a natural village. The average annual income per capita was given as 670 yuan in year 2000, but some informants said that the real figure was considerably lower.[28]

What is the Party's situation in a township of this type? Its total membership is only 760 people, or 2.3 per cent of the population, so the pattern appears to be that the more "rural" a place is, the lower its level of inclusion in the Party.[29] If we start at the bottom of the Guoqiao Party organisation, there are Party groups (*dang xiaozu*) at the level of the natural village, but they play a very limited role. The groups I heard of had 5-10 members each, and in one of them the latest newcomer had joined the Party in 1974. The groups had no activities of any importance and members described them as powerless. This is in line with complaints in the media about "paralysed" basic level Party organisations. Rather than any Party organ, it was the villagers' small group committees, which assisted in collecting taxes and statistics, guided visiting officials, bought fertilisers for the whole village, etc. Some small group heads were Party members, others were not, but they all acted in their capacity of elected representatives.

At the immediately higher level of the administrative village (a unit of 3,000-6,000 people) the presence of the Party becomes more substantial. In the *Organic Law on Villagers' Committees*, the exact relationship between the village Party secretary, who is appointed at the township level, and the elected village head is not crystal clear, but in Xuanwei I had the strong impression that the PS was generally the most important figure (*diyi ba shou*) at this level. This is probably a general trend.[30] I have no exact data on the political status of village heads in Guoqiao. But in another Xuanwei township, Rongcheng, all 12 village heads elected in the summer of 2000 were Party members, and 11 of them were concurrently members of the Party committee, which means that they were placed under the command of the PS in the most important political hierarchy.[31]

There was one significant difference between these two local authorities: the village head actually came from and lived in the village he ran. This is stipulated in the law, and it had forced the township to change a pre-2000 practice of moving village heads among villages. In contrast, the PS was not necessarily from the village, although he was always a native of the township.

In crucial matters such as tax collection, public works, and birth control, the PSs worked as the extended arm of the township administration with practically no possibility of adapting policies to the local situation. Their other main field of operation was economic construction where more was left to their own initiative.[32] The production of tobacco was in a state of crisis due to restrictions introduced by the national government on the amount of land to be planted with tobacco and the number of cigarettes to be produced. In order to revitalise a shrinking economy the village PSs were expected to find alternative sources of income to the villagers, and they tried hard to attract investments and enterprises and introduce new crops. In this sense the Party exercised leadership in the economic field, and the village PSs were in many ways classic rural Communist cadres: ordinary peasants who had their power base inside the Party apparatus and played a vanguard role in collective actions.

PSs in low-income villages are now in a very difficult position. They are pushed hard by the township to implement policies coming down from above, and they receive little support from the farmers. Some years back they could still hope to be promoted to a position in the township administration if they did their job well. This avenue of upward social mobility had now been blocked in Xuanwei as village PSs are not considered qualified for promotion due to their generally low level of education. By preventing village PSs from advancing to posts at higher levels, the Party clearly signals that they are not considered as members of the new managerial elite, and the absence of this incentive has had a very negative effect on their morale. Furthermore, their salary is modest, only 200-300 yuan a month, so there is actually little that ties them to the higher levels of authority.

Township Cadres

When we move up one more step to the township administration we meet a different type of cadre. In Guoqiao, officials working for Party and government organs lived together with their families in a relatively new compound on the edge of town. Not all of them were Communist Party members, but they clearly formed a separate community where the Party, in the final analysis, defined career opportunities and professional values. Also, in the eyes of the rest of the population they formed a distinct social group.

Among the cadres there was a clear hierarchy with the PS, the mayor, the head of the disciplinary committee, and the chief of police at the top. The "rule of avoidance" applied to these top-level cadres, so they were all recruited from outside the township. The two most powerful cadres in Guoqiao, the PS and the mayor were very similar in background and outlook. They were both men in their early 30s with college degrees, and they had both left wife and child behind them in the city, partly because their wives had jobs there, and partly because they did not want to send their child to a rural school. To them, Guoqiao was obviously a hardship post, a necessary stepping-stone in their career. Maybe they worked hard for Guoqiao while they were there, but they were primarily loyal to the county administration to which they would return after one or two years, and which would decide their future career.

Township top leaders may appear to be very powerful inside the government compound, but the county assigns practically all their tasks to them, and they have no more leeway for making their own decisions than the village party secretaries under their command. If village leaders are squeezed between farmers and township officials, the latter find themselves squeezed between despondent and underpaid village leaders and an ambitious county administration. Township officials are generally loathed in China, and everybody has stories about their greed and corrupt behaviour, but from their own perspective, they are caught between a rock and a hard place. They are assigned difficult and expensive tasks from above, such as guaranteeing nine years of education for all, building roads, attracting enterprises, etc., but these tasks are rarely followed up by external funding, so they have to rely on taxes and fees extracted from the villagers. If they squeeze "their" villagers too hard, however, there will be complaints to the higher levels, and as the authorities are very sensitive to all signs of social instability, a young cadre's career can be seriously damaged if his villagers "make trouble" (*naoshi*).

The position of the township cadres is strikingly similar to the situation during the collective era, when townships were people's communes. The careers of commune cadres also depended primarily on their relations with the county level administration; they were also rotated between posts outside their place of origin, and their loyalty to the localities under their administration was also dubious.[33] One difference, however, is that commune cadres had a strong guiding ideology in Maoism, which provided both internal and external legitimacy to their actions. In the following section, I discuss the ideas which recently replaced Maoism in this role.

INTERNAL LEGITIMACY: GIVING SENSE
AND DIRECTION TO PARTY WORK

How do township cadres legitimise their own leadership over local economic, social, and cultural life? To answer this question I interviewed township cadres and read local internal publications specifically aimed at boosting the *esprit de corps* of Party and government cadres. It appears from these materials that the cadres have a strong notion of belonging to an elite, which has received its mandate to rule by virtue of its higher level of education, insight, and competence. The perception of elite status is crystallised in the concept of human "quality" or "competence" (*suzhi*), a combination of educational and moral parameters, which also contributes to the formation of cadres' attitudes to political issues.[34] They saw the low quality of the villagers as one of the main obstacles to development, and were often sceptical about village elections. In the eyes of one young township PS, village elections had brought too much grassroots democracy to China. Because villagers were uneducated they were unable to elect the right leaders, so the outcome of some elections was based mainly on clan loyalties and personal connections rather than on the competence of the candidates. This view is quite common among township cadres, who are often identified as the most determined opponents of village level elections.[35] The same line of thought was strongly reflected in one Party secretary's attitude to birth control, which he shares with many educated Chinese: "Isn't it absurd" he said, "that people of low quality in the rural areas can have two children, while people of high quality in the cities can only have one? Where will this lead us?"

Such remarks demonstrate the cadres' strong belief in their own superiority in rural society. This belief forms an important part of the basis of the internal legitimacy of Party rule, as it answers the question of why the Party incarnated by its cadres has the right to rule even in those rural areas that have benefited little from the general economic growth, and it tallies well with the elitist aspects of Jiang Zemin's ideas about Party building. I shall suggest that the foundation of this belief rests on three clusters of ideas which are all related to the concept of human quality. The cadres see themselves as exemplifying:

(1)   a higher level of education and better access to information, which qualifies them for leadership in the economic field,

204

(2) a higher level of culture and civilisation, which qualifies them for a leading role in questions of values, public morality and lifestyle,

(3) a higher understanding of social organisation, which gives them the right to monopolise this field and exclude any organised potential competitors to the Party.

In all three fields, however, the villagers under their rule are challenging the Cadres' legitimacy.

EDUCATION, SCIENCE, AND ECONOMIC LEADERSHIP

Notions of superiority based on education have strong links to the traditional Chinese civil service examination system, but in their present form, they are linked particularly to post-May 4th ideas of peasant backwardness. Myron Cohen mentions how in the early decades of the 20th Century "the notion of the peasantry as a culturally distinct and alien 'other'… desperately in need of education and cultural reform, and… totally dependent on the leadership and efforts of rational and informed outsiders, became fixed in the outlook of China's modern intellectual and political elites".[36]

In recent years, the image of being educated has become extremely important for the status and self-perception of cadres in rural society. Presentations of new township and county officials in newspapers and on posters practically always start with a note about their educational level. The formulation of these announcements is significant: "XXX, *daxue wenhua,…*", or literally: "NN, at the cultural level of university…", reflecting the confluence of the concepts of education and culture. In contrast, the CVs of new village heads only note their earlier work experience, indicating that formal education means less at this level. Meritocratic selection is institutionalised through an increasing number of well-publicised exams and formal qualification standards. Tests are given to cadres from the county level and right down to the villagers' committees, and results are publicly announced in the local newspaper, on billboards, etc. In the summer of 2001, Xuanwei for the first time recruited new township level cadres through an open examination consisting of a written and oral test which was publicly announced, and which all citizens could sign up for. Almost 700 candidates competed for 22 positions, and the process was explicitly presented as a way to

205

make the cadre recruitment process more transparent and less corrupt.[37] By inscribing cadre appointment in the metaphor of scholarly competition, the CPC draws on the fact that the rural population sees the examination system as a relatively fair selection method despite all its flaws and social biases, because the alternative would be appointments based on personal connections.[38]

The new generation of township-level Party cadres can actually boast a relatively high formal level of education. Out of 14 township vice-PS appointed in Xuanwei in 2001, four were regular university graduates, nine had a short-cycle college background (*dazhuan*), and one was a graduate of a senior secondary specialised school (*zhongzhuan*). This does not mean, however, that they can be characterised as a technocratic elite. Their CVs show that most of them had followed a career path inside the political-administrative system. Seven of them had their degree in management (*guanli*), and six had graduated from a Party School. Three came from teachers' training schools, and two regular university graduates held degrees in mathematics and law.[39] All of them were thus generalists whose main strength was their familiarity with how the Chinese administration works, and except for the school teachers, the CVs show that they had achieved their academic credentials after they had started working for the Party. They were not technical experts who had been elected cadres but rather political cadres who had been equipped with academic qualifications. The CVs also reveal, however, that the new generation of Party cadres incarnate the dream of most villagers: they had been born in a village but managed to move from the category of "peasant" (*nongmin*) to the coveted group of "salary-men" (*na gongzide*) through a combination of education and political work.[40]

The journal *Rongcheng gongzuo tongxun* (Rongcheng Work Report) reflects particularly well the *esprit de corps* which the Party-state tries to foster in its cadres. It is mainly distributed to government and Party cadres in Rongcheng, the most urbanised township in Xuanwei, and graphically reflects the crucial role of education and culture in the formation of the cadres' identity. The content of the magazine is quite dry with official speeches and political reports, but the first page of each issue has a short piece written in a very different style. It is sometimes lyrical, sometimes more philosophical, but always filled with grammatical constructions and literary allusions from classical Chinese. It signals to its readers, I would suggest, that they belong to a cultural community of cadres who have common roots in a world of learning and culture, but must deal pragmatically with all the troublesome tasks of everyday life which fill the remaining pages of the magazine.

The image of educational and cultural superiority is projected onto the field of economic planning, where township cadres have been very active considering the fact that agriculture in principle has been privatised. Township leaders not only designed plans for local macro-level economic development, they also gave farmers very detailed guidance about which crops to grow, which varieties to use, when to sow, how to harvest, etc. The leadership in Guoqiao, for example, had decided that from 2002, tobacco should be planted earlier because the climate had warmed up over the last couple of years. They had also, in cooperation with the tobacco company, introduced a new variety of tobacco and insisted that every tobacco farmer grow it. They even gave detailed instructions about which leaves to pick first and how to bundle them. With all these different rules, their actual control over the production process was quite comprehensive.[41]

Tobacco is a special crop in this respect because, grown on the basis of contracts with tobacco stations, it is monopolised and state-controlled. However, other reports confirm a deep involvement of cadres in guiding the production of other crops as well.[42] As just mentioned, however, the leading cadres tend to be generalists rather than experts in agricultural production. Their strength lies in their link to the Party apparatus and a pool of updated knowledge and technology which becomes accessible through this channel. In practical terms, they gain information about new crops, technologies, and markets either from higher-level Party and state organs or through their personal networks. Both types of information can be quite unreliable, and I heard of several cases where township or village leaders had talked villagers into growing a particular crop only to find there was no real market for it, or that other villages had shifted to the same crop with the effect that the market became glutted and prices dropped.

In economic decision-making, farmers occasionally challenged the cadres' expertise and refused to follow their advice. Conflicts about which crops to grow appear to be common in rural China. In interviews, farmers were sceptical about the wisdom of many of the leadership's decisions, and said they tended to do things their own way, at least to a certain extent. When the cadres met this type of resistance, they believed the farmers' reaction was a reflection of their conservatism and ignorance. The cadres were generally so certain that their plans were supported by scientific evidence and deep insights into the mechanisms of the market that the farmers' resistance only further convinced them of their own enlightenment.

In spite of such contradictions, however, the farmers did not flatly refuse to be led by the cadres in the economic field. Demonstration fields where cadres planted new varieties of tobacco were watched with intense interest, and the results often convinced the villagers of the advantages of the new methods. One farmer who was generally very critical towards the local government specifically mentioned such demonstration fields as "an example of a positive relationship between the cadres and masses".

Moral Standards

There is a close link between educational level and moral standards in the traditional Chinese worldview, and township cadres construct themselves as the moral guides and supervisors of the rural population. In Guoqiao, this was most conspicuously done through a detailed evaluation system called the "Ten star grading system of civilised households". Briefly defined, under this system all households are evaluated in terms of their performance in such categories as respect for the law, sense of duty, birth control, family unity, children's upbringing, new (as opposed to "feudal") lifestyle, respect for teachers and education, hygiene, and wealth. Gold stars are granted (or not granted) to all families in each of these categories, and the stars are then attached to a red plate, which the villagers must place over their entrance gate. It is a way for the Party to mark its moral and political power in the villages.[43] Cadres and other "salary-men" are not evaluated in a similar way, so the system supports the cadres' perception of belonging to a higher moral category qualified to evaluate practically all aspects of the villagers' lives.

While challenges to the Party's supremacy in the field of education and science were relatively moderate, the Party-state was, in spite of all efforts, fighting a losing battle in the moral arena, where its credibility was low. The most obvious reason for this was the popular conception of widespread corruption and abuse of power among the cadres. Reports on cadre corruption in China are so many and detailed that they hardly need to be repeated here. Moreover, I have no precise data on the actual extent of the problem in Xuanwei. Xin Liu, however, who looked at allegations of corruption in a village in Shaanxi, makes the important point that "the issue is not whether the cadres are corrupt or not; rather, it is the extent to which these allegations of corruption have become part of a larger force reconstituting the public sphere by way of a moral discourse".[44] Corruption has become a metonym for all those aspects of the Party's exercise of power that the villagers dislike, and the critique of corruption in official as well as popular discourse has become so pervasive that it concerns both the Party's external and internal legitimacy.[45] When a cadre believes that his colleagues accept bribes or use their position to gain other advantages, he feels a fool if he does not do the same, so corruption tends to become the norm rather than the exception, which again leads to a high level of cynicism among many cadres.

Social Organisation

The third main component of the Party's internal legitimacy is its role in social organisation. The rural population is defined as being incapable of organizing *itself* from the bottom up. This point is actually an echo of similar arguments from the beginning of the 20th century when Sun Yat-sen and other reformers saw rural China as a "plate of loose sand" made up of families and clans that only considered their own narrow interests. As we have seen, Jiang Zemin plays on the same theme in his speeches on the "Three Represents". Local cadres fully agreed with Jiang that without the presence of the Party, rural society would either dissolve into autonomous units disregarding the common good, or form new types of organizations which would represent a step backwards (such as the clan system), or even have a criminal character (such as secret societies). Even a critical intellectual like Cao Jinqing repeatedly identifies the lack of organizational ability as the main weakness of Chinese villagers.[46]

In the local public sphere, the organisational monopoly is expressed in both a positive and negative form. The Party organises (or claims to organise) social activities, and also prevents others from doing so. Although the era of large, nationwide political campaigns that could change the life course of millions of people is over, it is remarkable how many small campaigns are still organised in local communities. The Party uses a standardised methodology and terminology in its presentation of all these attempts to change the outlook and social practice of the villagers. Two articles from the same issue of *Rongcheng gongzuo tongxun*, the journal for local cadres discussed earlier, may serve to illustrate this. One concerns economics and the other, health and lifestyle.

The first article was part of a campaign for growing potatoes in the autumn on fields where other crops, primarily tobacco, had already been harvested. It states that the success of this experiment was the result of the "importance attached to this issue by all leaders of different levels in the township". These leaders had "strengthened the leadership, intensified the propaganda, organised inspection trips to the fields, set up models, [and] led the way through examples". This had all been made possible because the leaders had increased their "understanding of the 'potato strategy' of the Qujing Municipality", which they then transmitted to the farmers:

> Under the serious attention of the [township] Party committee and government, and led by the vice township head responsible for agriculture, the relevant staff was organised to give technical training in all twelve agricultural villages of the township, and to go deep into each peasant family and each field to give guidance.[47]

So the introduction of new farming techniques is presented as a victory of the Party's organisational power as much as of modern science. The cadres' penetration of rural society, even down to the level of individual families, is seen as a precondition for technological progress.

The second article describes a campaign for making village toilets more hygienic. We get the same picture of a top-down process carried out with considerable difficulties:

> The transformation of the toilets from 1998 till today has been carried out level by level from the top down. The leaders of the county Party committee have frequently gone down to the villages to direct the work. The township mayor and officials in charge have regularly inspected the quality and strictly supervised and urged the work. Those who have been responsible for this process in the village committees in particular have worked day and night to solve the disputes set off by the reform of the toilets. They have, to the best of their abilities, established model toilets and let the good example lead the rest.[48]

As with the autumn potatoes, the Party does not present this as merely a practical matter. The township mayor places the toilet campaign in a larger perspective:

The reform of the toilets answers the need to develop human civilisation, the need of the health of the people, and the need of the construction of a spiritual civilisation.[49]

These are just two examples of a large number of very similar articles in local newspapers and magazines that portray a view of the world where even the most mundane actions in rural communities originate from policies designed by the higher levels of the Party. These policies are then transmitted down the administrative hierarchy and transformed into concrete social organisation and change by the local cadres who in this way civilise the villagers. In this construction of a cadre-organised and cadre-controlled world, the stereotyped villager and his inability to form stable social associations stand in the way of progress towards a modern world guided by rational and scientific principles.

As in the moral field, the Party's monopoly on social organisation is also being seriously challenged. Alternative organisations, primarily lineages and religious groups, sometimes put the Party in a state of alarm, but the most serious problems arise when villagers deny the Party the right to represent collective interests by extracting resources for public projects.[50] Farmers often refuse to pay taxes or take part in work projects organised by the local state, and frustrated village cadres described how they walked from door to door trying to collect money or make people take part in the construction of a new road. One informant described how tax collection had become increasingly difficult after the introduction of village elections:

> Relations between the cadres and masses have changed. The cadres cannot really collect taxes in a serious way now because they want to be re-elected. This year 70 per cent of the households in this village did not pay taxes. Before the reform, the cadres would have dragged these people's furniture or animals away if they did not pay, or they would have beaten them up. The cadres beat up the masses in those days [i.e., before the first village committee elections were held in this area in year 2000], beat them with clubs or boxed their ears. There were very sharp contradictions then. But if the 70 per cent who did not pay this year do not pay double next year there will really be trouble, because the 30 per cent who paid will feel cheated.

People refuse to pay because they do not trust that the money will be used for the common good. Met with this kind of resistance, the job of the village cadres becomes even more difficult, and they tend to be more lenient with their constituencies and less loyal to the higher levels.

CONCLUSION

The above observations indicate that top-level township cadres in poor rural areas to a large extent share Jiang Zemin's visions of an elite party. They base their claim to legitimacy on the perception that they, because of their personal competencies and links to the Party-state, represent a higher level of learning, information, and civilisation than the population in the rural communities they rule. They also believe that the Party they embody stands for modernity and progress and has the historical mission of leading the peasants to higher levels of economic development and social organisation, even when this means acting against the peasants' perceptions of their own interests. In addition to the personal benefits that cadres get from their positions, they find a sense of purpose believing they are part of a process which will eventually turn China into a strong and modern country. This can be seen as the logical conclusion to the state-promoted discourse which has been running for almost two decades on concepts like "human quality", "spiritual civilization", and "qualified people".

Some analysts have found serious cracks in the rural bureaucratic structure, namely, between the township and county levels with village and township cadres forming a close network that is equally hard for ordinary villagers to penetrate from below, as it is for county officials from above.[51] This may be the case in the richer rural areas where economic development has created a pool of resources for village and township leaders to share, but judging from the situation in a poor rural township like Guoqiao, the Party appears to be more fragile at the township-village interface. Here we find a serious cleft between, on the one hand, a leadership group of young, well-educated township cadres who identify with the higher levels of the state and base their claim to legitimacy on the elitist notions outlined above, and, on the other hand, village leaders, who increasingly identify with their communities. The further institutionalisation of village committee elections, which have only recently been implemented in Yunnan, and maybe even future democratic elections of village PSs, will give village-level leaders considerable legitimacy based on a popular mandate, rather than on the notion of belonging to an elite.

ENDNOTES

1 My research in China was made possible by a grant from the Danish Council for Development Research. I am grateful to Søren Clausen, Jørgen Delman, Jacques Hersh, Graham Young, and David Zweig for their comments on earlier drafts of this paper, and to Ole Aabenhus, Ane Bislev, Fan Jianhua, Mette Halskov Hansen, Li Xu, Frank Pieke, Sun Rui, Wang Ya'nan, and Zheng Hai for sharing their ideas with me during the time we spent in Xuanwei.

2 Cao Jinqing, *Huanghebian de Zhongguo. Yige xuezhe dui xiangcun shehui de guancha yu sikao* (China Along the Yellow River. A Scholar's Observations and Reflections on Rural Society) (Shanghai: Shanghai wenyi chubanshe, 2000), p. 448.

3 *Ibid.*, pp. 451-2.

4 Wang Gungwu and Zheng Yongnian, for example, summarise the three sources of legitimacy as development, stability and national unity. See their "Introduction", in Wang Gungwu and Zheng Yongnian, eds., *Reform, Legitimacy, and Dilemmas: China's Politics and Society* (Singapore: Singapore University Press and World Scientific, 2000), pp. 1-20.

5 Chalmers Johnson, for example, talks about "the shift from communism to Chinese nationalism as the regime's legitimating ideology", and similar views can be found in many other academic and journalist accounts. Chalmers Johnson, "Soft Totalitarianism in China", *New Perspectives Quarterly* 14, no. 3 (1997): 18-20.

6 Li Changping, *Wo xiang zongli shuo shihua* (I Will Tell the Truth to the Premier) (Beijing: Guangming ribao chubanshe, 2002), pp. 12-3.

7 Research on peasant protests and peasant resistance has been very popular in the last few years. Kevin O'Brien has recently reviewed much of this literature in his "Collective Action in the Chinese Countryside", *The China Journal* 48 (Jul. 2002): 139-54.

8 For these systems see in particular Susan H. Whiting, *Power and Wealth in Rural China: The Political Economy of Institutional Change* (Cambridge: Cambridge University Press, 2001), pp. 100-8, and Maria Edin, "State Capacity and Local Agent Control in China: Cadre Management from a Township Perspective", *The China Quarterly* 173 (Mar. 2003): 35-52.

9 For grotesque examples of local cadres' behaviour in connection with 'inspection' and evaluation from higher levels, see Cao Jinqing, *Huanghebian de Zhongguo*, pp. 590-2, 731-2, 735-40.

10 My discussion is based on Jiang Zemin, *Lun "sange daibiao"* (On the "Three Represents") (Beijing: Zhongyang wenxian chubanshe, 2001), which contains 12 speeches or excerpts from speeches by Jiang, arranged chronologically from a talk given in Feb. 2000 during an inspection tour of Guangdong, to his long speech on 1 Jul., on the occasion of the 80th anniversary of the founding of the CPC.

213

11 Jiang, *Lun "sange daibiao"*, pp. 169-70.

12 It should be added that other parts of Jiang's speeches sound more traditionally Leninist and emphasise the working classes as the "backbone" of the Party, but I think it is fair to say that any claim of originality must be based on the sections about the inclusion into the CPC of "outstanding elements" among the economic and managerial elite.

13 Jiang, *Lun "sange daibiao"*, pp. 163-4.

14 *Ibid.*, p. 120.

15 *Xinhua News Agency*, 2 Sep. 2002, from <www.china.org.cn/english/features/41251.htm> [10 Oct. 2002].

16 Ken Jowitt, *New World Disorder: The Leninist Extinction* (Berkeley: University of California Press, 1992), pp. 88-120.

17 *Asiaweek*, 2 Sep. 2001. Significantly, Yan tried to win over the sceptical old cadres by reminding them of their own privileges: "Many of them [i.e., the old cadres] are now living in housing of 200 square metres that the Party gave them, which they can sell for several million yuan. It was only after I pointed this out to them that they began to realise they, too, are owners of private property."

18 Jiang, *Lun "sange daibiao"*, pp. 31-2.

19 *Ibid.*, pp. 8-9, 12-3.

20 For a discussion of changes in the social integration of villages in Su-nan brought about by the transformation of collective enterprises into shareholding or private companies, see Dong Leiming, "Chuantong yu shanbian" (Tradition and Transmutation), *Shehuixue yanjiu* (Sociological Research), 1 (2002): 10-6.

21 Figures for Xuanwei are from *Xuanweibao* (Xuanwei News), 3 Jul. 2001, p. 1. In Jun. 2002, the CPC had 66.4 million members nationwide. See China Internet Information Centre, <www.china.org.cn/english/features/41930.htm> [2 Oct. 2002].

22 *Xuanwei shizhi* (Xuanwei City Gazetteer) (Kunming: Yunnan renmin chubanshe, 1999), p. 476.

23 *Xuanwei nianjian 2001* (Xuanwei Yearbook 2001) (Dehong: Dehong minzu chubanshe, 2001), p. 102.

24 *Xuanweibao*, 6 Sep. 2000, p. 1.

25 Interview with Yunnan Civil Affairs Bureau officials, Sep. 2000. There may be several reasons for this tendency, but it is reasonable to believe that part of the explanation can be found exactly in the need for legitimacy. Public support expressed through democratic elections has become a widely recognised base for claims of legitimacy also in China, and local Party secretaries have seen the writing on the wall. Once they are publicly elected as village heads through a secret ballot, they have at least partly and personally overcome the problem, well ahead of the Party leadership at the national level.

26 *Xuanweibao*, 6 Sep. 2000, p. 1.

27 I carried out interviews in Guoqiao in Jan. 2000 and Aug. 2001. I have changed the name of the township here.

28 The official figures are from Xuanwei shi tongjiju (Xuanwei Department of Statistics), *Xuanwei shi guomin jingji he shehui fazhan tongji ziliao, 2000 nian* (Statistical Materials on the Economy and Social Development of Xuanwei City, Year 2000) (Xuanwei, 2001), pp. 4 and 340. There was much discussion among cadres about this point. One village PS said the way in which rural income data is collected and reported is unreliable, and mainly reflects the targets set by the township.

29 Interview with the township Party Secretary, Aug. 2001.

30 See Kevin O'Brien, "Villagers, Elections, and Citizenship in Contemporary China", *Modern China* 27, no. 4 (2001): 407-35, particularly p. 422. According to the official formulation, the Party is supposed to "guide" (*zhidao*) rather than "lead" (*lingdao*) the work of the committee, but even the term guidance is open to interpretation. An interesting discussion of village leadership in action, including the relationship between the Party branch and villagers' committee, can be found in Björn Alpermann, "The Post-Election Administration of Chinese Villages", *The China Journal*, no. 46 (Jul. 2001): 45-67.

31 *Rongcheng gongzuo tongxun* (Rongcheng Work Report), no. 8 (2000): 11, 38-9.

32 This corresponds to what Alpermann found in Hebei. See his "The Post-Election Administration".

33 Jonathan Unger, *The Transformation of Rural China* (Armonk, New York: M.E. Sharpe, 2002), pp. 19-23.

34 *Suzhi* is normally translated into English as "quality", but some Chinese have started rendering it as "competence". For a more detailed discussion of *suzhi* see Ann Anagnost, *National Past-times. Narrative, Representation, and Power in Modern China* (Durham: Duke University Press, 1997), and Børge Bakken, *The Exemplary Society: Human Improvement, Social Control, and the Dangers of Modernity in China* (Oxford: Oxford University Press, 2000).

35 Cao, *Huanghebian de Zhongguo*, pp. 460-1. Kevin O'Brien has shown how the argument about "backward" villagers being unsuited to take part in politics is also used in the discussion on People's Congresses, see O'Brien, "Villagers, Elections, and Citizenship", pp. 413-4.

36 Myron L. Cohen, "Cultural and Political Inventions in Modern China: The Case of the Chinese 'Peasant'", in *China in Transformation*, ed. Tu Wei-ming (Cambridge, Mass.: Harvard University Press, 1994), pp. 151-70.

37 *Xuanweibao*, 8 Jun. 2001, p.1.

38 I have discussed this in more detail in Stig Thøgersen, *A County of Culture: China's Twentieth Century Seen From the Village Schools of Zouping, Shandong* (Ann Arbor: University of Michigan Press, 2002), pp. 206-10.

39 *Xuanweibao*, 3 Jan. 2001, p. 4; 2 May 2001, p. 4; 10 Aug. 2001, p. 4; 11 Dec. 2001, pp. 2-3. No information is given regarding the field of study of the remaining two university graduates.

40 In the minds of most villagers I talked to, the principle division line between the privileged and under-privileged was not between cadres and peasants,

but between those who received a fixed salary (including teachers, tobacco station staff, etc.) and those who depended on agriculture or temporary jobs.

41   In connection with our research in Xuanwei, Ole Aabenhus produced a video, "Tobacco on My Back", which features local tobacco politics, particularly the relationship between cadres and peasants. A DVD of the film can be obtained through the author.

42   The organisation and political economy of tobacco production is analysed in Yali Peng, "The Politics of Tobacco: Relations between Farmers and Local Governments in China's Southwest", *The China Journal*, no. 36 (Jul. 1996): 67-82. Peng finds that "local officialdom acts in a parasitic, predatory fashion as tax maximisers" (p. 82), because the tobacco tax is practically the only source of income for governments in some poor areas. Other examples of local governments forcing farmers to grow particular crops can be found in Alpermann, "The Post-Election Administration", pp. 59-66, and in Cao, *Huangbebian de Zhongguo*, pp. 651-2, 728.

43   Stig Thøgersen, "Cultural Life and Cultural Control in China: Where is the Party?" *The China Journal*, no. 44 (Jul. 2000): 129-41.

44   Xin Liu, *In One's Own Shadow: An Ethnographic Account of the Condition of Post-reform Rural China* (Berkeley: University of California Press, 2000), pp. 177-8.

45   The most extensive discussion of the phenomenon of cadre corruption is probably Xiaobo Lü, *Cadres and Corruption: The Organizational Involution of the Chinese Communist Party* (Stanford: Stanford University Press, 2000). He characterises the process which the Chinese administration has gone through as one of "organisational involution", which "produces neither modern bureaucrats who are rational, role-conscious, and rule-oriented,... nor well-maintained, disciplined and committed revolutionary cadres;... instead it produces disillusioned, status-conscious, and undisciplined cadres..." (p. 23).

46   Cao, *Huangbebian de Zhongguo*, pp. 432, 491, 586.

47   Yang Guangyu, "Rongcheng zhen qiu yangyu zhongzhi" (Growing Autumn Potatoes in Rongcheng Town), *Rongcheng gongzuo tongxun*, no. 11 (2000): 18.

48   Wang Yumei, "Rongcheng zhen WES xiangmu zhong moqi shenping zhunbei gongzuo zhashi youxiao" (The Preparation Work for the Final Evaluation of the WES Project in Rongcheng Has Been Solid and Efficient), *Rongcheng gongzuo tongxun*, no. 11 (2000): 10-12.

49   *Ibid.*, p. 10.

50   For conflicts between cadres and villagers on the land issue in Xuanwei see Xiaolin Guo, "Land Expropriation and Rural Conflicts in China", *The China Quarterly*, no. 166 (Jun. 2001): 422-39.

51   An example of an interesting analysis along these lines is Zhang Jing, *Jiceng zhengquan - xiangcun zhidu zhu wenti* (Problems of Rural Basic Level Governance) (Hangzhou: Zhejiang renmin chubanshe, 2000), pp. 186-90.

CHAPTER 8

The '*Shequ* Construction' Programme and the Chinese Communist Party

KAZUKO KOJIMA AND RYOSEI KOKUBUN

INTRODUCTION: GOVERNMENTAL AND SOCIAL SECTORS IN '*SHEQU* CONSTRUCTION'

In recent years, the community development programme called '*shequ* construction' has been making rapid progress in China. This paper analyses the position and actions of the Chinese Communist Party concerning the *shequ* construction programme as an essential process from the viewpoint of political science.

Shequ is a Chinese word for 'community' and it means a co-operative unit of people who live in a certain defined area. Although the word *shequ* itself does not formally define size or scale, since the founding of the People's Republic of China, each *shequ* governance has been handled by a 'street office' (*jiedao banshichu*), an outpost agency of a district government and by a 'residents' committee' (*jumin weiyuanhui*) under the street office, governed by residents. However, under the planned economy system, administering residents and providing services for residents was actually handled by work units (*danwei*) of government offices and enterprises to which the residents belonged. In reality, the authority and roles of street offices and residents' committees were very limited. Since the street offices are the outpost agencies of district governments, and are segmented according to the established vertical chains of command into sections and departments, they hardly played a

217

role in policy management as united entities. The residents' committees, consisting of several elderly ladies who worked without monetary compensation, got no further than to publicize government propaganda and to mediate disputes among residents.

In the market economy, however, the work unit management system no longer functions well due to diversified corporate structure, reforms of state-owned enterprises, housing reforms and increased population mobility. As a result, the *shequ* began to gain attention as an alternative unit to the work units that used to fulfil various important roles. For example, payments of various social benefits such as the pensions for the elderly and unemployment insurance as well as daily management of the insured that were formerly handled by the work units became one of the important duties of *shequ*.[1] Regarding the urban residents' minimum living allowance payments, the roles of the street offices and the residents' committees have already been stipulated in statutory provisions.[2] Also, managing migrated workers, maintaining public order, medical and public health, environmental issues, care for the elderly, daycare centres, household management, employment agencies and a wide range of other needs and functions are expected to be provided by the *shequ*.

TABLE 1   *SHEQU* CHRONOLOGY

1986	The Ministry of Civil Affairs (MoCA) proposed the necessity of shequ services provided by street offices and residents' committees.
May 1991	MoCA proposed construction of shequ. 'Notice regarding the hearing about "*Shequ* Construction Plan".
	They appointed Hebel district in the city of Tian jin and Xiacheng district in the city of Hangzhou as nationwide shequ construction pilot units and commenced experimental "*shequ* construction'.
1991-1992	MoCa held three symposiums on the nationwide *shequ* construction theory.

TABLE 1 *SHEQU* CHRONOLOGY (cont'd)

1996-present	Jiang Zemin said that 'intensification of *shequ* construction in urban areas and full exertion of the roles of street offices and residents' committees are needed'.
	The city of Shanghai attempted an arrangement of the duties and authorities of city, district and street offices based on the city's reform plan on administrative system under 'Two Tier Government and Three Tier Management'.
June 1998	The city of Qingdao held a meeting to discuss shequ construction in all cities.
July 1998	As part of the reform of the central government administration system, the Bureau for the Construction of Basic Government of MoCA was renamed the Bureau for the Construction of Basic Government and Community (*shequ*).
1999	The city of Shenyang promoted the reform of *shequ* system at the expiration of the members' term of the residents' committees.
	Cities such as Beijing, Tianjin, Chongqing and Nanjing commenced reform of all-city-level administrative system and '*shequ*' construction activities.
	MoCA appointed the following 11 districts as nationwide shequ construction test-case districts in urban areas: Capital Times Square in the city of Beijing, Luwan district in the city of Shanghai, Jiangbei district in the city of Chongqing, Gulou district in the city of Nanjing, Xiacheng district in the city of Hangzhou, Shinan district and Sifang district in the city of Qingdao, Chang'an district in the city of Shijiazhuang, Zhendong district in the city of Haikou, Shenhe district in the city of Shenyang, and Hexi district in the city of Tianjin.
	MoCA established the Research Centre for Urban *Shequ* Construction in China in Beijing (Beijing Academy of Social Sciences), Shanghai (East China Normal University), Tianjin (Nankai University) and Wuhan (Central China Normal University).

TABLE 1 *SHEQU* CHRONOLOGY (cont'd)

August 1999   MoCA held the first joint meeting among nationwide shequ construction test-case districts in Xiacheng district in the city of Hangzhou.

August 1999   MoCA appointed additional 15 districts including the following as nationwide shequ construction test-case districts in urban areas: Xuanwu district in the city of Nanjing, Heping district in the city of Shenyang, Xishi district in the city of Hefei, Heping district in the city of Tianjin, Nangang district and Daoli district in the city of Ha'erbin, Xilui district in the city of Benxi and Xincheng district in the city of Xi'an, as well as provinces such as Liaoning and Hubei as province-level *shequ* construction test cases.

January 2000   MoCA held the second joint meeting among nationwide *shequ* construction test-case districts in Zhendong district in the city of Haikou.

November   General Office of the Central CCP and State Council Agency
2000   transferred the 'Opinion of the Ministry of Civil Affairs (MoCA) on Promoting *Shequ* Construction Nationwide'.

April 2001   MoCA held the third joint meeting among nationwide *shequ* construction tes-case districts in Lixia district in the city of Jinan in Shandong province.

July 2001   MoCA held the first conference on nationwide *shequ* construction operation in the city of Qingdao, Shandong province.

               MoCA issued 'Outline of model activity guidance in constucting *shequ* nationwide'.

Source: prepared by the authors

Under these circumstances, the major concern of the Chinese government is how to extend the functions of the street offices and the residents' committees and allow them to play an important role administering residents and providing services for residents. As shown

220

in Table 1, various *shequ* construction programmes have been attempted throughout the 1990s at various places.

Based on the results of test cases in various areas, the 'Opinion of the Ministry of Civil Affairs (MoCA) on Promoting *Shequ* Construction Nationwide' (hereafter referred to as 'the Opinion' was made public with the approval of the Central Party and the State Council in December 2000.[3] Regarding the scope of the *shequ*, the Opinion stated that the area covered by a residents' committee (100-700 family units in accordance with the Residents' Committee Organizing Act) should be adjusted to facilitate the administrative needs, conveniences and people's sense of attachment. After such adjustments, residents' committees should be renamed the '*shequ* residents' committees' and the area covered by *shequ* residents' committees as *shequ* (with 1,000-3,000 family units). In addition, 'the Opinion' stated that a *Shequ* Members' Representative Congress (*shequ chengyuan daibiaohui*) as a policy-making entity, should be established in each *shequ*, formed by representatives of residents and of work units within each *shequ*, and the *shequ* residents' committee should act as the administrative entity with members elected by people after soliciting their candidacy publicly.[4] Each district is independently setting its own standards to operate and manage its *shequ* efficiently, by preparing its budget and asking for financial provision and increments for *shequ* residents' committee officers for their supplementary income and better working environment from the district government.

As stated before, a uniform policy for *shequ* construction seemed to be finally established by the end of 2000, but each district has its own way of meeting the specific needs of the district. What had been tried in the city of Shanghai, the city of Shenyang in Liaoning province, Jianghan district in the city of Wuhan in Hubei province, and the city of Qingdao in Shandong province are often quoted as the four models for *shequ* construction.[5] After reviewing the four different models, the discussion focused on the issue of the relation between the street offices under the jurisdiction of the government and the residents' committees which form the people's self-governing entity. In other words, the issue raised is whether *shequ* construction should proceed with a 'governmental' or 'social' entity at its helm, and whether 'control' or 'autonomy' should have priority.

For example, Shanghai adopted the 'two-tier government' (district and city), 'three-tier management' (street, district and city) and 'four-tier network' (*shequ* residents' committee, street, district and city). Under this system, the function of the street offices was reinforced, and the function of the autonomous *shequ* residents' committees was expanded for the street offices actively participating. And as a result, improvements have been made on administrative matters and resident services. '*Shequ* construction' using the method of 'consolidating governmental (street) and social (resident) sectors' (*jieju yitihua*), which has been adopted in Shanghai, is also under way in Beijing, Chongqing, Hangzhou, Shijiazhuang, Xi'an and Chengdu. In Shanghai and Beijing, staff members that specialize in *shequ* services (called '*shequ* workers') are sent from the street offices to the *shequ* residents' committee.[6] Under the policy of 'consolidating governmental and social sectors', it remains normal practice in certain places for the street offices to appoint elected persons as the members of *shequ* residents' committee. This is one of the ways in which the street offices are involved in the personnel affairs of the *shequ* residents' committee.

In the case of the city of Shenyang, its '*shequ* construction' has an established record of establishing strong self-governing *shequ*. The city has made large-scale reforms of its *shequ* system, starting in 1999 when the term of offices of the members of the residents' committees expired. By means of this reform, *shequ* with 1,000-2,000 family units were created by combining several residents' committees. The newly created *shequ* were allowed to have rights to self-govern, administer, manage and supervise in accordance with the 'Opinion to Establish Clear-cut Lines of Authority and Responsibility of *Shequ*', and '*shequ* construction' with the principle of 'residents' autonomy' is under way.[7] In Shenyang, it is not allowed to send personnel from the street or district offices to *shequ* except for civil law enforcement personnel.

In the case of the Jianghan district of the city of Wuhan, a clear division of functions between the street offices and *shequ* residents' committee was made in order to build a relationship that is mutually complementary between government-controlled functions and the *shequ*'s autonomy.[8] Owing to changes in their functions, the street offices transferred 17 of their duties and authorities to the *shequ*, i.e., 1) personnel matters; 2) control of funds; 3) management of *shequ* service networks; 4) minimum living allowance, social relief funds, special reduction of rents for poor families, preliminary hearings on various applications such as application for certificates for the disabled, etc.[9]

Transfer of appropriate authorities and duties from the city to districts, from districts to streets and from streets to the *shequ*, as witnessed in Jianghan, seems to have become the prevalent practice. However, the process of transfer does not always run smoothly, as each section or office tries to protect its acquired rights and interests. On the contrary, under the pretext of making the *shequ*'s functions substantial, several government offices and departments at all levels are creating their own clique or groups within the *shequ*, and are forcing upon the *shequ* a number of jobs and duties as well as various quotas that must be fulfilled by the governmental sectors. As a result, it is said that the *shequ* residents' committees are overloaded with hundreds of duties. Some members of the MoCA are voicing their concern over this situation, warning that the *shequ* residents' committee may become a part of government, and may lose its autonomous character.[10]

However, those actors and agencies who could make the autonomous *shequ* successful have not been fully developed or matured. Even if the process of transferring authorities from the street offices to the *shequ* takes place, the '*shequ* construction' programme will face financial difficulties without the support of work units providing human and material resources. In this case, the '*shequ* construction' programme will not be able to remain autonomous without the support and participation of the residents at large. What all the districts and areas that have been proceeding with the '*shequ* construction' first face is the harsh reality that there are insufficient financial and human resources as well as know-how, while duties such as urban administration and resident services pile up. Under these circumstances, being dependent on the governmental sector is unavoidable at the initial stages, even though it is not consistent with the administrative reforms and the change to the market economy.

Wang Sibin, a Professor of Department of Sociology at the Peking University, speculates that the process of '*shequ* construction' from *shequ* managed by the administration to *shequ* with autonomy will take place as follows:[11]

- Pre-'*shequ* construction': In choosing the *shequ* system instead of the *danwei* (unit) system, the government expands the duties and responsibilities of *shequ* and transfers authorities.
- Primary stage of '*shequ* construction': Under the government directives, grassroots organizations such as the street offices and the residents' committees become the administrative bodies of *shequ* management, and organize *shequ* residents to participate in '*shequ* construction'.

- Developing stage of '*shequ* construction': The street offices, the residents' committees and *shequ* members co-operate in services and management; consequently social elements in *shequ* mature at a remarkable pace.
- Maturity of '*shequ* construction': A relatively strong *shequ* autonomous system will be formed and the street office as the government's agency will become a separate entity from the autonomous residents' committee. A co-operative/mutual control system will be established among the street offices, the residents' committees (autonomous entity), *shequ* social organizations and *shequ* members (residents and work units within shequ).

A further essential factor (player) cannot be excluded when examining the issue of whether the constructed *shequ* is a 'governmental' or 'social' entity. We refer here to the Chinese Communist Party (CCP), whose comprehensive network reaches all over the country beyond the boundary of 'governmental' and 'social'. It is clearly stated in the Organizing Rural Residents' Committee Act that the CCP should take the leading role in the rural community's autonomy, but the Organizing Urban Residents Committee Act has no such stipulations. However, the aforementioned 'Opinion' formulated the following cohesive policy concerning various players and their roles to push forward the '*shequ* construction'. The basic policy stated in 'the Opinion' is as follows:

> Under the guidance of the Party Committee and the government, *shequ* residents' committees are to take the helm for "*shequ* construction", supported by the society and with the participation of the people at large, under the leadership of the Department of Civil Affairs and the assistance and co-operation of all concerned sections of the government.

Here, the role of the CCP in the '*shequ* construction' is clearly stated as 'the guidance core'. To understand how the CCP plays this role effectively, the following observations were noted when reviewing several publications.

THE BACKGROUND AND HISTORY
OF 'SHEQU PARTY CONSTRUCTION'

Under the planned economy system, the grassroots organizations of the CCP were divided into two systems, i.e., work units and the street offices. Incumbent party members residing in a *shequ* belonged to the party organization within their work units and had no direct contacts with *shequ* party organizations in the street offices. Those who were under the *shequ* party organizations were limited to: retired and elderly party members; party members who worked for private corporations or for foreign corporations in the *shequ*; party members in the mobile population; and unemployed party members. But *shequ* party organizations did not have sufficient organizing ability to manage those party members. *Shequ* was a kind of 'void' for the party, so to speak. As the market economy began to flourish and private enterprises, foreign companies and various social organizations have increased since 1990s, unsettled party members, laid off and/or unemployed party members increased drastically, and the 'void' was further enlarged.[12] In the mid-1990s, alarmed by the trend that could threaten the maintenance and expansion of the party leadership, the Central Party began to build up *shequ* party organizations and strengthen their functions. Especially as the Falun Gong became so popular and widespread among people and party members, the Central Party strongly felt the need to strengthen the party members' organizations at the grassroots level of society, as well as the management capacity and influence of party organizations.

In 1996, the ODoCCP (Organization Department of the CCP) issued the 'Opinion to Strengthen the Street Party Organizations'. It specified the duties of the street party organizations and *shequ* party organizations and urged measures to strengthen the party organization. Various conferences and symposiums were conducted to actively promote '*shequ* party construction', e.g. in Shanghai in 1999, Beijing in 2000 and the city of Haikou in Hainan province in 2002. The themes of conferences and symposiums included: 'National Street and *Shequ* Party Construction Workshops'; 'National Symposium on Building-up Street and *Shequ* Party Organizations in Municipalities under the Direct Control and Other Municipalities'; and 'National Conference and Exchange of Experiences of Organizing Street and *Shequ* Party Organizations in Medium- to Small-Size Cities'.

Based on cases in different cities, the following is the summary of main policies in 'shequ party construction'.

Improving the systematization rate

According to the 'Charters of the Chinese Communist Party', a party committee should be formed wherever there are more than 100 party members who belong to organizations within the jurisdiction; a party main branch should be set up wherever there are more than 50 party members; and a party cell should be established wherever there are more than three party members. In order to adhere to the charter, shequ party cells were established at many places. As a result, the percentage of party cells established under the jurisdiction of the residents' committees nationwide increased to 78 percent in 2001 compared to 65 percent in 1993.[13]

Improving the quality of party organization officers

One of the major elements that hinder the organizational ability and leadership of any shequ party organization is the low quality of its officers. Many of them are elderly without higher education and the necessary management skills. In order to resolve the problem, each area is trying to secure capable party members for its key positions. The following methods are used in selecting persons for the position of secretaries of shequ party cells. First, capable officers of the residents' committees who are trusted by the people at large and popular among them are selected as secretaries of shequ party cells. According to year 2000 statistics, 56 percent (196 persons) of the shequ party branch secretaries in the city of Jinan in Shandong province were chosen in this way (officers of the residents' committees holding concurrent posts in the shequ party branch as secretaries will be explained later). Second, the district party committees choose young and capable party members in the districts/street agencies or companies who are familiar with the tasks of the shequ and have them assume the position of the shequ party branch secretaries. In other words, the higher-level party organizations appoint members to the lower-party organizations. Third, they recruit party members who are laid-off labourers, retired military personnel and university students to take qualifying examinations and appoint to the positions.[14]

To secure highly qualified personnel, remuneration for the party branch officers has been improved. Previously, while the party main branch secretaries were full-time personnel, the party branch secretaries under them held concurrent posts and were not remunerated. Therefore, whether the work at the party cells could be carried out successfully or not depended on the personal relationship between the party main branch secretaries and the party branch secretaries. But grievances for working without compensation have been reported. According to the survey taken in Xihu district of the city of Hangzhou in Zhejiang province, the *shequ* party branch secretaries, dissatisfied by the fact that they were not given any remuneration while doing the same job as the residents' committee officers who were remunerated, became unmotivated in carrying out their duties.[15] To avoid this type of situation and to recruit capable party members for *shequ* activities from all areas and fields, the Organization Department of the party committee in the city of Jinan (Shandong province) came up with provisions, by which the party members recruited to work in the *shequ* party branch or the residents' committee who are officers of national agencies or collective-owned agencies receive the same remuneration and are allowed to receive additional compensation offered by the residents' committee. The provision also stipulated that in the case that collective-owned agency officers are employed by *shequ* and apply to qualify as civil servants, they should take priority for appointment.[16] As the remuneration for the residents' committee officers is improved, the compensation for the *shequ* party branch secretaries is being revised to be on a par with residents' committee directors.

Improved work environment

Difficulties that the *shequ* party organizations used to face were the shortage of office space and an insufficient budget to manage their offices. In order to improve this situation, several measures have been taken together with the current reforms, e.g. offices of the *shequ* party cells are constructed with the co-operation of the urban construction sections, and telephones are installed in offices.

227

Increasing organizational strength through network building

The street party organizations being the core, building the network of all party organizations in government agencies and work units within the *shequ* is taking place so that the vertical chain of command by work units and the horizontal ones rooted in the community can come together and co-operate. Members of *shequ* party organizations used to be retired and elderly members, members in private enterprises or foreign corporations, members in mobile population and unemployed members. According to the re-organization plan, those who were laid off are included in *shequ* party organizations and the incumbent party members under the jurisdiction of municipalities and of districts are placed under the co-operative control of party organizations by work unit and *shequ*. Thus these party members can be mobilized to participate in various activities in the *shequ*.[17] For example, in 2001, the Kecheng district of the city of Quzhou in Zhejiang province issued an 'Opinion Concerning Mobilizing Incumbent Party Members to Organize and Participate in *Shequ* Works'. In it, incumbent party members residing in the district were encouraged to go to the party branch to register in the 'Registration of Incumbent Party Members' and to participate in one or two *shequ* service activities. They were also asked to volunteer for propaganda education, environmental hygiene, crime watch patrol, medical and public health, the repair of household appliances, maintenance of housing environment, etc., through such initiatives as 'Party Member Volunteer Service Groups', 'Apartment Buildings in the Responsible Area of Party Members', 'Act as the Spearhead of the Communist Party', etc. As a result, more than 3,000 incumbent party members in the district registered at the *shequ* party branch by the end of 2001, more than 100 service groups of various sorts were set up, and more than 2,000 incumbent party members are able to participate in the *shequ* services at all times.[18] In order to encourage the incumbent party members to participate in voluntary activities, the party committee of Xuanwu district in the city of Nanjing reports the party members' rate of activity participation to their work unit every year, and has implemented a measure to use these data as a criterion for the evaluation of advanced units.[19]

This progress is not limited to the activities of party members; the systematic building of co-operative networks combining the vertical and horizontal chains of control has also been successful. Party construction joint meetings and party construction seminars have been held. For example, the party committee of Xueyuan street in the Xiling district of the city of Yichang (Hubei province) started the *shequ* party construction joint meeting involving 59 agencies and party organizations of work units in the *shequ*. The party members come together to decide the party's work plan and other matters.[20] Also, the party work committee of Yinxing street in the Yangpu district in Shanghai initiated the *shequ* party construction joint meeting system with the participation of 32 units in the *shequ* (the street party work committee; four government departments and agencies; six work units; five group units; twelve schools and scientific research centres, and four public utility units).

Intensifying theoretical study for party members

Educational activities are intensified for party members to strengthen their ideology and conviction as Communist Party members so that they are successful in accomplishing their role in the *shequ*. *Shequ* party organizations hold study sessions at least once a month and are encouraged to hold a seminar every 6 months for party members, inviting leaders of cities or districts, or members of the Organization Department, the Propaganda Department and the Party School as guest speakers. What they study is mainly Marxism-Leninism, Mao Zedong Thought, Deng Xiaoping Theory, Important Strategies and Policies of the Party and the Nation, various issues concerning China's entry into WTO and reforms of state-owned enterprises, improvement of knowledge and skills, etc. In addition to these study sessions, some are conducting ideological political projects in several organizations within their jurisdiction. For example, the party committee of the Xueyuan street in the district of Xiling, Yichang city, is sending 24 party construction coordinators to 58 *shequ* economic, business and social organizations to assist their ideological political activities.[21]

Active participation in services for residents

In order to have a wide range of residents recognize the party leadership in *shequ*, services for residents are provided by the *shequ* party organizations. 'The Opinion' issued in September 1996 stipulated that one of the main duties of the street party organizations is to discuss issues such as the dissemination and implementation of party lines and control of party members, as well as issues concerning the street's urban management, social services, economic development, social safety and general management, etc. The *shequ* party organizations are obligated to work with the general public and provide various services. Providing services for residents is done through the *Shequ* Party Members' Service Volunteer Society, *Shequ* Party Members' Security Service Group, *Shequ* Party Members' Environment Protection and Hygiene Group, *Shequ* Party Members' Crime Watch Patrol Group, and *Shequ* Party Members' Support and Assistance for the Poor.

Party branch secretaries holding concurrent positions as the *shequ* residents' committee officers

According to the *Complete Book of Administration*, published in June 2000, out of 300 *shequ* party cells of a certain district in a certain city, 133 (44.3 percent) were not in the residents' committees and 122 party branch secretaries (40.7 percent) were not holding concurrent posts as director or committee member of residents' committees. As a result, activities of the *shequ* party cells were rather stagnant. In many areas, one person's concurrently holding two posts: *shequ* party branch secretary and director of the *shequ* residents' committee is encouraged for long-term stability and to ensure continuous party leadership in the *shequ* party organizations.

Holding a concurrent post as *shequ* party branch secretary and director of the *shequ* residents' committee was normal practice when the members of residents' committees used to be chosen by the street party organizations and when party cells were organized by party members who were also officers in the residents' committees. But in recent years, as the party centre's guidelines call for election of officers of *shequ* residents' committees by the direct vote of residents, it becomes risky to continue this practice. If the party members sent by the district or street party organizations to assume the position of secretary of *shequ* party cells do not reside in the *shequ*, they are not entitled to run for election. On the other hand, there is a greater possibility that non-party members may be elected.

According to a survey taken (probably in the year 2000), the majority of 56 secretaries of the *shequ* party cells of Yinxing street in the Yangpu district in Shanghai responded that the direct election of residents' committee officers should take place but that the time was not ripe; or that direct elections would be disadvantageous for the leadership of the party and should not be allowed. Some also responded that reasons should not be revealed but that these direct elections should not be conducted.[22] A comprehensive book on *shequ* published in June 2000 refers to this issue as follows:

> In other words, the street offices should lay the groundwork firmly for the election of residents' committees so that residents elect party members as directors or members of residents' committees. Street party committees (or *shequ* party main cells) should lay the groundwork so that party members will elect officers of the residents' committees as branch secretaries or branch committee members.[23]

The aforementioned fundamental idea that supports the '*shequ* party construction' programme by the party's Organization Department can be summarized as follows: To maintain long-term stability and continuous leadership of the *shequ* party organization, all the party members should be organized into the street party branches, and the personnel and duty aspects of the party branches should be unified into *shequ* residents' committees. Under the policy, the holding of posts concurrently as *shequ* party branch secretary and director of the *shequ* residents' committees is aimed at in many areas. Party cells are established in the *shequ* residents' committees and party branch secretaries who hold concurrent posts as directors (or committee member) of *shequ* residents' committees are managing residents and providing services for residents. For example, in Yinxing street of Yangpu district, 41.5 percent of the 56 party branch secretaries hold a concurrent post as director of the residents' committees, and 9.4 percent of those who do not hold concurrent posts stated that their job title may be different but the work itself is the same. Likewise, 5.7 percent stated that they are mainly engaged in the administrative work of the residents' committees and there is less party administrative work.[24]

At the 99 Long *shequ* of Zhongyuan Lu in the same street, all activities of the party branch except the party's organizational work are basically identical to those of the residents' committee. The job of Ms. Jin Cheng Hong, who is the party branch secretary, is general management of the *shequ* and she assumes responsibility for a great many of the residents' committee's activities, e.g. as group leader for Safe Area Construction Group, Public Health Group, etc. She is also in charge of managing seven floors of a certain residential unit with a residents' committee officer. She has her desk inside the office of the residents' committee where she works with the residents' committee officers and attends all meetings of the residents' committee. There is no clear division of work between the party branch and the residents' committee.[25]

Unification in the personnel and duty aspects naturally leads to financial confusion. Under the policy, which encourages the party branch to be engaged in the resident management and service activities that were originally the duties of the *shequ* residents' committee, some areas have begun to pay the party branch secretaries remuneration equivalent to that of directors of *shequ* residents' committee. And it should be noted that the activity expenses of the party branches, including labour costs, are covered by the contributions from district/ street offices' finances as well as by the party expenses.[26] The current reform calls for an increase in the office expenses of *shequ* residents' committees as well as budget increases for activities of *shequ* party branch by means of financial support from districts and street offices. This gives the impression that the unification of the party, the government, and the *shequ* residents' committee is proceeding in all of the personnel, fund and duty aspects.

ISSUES OF '*SHEQU* PARTY CONSTRUCTION'

In the preceding section, the *shequ* construction policies of ODoCCP were introduced. Some members of the CCP, however, have raised objections against these policies, as follows.

First, CCP members who have little interest in *shequ* activities make the point that many incumbent party members are preoccupied with their own lives and do not have time to spare for the activities of *shequ* party organizations. According to a survey made in Yinxing street of Yangpu district, the sense of attachment to *shequ* of incumbent party members was weak and they seemed to be indifferent toward the issue of '*shequ* construction'. Some of the party members do not transfer their membership to street party organizations even after retirement, for fear of getting involved in problematic situations.[27] In surveys of incumbent party members, 24.5 percent of 56 party branch secretaries met party members who tried to hide the fact that they were party members. Consequently, *shequ* party branch secretaries in general are rather cautious in urging incumbent party members to participate in branch activities. When asked whether they agreed or disagreed with the statement that 'the activities of *shequ* party organizations were basically for unemployed or retired party members and it would not be necessary for incumbent party members to participate', 56.6 percent responded that they did not agree. But 37.8 percent responded that they agreed or they agreed basically. Furthermore, 86.8 percent agreed or basically agreed that 'it would be difficult to control incumbent party members as their organizational relationship was based on their work units'. The findings of these surveys show that many branch secretaries are aware that incumbent party members should be involved in '*shequ* party construction' but feel that this is unrealistic.[28] Moreover, it is very interesting to find that people who are not party members are more aware of activities of street party work committees and of *shequ* residents' committees.[29] The ratio of party members for open candidates for *shequ* workers is less compared to non-party members. In the survey taken in the Xihu district of the city of Hangzhou, out of 343 who passed the open test of candidates for *shequ* workers, only 50 persons (14.58 percent) were party members.[30] As shown in the data, many party members have neither the time to spend on the *shequ* work nor have greater interest than non-party-members in *shequ* work. At the National Conference and Exchange of Experiences of Street and *Shequ* Party Constructions in Medium to Small Size Cities, held in January 2002, some representatives expressed their opinions in the discussion titled 'Strengthening and Improving the Street *Shequ* Party Construction Works' that the *shequ* was the place for people to live and rest and it would not be desirable to organize *shequ* patrol units by party members, etc.[31]

The other objections are raised by those who are reconsidering the ideal stand of the party. As the personnel of *shequ* party cells and *shequ* residents' committees are either duplicated or have no distinction in their functions, *shequ* party cells have to deal with various matters including mediation of civil disputes, maintenance of public order, civil administrative services, environmental hygiene, women's affairs, etc. And they hardly have any time to spare for the duties they are supposed to perform for the party and to organize and develop party organizations.

Moreover, the results of the studies made by Lin Shangli indicate another major problem brought about by the unification with *shequ* residents' committees. The greatest advantage of the Communist Party essentially is that it is the embodiment of the social power and it is not the non-socialistic external authority or power like the administrative organ. But the positioning of the party becomes vague by carrying out administrative functions at *shequ*. Under these circumstances, organizing party cells in the *shequ* is seen as the government's intervention into societal affairs, contradicting its position to make the *shequ* autonomous. Additionally, as residents cannot make a clear distinction between party cells and the *shequ* residents' committees, they may not associate the efforts made by the party for public interests with the successful infiltration of the party's authority or with improving their opinion with respect to the party.

In fact, surveys taken via interviews show that most residents identified the party cell secretary as 'another director of their residents' committee' and did not know whether the director was a party member or not.[32] This is why Lin Shangli proposes that a clear distinction should be made between the *shequ* party organization and the *shequ* residents' committee. In other words, as long as the circumstances allow, holding concurrent posts, being party cell secretary and *shequ* residents' committee director at the same time should be avoided and *shequ* party organizations should stay away from cumbersome public services and administrative activities. By doing so, *shequ* party organizations, not being entangled in the dispute as to whether the '*shequ* construction' should be led by 'governmental' (the administration) or 'social' (or autonomy) directions, can demonstrate their leadership as the social power in '*shequ* construction' by building up the organizational ability of the *shequ* party members and by expanding their network in *shequ*. Indeed, the intention of organizing *shequ* party cells meets the goal of residents' autonomy and democracy at the grassroots level.[33] At the National Conference and Exchange of Experiences of Street and *Shequ* Party Constructions in Medium- to Small-Size Cities, mentioned earlier, the role of the party for the *shequ* residents' autonomy was discussed and the proposal was made to have the content of the discussion included in the written document. What had been said is that the party's directives should be considered as 'guidelines' and that the party and the *shequ* residents' autonomous organizations are two independent organizations in the streets and *shequ*; and that the party should not undertake all the activities of the residents' autonomous organizations.[34]

CONCLUSION: SOME OBSERVATIONS

The role of the Chinese Communist Party in '*shequ* construction' has not yet been defined. One direction is to aim for coalescence with the *shequ* residents' committee. The other is to differentiate itself from the *shequ* residents' committee, which is still viewed as the arm or agent of the district or street administrations and to adhere to the standpoint as a driving force of society.

The discussions being made regarding the CCP's position related to the '*shequ* construction' have brought into relief some points of contention as to the specific direction and guidance for the future and the ideal state of the party. The first point is on the separation of party and government. The aforementioned two opinions are presented based on the same recognition of the current situation where the *shequ* residents' committee has, at this point, a stronger function as terminal agent of the government to determine whether the party should directly perform the administrative duties of *shequ* residents' committees or whether the direction and guidance should be indirectly given through the model roles demonstrated by individual party members. The argument is similar to those related to the separation of party and government that have been repeatedly made in the political system reforms. However, the ideal state of the party that has been presented by Lin Shangli et al. introduces a second question: In what way should the party change the course of its direction and guidance under the conditions for separation of government and society? The separation is slowly but constantly taking place, and the *shequ* residents' committees and social associations will gradually lose their characteristics as the proxies of the government and strengthen the functions as representatives of social forces. To this question, Lin et al. answers: 'The greatest advantage of the Communist Party is that it is the embodiment of the social power and it is not the non-socialistic external authority or power like the administrative organ.' Then, when the separation of party and government is accomplished, can the party really provide society with direction and guidance effectively? This third point is a difficult question to answer. However, considering only the attitudes of incumbent party members toward the *shequ* work introduced in this text, the claim that the party has a persistent organizational power that enables provision of effective direction and guidance to society is unconvincing.

ENDNOTES

1   For example, the method of the payments of pensions for the elderly had changed, i.e., it used to be paid through work units to which people belonged, but payments are now made at banks or post offices in the neighbourhood. And for those who are retired and cannot go to banks or post offices on their own, the Social Insurance Agency has decided to deliver pension payments directly to the payee or ask the *shequ* service agency to deliver the payments. *Renmin ribao* (wangluoban), 26 April 2000.

2   Article 4 of the 'Urban Residents Minimum Living Allowance Act' (effective as of October 1999) states that the county departments of civil affairs, street offices and township authorities should be responsible for administration and evaluation for the urban residents' minimum living allowance. It also states that upon request of the administration and evaluation agencies, the residents' committees can provide daily administration and services.

3   *Renmin ribao*, 13 December 2000.

4   Although it is not stated in 'the Opinion', there are many cases whereby, during the period when the Community Members' Representative Congress is not in session, the *Shequ* Consultative Councils are established as the consultative supervisory agency, consisting of representatives of residents, units and members of People's Congress and the Chinese People's Political Consultative Conference.

5   See for example Mao Minghua, '*Shequ* guangli moshi zhi xuanze' [Choice of *Shequ* Construction Models], *Shehui* [Society], no. 3 (2001); Hu Zongshan, 'Quanguo *shequ* jianshe moshi pingxi' [Evaluation of *Shequ* Construction Models], *Zhongguo Minzheng* [China Civil Affairs](June 2001).

6   In Beijing, for example, the street offices hire one *shequ* business staff member per 300 family units to serve in the *shequ*. Those who are hired run for elections of the *shequ* residents' committees as directors, deputy directors or committee members. Once elected, they enter into contracts called 'Beijing *Shequ* Business Staff Employment Contracts' with the street offices.

7   In the case of Quanyuan street of Dongling district in the city of Shenyang, 16 *shequ* within the street office are given (a) the right of self-government (the right of democratic election, the right of decision-making in internal affairs, the right to manage daily affairs, financial/budgetary autonomy, the right to reject unreasonable allocation and the right to internal supervision); (b) the right to co-operate with the government and manage affairs (the rights to co-operate in carrying out duties/jobs such as urban development, environmental protection, garbage collection/disposal, affairs of the elderly, medical and public health, public safety, jurisprudence, family planning, employment, social welfare. In co-operating with the government, they are to be compensated financially); (c) the right to supervise the government (supervising government offices of all levels, street offices, personnel and their work and operations, as well as supervising public utilities such as water, gas, electricity and heating, including the activities of the real estate management firms and public

remarks made by the key Communist Party members within the *shequ*). See the Director of Civil Affairs Agency of Liaoning Province, Zhang Yongyin, 'Shenyang songbang fangquan kan zizhi' [City of Shenyang Transferred Its Authorities Downward and Lays Stress on Autonomy], *Shequ* (January 2001), p. 8.

8   (a) Tasks of the street offices include: establishing and evaluating administrative goals, enforcement of administrative matters, improving the investment environment, providing care and support to poor families, receiving and dealing with grievances, registration of corporations, etc.; (b) tasks of the street offices in which the *shequ* co-operates include: education and dissemination of lawful acts, propaganda of the national policies, managing influx of people, family planning, payment of minimum living allowances, etc.; (c) joint tasks of the street offices and *shequ* include: mediation/arbitration of civil disputes, marital status certificates, etc.; (d) tasks to be carried out by *shequ* under the leadership of the street offices include: *shequ* service works, managing *shequ* service groups, etc. Similar attempts can be seen in other districts.

9   Jing Yao, 'Jiedao fenquan de jixiao yu jiazhi _ Jianghan qu *shequ* zizhizuzhi ceping jiedao de diaocha' [The Street Offices and *Shequ* _ the Case of Jianghan], *Zhongguo Minzheng* [China Civil Affairs] (November 2001), p. 22.

10 For example, Li Baoku, the Deputy Minister of the MoCA stated during the conference on *shequ* construction in Beijing. *Shequ* (January 2001) p. 6.

11 Wang Sibin, 'Tizhi gaige zhong de chengshi *shequ* jianshe de lilun fenxi' [Analysis Related to Urban Community Constructions during the System Reform], *Shehuixue* [Sociology], no. 2 (2001), pp. 64-65.

12 According to a handbook published in April 2001, sample research conducted in Shanghai indicates that less than 5 percent of employees in Shanghai's private science and technology corporations were party members. Out of 8,326 foreign corporations in Shanghai, only 2,557 had party organizations. Out of more than 80,000 private enterprises, less than 10 percent had party organizations. It is said that those party organizations are rather inactive. Zhong Xiangting, *Jiedao shequ dangjian gongzuo shouce* [Handbook of party construction in *shequ*] (Shanxi Renmin Press, 2001), p. 16.

13 Zhong Shu, '*Shequ* dangjian shi jianqiang de zuzhi baozheng' [*Shequ* Party Construction Guarantees the Party's Organizational Strength], *Shequ* (May/June 2001), p. 8.

14 Bureau for the Organization, ODoCCP, '*Jiedao shequ dangjian gongzuo zhidao*' [Directives in Street and *Shequ* Party Construction] (Dangjian Duwu Press, 2000), pp. 135-36. Party Committee of Shijingshan District in Beijing, 'Yi "liumin" gongcheng wei zaiti jiaqiang *shequ* dangjian' [Strengthen the Activity Toward *Shequ* Party Construction by Means of Six Projects for the People], *Dangjian yanjiu neican* [Internal Reference Material of the Party Construction Study], no. 1-2 (2001).

15 Office of the Party Committee of Xihu District in the City of Hangzhou, 'Dangjian daodi zenme nan' [Why is Party Construction Difficult?], *Shequ* (December 2001), p. 14.

16   *Jiedao Shequ dangjian gongzuo zhidao*, pp. 141-42.

17   Liang Shan, '*Shequ* dangjian zenyang changhao "sanbuqu"' [How can *Shequ* Party Construction Sing Trilogy Well?], *Shequ* (December 2001), p. 15.

18   Jiang Wenxian, '*Shequ* dangjian juqile renxin' [*Shequ* Party Construction Occupied People's Minds), *Shequ*, no. 2-3 (2002), p. 9.

19   Organization Department of the Party Committee in the City of Nanjing, 'Redian zhuazhule dangjian gaohuole' [If You Have a Knack For It, The Party Construction Can be Vitalized], *Shequ*, no. 3-5 (2002), p. 9.

20   *Jiedao Shequ dangjian gongzuo zhidao*, p. 39.

21   *Ibid.*, p. 40.

22   Lin Shangli et al., *Shanghai shequ jianshe yanjiu baogao congshu, shequ dangjian yu qunzhong gongzuo, Shanghai Yangpu qu Yinxing jiedao yanjiu baogao* [Reports on *Shequ* Construction in Shanghai] (hereafter referred to as *Shequ dangjian yu qunzhong gongzuo*) (Shanghai: Shanghai daxue chubanshe, (2000), p. 73.

23   Du Zhiming, *Xin shiqi jiedao juweihui gongzuo shiwu quanshu* [Complete Administrative Book of Street Office and Residents' Committee Works in New Era] (Zhongyang Dadi Press, 2000), p. 175.

24   *Shequ dangjian yu qunzhong gongzuo*, p. 61.

25   *Ibid.*, p. 92.

26   As for the budget or financial resources to cover activities and expenses of party branches, the *Handbook for Shequ Party Construction Works*, published in April 2001, affirms that the districts, party and street offices share this responsibility. *Jiedao shequ dangjian gongzuo shouce*, p. 152.

27   *Shequ dangjian yu qunzhong gongzuo*, p. 282.

28   *Ibid.*, p. 60.

29   *Ibid.*, p. 74.

30   'Dangjian daodi zenme nan'.

31   *Shequ*, no. 2-3 (2002), p. 8.

32   *Shequ dangjian yu qunzhong gongzuo*, p. 95.

33   *Ibid.*, pp. 42, 95 and 102.

34   *Shequ*, no. 2-3 (2002), p. 8.

CHAPTER **9**

The Party and Private Entrepreneurs in the PRC

HEIKE HOLBIG

ADMITTING PRIVATE ENTREPRENEURS INTO THE CCP: DOES IT MAKE A DIFFERENCE?

In his now legendary speech of 1 July 2001, to mark the Chinese Communist Party's 80th anniversary, Party Secretary Jiang Zemin announced that the CCP would open its doors wide to admit 'outstanding elements' from the 'new social strata'. Many observers were surprised by the ideologically acrobatic speech which was purported in the international press to signify a eulogized invitation of private entrepreneurs into the CCP. Particularly in Western countries, the step was interpreted as a heartened acknowledgement by the communist party leadership that the country had finally found its way home back into the capitalist world. Strong criticism voiced by alleged 'hardliners' such as Deng Liqun and others who accused Jiang Zemin of betraying the CCP by admitting 'capitalists' and 'exploiters' seemed to confirm that this indeed represented a major breakthrough in the party's ideological and organizational design.[1]

Conventional wisdom had it that the party leadership finally had decided to acknowledge the enormous contributions of the private sector and to broaden its own social base by representing the interests not only of the 'proletariat' but also of the new social elites. This move was said to aim at preventing the defection of a new bourgeois middle class, pre-empting the emergence of a potential political opposition and bolstering the power of the one-party state. With this 'revolutionary' step, Jiang Zemin was seen to have created a personal hallmark that would stand

239

out in party history before handing over the reins to the next generation of leaders.

However, when the moment of surprise was over, observers who looked more closely at the event had to realize that the admittance of entrepreneurs into the party was, after all, not such a new thing. In fact, quite a number of private entrepreneurs seem to have joined the party before, indicating that the CCP doors had actually been open to this group for a while already. As Jiang Zemin's proposal is going to be enshrined officially as the CCP's new policy, it seems worthwhile to test the conventional assumptions and to ask whether it really does make a difference, and, if so, what kind of difference.

To address this question, this paper first seeks to analyse in some depth the various statistical categories and numbers to elucidate the not so clear-cut notions of 'private entrepreneur', 'private enterprise', 'private sector', etc. A second section will piece together the information we have about CCP membership among various kinds of entrepreneurs. Based on these findings, a third section will then discuss various motives and strategies which may be behind the decision of the party to admit private entrepreneurs, and their implications for representing the interests and political participation of the new economic elites. Here, ideological, financial and organizational aspects will be taken into account. It will be suggested that, although there are serious ideological barriers to the inclusion of 'capitalists' into the party, the move can be seen as a rational organizational strategy to secure the CCP's status as 'vanguard of the working class' - albeit with an extended definition of the term. Yet, the main goal of this paper is not to answer questions but to identify relevant new questions and analytical topics which could or should be addressed in future research on the relations between the party and private entrepreneurs.

DECONSTRUCTING THE PRIVATE SECTOR: CATEGORIES AND NUMBERS

At first glance, it seems quite clear what is meant by the 'private sector' in China. As the English language service of Xinhua reported in April 2002, 'the share of the private sector in China's GDP has reached 33 percent, a little lower than the 37 percent of the state-owned economy'.[2]

Unfortunately, as is the case in many English media reports, a definition of the 'private sector' or of 'private enterprise' is not given.

Traditionally, PRC statistics used to differentiate four sectors of the economy by the criterion of ownership of the means of production, namely the state-owned, the collective, the private and the foreign-funded. Among them, the category 'private' was always the hardest to define. In the Chinese language, the term that comes closest to 'private enterprise' is *siying qiye*, a notion that was sanctioned for official use in 1988 to signify enterprises with privately owned assets employing at least eight people. The latter criterion was to distinguish them from the smaller *geti gongshanghu (getihu)*, the 'single industrial and commercial proprietors' or 'self-employed entrepreneurs' who employ less than eight persons and do not represent formal enterprises in the sense of legal entities. Together, these two categories form the core entities of what is understood as the 'private sector' proper, reported to comprise more than 20 percent of China's GDP.[3] These 'private entrepreneurs' are still today often imagined as rural and urban self-made men, stereotypically lowly educated but with lots of entrepreneurial wit who have braved the storms of the emerging Chinese market economy.

Statistical numbers for the private enterprises (*siying qiye*) are the most unambiguous and easy to access. According to official statistics, at the end of 2000, 1.76 million *siying qiye* were registered across the country, employing 24.06 million persons.[4] The most recent figure reported for the end of 2001 is 2.03 million private enterprises, an increase which continues the rapid growth trend of the 1990s when the number of private enterprises on average increased by 35 percent per year (see figures below).[5] Concerning the numbers of self-employed individuals (*getihu*), official statistics reported a decrease over the past two years. While the number of registered *getihu* had been growing steadily over the past two decades to reach 31 million in 1999, the figure decreased to 25.71 million at the end of 2000, and further to 24.23 million at the end of 2001.[6] This reversal of the trend - which seems to be caused by a technical change in statistical recording - has produced no little confusion. Some Chinese sources tend to ignore the decrease and instead extrapolate the former figures; others seem to treat *getihu* as a residual category; still others exclude the category of *getihu* altogether without making clear where the 'self-employed individuals' have gone.[7]

FIGURE 1 NUMBER OF REGISTERED PRIVATE ENTERPRISES
(*SIYING QIYE*), 1989

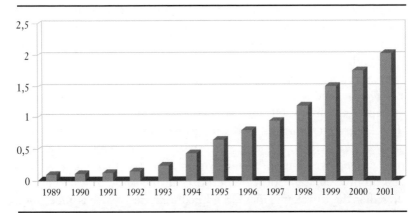

Source: Data made available by the Administration for Industry and
Commerce (*Gongshangju*) in July 2001; data for 2001: *Renmin ribao* website,
15 September 2002.

FIGURE 2   NUMBER OF EMPLOYEES IN PRIVATE
ENTERPRISES (*SIYING QIYE*), 1989-2000 (IN MILLIONS)

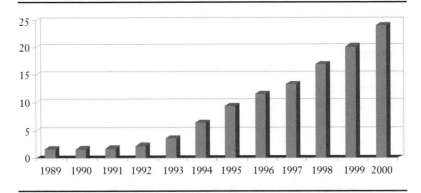

Source: Data made available by the Administration for Industry and Commerce
(*Gongshangju*) in July 2001.

Less unambiguous are the data available for the number of people
employed in the *siying jingji*, the 'private economy', comprising both
private enterprises (*siying qiye*) and self-employed individuals' (*getihu*)

enterprises. Official statistics reported 82.63 million people employed by *siying qiye* and *getihu* at the end of 1999, and 74.77 million one year later - the decrease being due to the shrinking number of *getihu* in the same period.[8] A recent report published in the official media gave a figure of 74.74 million employees in the private economy for the end of 2001.[9] Quite differently, an article published in late 2001 in *Zhonggongdangshi yanjiu* puts the total of people working in private enterprises and self-employed enterprises (*jiuye renshu*) at 130 million – without explaining how this high number is derived.[10] Concerning the number of employees in private enterprises (*siying qiye*), there is also some ambiguity. According to the *Statistical Yearbook*, in late 2000, one private enterprise employed 13.66 persons on average.[11] A recent study of the private sector presented by the Chinese Academy for Social Sciences (CASS) reports a ratio of 11.38 employees per private enterprise, based on official registration figures. The same source, however, also cites a nationwide sampling survey which found that one private enterprise employed 55 people on average (with more than 90 percent of them working as low-skilled blue-collar workers in labour-intensive sectors).[12] Nobody really seems to know how many people are employed in the private economy.

Things become even more ambiguous when alternative concepts of the 'private economy' are taken into account. As a rule, the more ideologically correct a term is, the more statistically vague it becomes. While the term *siying jingji* (literally 'privately operated economy') is used without much reservation in coastal regions, representatives from less developed regions often prefer the term *minying jingji*, or 'economy operated by the people', to avoid the capitalist connotations of the word *si*, private.[13] Should the *minying jingji*, at some point in the future, account for the largest share of GDP, then this would be much more palatable than a dominant 'private' (*siying*) sector.

An ideologically still more cautious notion is the term *fei gongyouzhi jingji*, or 'not publicly-owned economy'. It defines the private sector in a negative manner, including all ownership forms that are not state-owned, thus comprising not only *getihu* and *siying qiye*, but also foreign-invested enterprises and a large variety of mixed ownership forms (among them shareholding companies, 'red hat' and other forms of nominally collective enterprises which will be discussed below). Although these latter types are in many cases actually run as private enterprises, they are not formally acknowledged as belonging to the 'private economy' (*siying jingi*), a term that still is reserved for enterprises with private capital assets of at least 90 percent. Thus, the term *fei gongyouzhi jingji* is ideologically more correct but statistically less transparent. As parts of the hybrid ownership forms are included, the category produces much higher figures than the category *siying jingji*. Already in 1996, the *fei gongyouzhi jingji* was reported to account for 31 percent of industrial output value and 53 percent of consumer goods retail sales; the shares are said to have been growing year by year since then.[14] According to recent word-of-mouth information, the figures have risen to 38 and 62 percent respectively in 2001.

The statistical deviations between these various categories reflect a high degree of ambiguity in the classification of enterprises. Of course, to some degree the deviations result from the reformulation of statistical concepts in the official process of diversification of ownership forms. However, they are also the outcome of strategies used intentionally by entrepreneurs to cover themselves in a cloak of ambiguity. Various strategies have allowed them to circumvent the discriminations against private firms which, to a greater or lesser degree, are still prevailing today, such as limited access to finance, regulatory restrictions of enterprise size and operation, and ideological harassments by the party-state. Among the most popular strategies have been the following:

- *Leasing collective firms*: Starting from the early 1980s, many ailing collective enterprises were leased out for private operation. The entrepreneur paid the collective a fixed rent and operated the firm as if it were his own private enterprise. Quite often, these entrepreneurs accumulated large capital assets, thus gradually reducing the share of the collective assets. In some cases, this led to the transformation into a solely privately owned firm. Others, however, preferred to stay in disguise and to continue to operate as leased collectives.
- *'Wearing a red hat'*: Particularly in the countryside, many firms that were actually privately owned were registered as collectively owned enterprises, among them most township and village enterprises (TVEs, Chinese: *xiangzhen qiye*). This prevalent strategy of 'wearing a red hat' (*dai hong maozi*) secured them access to land, assets, finance and markets, as well as tax breaks, favourable contracts, loans on preferential terms or other forms

of subsidies by the local governments who, in turn, participated in the profits these firms made. Although local governments started in the middle of the 1990s to encourage the transformation of these firms into private enterprises in order to reduce the budgetary costs, 'red hat' enterprises still exist in large numbers today, owing to the continuing advantages of local government involvement.

• *'Roundtripping' of domestic capital*: Other domestic entrepreneurs (re)invested their capital on the mainland through offshore companies - often existing as mere 'letterbox companies' in Hong Kong - in order to qualify as foreign investors. As the Chinese government decided very early in the reform process to offer significant tax breaks and other advantages to foreign enterprises (joint ventures or Sino-foreign co-operation enterprises with domestic state-owned or collective enterprises), the roundtripping of capital allowed domestic entrepreneurs to partake in these privileges. With China's accession to the World Trade Organization in 2001 and the application of the 'national treatment' requirement, however, privileges to foreign investors should be reduced considerably over the next years, and with them the incentives for this kind of roundtripping of domestic capital.

• *Co-investing with state and collective firms*: Last but not least, many private entrepreneurs have decided to co-invest with state or collective firms to create larger mixed-ownership companies, mostly under the legal form of limited joint-stock or shareholding companies. Co-investing with public sector actors may have the advantage of overcoming entry barriers set for private firms in particular sectors (industries considered vital to the national economy; industries whose products entail certain public hazards; and industries using scarce resources - though some restrictions have been abolished during the past two years). Giving shares to local government and party cadres or paying them positions as advisors or board members may also induce other more informal advantages. A Jiangsu entrepreneur explained in an interview in Spring 2001 how he had tactically and elegantly distributed the shares of his firm between his wife, various other family members and key figures in the local government, not neglecting the local community authority which obtained 0.5 percent of his company's shares.[15]

These strategies demonstrate that the private sector in China is far from presenting a clear-cut entity. Instead, the regulatory and ideological restrictions confronting private entrepreneurship have produced many incentives to create tactical ambiguity about the firm's ownership form. The more successful private entrepreneurs are, the more they will be inclined to obscure their categorization as part of the 'private sector' and to join the hybrid sector of mixed ownership and management forms. To tackle this ambiguity, administrators have started to give up the increasingly obsolete ownership categories and instead to lump the various categories together by simply distinguishing between 'small and medium enterprises' (*zhong xiao qiye*, which are reported to make up 80-90 percent of Chinese enterprises) and 'large enterprises' (most of which are state-owned enterprises).[16] Although this might be a more realistic approach, it does not help to clarify the existence of 'true private entrepreneurship' in China.

David Goodman presents an even more disturbing message. In a study on entrepreneurs conducted during 1996-98 in Shanxi province, he argues that a complex sector of the economy has emerged between the state-planned and the privately owned sector which has to be acknowledged as a key feature of provincial economic development. Apart from the traditional state-run enterprises on the one side and the formal private sector enterprises on the other, a hybrid variety of ownership structures, management systems, registration and incorporation systems and scales of operation has sprung into existence over the past decade. Goodman characterizes this hybrid sector as the new 'public sector' of the economy in the sense that it is relatively open to market forces and public equity. Among them, he identifies:

- *urban enterprises* including collectives and share-based companies established by state-run enterprises and social units, as well as urban collectives of more pre-reform types;
- *rural enterprises* including collectives and stock companies established by townships, villages and rural districts, taking advantage of the rural sector's preferential economic regulations;
- *wholly or partly foreign-funded enterprises*, often former private sector or state-run enterprises which have been transformed into larger firms through foreign investment;
- *so-called 'public sector private enterprises'* private enterprises which have become either collective enterprises through co-operation with local

governments or which have become share-based public companies, but where the original individual entrepreneur remains in the senior management position.[17]

Looking at the personal backgrounds and risk-taking approaches among the entrepreneurs and managers of the different types of state-run, private and 'public sector' enterprises, Goodman concludes:

> Indeed, whilst entrepreneurship is certainly to be found in the private sector of the economy, the more successful entrepreneurship is located outside the formal private sector in the new hybrid series of arrangements that exists between the state-run and private sector.[18]

With this finding, Goodman indeed shakes the myth of the dynamism of the private economy contrasting with the inertia of the public economy. According to his study, the most outstanding entrepreneurs are to be found not in the private sector but in the hybrid public-private ownership sector. If his observation is true not only for Shanxi province but for other regions too, then the question arises: Who exactly does the CCP leadership have in mind when extending the invitation to join the party? The question becomes all the more tricky when we realize that a large number of entrepreneurs are already in the party.

WHO IS CO-OPTING WHOM?
PARTY BACKGROUND OF ENTREPRENEURS

Statistics on the percentage of party members among entrepreneurs are available but rather scattered. Relevant data can be found in the secondary literature of the past years and in some recent official and semi-official Chinese publications.

Starting at the bottom end of percentage shares, Andrew Walder found in a nationwide representative sample conducted in 1996 that 2.6 percent of those classified as *getihu* and 14.8 percent of private entrepreneurs (obviously *siying qiye*) were party members.[19] These numbers seem quite low, but things look different when we take the firms' scale of operation into account. As various business associations are competing with one another at the local level to induce the larger and more 'representative' enterprises to become members, their membership data are quite revealing here. In particular, the All-China Federation of Industry and Commerce (ACFIC) and its provincial and local subsidiaries (also called *minjian shanghui* or 'non-governmental chambers of commerce'), which have been mandated by the CCP's United Front department specifically to represent the private sector enterprises, offer relevant information. Thus, recent ACFIC data reveal that the share of CCP members among its own members has already increased beyond 20 percent. For Anhui province, the provincial chamber data set for 2001 gives a number of 22 percent of member entrepreneurs who belong to the party.[20] These numbers are confirmed by other recent Chinese data. The *Almanac of Private Economy in China 2000* reported that 19.8 percent (or 4.3 million) of China's private entrepreneurs (obviously *siying qiye*) in 1999 were party members.[21]

Still higher shares of party members have been reported by Bruce Dickson, who conducted a survey in eight counties in Zhejiang, Shandong, Hebei and Hunan in 1997 and 1999 which included, among others, more than 500 private entrepreneurs. In this survey, which was not conceived as a random sample but intentionally designed to represent the local economic and political elites, Dickson found that almost 40 percent of all responding entrepreneurs were already CCP members; among them, 24.6 percent were *xiahai* entrepreneurs, or former officials who had left their posts and 'plunged into the sea' of the private economy; 13.4 percent were formal private entrepreneurs who had been co-opted into the CCP as a result of their business success at some point in the past. Among the members of various business associations, he found the highest percentage shares of CCP members among members of local subsidiaries of the ACFIC; among them, 34.7 percent had a background as *xiahai* entrepreneurs and 16.8 percent as private entrepreneurs who were later co-opted into the CCP. Together, more than half of the responding ACFIC members were CCP members when the survey was conducted. Also quite strikingly, more than one-quarter (26.7 percent) of the entrepreneurs in the sample responded that they wanted to join the party, with about the half of them having applied for CCP membership already.[22]

As we understand now, growing numbers of entrepreneurs had de facto been admitted as party members at the local level by various 'flexible methods' (*biantong fangshi*) since the 1980s[23] - despite the fact that Article 1 of the CCP statute excludes entrepreneurs as possible

CCP members, and despite a Central Committee document of 1989, which explicitly banned private entrepreneurs from joining the party (see below). Municipal and county party committees decided high-handedly to recruit local magnates for pragmatic reasons - be it to participate more effectively in the wealth of private entrepreneurs, or because they realized that they could not find enough competent people to run as village party secretaries if they excluded private entrepreneurs. In order to circumvent the official ban, some private entrepreneurs signed their firms over to their spouses and applied for party membership as 'employees' of their own firm.[24]

Percentage shares rise further when we do not focus on the formal private sector, but look at the various hybrid enterprise forms identified above. Many of these hybrid enterprises are not run by entrepreneurs in the sense of private owner-operators but by managers taking entrepreneurial risks and contributing with entrepreneurial skills. It seems to be this wider group of managers and entrepreneurs in the hybrid private-public sector which Jiang Zemin had in mind when he invited into the CCP 'outstanding elements' of the 'new social strata'. In his speech, he named 'among others, entrepreneurs and technical personnel employed by scientific and technical enterprises of the non-public sector, managerial and technical staff employed by foreign-funded enterprises, the self-employed, private entrepreneurs, employees in intermediaries, and freelance professionals'.[25]

In the above-mentioned study conducted by David Goodman among Shanxi business people, he found that 39 percent of owner-operators in the formal private sector (many of them confirming the stereotype of young and lowly-educated self-made men) were CCP members. While this share is already high, he found significantly larger shares among the generally better educated, and sometimes older, managers and entrepreneurs in what he identified as the hybrid 'public sector'. Thus, 71 percent of urban enterprise managers, 77 percent of rural entrepreneurs, 73 percent of joint venture managers and 56 percent of 'public sector private entrepreneurs' were found to be party members. Also, among the mostly young and highly educated people who were hired by formal private enterprises as managers due to their specialized professional skills, 66 percent were CCP members; all of them had entered the party after 1978.[26]

The above-mentioned *Research Report on Social Strata in Contemporary China* published by CASS in late 2001, which is based on samples from four different localities in China, offers some revealing and somewhat surprising information in this context. The study found that the share of CCP members ranged between 5.2 and 13.7 percent among self-employed entrepreneurs, and between 0 and 24.4 percent among private entrepreneurs (with 85.2 percent of private entrepreneurs in Shenzhen found to be members of the Communist Youth League, the CCP's traditional recruitment pool). Strikingly, the figures are significantly higher among managers (*jingli renyuan*): here, shares of CCP members vary from 35.7 to 58.8 percent (with a record high of 97.1 percent of managers in Hefei, Anhui province, found to be present or former members of the Communist Youth League). Clearly, these percentage shares are much higher than among industrial workers, where the share of CCP members ranges between 5.9-13.3 percent, and among agricultural workers with a range of 4.3-5.2 percent).[27]

Confronted with these figures, and recollecting the fact that the ratio of CCP members among the overall populace is less than 5 percent, the party seems to have attracted managers and entrepreneurs quite successfully in the past already. Why, if the new economic elites - or, at least, their most outstanding representatives - are already party members, should the CCP be interested in 'opening the doors wide' to the 'new social strata' in the future?

EX-POST LEGITIMIZATION OF A LONG-STANDING FACT: IDEOLOGICAL STRATEGIES

The simple answer to the question why private entrepreneurs are now officially admitted into the CCP is that the party leadership is attempting to legitimize what has already been occurring for many years. The need for an ex-post legitimization might have seemed all the more pressing as the ideological revaluation of private entrepreneurs has been increasingly lagging behind the rise of their constitutional status in recent years. Since the start of economic reforms, the most important steps in the constitutional career of the private sector were the recognition of individual economic activities as being complementary to the state sector in 1982, the recognition of the private economy as being a complement to the socialist public economy in 1988, and the recognition of the private economy (*feigongyouzhi jingji*) as an 'important component of the socialist market economy' (*shehuizhuyi shichang jingji de zhongyao zucheng bufen*) plus the provision of constitutional protection of this sector (Art. 11) in 1999.

Party ideology with its inbuilt safeguards against 'capitalists', 'exploiters' etc. found it hard to parallel the steady economic and constitutional rise of the private sector, although there were some earlier attempts to bolster the ideological status of private entrepreneurs. During the 13th Party Congress in 1987, Zhao Ziyang, then General-Secretary of the CCP, arranged for the 'Guan Guangmei phenomenon' to be presented as a showcase to the public. Guan Guangmei was a Liaoning party member who had taken the lead in leasing an ailing state-owned enterprise and turning it into a profitable private enterprise. Since then, private entrepreneurs started to join the party in significant numbers, provoking an intra-party controversy on the topic of 'exploitation'.[28] The Tiananmen protests in 1989 caused a setback; in August of this year, the Central Committee published its Document 1989 No. 9, which explicitly banned private entrepreneurs from joining the CCP (Jiang Zemin, then incoming Party Secretary, supported the ban explicitly at the time). Starting in the early 1990s, Deng Xiaoping helped to step up the political status of private entrepreneurs. In his theory of the 'three benefits' (*sange liyu*), which was also incorporated in the official document of the15th Party Congress in 1997, he argued that the standard to measure whether an ownership system was good or bad was 'whether or not it benefits the development of productive forces in a socialist society, the improvement of overall national strength, and the improvement of people's lives.'[29] What he refrained from doing, however, was establishing criteria for representatives from the private sector to qualify as CCP members.

Since early 2000, when Jiang Zemin introduced to the public the so-called 'requirements of the three representations' (*sange daibiao*), he has paved the way for a full ideological emancipation of private entrepreneurs. Claiming that the CCP has always to 'represent the development trend of China's advanced productive forces (1), the orientation of China's advanced culture (2), and the fundamental interests of the overwhelming majority of the people in China (*zui guangda renmin de genben liyi*) (3)', he builds upon Deng Xiaoping's 'three benefits'. By putting the stress of the argument on the development of the 'productive forces' (1), attention is shifted away from the notion of the 'relations of production', which, according to Marxism-Leninism, creates the contradictions between classes and determines whether a social system is either capitalist (exploitative) or socialist (non-exploitative). By actively supporting the development of the most 'advanced' production forces, class struggle becomes irrelevant. The other crucial manipulation of party ideology is the notion of the 'overwhelming majority of the people' which the CCP is required to represent. As sensitive readers in China seem to have understood very early on, this notion - which at first glance simply seems to reaffirm the CCP's 'mass line' idea - has been intentionally formulated by Jiang Zemin to include basically *all* social classes, or, as the concept of 'class' has been made irrelevant, all social strata.[30]

Also, obviously in an effort to bolster the image of private entrepreneurs who are still widely seen as stingy rustics with a low 'cultural calibre' (*wenhua suzhi*), a hierarchy is being created among new social strata: Situated at the top of this hierarchy are 'entrepreneurs and technical personnel employed by scientific and technical enterprises of the non-public sector'. Next come 'managerial and technical staff employed by foreign-funded enterprises', and only then are the self-made type of private entrepreneur, the self-employed and others mentioned. This preoccupation with the higher realms of science and technology (S&T) seems to resonate with older mystical beliefs in the modernizing power and scientistic debates of the late nineteenth and the early twentieth centuries in China. This aspect becomes very obvious in a *Qiushi* article of November 2001, which describes the 'key contribution' of the new social strata to the 'building of a socialist economy':

> The broad masses in the new social strata are all engaged in economic operations to adapt to the objective needs of the development of a socialist market economy. Private S&T enterprises and their leading technicians with their flexible and efficient operating forces are engaged in market economy operations, with their entrepreneurs and technicians applying leading S&T to the development of new products. ... The broad masses in such new social strata are playing a key role in promoting S&T progress, revitalizing the market, optimizing the disposition of resources, expanding job avenues, meeting diverse social needs, and increasing overall social productivity, to promote the development of the national economy.[31]

Perhaps the most important element in this legitimization strategy is the establishment of a set of criteria for admitting entrepreneurs into the party. Here, the somewhat tautological formula presented in Jiang Zemin's July speech goes: 'The main criteria to admit a person into the Party are whether he or she works wholeheartedly for the implementation of the party's line and programme and meets the requirements for party membership.'[32] This formula obviously was regarded as too vague; consequently, party organs in the following months set out to clarify the criteria for party membership. Thus, at the end of August, a much more specific set of requirements was made public. According to a Xinhua report, entrepreneurs who wanted to join the party would have to (1) be law-abiding patriotic citizens, (2) not be guilty of tax-evasion, (3) reinvest the major part of their profits, and (4) to repay society out of the wealth they have accumulated.[33] Here, the delegation of socio-economic responsibilities to the 'new rich' appears as an important rationale behind the move to invite entrepreneurs into the CCP. Another *Qiushi* article of November 2001 offers a major discussion of the criteria of party membership, recommending rules to establish a person's qualification to join the party. The core passage goes:

> The introduction of these principal criteria for recruiting new party members requires that we be strict in guarding the gates to the party as well as the gates of ideology. ...The two basic requirements of "wholeheartedly struggling for the implementation of the party's line and programme" and of "meeting the requirements for party membership" should be handled as one single criterion; observation of practical performance, as well as the motive for joining the party, should be integrated, while one-sidedness should be avoided. ...Efforts should be made to strictly prevent those with impure motives from being admitted into the party and to avoid using erroneous methods to measure the new requirements for party membership, such as admission based on economic strength, on the amount of material donation to society, and on personal reputation.[34]

The main thrust of this argument seems to be to pacify those who fear that the CCP might admit persons simply for the sake of their wealth and business success, or persons whose main motive is to abuse the party's organizational network for their own commercial interests - a fear that seems quite reasonable. The attempt of ideological justification comes very close to more pragmatic motives of admitting entrepreneurs into the party, which will be discussed below.

253

The CCP leadership is conscious of the fact that many regard the party's efforts to justify itself ideologically as highly cynical. As Børge Bakken points out, the 'three representations' imply the revision of the Marxist theory of labour and labour value which has formed the core theory of Marxism and thus lie at the heart of the CCP's identity as the 'vanguard of the working class'.[35] The fundamental contradiction between 'capitalists' and 'proletarian masses', between 'exploiters' and 'exploited', which has been internalized in China's socialist discourse over decades, clearly stands in the way of accepting the CCP's new claim to represent *both* - labour *and* capital, workers *and* entrepreneurs. Party theorists and social scientists have recently collaborated intensively to find a formula to reconcile the contradictions, at least rhetorically, and they have come up recently with a pair of innovatively coined concepts. Workers and peasants are classified as 'basic labourers' (*jichu laodong*), while entrepreneurs and managers, the new economic elites, are coined as 'management labourers' (*guanli laodong*, or *jingying guanli laodong*) with their specific, and in fact, qualitatively more valuable contributions to social and economic progress. The CCP of course, according to its traditional mission as the 'vanguard of the working class', has to represent all workers of the modern economy, basic labourers as well as management labourers.[36]

Whether one reads this formula as an enlightened departure from Marxist dogmatism or as pure cynicism depends on one's own ideological standpoint. Theoretically, the concept of social(ist) democracy, which has been debated in Chinese leadership circles for several years, could offer a framework for a broad representation of all social strata in the CCP. Yet, acceptance of the new formula should hinge not so much on the adequate use of ideological labels but on the perception of real opportunities. Even those social groups who have lost out most in the reform process would probably not cite the classical Marxist concepts of exploitation of surplus value to prove the party regime wrong, but rather demand that they themselves, or their children, get better chances to participate in the country's economic growth and catch up with the new economic elites whatever they are called. Here, I would argue in line with Torstein Hjellum that the party regime will have a basis of legitimacy as long as it allows sufficient upward mobility for workers and peasants to enter the elite ranks.[37] However, should the 'three representations' aim not so much at opening the party up to the 'new social strata' but rather, as Børge Bakken suggests, at 'closing the door to groups further down in the social hierarchy',[38] then the CCP's basis of legitimacy may indeed crumble rapidly.

REPAYING SOCIETY: MATERIAL MOTIVES

Considering more pragmatic reasons for the CCP to invite entrepreneurs, of course, one would first of all think of financial motives. As it is always advantageous to be in the company of rich people, local party committees might wish to participate more in the wealth of the new economic elites and the charisma that radiates from it. More specifically, while the party-state as a whole will not have any difficulty in financing its own activities, it should be interested in devolving some of its social tasks to the newly rich.

Thus, in the first half of 2001, chambers of the All-China Federation of Industry and Commerce mobilized their members to take part in a public relations campaign titled 'Two think-ofs' (*liang si*). With its motto 'Being wealthy, yet think of the sources [of wealth], enjoying prosperity, yet think of development', the campaign appealed to private entrepreneurs to be cognizant of their social responsibility and pay their share for social, educational, cultural and infrastructure projects in their communities or in other parts of the country - some in the far West. The so-called 'Glorious Cause' (*guangcai shiye*) activities organized by party and mass organizations and financed by more or less voluntary philanthropists among the newly rich have, in the meantime, grown into a nationwide network which involves significant 'private' financial transactions.[39]

Also, by inducing more private entrepreneurs into the reach of the party-state, some might hope to improve the tax discipline of the new economic elites. While tax evasion seems to have been a kind of sport among private and self-employed entrepreneurs since the 1980s, the state has tried since the mid-1990s to consolidate the legal basis of tax collection in the private and the hybrid public-private sector, but with mixed success. Although private enterprises and individually owned enterprises together account for more than 20 percent of GDP, they are reported to contribute less than 10 percent (in some places less than 5 percent) to the local coffers.[40]

Connected with these financial aspects is the fear of some that admitting private entrepreneurs into the CCP will strengthen the role of 'money politics', making corruption even more widespread than it already is.[41] As the above-mentioned CASS report complains, there are already quite a number of private entrepreneurs who regard themselves as 'special citizens' (*teshu gongmin*) or are so regarded in their local communities. Thus, they bribe local officials in order to obtain 'political loans' (*zhengzhixing daikuan*) and other preferential treatment, and show off their wealth through conspicuous consumption, which leads to moral decay. Some of them even link up with triads and other criminal organizations, exerting a very bad influence on local politics.[42] Of course, with more financial capacity entering the party, to fear that this will inflate corruption seems a legitimate concern. On the other hand, one could argue that, compared to the bribery and red tape practised at present, corruption will not necessarily increase in the wake of more entrepreneurs joining the party. As entrepreneurs will not have to 'take the back entrance' (*zou houmen*) but will be able, as party members now themselves, to 'take the front entrance' ('*zou qianmen*') to realize their goals, overall corruption may well diminish and 'money politics' may become more transparent than it used to be in the past.

CO-OPTING THE NEW ELITES: STRATEGIES OF INCLUSION

Another prevailing argument is that the admission of entrepreneurs into the CCP is to be interpreted as a strategy to co-opt the new elites: a strategy of inclusion that allows an organization to add new skills and resources, enhance its performance, increase political support etc., thereby 'avert[ing] threats to its stability or existence'.[43] According to this interpretation, by incorporating private entrepreneurs, the party mitigates the political pressures from these people. By bestowing on entrepreneurs the prestige of being part of the ruling party and giving them a say in decision-making, the CCP ultimately aims at preventing the emergence of a bourgeois middle class which could form an autonomous political force and thus challenge the CCP's power. In a word, the co-optation of new economic elites is designed to pre-empt a potential political threat which a future middle class or bourgeoisie could pose to the CCP's one-party dominance.[44]

This argument is used by CCP ideologues, too, whose mission is to promote the admission of the new 'outstanding elements'. Thus, some of them warn that if the party does not reach out to the new elites, they could, at some point in the future, form an organized oppositional force challenging the party's authority. As one article published in late 2001 in *Zhonggongdangshi yanjiu* argued, the CCP has to learn a lesson from the worldwide decay of communism: The reason why the power of the Soviet Union's and other countries' communist regimes collapsed was the fact that they had failed to adapt their social base in accordance with the structural change of the social strata, thus 'losing the support of the youth, particularly of young entrepreneurs active in the new economy and of young intellectuals'. To prevent a collapse of power similar to that of the Soviet Union, the CCP should follow the trend of the more successful socialist democratic parties worldwide and adapt its social base to absorb outstanding elements from the newly emerging middle strata (*xinxing zhongjian jieceng*), among them entrepreneurs, white-collar workers and intellectuals. Should the party fail to do so, the author warns, these people 'will necessarily develop this or that idea' (*shibi hui chancheng zheyang nayang de xiangfa*), some will join one of the democratic parties, or even join forces with other parties to form an opposition party (*chengwei yige fanduipai*)'.[45]

Now, we should ask ourselves how realistic such a scenario is indeed. More specifically, is there really something like a new middle class in the making, with an independent bourgeois mindset and political ambitions of its own, which the party has to prevent from taking over its power? As we have seen above, there are large differences in the social, educational and professional backgrounds of the various groups of entrepreneurs and managers, with the sidewalk shoe-shine *getihu* at one extreme, and the US-trained manager of a modern 'S&T' enterprise, investment corporation or foreign-invested firm at the other. Also, the oft-cited discrimination against the private economy does not apply uniformly across the various ownership and management forms. While some enterprises may find it hard to access bank credit, land or raw materials, others may have found a viable mode of symbiosis with the local authorities which secures them privileged access to finance and other resources as well as political insurance. With the enormous differences in mind, it still seems hard to imagine the emergence of a homogeneous social group pursuing a collective set of strategies in a consistent manner, at least for the time being. As Bruce Dickson maintains: 'So far, China's private entrepreneurs have not asserted themselves as an organized or coherent interest group.'[46]

Yet, according to the CASS report, a social identity of private entrepreneurs is in the making. Although they do not yet form a political force of their own, private entrepreneurs are found to gradually develop a sense of common bonds and belonging. What binds them together is, after decades of repeated class struggle, the desire to regain full social and political acceptance as well as legal protection of their properties and activities. Only if they can trust that the severe ideological discrimination against 'capitalists' in the past will not be repeated in the future, the report argues, will entrepreneurs be ready to reinvest substantial parts of their profits. Also, the study finds, while the majority of entrepreneurs are restricting their activities to speaking business (*zai shang yan shang*), aiming just to protect or promote their individual status, a minority has become politically active, articulating specific political demands. Thus, for example, they lobby for a positive business environment and a stable implementation of economic policies, for the enhancement of their social and political status (e.g. for the right to be eligible as 'model workers'), for legal guarantees and for more direct participation in the party-state's decision-making process.[47]

If these findings are true, a rationale might indeed have taken shape in CCP leadership circles to include the more active and articulate elements among the new social strata into the party rather than risk their political defection. However, we have to ask ourselves again whether the new policy of admitting entrepreneurs into the party does indeed make a difference here. Inclusionary politics have been practised by the party-state in the past. Various mechanisms of inclusion have existed for a long time, such as 'arranging' (*anpai*) for entrepreneurs to serve as delegates to people's congresses or the political consultative congresses at all administrative levels, to let them articulate their interests via the ACFIC and its local subsidiaries, or via other associations and mass organizations, etc. Strikingly, many of these traditionally 'arranged' political representatives of the private economy are already CCP members - which can be easily explained by the fact that it is always the most prestigious entrepreneurs who are selected for 'political' posts. As Bruce Dickson found in his sample of eight counties, 78 percent of private entrepreneurs in people's congresses and 61 percent in political consultative congresses were party members.[48] Therefore one could argue that the strategy of co-optation has been applied quite successfully already.

Given such a high degree of overlapping political roles among private entrepreneurs, the question arises whether the admission of more entrepreneurs into the CCP might not merely lead to a duplication of leverage of those groups who have already been politically active in the past. Of course, the new policy would make a difference if it were to allow representatives of the private sector to take over politically influential party or government posts. Otherwise, bestowing the most prestigious private entrepreneurs with CCP membership, for them could just mean another honorary ornament without much significance for political participation. Much more detailed information will be needed to find out more about the reality of inclusionary politics vis-à-vis the private sector.

STRETCHING THE CCP GRASSROOTS: ORGANIZATIONAL MOTIVES

Another - more tangible and perhaps more decisive - motive for inviting private entrepreneurs into the CCP may be the steady decline of the party's organizational influence in the economy which has been recorded over the past two decades. In the traditional state-owned sector, the party was not only omnipresent but in most cases dominant in the firms' management. With the growth of the private and hybrid sectors, however, the party's presence has been reduced quite dramatically. While the total number of party members has developed proportionally with the increase of population (June 2002: 66.4 million members, which equals about 5 percent of the population), the CCP's organizational reach has been shrinking significantly in the growing private sector of the economy. As the establishment of CCP grassroots organizations has not been obligatory here, the mobilizational capacity of the party seems to have been severely reduced in this sector. With it, the party has, over the years, been cut off from access to even larger parts of the country's workforce.

To tackle this problem, Jiang Zemin announced in May 2000 that party grassroots organizations should be established in those firms of the non-public economy where 'conditions were ripe'.[49] According to the plans of the CCP's Organization Department, enterprises with at least three party members among their employees were expected to establish a CCP grassroots organization (*jiceng zuzhi*), those with more than three but less than 50 party members should form a regular party branch (*dang zhibu*), and those with more than 50 party members should establish a general branch (*zong zhibu*). If 'conditions were not ripe yet', trade unions, youth leagues and other mass organizations' branches should be set up first to pave the way for the later establishment of party cells in private firms.[50]

According to an article published in *Zhonggongdangshi yanjiu* in the autumn of 2001, among the 1.76 million private enterprises registered in late 2000, 86 percent had no party members among their employees at all, and only 0.9 percent had established CCP grassroots organizations in their firms. The author lists various reasons for this dire situation: First of all, it is hard for party organizations in private enterprises to play their proper role. Although some firms have established party cells, they did so only to get access to party channels for the recruitment of qualified personnel; some party cells were 'dependent on the entrepreneur' (*yifu yu qiyezhu*) - obviously a euphemism for being an instrument of the entrepreneur - while others existed on paper only.[51]

The case of Zhang Ruimin, director of the famous Hai'er joint stock company, is a case in point: When asked by a foreign journalist about who was the party secretary in his company, and whether were there any contradictions between the party's goals and the shareholders' interests, Zhang replied: 'Well, the party secretary, that's me... there won't ever arise any contradictions, 'cause how can I be in contradiction with myself?'[52] Our own interviews with private and 'red-hat' (*hongmao*) entrepreneurs in Jiangsu in May 2001 have revealed that this type of entrepreneur-cum-party secretary has indeed become quite widespread in recent years.[53] Thus, often, where there are party cells, they seem to be instrumentalized as a mere management tool by the *laoban*, the 'boss'. In a sense, one can recognize here a strategy of 'counter co-optation' where the entrepreneur co-opts the party in order to safeguard the organizational stability of his firm.

The *Zhonggongdangshi yanjiu* article offers another reason for the troubles of establishing party cells in private firms, which is the 'incomplete ideological understanding' (*sixiang renshi bu daowei*) on the side of some party members. For example, some believe (wrongly, of course) that the principle of striving for profits is fundamentally incompatible with the overall goals of the party, and therefore lack self-confidence to do a good party-building job. Others believe that although private entrepreneurs have experienced a rapid development, they still hold a marginal position in social respects. From this perspective therefore, whether party organizations are active there or not does not really matter so much. Still others believe (again, wrongly) that private entrepreneurs only strive for economic success and do not care at all about the development of party cells.

On the side of the private entrepreneurs, the article finds the following 'one-sided opinions' which can be explained by their 'different personal backgrounds and knowledge levels': First, some entrepreneurs fear that party grassroots organizations, once they are established in their firm, could 'use their political influence to interfere with the economic decision-making and disturb the regular production order of the firm, thus impairing the profit goals'. Second, some believe that there are too many non-economic activities being initiated by grassroots organizations, increasing the financial burden and driving up the firm's expenditures. Third, some associate the party mainly with lavish banquets, red-tape and corruption in general and therefore 'have no trust in the party' (*dui dang mei you xinrengan*) - a peculiar reversal of orthodox party members' fear that admitting private entrepreneurs into the CCP could increase corruption.[54]

As these observations demonstrate, the author is quite sensitive to the potential barriers hindering the establishment of party grassroots organizations in private enterprises. The precautions found on the side of entrepreneurs seem all the more realistic as the prescribed tasks of party organizations in private firms comprise not only ideological education and the protection and mediation of workers' interests, but also participation in the firm's decision-making on crucial production and operation matters. The article emphasizes over and over again that the party organizations, in order to win the trust of the entrepreneurs, should refrain from old-style 'commandism', bureaucratic interference and compulsion. Rather, they should play a participatory role by making suggestions and giving advice, co-operating with the management to ensure a healthy development of the firm. The relation between party organization and entrepreneur should not be 'hierarchical' (*dengji*) or 'antagonistic' (*duili*), but rather one of 'compatibility' (*xiangrong*) – whatever this might signify in terms of power relations.

What we find in this description is a potential source of growing problems, tensions and contradictions between the *laoban* and party representatives inside private enterprises. As the article states explicitly, if the entrepreneur is not willing to recruit party members as employees, he cannot be forced to do so. Thus, to attain the goal of establishing party cells and increase the CCP's organizational presence in private companies, it is crucial to win the sympathy of the entrepreneurs at first hand.

The nexus between the inclusion of entrepreneurs and the mobilization of private sector's workforce outlined seems very important and might have significantly motivated Jiang Zemin's July speech: While the co-optation of private entrepreneurs into the CCP is often seen to work at the expense of the traditional focus of party-building on workers and peasants,[55] one could also make the reverse argument: In line with the logic just presented, co-optation of the new elites is not so much an end in itself, but rather a necessary precondition for ensuring the continued success of traditional party-building measures among the working masses. As an ever larger share of the country's workers is and will be employed by the private or hybrid sector of the economy, the CCP needs to secure its foothold in these sectors in order to gain access to these parts of the workforce. In this sense, co-opting the new 'management labourers' can be seen as the best and only strategy for the party to reach out to the masses of the 'basic labourers' who otherwise would go astray. Paradoxical though it may sound, in order to uphold its nature as the 'vanguard of the working class', the CCP might have decided to tolerate 'capitalists' within its own ranks.

CONCLUSION: WHAT WE DO NOT KNOW

Concluding this paper, it would be a very satisfying thing to sum up the results and use them to philosophize about the outlook for the party's future development. Suitable topics for discussion might include: the possible evolution of the CCP into a 'people's party' or whatever other labels one might invent; the change in the party's identity and the ideological and psychological reverberations of this change; the future political role of entrepreneurs and other new economic elites; or the prospects for democracy inside and outside the party. However, for the time being, it seems premature to tackle these 'big questions' when our knowledge of the 'small questions' remains insufficient. Thus, as I hope to have shown, some assumptions concerning basic concepts and categories of the 'private sector', as well as motives and strategies of the party, should be (re-)tested on the microscopic level before drawing macro-political conclusions. According to my understanding, conceptual vagueness or insufficient knowledge prevails regarding the following aspects:

- The concepts of 'private sector', 'private entrepreneur' etc. are not such clear notions in Chinese discourse as the English-language media coverage seems to suggest. This is not only due to statistical inconsistencies, but more importantly, to inbuilt incentives for actors in the Chinese political economy to disguise what is 'private'. Looking only at the formal private sector (*getihu* and *siying qiye*) seems substantially to misrepresent the dynamics of entrepreneurial activities. Therefore, it would be highly desirable to get more concrete insights into the hybrid public-private sectors of the economy, particularly at the local level, and to understand better which among the various types of entrepreneur-managers the CCP in fact wishes to co-opt.

- To speak of 'private entrepreneurs' as a homogeneous group, suggesting that they have similar backgrounds and pursue consistent interests and strategies, seems to ignore the large divergencies in personal, educational and occupational backgrounds of entrepreneurs as well as in their attitudes and behaviour. Therefore, the notion of an emerging 'middle class' seems somewhat premature, particularly if it is ascribed the mythical role of a harbinger of pluralist democracy. Before lumping everybody together to form a 'bourgeoisie with Chinese characteristics', it seems more promising to analyse in more detail the variations in backgrounds, interests and strategies among the different groups of entrepreneurs and managers active in present-day China. Some recent studies of social scientists inside and outside China have done pioneering work in this field which can form a fundament for further research.

- Analysing the CCP's strategies of inclusion, we should take into account the various modes of co-optation and organizational linkage which exist inside and outside the party (as scholars such as Bruce Dickson, Thomas Heberer, Kellee Tsai, Zheng Yongnian and others have already been doing). To remind ourselves, various formal channels of political representation of entrepreneurial interests have already been in existence for many years, such as serving as delegates in people's congresses and political consultative congresses, or lobbying through business associations and mass organizations. Realizing that most entrepreneurs who have been politically active via these channels are already CCP members, the question arises how the admission of more entrepreneurs into

263

the party will impact on those formal channels of participation. Will party membership of new groups of entrepreneurs indeed increase their leverage, or will it merely duplicate existing structures of political participation?

- Besides the formal channels, there are many informal ways of representing group interests, which entrepreneurs seem to have found effective in the past. Among them are, of course, various time-honoured networking (*guanxi*) strategies, but also some innovative methods. The emergence of the 'private entrepreneur-cum-party secretary model' is but one example of what I would call a 'counter co-optation' strategy pursued by entrepreneurs to cope with the CCP's co-optation strategy. If we want to understand the motives and strategies behind the party's attitude toward entrepreneurs, we should analyse the entrepreneurs' motives and strategies as well. Hopefully in the wake of the 16th Party Congress, when more entrepreneurs might be admitted into the CCP, more detailed information will become available about their role in the game.

ENDNOTES

1   Zhang Dejiang, 'Several Issues to be Studied and Resolved in Strengthening the Work of Party Building in Non-public Enterprises', originally published in *Dangjian yanjiu* [Research on Party Building], no. 4 (2000), excerpted in *Zhenli de zhuiqiu* [Pursuit of Truth] (May 2001), translated in BBC Monitoring Global Newsline Asia Pacific Political File, 15 July 2001; Lin Yanzhi, 'How the Communist Party Should "Lead" the Capitalist Class', in *Shehui kexue zhanxian* [Social Sciences Battlefront] (June 2001), translated in BBC Monitoring Global Newsline Asia Pacific Political File, 16 July 2001, Deng Liqun et al., 'Deng Liqun dengren pi Jiang Zemin gongkai xin' (Open Letter by Deng Liqun and Others Critizing Jiang Zemin), unpublished document, cited by Joseph Fewsmith, 'Is Political Reform Ahead? - Beijing Confronts Problems Facing Society - and the CCP', *China Leadership Monitor*, no. 1 (2002), p. 9, fn. 8. The contents of these critical articles have been purported widely; cf. Fewsmith, 'Is Political Reform Ahead? - Beijing Confronts Problems Facing Society - and the CCP'; Heike Holbig, 'Die KPCh öffnet sich für Privatunternehmer. Jiang Zemins theoretischer "Durchbruch" und die praktischen Konsequenzen' [The CCP Opens Its Doors to Private Entrepreneurs: Jiang Zemin's Theoretical "Breakthrough" and the Practical Consequences], *China aktuell*, no. 7 (2001), pp. 739-46; see also Zheng Yongnian, 'Interests, Interest Representation and the Transformation of the Chinese Communist Party'. Paper prepared for the conference 'Bringing the Party Back In: How China is Governed' held in Copenhagen, June 2002.

2   http://english.peopledaily.com.cn/200204/07/print20020407_93626.html.

3   *Renmin ribao* [People's Daily] website, 19 March 2002.

4   *Zhongguo tongji nianjian 2001* [China Statistical Yearbook 2001] (Beijing: Zhongguo tongji chubanshe, 2001), pp. 128-31.

5   Lu Xueyi (ed.), *Dangdai Zhongguo shehui jieceng yanjiu baogao* [Research Report on Social Strata in Contemporary China] (Beijing: Shehui kexue wenxian chubanshe, 2001), pp. 213-15. I would like to thank Torstein Hjellum and Kjeld Erik Brødsgaard for making the report available to me.

6   *Zhongguo tongji nianjian 2000*, p. 140; *Zhongguo tongji nianjian 2001*, p. 131; *Renmin ribao* website, 19 March 2002.

7   For example, Zhang Yuanbao, 'Xiang shehui youxiu fenzi zhangkai damen shi jiaqiang dang de jianshe de zhanlüe jucuo' [To Open the Doors Wide to Outstanding Elements of Society is a Strategic Move to Strengthen Party Building], *Zhonggongdangshi yanjiu* [Research on the CCP's Contemporary History], no. 6 (2001), p. 11.

8   *Zhongguo tongji nianjian 2000*, pp. 138, 140; *Zhongguo tongji nianjian 2001*, pp. 130, 133; *Renmin ribao* website, 19 March 2002.

9   *Renmin ribao* website, 19 March 2002.

10 Zhang Yuanbao, 'Xiang shehui youxiu fenzi zhangkai damen shi jiaqiang dang de jianshe de zhanlüe jucuo', pp. 10-15; see also *Xinhua News Agency*, 22 May 2002; even if the official figures for private entrepreneurs and self-employed entrepreneurs, whose incomes are generated on the private economy, are included in the term '*jiuye renshu*', this would only amount to 102.26 million persons for late 2000 - still a large gap to the figure of 130 million.

11 *Zhongguo tongji nianjian 2001*, p. 132.

12 Four sampling surveys conducted by the CCP United Front Department, the All-China Federation of Industry and Commerce, the China Private Economy Research Group and the Chinese Academy of Social Sciences since 1993 are mentioned in Lu Xueyi, *Dangdai Zhongguo shehui jieceng yanjiu baogao*, pp. 216-17.

13 See, for example, *Renmin ribao*, 19 March 2002.

14 Zhang Yuanbao, 'Xiang shehui youxiu fenzi zhangkai damen shi jiaqiang dang de jianshe de zhanlüe jucuo'.

15 See International Finance Corporation (IFC), *China's Emerging Private Enterprises. Prospects for the New Century*, (Washington, DC: IFC, 2000), pp. 7-44; Organization for Economic Cooperation and Development, *China in the Global Economy. Reforming China's Enterprises*, (Paris: OECD, 2000), pp. 17-32; interviews with private entrepreneurs conducted with Thomas Reichenbach in Wuxi, May 2001. Thomas Reichenbach is my project partner in a research project on the All-China Federation of Industry and Commerce and its role in the changing structures of interest representation of entrepreneurs in various regions of China. The project, which is funded by the Volkswagen Stiftung, commenced in April 2000.

16 See, for example, 'Report on expanding SMEs' in *Zhongguo jingji shibao* [China Economic Times], 19 April 2001, p. 7; *Xinhua News Agency*, 20 February 2002, 26 June 2002.

17 David S. G. Goodman, 'The Emerging Public Sector in Shanxi. Entrepreneurs and Enterprise as Risk under Reform'. Paper prepared for

UNSW-UTS Centre for Research on Provincial China, Provincial China Workshop, Taiyuan, October 2000, pp. 7-11. I would like to thank Prof. Goodman for making the paper available to me.

18   *Ibid.*, p. 5.

19   Email correspondence with Prof. Andrew G. Walder in May 2002; percentages cited from Bruce Dickson, 'Economics as the Central Task: Do Entrepreneurs Matter?' Paper prepared for the 'China's Leadership Transition: Prospects and Implications' conference, Virginia, December 2001, p. 20, fn. 9. I would like to thank Prof. Walder and Prof. Dickson for sharing their data.

20   Data obtained from my project partner Thomas Reichenbach.

21   Cited by Ignatius Wibowo, 'Party Recruitment and the Future of the Chinese Communist Party', *EAI Background Brief No. 101* (September 2001).

22   Dickson, 'Economics as the Central Task', pp. 13-15, and separate Table 5.

23   This is a term used in a recently published party source: Shi Zhongquan et al., 'Guanyu youxiu qiyezhu rudang wenti de diaocha' [Investigation into the question of outstanding entrepreneurs joining the CCP], *Zhonggong dangshi yanjiu*, no. 3 (2002), pp. 66-75.

24   Cf. Thomas Heberer, 'Die Privatwirtschaft als Wachstumsmotor. Weshalb öffnet sich die Kommunistische Partei Chinas privaten Unternehmern?' [The Private Economy as Motor of Growth. Why Does the CCP Open Its Doors to Private Entrepreneurs?], *Frankfurter Algemeiner Zeitung*, 25 March 2002, p. 8; *Yeguang Xinwen*, 17 August 2001, accessed 24 May 2002 via: http://news.1chinastar.com/news.shtml?l=chinese&a=express&p=1090047.

25   Cited from the official English translation by *Xinhua News Agency*, 1 July 2001, section 29.

26   Goodman, 'The Emerging Public Sector in Shanxi', p. 17.

27   Lu Xueyi, *Dangdai Zhongguo shehui jieceng yanjiu baogao*, p. 36; an overview of the report is given in the Hong Kong monthly *Guangjiaojing*, no. 2 (2002), pp. 14-17; and no. 3 (2002), pp. 14-17; see also *The Straits Times*, 15 May 2002.

28   *Washington Post*, 31 October 1987. See also Fewsmith, 'Is Political Reform Ahead?'.

29   Interestingly, the 'three benefits' theory of Deng Xiaoping has been cited in recent articles in the official press. See, for example, *Renmin ribao*, 19 March 2002; *Zhonggong dangshi yanjiu*, no. 5 (2001), p. 52.

30   For an analysis of the 'three representations' concept, see Holbig, 'Die KPCh öffnet sich für Privatunternehmer'.

31   'New Social Strata Play Bigger Role in China's Economic Development', *Qiushi*, 16 November 2001, translated in BBC Monitoring Global Newsline Asia Pacific Political File, 4 December 2001.

32   English translation by *Xinhua News Agency*, 1 July 2001, p. 29.

33   *Xinhua*, 28 August 2001, cited from http://news.1chinastar.com/news.shtmal?l=chinese&a=express&p=1092012 (visited 12 May 2002).

34   Song Haiqing, 'Zenyang lijie nengfou zijue de wei shixian dang de luxian he gangling er fendou, shifou fuhe dangyuan tiaojian, she xishou xin dangyuan de zhuyao biazhun?' [How to Understand that the Most Important Criteria for Absorbing New Party Members are Whether They Struggle Wholeheartedly for the Implementation of the Party's Line and Programme and Whether They Meet the Requirements for Party Membership?], *Qiushi*, no. 22 (16 November 2001), pp. 35-36.

35   See Børge Bakken, 'Norms, Values and Cynical Games with Party Ideology'. Paper presented at the conference 'Bringing the Party Back In: How China is Governed' in Copenhagen, June 2002, pp. 14 ff.

36   For the use of this new concept see Lu Xueyi, *Dangdai Zhongguo shehui jieceng yanjiu baogao*, pp. 233-38; *South China Morning Post*, 30 July 2002.

37   Torstein Hjellum, 'Features of Capitalism and the Restructuring of Ruling Classes in China', *The Copenhagen Journal of Asian Studies*, no. 14 (2001). Accessible via: http://www.uib.no/people/sspth/CapitalistclassChina.htm (visited on 21 May 2002).

38   See Bakken, 'Norms, Values, and Cynical Games with Party Ideology', p. 33.

39   Information from interviews with private entrepreneurs and representatives from All-China Federation of Industry and Commerce subsidiaries in May 2001.

40   Hu Angang (ed.), *Zhongguo tiaozhan fubai* [Challenging Corruption in China] (Hangzhou: Zhejiang renmin chubanshe, 2001), pp. 49-50; see also, Lu Xueyi, *Dangdai Zhongguo shehui jieceng yanjiu baogao*, p. 215.

41   Increasing corruption is one of the consequences Zheng Yongnian sees as arising from the admittance of private entrepreneurs into the CCP; see Zheng Yongnian, 'Interests, Interest Representation and the Transformation of the Chinese Communist Party'.

42   Lu Xueyi, *Dangdai Zhongguo shehui jieceng yanjiu baogao*, pp. 242-43.

43   Definition by Philip Selznick, cited from Ignatius Wibowo, 'Inducting Capitalists into the CCP: A Case of Hobson's Choice', *EAI Bulletin*, vol. 3, no. 2 (September 2001), pp. 1-2; see also Bruce J. Dickson, 'Cooptation and Corporatism in China: The Logic of Party Adaptation', *Political Science Quarterly*, vol. 114, no. 4 (Winter 2000/01), pp. 517-40.

44   *Ibid.*; similar arguments can be found widely in the secondary literature.

45   Zhang Yuanbao, 'Xiang shehui youxiu fenzi zhangkai damen shi jiaqiang dang de jianshe de zhanlüe jucuo", pp.10-11.

46   Dickson, 'Economics as the Central Task', p. 4.

47   Lu Xueyi, *Dangdai Zhongguo shehui jieceng yanjiu baogao*, pp. 219-24.

48   Dickson, 'Economics as the Central Task,' p. 16.

49   *Xinhua News Agency*, 16 May 2000.

50   Cited from Yin Fuying, 'Jiaqiang siying qiye dangjian gongzuo, cujin siying jingji jiankang fazhan' [Strengthen Party Building in Private Enterprises and Promote the Healthy Development of the Private Economy], *Zhonggong dangshi yanjiu*, no. 5 (2001), pp. 51-56, at p. 53.

51   *Ibid.*, p. 51.

52 'Hai'er: Dangyuan laoban bu maodun' [Hai'er: Being a Party Member Boss is not a Contradiction], *Yeguang xinwen*, 5 July 2001, accessible via: http://news.1chinastar.com/news.shtml?l_fanti&a=express&p=1081115 (visited on 24 May 2002).

53 Interviews conducted with my project partner Thomas Reichenbach in May 2001.

54 Yin Fuying, 'Jiaqiang siying qiye dangjian gongzuo,' pp. 51-52.

55 Similar arguments are made by Dickson, 'Economics as the Central Task', p. 15, or by Bakken, 'Norms, Values and Cynical Games'.

10

Interest Representation and the Transformation of the Chinese Communist Party

ZHENG YONGNIAN

INTRODUCTION

In his controversial speech celebrating the 80th anniversary of the Chinese Communist Party (CCP) on 1 July 2001, Jiang Zemin called on the party to admit those 'outstanding elements' of society such as private entrepreneurs, professionals, technical and managerial personnel from various non-state sectors, including those employed by MNCs.[1] According to Jiang, these are people who can also make a positive contribution to the rebuilding of China's socialism, and should therefore not be excluded from the party. Whether they are politically progressive (*xianjin*) or backward (*luohou*) should not be judged purely on whether they are property-owning classes. 'Private entrepreneurs' - actually an official euphemism for 'capitalists' or 'private businessmen' - were hitherto publicly barred from the party. The proposed membership relaxation has generated much enthusiasm from many private businessmen wanting to join the party. Immediately after Jiang's speech, more than '100,000 private entrepreneurs' were reported to have submitted applications to join the party. The party's organization department (headed by Zeng Qinghong) is planning to recruit 200,000 private entrepreneurs before the 16th Congress in September 2002.[2]

Traditionally, the CCP was supposed to represent the interests of only five major groups, i.e., workers, peasants, intellectuals, members of the PLA (People's Liberation Army), and government officials and cadres.

The majority of the original rank and file of the party was basically drawn from the 'proletariat' background. In championing the causes of capitalists, Jiang's initiative has been hailed by supporters as a theoretical breakthrough, throwing off the party's old dogmas, particularly the shackle of class. At the same time, for Jiang as General Secretary to openly embrace capitalists - the antithesis of the proletariat class - amounts to dropping an ideological bombshell on the conservative wing of the party. Naturally, the party's ideologues have raised a great hue and cry. The strength of the opposition from these party diehards seems to have taken Jiang by surprise.

The opposition came into the open with the publication on the Chinese Internet of a widely circulated *Wanyan-shu* or 'a petition of ten-thousand words,' attributed to a group of conservative party veterans led by long-time leftist critic Deng Liqun. Prior to Jiang's 'July 1 speech,' several provincial party leaders, such as deputy party secretary of Jilin Province Lin Yanzhi, had already spoken out against Jiang's scheme.[3] Zhang Dejiang, party secretary of Zhejiang Provincial Committee of the CCP, had also strongly argued that private entrepreneurs should not be allowed to join the CCP.[4] Zhejiang is among the few provinces in China where the private sector has made rapid inroads and has played an increasingly important role in the local economy and even politics. Zhang's strong opposition suggested that there was no consensus within the party leadership on the political role of the private sector. Indeed, the arguments presented by Lin and Zhang are representative of and are popular among old-style leftists. In brief, apart from being accused of breaching the party's cardinal principle by courting members of the exploitative class, Jiang was blamed for his failure to address the burning issues of growing unemployment and widening income disparities, and his failure to hold formal consultations within the party before making the announcement.

In response, Jiang quickly ordered the closure of the two 'theoretical' (i.e. ideological) magazines, *Zhenli de zhuiqiu* [Seeking Truth] and *Zhongliu* [The Central Pillar], which were well-known mouthpieces of the leftists.[5] Subsequently, some leftist websites were also shut down.[6] Since then, party cadres throughout China, including officers of the PLA, have been instructed to hold study sessions of Jiang's 'July 1 Speech.'[7] Not too long ago, the CCP had continued to proclaim that its ultimate goal was to eliminate capitalism; and all forms of politically and ideologically incorrect 'elements' such as 'private entrepreneurs' or capitalists were not allowed to exist in the party. Although it is still not certain today what political role the rising new capitalist class will play, the party seems to have begun its transformation from traditional Marxism and Leninism to something else. This paper attempts to examine this transformation by employing the concept 'interest' based on Albert Hirschman's definition. The paper is divided into sections. The first section discusses the concept 'interest.' The second section examines the rise of an interest-based social order and its impact on Chinese politics. The third section highlights how the party leadership has adjusted the party to accommodate a rising interest-based social order. Finally, I shall discuss what difficulties lie ahead in the process of transformation.

'INTEREST'

'Interest' has been a fundamental force that motivates the action of the actor. The concept of 'interest' used here is drawn largely from Hirschman's definition.[8] 'Interest' motivates action, but actors define 'interest' differently, including interest in honour, glory, self-respect, in an afterlife, in economic advantage, etc.[9] Regardless of the various definitions of 'interest,' this paper regards 'interest' as a 'methodical pursuit and accumulation of private wealth.'[10] According to Hirschman, an interest-propelled action is characterized by *self-centredness*, that is, 'predominant attention of the actor to the consequences of any contemplated action for himself,' and *rational calculation*, that is, 'a systematic attempt at evaluating prospective costs, benefits, satisfactions, and the like.'[11]

There are political benefits of an interest-based social order. First of all, an interest-based social order is more governable than one based on other non-interest-based factors, such as various forms of passion, since interest-guided individual behaviour is more predictable than a passion-guided act. As Hirschman noted, 'A world where people methodically pursue their private interests was... far more predictable, and hence *more governable*, than one where the citizens are vying with each other for honor and glory' (emphasis original).[12] Second, in an interest-based social order, individual behaviour is expected to be stable and continuous. When individuals pursue 'single-mindedly material interests,' their behaviour will not experience any turbulent change.

Third, economic expansion and the coming of an interest-based social order can make individual behaviour increasingly peaceful. In what Hirschman called the French thesis of the *doux commerce*, 'commerce was often regarded as a powerful civilizing agent diffusing prudence, probity, and similar virtues within and among trading societies.'[13] This theme was expressed by Montesquieu in the *Spirit of Laws* when he declared,

> [I]t is almost a general rule that wherever manners are gentle there is commerce; and wherever there is commerce, manners are gentle. [C]ommerce... polishes and softens barbaric ways as we can see everyday.[14]

Fourth and even more relevant to this paper, the principle of *doux commerce* is applicable not only to democracy, but also to other types of regime such as monarchy and despotism. Economic expansion can soften a regime's use of coercion. It can even lead to regime changes by eliminating arbitrary and authoritarian decision-making by the sovereign. For Montesquieu, with the rise of specific new economic institutions resulting from economic expansion, the state will be largely deprived of its traditional power such as the power 'to seize property and to debase the currency at will.' For Steuart, 'it is rather the overall complexity and vulnerability of the 'modern economy' that make arbitrary decisions and interferences unthinkable - that is, exorbitantly costly and disruptive.'[15] Furthermore, economic expansion can also empower the people. According to Millar, the advance of commerce and manufacturing gives rise to a general diffusion of the spirit of liberty. This is so because it enhances the ability of certain social groups to resort to collective action against oppression and mismanagement.[16]

Finally, many scholars have argued that the economic benefits from economic expansion will make the state soften its rule over economic activities and respect people's basic economic freedom. Smith argued that economic expansion and individuals' pursuit of wealth and interest could lead to a spontaneous social order. According to him, market exchange can produce a 'natural progress of things toward improvement' because it induces individuals to consume and produce in rational ways. Free market exchange thus can ensure that the consumer is 'led by an invisible hand to promote an end which was no part of his intention.'[17] In other words, the market generates a 'public interest' that encompasses national wealth, a non-coercive society, and the freedom to choose and co-operate that emerges when individuals have the option and incentive to make rational choices.[18]

The logic behind the transformation of the CCP is based on the simple notion of preserving its 'interest.' It is all these advantages of 'interest' defined above that have led the Chinese leadership to justify a market economy and capitalistic development and allow capitalists to join the party.

FROM 'IDEOLOGY' TO 'INTEREST'

In the pre-reform era, China can be regarded as an ideologically and politically constructed society based on the concept of 'class.' It was organized in accordance with major political leaders' perceptions of what a society should be and realized by forceful organizational weapons. As Schurmann correctly pointed out in the 1960s, 'Communist China is like a vast building made of different kinds of brick and stone. However it was put together, it stands. What holds it together is ideology and organization.'[19]

The leadership under Mao Zedong initiated various political experiments, especially during the Cultural Revolution from 1966 to 1976, to reorganize China, according to Mao's own utopian ideals of what society should be like. Whatever Mao did, his aim was to destroy all possible private space and politicize the Chinese society. Totalitarian state power penetrated every corner of society and coercive institutional mechanisms were used to eliminate private space and manage public space.[20]

The household registration (*hukou*) system was used to control population movement and bind people to their place of birth and work. Since without a household registration booklet, no one could obtain food, clothing, housing, employment, schooling for children or the right to marry or enlist in the army, the system created a spatial hierarchy of urban places, priority of urban over rural areas, and where large cities took precedence over smaller ones in terms of the allocation of state resources.[21] A related institution for controlling population was the work unit (*danwei*) system, in which the party-state implemented ideological indoctrination and administrative disciplining such as warning, public criticism and negative records in the dossier.[22] The *danwei* system was also a mechanism in which the party-state solicited political compliance and allegiance from individual citizens by providing them with economic

273

and social security such as inexpensive housing, free medical care, generous retirement pensions, and a wide range of subsidies covering virtually every household need from transportation to nutrition.

Furthermore, enormous mass organizations were created in order to mobilize millions of people to implement public policies, and to achieve the party's and even Mao's personal purposes. All these organizations were administrated and monitored by the party-state and were used to organize youths, workers, women and other social groups into bodies resembling 'a conscription society.'[23] Meanwhile, the party-state banned all functional organizations, which were regarded or even suspected to be 'counter-revolutionary.' All autonomous and independent organizations were prohibited.

A highly organized and politicized society, together with a planned economy, enabled the party-state to mobilize numerous social groups into the political arena, and thus created new power resources within the Chinese society to implement profound tasks of social engineering such as land reform, collectivization and nationalization of business and commerce. Nevertheless, over time, the reach of the party-state was shortened. As Shue has pointed out, the highly organized and efficacious party-state gradually degenerated into a regime obsessed with ideology and lacking almost any genuine social base beyond its party-state apparatus. No wonder then that it becomes increasingly difficult to govern either legitimately or effectively.[24]

In the late 1970s, the Deng Xiaoping leadership began to shift its emphasis to economics as a way of reorganizing the country.[25] In the 1980s, China achieved high rates of economic growth by expanding its market space.[26] But it was only after Deng's southern tour (*nanxun*) in 1992 that the Chinese leadership legitimized capitalism as a way of promoting economic expansion.

Why was the CCP not able to legitimize capitalism in the 1980s? Capitalism could have been legitimized in that period. After the bitter and uncertain 30 years of experimentation following 1949, many leaders realized that learning from capitalism conforms to historical necessity, and capitalism is a stage that cannot be skipped on the way to socialism. Although the party had an idea of the nineteenth-century capitalism from which Marx drew inspiration, the reform and open-door policy enabled party cadres and government officials to see what had happened to capitalism recently from China's neighbouring countries, especially the four little dragons, i.e., Hong Kong, Taiwan, Singapore and South

Korea, in addition to Japan and the United States. From all these countries, the leadership saw how capitalism had helped raise the standard of living of the vast majority of the people there, and enhanced their status in international arenas, which were goals that the CCP had fought for since its establishment. The impact of the four little dragons on China's leaders should not be underestimated since the experiences of Hong Kong, Taiwan and Singapore showed that Chinese culture was not a barrier but a catalyst to economic growth.[27] The leaders realized what was important was not cultural but institutional factors, and if the country wanted to achieve rapid economic growth, its economic system had to be overhauled. This was the motivation behind the decision of the leadership to implement economic reforms. Many social groups, especially young intellectuals, advocated publicly for capitalism, genuinely believing that capitalism could pave the way for China to grow into a strong and affluent nation. Spurring the country on was the capitalist West, which was quite friendly to China in the 1980s, as they believed China's market-oriented economic reform and open-door policy would eventually lead to two transformations, that is, from a planned economy to a free market system, and from political authoritarianism to democracy.

However, in that decade, the Chinese revolutionary leaders had quite different perceptions of the market economy and capitalism.[28] While at the practical level they did not oppose carrying out different forms of capitalistic experiment, ideologically, they were unwilling to legitimize capitalism.[29] It was only after they saw that market economy did not harm the socialist system which they had fought for that they became willing to recognize its legitimacy. This can be seen from changes in the official definition of China's economic system. At the CCP's 12th Congress in 1982, the leadership defined the country's economic system as one in which the 'planned economy is the main pillar and market economy a supplementary element.' The market economy failed to gain theoretical legitimacy then. Five years later in 1987, at the 13th Congress, the leadership defined the economic system as one 'combining planned and market economies'; and here the market economy gained an ideological status equal to that of the planned economy. However, with the coming and in the aftermath of the 1989 pro-democracy movement, capitalism came under serious attack. Conservative leaders regarded the pro-democracy movement as the result of the spread of capitalism as an idea and as a practice.[30]

Why then did a sudden change take place after Deng Xiaoping's *nanxun*? Two important and subtle factors can be identified. First, the political interests of the regime were reconstructed in the early 1990s. Second, the reconstruction of political interests created an ideological room for capitalism as a way to reorganize society. In the early 1990s, a serious political legitimacy crisis hit the CCP, following the crackdown of the 1989 pro-democracy movement and the collapse of communism in the Soviet Union and East European countries. Initially, regime survival became the highest priority, and consequently, the leadership tightened its control by engaging in both political and economic rectification. Nevertheless, Chinese leaders, especially Deng Xiaoping, also realized that the fall of the Soviet Union and the collapse of East European communism was mainly due to the failure of economic development there. Therefore, the party needed to achieve radical economic growth if it wanted to avoid such a misfortune and rebuild its political legitimacy. Deng Xiaoping chose the path of initiating radical economic reforms.[31]

While the leadership decided to implement radical economic reform, it also began to build a new social order in accordance with the capitalist economic changes. Although the leadership tightened its political control in the aftermath of the 1989 movement, social demands for political reform were still prevalent. In order to transform popular passions for political interests to those for economic interests, the leadership had to provide social members with an economic 'exit.' While the crackdown of the 1989 movement showed social members the high cost of pursuing political interests, the opening of an economic 'exit' led them to realize that the shift from political interests to economic interests would be beneficial. In Hirschman's term, this is a strategy to transform people's 'public action' (demands for political reform) to 'private interest' (economic activities).[32] The political significance of such an economic 'exit' motivated the leadership to de-ideologize capitalism as a means of economic expansion. This strategy resulted in almost a decade of rapid development and socio-political stability.

A RISING INTEREST-BASED SOCIAL ORDER

An interest-based social order is not a natural result of economic expansion, but was consciously pursued by the party leadership. What the leadership wants is not only economic expansion *per se*, but also the beneficial political consequences arising from rapid economic expansion. Economic expansion has generated enormous political benefits, not only because it has increased the regime's political legitimacy, but also because it has changed the space structure in the country. The conscious pursuit of economic expansion has led to the emergence of an interest-based social order,[33] which in turn has resulted in the creation and expansion of a private arena.[34]

The rapid expansion of the private space is reflected in the decline of the state sector and the development of the non-state sector, as shown in Tables 1 and 2. From Table 1, we can see that the gross industrial output by the state-owned enterprises declined from 55 percent in 1990 to 27 percent in 1998, while that by individually owned enterprises increased from 5 percent to 16 percent during the same period. The non-state sector has overwhelmingly surpassed the state sector.

TABLE 1 GROSS INDUSTRIAL OUTPUT IN CHINA, 1980-98

Year	Total %	State-owned enterprises %	Collective-owned enterprises %	Individually-owned enterprises %	Other types of enterprises %
1980	100	76.0	23.5	0	0.5
1985	100	64.9	32.1	1.9	1.2
1990	100	54.6	35.6	5.4	4.4
1991	100	56.2	33.0	4.8	6.0
1992	100	51.5	35.1	5.8	7.6
1993	100	47.0	34.0	8.0	11.1
1994	100	37.3	37.7	10.1	14.8
1995	100	34.0	36.6	12.9	16.6
1996	100	33.7	36.5	14.4	15.4
1997	100	29.8	35.9	16.9	17.4
1998	100	26.5	36.0	16.0	21.5

Source: Calculated from *Zhongguo tongji nianjian* 1999 [China Statistical Yearbook 1999] (Beijing: Zhongguo tongji chubanshe, 1999), p. 423.

TABLE 2   THE DEVELOPMENT OF THE PRIVATE SECTOR
IN CHINA, 1989-97

	Private enterprises*				Individually owned and operated enterprises**			
	No.	Change %	Employees (million)	Change %	No. (million)	Change %	Employees (million)	Change %
1989	90,581		1.6		12.5		19.4	
1990	98,141	8.3	1.7	3.7	13.3	6.5	20.9	7.8
1991	107,843	9.9	1.8	8.2	14.2	6.7	22.6	7.9
1992	139,633	29.5	2.3	26.1	15.3	8.3	24.7	9.3
1993	237,919	70.4	3.7	60.8	17.7	15.2	29.4	19.1
1994	432,240	81.7	6.5	73.3	21.9	23.8	37.8	28.5
1995	654,531	51.4	9.6	47.5	25.3	15.6	46.2	22.2
1996	819,252	25.2	11.7	22.2	27.1	7.0	50.2	8.7
1997	960,726	17.3	13.5	15.2	28.5	5.4	5.4	8.5
1998	1200,978	25.0	17.1	26.7	n.a	n.a	n.a	n.a
1999	1508,857	25.6	20.2	18.8				

*   Refers to those with more than eight employees
**   Refers to those with less than eight employees
Note: Annual percentage change in number of employees may not be exact due to rounding off of figures.
Source: Adapted from Zhang Houyi and Ming Zhili (eds.), Zhongguo siying qiye fuzhan baogao 1978-1998 [A Report on the Development of Private Enterprises in China, 1978-1998] (Bejing: Shehui kexue wenxuan chubanshe, 1999), pp 60,66: zhangguo siying jingju mainjain The Year book of Private Businesses in China. 2000] (Beijing Hwuawen chubanshe, 2000).p.402

Table 3 shows the economic significance of the private sector. The private sector consumed 4 percent of the total retail sales in 1996, and the figure increased to 13.5 percent in 1999. During the same period, the industrial and commercial taxes paid by the private sector in national total increased from 1 percent to 2.6 percent. The private sector has become even more important in revenue contribution at local levels. According to one calculation, as of the mid-1990s, the private sector had contributed about 10 percent of the total tax revenue at the provincial level, 20 percent at the prefectural level, and 30 percent at the county level.[35] For instance, in 1996, the private sector in Zhejiang contributed

4.4 billion *yuan* industrial and commercial taxes, or 13.4 percent of the total industrial and commercial taxes in that province. In some rich areas, the private sector contributes township revenue as high as 60 percent.[36]

TABLE 3   THE ECONOMIC SIGNIFICANCE OF THE PRIVATE
SECTOR IN CHINA, 1996-99

	1996	1997	1998	1999
Percentage of goods consumed by the private Sector in total retail sales	4.1	6.8	10.5	13.5
Percentage of industrial and commercial taxes by the private sector in total industrial and commercial taxes	1.11	1.31	2.14	2.63

Sources: **Zhongguo siyingingji mianjian, 2000; and zhongguo shuiwu mianjian, 1994-97.**

Nevertheless, it is worthwhile to point out that while the private sector has become increasingly important, its motivation to pay tax revenue to the state is low. Table 3 shows that in 1999, the private sector consumed 13.5 percent of retail sales of consumer goods, but its revenue contribution to the total industrial and commercial taxes was only 2.6 percent. Low incentive to contribute revenue is also reflected in Table 4. From 1986 to 1992, revenue contribution by the private sector was largely in accordance with its share of the total national industrial output. After 1992, the gap between the two widened dramatically. For instance, in 1998, while the private sector contributed only 7 percent of the total national budgetary revenue, it accounted for more than 17 percent of the total industrial output.[37]

The rapid expansion of private space has undermined, or even destroyed, the old ideologically constructed social order. The household registration system has faced gradual erosion since the introduction of a market economy in the 1980s. With basic daily necessities available through the market, the state was no longer able effectively to control population movement from rural to urban areas, from interior to coastal areas, and from small to large cities. The system was further undermined by intensive economic competition among regions. To attract talented

279

people, many cities have substantially relaxed the original registrations required for the employment of non-local residents.[38]

TABLE 4   REVENUE CONTRIBUTION BY THE PRIVATE ENTERPRISES, AND INDIVIDUALLY OWNED ENTERPRISES, 1986-98*

	Tax revenue (billion,yuan)	% Total budgetary revenue	% Total GDP	% Total industrial output
1986	4.93	2.32	0.48	2.76
1990	14.57	4.96	0.79	5.39
1991	17.42	5.53	0.81	4.83
1992	20.33	5.84	0.76	5.80
1993	29.34	6.75	0.85	7.98
1994	37.03	7.10	0.79	10.09
1995	42.96	6.88	0.73	12.86
1996	46.96	6.34	0.69	15.48
1997	56.79	6.56	0.76	17.92
1998	70.00	7.09	0.89	17.11

* 'Private enterprise' and 'individually owned enterprise' are two different concepts in China, the former refers to those enterprises that have more than eight employees, while the latter refers to those enterprises that less than eight employees.
Source: Ho Angang (ed.), Zhongguo tianzhuo fazhan (China: Fighting against Corruption, (Hangzhou: Zhejiang renmin chubanshe, 2000), p.50.

In Russia and some other East European communist states, the collapse of the ideologically constructed social order had resulted in socio-economic chaos. But this is not the case in China. The creation and expansion of a private arena is what distinguishes China from the fate of the other communist states. Although the expanding private space is confined to the non-political arena, it is politically significant. First of all, it provides social members with an 'exit' from the public arena. Without such a private exit, social members would have to struggle for what they want in a highly politicized public arena. Since there was no private arena, they would have to fight to win in this public arena; otherwise, they would lose everything. This would undoubtedly intensify political conflicts among social members. Therefore, the expansion of a private arena reduces greatly the intensity of political conflicts, and thus the political burden of the party and the government.

Second, the existence of a private arena makes it possible for citizens to remain apolitical, if they do not want to be involved in politics. In an ideologically constructed society, political indifference is possible, but politically risky. Since all economic benefits are distributed through political means, social members had to engage in politics. In contrast, an interest-based social order not only allows people to pay less attention to politics, but also encourages them to devote themselves whole-heartedly to economic activities. In other words, political indifference is no longer risky, and politically indifferent citizens can obtain their basic necessities through the market.

Third, with the dawn of an interest-based social order, China's economic development has gained a spontaneous and natural momentum. In an ideologically constructed social order, any political change would inevitably affect economic activities. But in an interest-based social order, economic activities are less affected by political changes. An interest-based social order has an inherent capability to resist the impact of political changes. Government intervention in economic activities is reduced, but economic development continues. This in turn increases the legitimacy of the government, though it is now less responsible for economic development.

POLITICAL ORDER AFFECTED

The rise of an interest-based social order is beneficial for the legitimacy of the party-state at an early stage. Nonetheless, a continuously expanding social order has come to produce enormous unexpected political consequences that affect the existing political order. In other words, an interest-based social order has gradually undermined the existing political order and thus created pressure for interest representation.

With rapid economic expansion, the private arena has become more profitable than the public arena. The nascent interest-based social order has thus attracted not only social members, but also party cadres and government officials. This is especially true in the period after Deng Xiaoping's southern tour. Party cadres and government officials were allowed, even encouraged, by the reformist leadership to turn to business. This soon resulted in a nationwide wave of *xiahai* (literally 'plunging into the sea').[39] As shown in Table 5, in 1992, party cadres and government officials were the second largest group (25.5 percent) who established private businesses, following household-business owners (38.2 percent). By the mid-1990s, as shown in Table 6, they had become the largest group in private enterprises.

TABLE 5   BACKGROUND OF OWNERS OF PRIVATE ENTERPRISES IN CHINA(PERCENT)

Original Position	Business established before 1998	Business established 1989-92	Business established 1992	Percentage share
Professionals	1.9	4.3	4.9	4.6
Party cadres	19.8	16.0	25.5	25.5
Workers	13.2	8.6	10.8	10.7
Peasants	20.8	17.9	15.8	16.7
Household-Business owners	35.8	46.3	36.9	38.2
Others	8.5	6.8	6.1	6.5
Total	100	100	100	100

Source: Zhang Houyi and Ming Zhili (eds.), Zhongguo siying qiye fuzhan baogao 1978-1998, p.153.

By encouraging party cadres and government officials to turn to business, the party leadership aimed to reduce their political resistance to radical economic reforms. To a great degree, this goal was realized. But it was achieved at great costs. First of all, many talents 'exited' from the state to the private arena, especially those who had promoted China's market reform. Since they had been involved in new forms of economic activities, they were more knowledgeable than others on how to make profits through an emerging market. Such an 'exit' indeed weakened the reformist forces in the country. Second, party cadres and government officials were given opportunities to utilize their public power to gain private economic benefits. For example, party cadres and government officials have attempted to build up their connections (*guanxi*) with the private sector. In a survey conducted in 1993, when private entrepreneurs were asked to name their closest friends, the distribution was as follows: professionals (16.6 percent), cadres in the government sector (24.4

percent); cadres in SOEs (18 percent), workers (1.3 percent), farmers (3.7 percent), specialized artisans (6.4 percent), staff in the service sector (9.5 percent), and small enterprise owners (8.9), and others (2.9).[40] According to the study, to build their connections with the private sector, party cadres and government officials aimed to: (a) gain economic benefits for themselves and their family members; (b) search for opportunities to *xiahai*, i.e., to leave the government sector and turn to business; and (c) seek political support from the private sector due to its increasing political importance.[41]

TABLE 6   BACKGROUND OF OWNERS OF PRIVATE ENTERPRISES IN CHINA(PERCENT)

	1993 survey			1995 survey		
	Urban areas	Rural areas	Percentage share	Urban areas	Rural areas	Percentage share
Professionals	3.9	1.6	3.3	4.1	2.3	3.3
Cadres in urban State & Collective sectors	43.2	16.6	36.3	33.2	11.8	24.0
Rural cadres	4.1	16.9	7.5	3.5	11.2	6.8
Cadres in the non-State sectors	11.2	17.9	13.0	11.0	17.9	14.0
Peasants	4.4	16.3	7.5	6.3	17.3	11.0
Workers	22.9	11.4	19.7	21.7	17.5	19.9
Small-scale Individual business Owners	8.8	18.2	11.2	15.8	18.1	16.8
No occupation	1.5	1.0	1.4	4.5	3.8	4.2

Source: Lau Siu-Kai et al. (eds.), shichang, jieji yu zhengzhi (Market, Class and Politics) (Hong Kong: Hong Kong Institute of Asian-Pacific Studies, The Chinese University of Hong Kong, 2000), p.328.

When public power is used for economic benefits, corruption becomes inevitable and increasingly serious. While in the old days political loyalty was the most important standard used to evaluate the political achievements of party cadres and government officials, 'money' has now come to replace political loyalty. Corruption has undermined not only the effectiveness of the government, but also popular confidence in the government. Shoring up political legitimacy has thus become once again a serious challenge for the party and the government. The Chinese state has played an extremely important role in pushing the process of economic transformation. But the close linkages between the government and businesses have led to widespread corruption among party cadres and government officials. Corruption has become increasingly serious since the early 1990s, as shown in Table 7. Between 1993 and 2000, the number of cases investigated and handled by discipline inspection and procuratorial organs throughout the country increased 9 percent annually, and the number of officials given party and administrative disciplinary punishments went up 12 percent. Between 1990 and 1998, procuratorial organs nationwide accepted and handled more than 1.1 million corruption cases, of which over 500,000 cases were placed on file for investigation and prosecution. More than 600,000 offenders were involved.[42] From January to August 2000 alone, the procuratorates throughout the country prosecuted 23,464 criminal cases involving graft and embezzlement. [43] The 2000 Corruption Perceptions Index of Transparency International ranked China as 63rd among 90 countries.[44]

Since the early 1990s, the Chinese state has initiated a series of anti-corruption measures. Nevertheless, corruption is still rampant. Even Premier Zhu Rongji had to admit, in his Work Report to the National People's Congress in March 2000, that 'the emergence and spread of corruption and undesirable practices have not been brought under control.'[45] Corruption has caused social and political instability. It also aroused people's ire against the party's inability to ensure fairness and cast doubts on its legitimacy to rule the country.

All these economic and social problems have further eroded social morale. Ordinary citizens see the abundance of wealth and greed of party cadres and government officials, and find it difficult to rationalize why they should hold back. Gradually, they no longer regard the system in which they live as being fair to them. Meanwhile, government officials at different levels have also found that it is increasingly difficult to maintain a sense of morality and social community among both urban and rural residents. Moreover, as corruption becomes rampant among party cadres and government officials, crime has also become widespread among ordinary citizens.[46] Robbery and armed assault, which were unthinkable during Mao's time, have become a part of daily life.

TABLE 7 THE DEVELOPMENT OF CORRUPTION AMONG LEADING CADRES IN THE 1990s

		1993	1994	1995	1996	1997	Jan-Sept 1998	1999
Punished by party & gov.disciplines	Provincial level	6	17	24	23	7	10	17
	Prefectural level	205	309	429	467	576	219	327
	County level	2,793	3,528	4,880	5,868	6,585	2,955	4,029
Investigated by Procuratorial Organs	Provincial level	1	1	2	5	3	3	3
	Prefectural level	7	88	145	143	148	85	136
	County level	1,141	1,826	2,306	2,551	2,426	1,462	2,200
Sentenced by law	Provincial level		1		1	5	2	2
	Prefectural level	7	28	35	43	58	30	65
	County level	69	202	396	364	403	271	367

Source: The Research Group of the Department of Organization, the CCP Central Committee (ed), 2000-2001 Zhongguo diaocha baoguo: xin xingshi xia review neibu modern yanjiu China Investigation Report, 2000-2001: Studies of Contradications within the People under Ned Conditions, (Beijing, Zhongyang bianyi chubanshe, 2001).p.86

Various surveys show that since the early 1990s, 'serious corruption committed by government officials' and 'public disorder' were among the issues of concern among ordinary citizens in China.[47] When the government becomes corrupt and public order becomes problematic, people tend to become discontented and anxious. According to a 1998 survey, nearly 93 percent of the respondents did not regard China as a country ruled by law. When asked what they would do if conflict or disputes with others occurred, 74.7 percent indicated that they would turn to legal means for a resolution. Nevertheless, they also believed that such means would be ineffective since power was still above the law in China, so they would appeal through other non-legal means. About 49 percent said that they would seek help from the media, and 24.7 percent would turn to individual leaders. Furthermore, about 16 percent of the people would turn to some form of collective action for justice such as petition, demonstration, and collective visit to higher authorities for their intervention (*shang fang*).[48]

TABLE 8   KEY POLITICAL FACTORS THAT AFFECT
PRIVATE BUSINESSES (PERCENT)

	1996	1997
Legal protection of property rights	5.1	4.1
Government propaganda	5.0	6.0
Taxation policy	18.8	n.a.
Credit policy	31.8	27.2
Government macro-economic adjustment	23.6	17.9
Industrial and commercial management	2.6	31.9
Household system	0.6	5.2
Ownership	5.0	0.4
Others	7.5	7.2
Total	100	100

Source: Zhang Houyi and Ming Zhili, (eds), *Zhougguo saying qiye fuzhan baogao 1978-1998*. p.150

The most serious threat is that the party is increasingly facing pressure to incorporate newly rising social forces into its political order. The nascent social order has a strong justification to request that its voice be heard since government policies have an impact on its rise and fall. Table 8 shows the results of two nationwide surveys conducted in 1995 and 1997 respectively. We can see that taxation policy, credit policy, government macro-economic adjustment, and industrial and commercial management, among others, have been the most important political factors affecting their business activities. More and more, private business people expect to participate in policy-making or at least have some input in policy-making. Moreover, the private sector has been affected not only by relevant government policies, but also by various forms of social and political practices prevalent in China. As shown in Table 9, 'exchange between power and money,' 'worsening public order' and 'arbitrary collection of fees, fines and levies' have been regarded as the factors that have had the most serious impact on private businesses. To change such social and political practices is no easy task and would require the political participation of private business persons.

**TABLE 9   SOCIAL PROBLEMS WITH MOST SERIOUS
NEGATIVE IMPACT ON PRIVATE BUSINESSES (PERCENT)**

	1995	1997
Unjust income distribution	5.1	9.9
Exchange between power and money	37.3	37.6
Worsening public order	20.6	41.1
Arbitrary fees, arbitrary fines, and arbitrary levies	31.4	6.3
Business involvement of government and military in businesses	2.6	3.9
Others	8.1	1.3
Total	100	100

Source: **Zhang Houyi and Ming Zhili, (eds), Zhougguo saying qiye fuzhan
baogao 1978-1998. p.148**

Indeed, private entrepreneurs have been making great efforts to
participate in the political process, especially in local politics. No
systematic national statistics are available to show the degree of political
participation by private businesspeople. But as shown in Table 10, a rapid
expansion of their involvement in local politics took place in the early
1990s. According to a survey conducted in 1993, on average, each private
entrepreneur had membership in 2.75 organizations such as private
enterprise associations, guilds, different democratic parties, Youth League,
and even the Chinese Communist Party. Almost 84 percent of private
entrepreneurs argued that it was imperative to establish their own
organizations.[49] Another means for private entrepreneurs to influence
China's political process was for them to join the CCP. According to
various surveys, more and more private entrepreneurs have become party
members. In 1993, among all private entrepreneurs, 13 percent were
CCP members, and this figure was 17 percent in 1995, and 16.6 percent
in 1997. In 2000, this figure increased to almost 20 percent, far higher
than other social groups such as workers and farmers.[50]

Political participation by private entrepreneurs is still extremely
limited at the national level. For example, only 46 out of more than 2,000
representatives of the 9th Chinese People's Political Consultative
Conference (CPPCC) in 1998 were private businesspeople.[51] A low degree
of political participation indeed has caused dissatisfaction among this
sector. As shown in Table 11, while self-evaluation by private
businesspeople about their economic and social status has been consistent,

287

that of their political status has deteriorated. It is worthwhile to note that their self-evaluation for political status was lowest in 1997, the year the private sector was formally legalized by China's Constitution.[52]

TABLE 10   REPRESENTATIVES FROM THE PRIVATE SECTOR IN POLITICAL ORGANIZATIONS

Year	Representatives in the People's Congress at the Country level and above	Representatives in the CPPCC at the country level and above*	Representatives' mass organizations**
1990	5,114	7,238	4,603
1994	7,296	11,721	7,671
Increase	42%	62%	67%

* CPPCC: The Chinese People's Political Consultative Conference
** Such as the Communist Youth League and the Women's Federation
Source: Zhonghua gongshang shinbao China Industrial and Commercial Daily, 29 April 1996

TABLE 11   SELF-EVALUATION BY PRIVATE BUSINESS PEOPLE OF THEIR ECONOMIC, SOCIAL AND POLITICAL STATUS

	Economic Status	Social Status	Political Status
1993	4.5	4.0	4.6
1995	4.5	4.2	5.1
1997	4.7	4.6	5.7

The highest score: 1.0
The lowest score: 10.0
Source: Zhang Houyi and Ming Zhili (eds.), Zhonghua siying qiye fuzhan baogao 1977-1998, p. 163.

ACCOMMODATION AND REPRESENTATION

The response of the CCP is to co-opt rising social forces into the regime. Since the southern tour, the new leadership has made great efforts not only to legitimize and institutionalize the emerging interest-based social order, but also to search for a proper political order which will be compatible with this emerging social order. While the party-state has attempted, albeit without success, to incorporate some social groups into the regime, it still remains intolerant of any direct democratic challenge, which became apparent towards the end of the 1990s, as exemplified by the attempts of Chinese pro-democracy activists to organize an opposition party. In the last few months of 1998, the preparatory committees of China's Democracy Party were established in 23 out of China's 31 provinces and major cities. Applications to register the new party were made in 14 provinces and cities.[53] As long as the party-state 'refuses' to address the democratic challenge head-on, it will stay irrelevant to newly emerging democratic forces. The CCP leadership is intolerant of direct political challenges mounted by social groups, but attempts have been made to accommodate newly rising social forces. This can be shown by changes introduced into the country's Constitution.

Constitutional changes in China could mean two things, first, a replacement of the existing constitution with a new one (1954-82), and second, making amendments to the Constitution (1982-99). When the political situation changes, the old Constitution is likely to be replaced by a new one. Thus the 1975 Constitution is called the 'Cultural Revolution Constitution,' the 1978 Constitution the 'Four-Modernization Constitution,' and the 1982 Constitution the 'Reform and Open-Door Constitution.' Similarly, each revision of the Constitution was motivated by strong political concerns and heavily influenced by the leadership's intention to adjust the political system to changing situations. It is worthwhile to briefly examine the constitutional changes related to the private sector.

According to the 1954 Constitution, the first one in the history of People's Republic, China's political system was led by the working class as its leading class and the worker-peasant alliance as its foundation (Article 1). Regarding the economic system, the Constitution decreed that the state would aim at eliminating the exploitative system and building a socialist system. While the state sector should be in a dominant position, other sectors such as collective cooperatives, individually owned enterprises, private capitalist economy, and state capitalism were allowed to co-exist (Articles 5 and 10). Furthermore, the Constitution also provided protection to citizens' ownership of legal incomes, savings, properties and other forms of productive materials (Article 11), and protection to the right of inheritance of private properties (Article 12). Meanwhile, the state would collect and even confiscate land and other forms of productive materials in accordance with laws and regulations in order to meet the needs of public interests (Article 13), and everyone was prohibited from utilizing his/her private properties to undermine public interests (Article 14). The Constitution also declared that public properties were sacred and inviolable, and it was every citizen's duty to protect public properties (Article 101).

Many waves of political movements such as the Anti-Rightist Movement and the Cultural Revolution almost completely nullified the 1954 Constitution. In 1975, the party leadership under the 'Gang of Four' drew up a new Constitution. The 1975 Constitution formally nullified many articles regarding citizens' rights in the 1954 Constitution, and added some articles to meet the political needs of that time. To support the party became the citizens' rights, although citizens were also granted the right to rebel. The revised Constitution was reduced to 30 articles from the original 106.

After the death of Mao Zedong and the overthrow of the Gang of Four in 1976, the CCP leadership under Hua Guofeng decided to make a constitutional revision in 1978. Though the Constitution was expanded to 60 articles by restoring some articles of the 1954 Constitution, it was still based on the 1975 Constitution. In accordance with political changes in train at that time, the use of material incentives to promote the four-modernizations was legalized.

After Deng Xiaoping returned to power, the CCP leadership passed an entirely new constitution, i.e., the 1982 Constitution. The new Constitution restored almost all the articles of the 1954 Constitution. New ones were added (from 106 articles in 1954 to 138) to meet new political and economic needs. Though the 1982 Constitution still emphasized that the state sector had to be dominant in China's economy, it recognized that individually engaged economic activities in both rural and urban areas were complementary to the state sector (Article 11). What was later called the private enterprise (which employed more than eight workers) was not legalized.

In 1988, the first constitutional amendment was made. Two significant changes were made regarding China's economic system. First, one paragraph was added to Article 11:

> The state allows the private economy to exist and develop within the legal boundary. The private economy is a complement to the socialist public economy. The state protects legal rights and

interests of the private economy, provides it with leadership, supervision and management (Article 11, para. 3).

Second, para. 4 of Article 10 was revised: The state recognized that 'land use right can be transferred in accordance with legal regulations.' This change was significant since it meant that the state legalized employment, capital accumulation, land commercialization and other newly rising economic activities. Five years later, in 1993, the second constitutional amendment was made. The 1993 amendment gave up the planned economic system, and formally declared that a socialist market economy was to be established.

The official confirmation of the market economy led to serious criticisms against capitalistic development by the Leftists, both old and new, in the mid-1990s. Despite controversies, the leadership decided to press on. The 15th Party Congress in 1997 further pointed to how a market economy could be rooted in China, and declared a programme of partial privatization of state-owned enterprises. Further, based on the 1993 amendment, the Second Session of the 9th National People's Congress (NPC) in 1999 made a constitutional amendment, which, for the first time since the establishment of the People's Republic, provided constitutional protection for the private economy.[54]

While it will take a long time for the CCP to establish an interest-based political order, all these constitutional changes in the 1990s show that the party leadership has made great efforts to adjust China's political system not only to promote further economic development, but also to accommodate capitalist economic institutions. In February 2000, Jiang Zemin raised a new concept of *sange daibiao* (literally 'Three Representations'). According to this concept, the CCP represents the 'most advanced mode of productive force, the most advanced culture, and the interests of the majority of the population.'[55] The 'Three Representations' theory is undoubtedly the clearest sign yet of the CCP's affirmation of the non-state sector in the economy. More importantly, it also shows that the CCP has begun to consider how the interests of newly rising classes or social groups can be represented. As discussed at the beginning of this paper, the CCP leadership has also legitimized party membership of private entrepreneurs or capitalists. All these changes have been warmly received by the private sector, and are widely regarded as a symbol of the CCP's transformation from a communist party to one containing some social democratic elements.

TRANSFORMATION AND POLITICAL RISKS

What the CCP has done provides clear indications that the party is jettisoning its past ideological rigidity by willingly embracing rising economic and social elites. The party's initiative is apparently motivated by pragmatic political considerations. First, admitting private entrepreneurs is a means for the party to adapt itself to China's changing political and social realities. As mentioned earlier, many private entrepreneurs are already party members. What the party leadership proposes to do today is formally to endorse their party membership while allowing others to join as new members. Second, by so doing, the leadership wants to expand the party's social base in order to revitalize itself. Over the years, the capitalist mode of economic development has radically changed China's class structure. With the decline of the political and ideological importance of workers and peasants, the party has to embrace the rising new elites, from industrialists and international businessmen to property magnates and 'dotcom' venture capitalists, in order to stay socially relevant. China today has 60 million registered stock and share buyers, roughly equal to the total party membership.

Politically, the party's initiative to embrace these new social elites or new economic interest groups is clearly calculated to bolster its one-party domination. Mao could depend on class struggle and mass movements to govern China, and he could count on the support of millions of poor peasants and workers. China was then a backward agricultural economy, with peasants accounting for 80 percent of the total labour force. Today, China is a growing industrial economy, with peasants constituting less than 50 percent of the labour force and many of them not even full-time farmers.

Specifically, the party leadership simply cannot rule China today by mass political mobilization as Mao once did, since the party's original power base has fast eroded. China is rapidly developing into a modern society, with 130 million hand-phones and close to 30 million Internet users. The economy is increasingly integrated with international capitalism on account of China's growing foreign trade, foreign investment and foreign tourism. The populace is also becoming increasingly literate, especially in urban areas.

Furthermore, state governance in China is not yet highly institutionalized, and the rule of law not firmly rooted. For the party effectively to rule such a vast and diverse country without sound democratic foundations, it is all the more crucial for the party leadership to build up a broad social consensus and a coalition of various interests. Clearly, the party cannot exclude the 'outstanding elements' of society from the private sector. For China's emerging political order to remain viable, the party has to be socially more broad-based.

However, the party will have to bear some long-term costs for admitting capitalists and professionals. Leftist critics have warned that the recruitment of the bourgeoisie into the party will inevitably create more corruption in the party, making it easier for the 'money for power' phenomenon to take place. Some critics have even suggested that capitalists may eventually take over the party's leadership.[56]

This is actually already happening in many party branches in the rural areas where businessmen are reported to have used their financial power to manipulate local elections or simply take over local party branches. Suffice it to say that with capitalists inside the party, they will certainly act as potential catalysts to quicken the transformation of the party. Judging by the way Chinese society is evolving, there is a real possibility that the party, in admitting capitalists, has also let in the Trojan horse.

This top-down transformation is not without any political risks. The most serious challenge for the CCP is to determine whose interests it should represent. During Mao Zedong's time, the CCP was genuinely a revolutionary party with its members drawn overwhelmingly from workers and peasants, who constituted 83 percent of the total membership in 1956. But this figure dropped to 52 percent in 1994.[57] After his return to power, Deng started what may be called a 'technocratic movement,' replacing revolutionary cadres in party leadership positions with technocrats, with an essential proportion increasingly coming from the non-state sector.[58] When the party associates itself with capitalists, workers and farmers tend to feel alienated. Scholars have found that SOE workers and rural farmers are rapidly becoming the two biggest losers of capitalistic development.[59] Rapidly growing new leftists are fearful that the party might favour these new entrepreneur-members at the expense of its traditional clients, i.e., workers and farmers. While in the past the party protected the workers, the present may see the party colluding with the entrepreneur to clamp down on the workers. They argue that being wealthier and wielding greater influence, these capitalists would exert an unhealthy bias in the formulation of party policies. Worse, the close links between the CCP and the capitalists would breed new types of cronyism and corruption. New leftists thus have called on workers and farmers with democratic mechanisms to articulate their interests.

CAN 'VOICE' MECHANISMS BE ESTABLISHED?

So, the key question is: What choices do the party-state face in transforming itself into a democratic mechanism? This question can be answered in different ways, but in terms of the representation of class interests, three options can be identified.

MULTI-PARTY SYSTEM

This is the alternative that most scholars have called for. It has been argued that democracy means a multi-party system. Without political competition among parties, there will be no democracy. For the CCP, this choice is to have parties outside the party (*dangwai youdang*). Demands for establishing opposition parties were there and became apparent towards the end of the 1990s, as exemplified by the attempt of Chinese pro-democracy activists to organize an opposition party. In a few months of 1998, the preparatory committees of China's Democracy Party were established in 23 out of China's 31 provinces and major cities. Applications to register the new party were made in 14 provinces and cities.[60]

The unfolding of this event also shows that different opinions existed among CCP leaders regarding opposition parties. A multi-party system undoubtedly is ideal, but realistically speaking, it is less likely. Except for dissidents inside and outside China, the majority of the population are not demanding a multi-party system. Democratization characterized by the emergence of a multi-party system in Russia, Taiwan and Indonesia has not enabled the regimes there to improve people's living standards. Instead, social decay and economic chaos have become prevalent there. The majority is more likely to choose other alternatives, if they exist. Furthermore, the party-state favours a top-down approach. The leadership is intolerant of direct political challenges mounted by social groups, although attempts have been made to accommodate newly rising social groups. To a great degree, democracy is not an option decided by social groups.

FACTIONAL POLITICS WITHIN THE PARTY

More feasible than a multi-party system is the option to legitimize and institutionalize factions within the party (*dangnei youpai*). Like elsewhere, factions existed within the CCP. Even under Maoist coercive rule, factional struggles never disappeared among top leaders. Certainly, under Mao, factions were unlikely to be institutionalized. Since the passing of the Deng-centred generation leadership, factional politics has been institutionalized to some degree and many organization-based factions have been formed, such as the party, the National People's Congress and the State Council. Other factions have also co-existed such as the Shanghai Clique, the Qinghua Clique (those who graduated from Qinghua University), the *Tuanpai* (officials related to the Communist Youth League), the *Taizidang* (the princelings), and so forth. These factions have their own interests and identity, their own ways for interest articulation.

All these factions will not help in establishing 'voice' mechanisms for different social groups. To materialize interest articulation, the leadership has, first, to legalize factional politics, and second, to address class interests. Without the legitimization of factional politics, factional competition can only be engaged informally. The legitimization and institutionalization of factions help make the political process transparent. Social classes therefore will be able to identify their interests with certain factions. Certainly, more important is that the party has to allow different factions to represent the interests of different social classes. Organization-based factions only represent the interests of these organizations, not those of the social classes. Once factions are legitimized, these factions will appeal to different social classes in their competition for political power. Power competition will further push the party to establish inter-party democratic mechanisms since without such mechanisms, the party will fall apart. While factions enable the party to represent different social interests, inter-party democracy enables the party to remain united.

REFORMING THE EXISTING SYSTEM

The most feasible but less effective option in representing different social interests is to reform the existing political system. The Chinese political system is not without any advantages. The problem is that the leadership never considers the issue of interest representation. Many mechanisms are actually available for interest representation. Among others, three reforms have to be made. First, the People's Congress is the most feasible mechanism for different social classes to articulate their interests. To achieve this goal, reforms have to be introduced to transform the People's Congress into a real institution for people's representatives. Needless to say, people's representatives have to be selected and elected by people.[61]

Second, the People's Consultative Conference (PCC) system has to be re-organized and indeed re-politicized. Before the People's Congress was established in 1954, the PCC played an important political role in representing the interests of different political parties and functional groups. China did not have a multi-party system after 1949. The PCC, instead of political parties, played the role of interest articulation and integration. This model used to inspire the first Indonesian President Sukarno in designing Indonesia's political system. In order to avoid political chaos and instability caused by intensive competition among enormous parties, Indonesia established GOLKAR (functional groups) for interest articulation and representation.[62] In China, after 1954, the PCC was sidelined. Even after the reform began, the PCC is still an institution for retired government officials and social elites. Today, the PCC is only a forum for these representatives: it has the right to discuss the issues, but no right to vote. To a great degree, it is a political organization without any political significance. To revive the PCC, it has to be granted the right to vote. Furthermore, it has to go back to its previous role of representing different functional groups (social interests). Its relationship with the People's Congress has also to be sorted out.

Third, at the next level, civil society and social organizations have to adjust their functions. Throughout the reform period, social groups have mushroomed.[63] But at present, all those social organizations are not able to aggregate and articulate social interests, even their own interests. The development of social organizations has been extremely uneven. There are more economic and social organizations are than political ones, and more urban organizations than rural ones. Furthermore, all these social organizations are highly dependent on the party-state. To empower them to articulate social interests, the party-state has to, first, grant them a greater degree of autonomy, and second, allow them to form their own class identity.

CONCLUSION

Interest representation requires a systematic transformation of the CCP-dominated Chinese political system. The CCP has claimed that it would represent the interests of the majority of people. This is easier said than done. Moreover, interest representation requires institutions for interest aggregation and articulation, and aggregating and articulating diverse social interests requires political participation. In the long haul, democratization appears to be the only option for the CCP to achieve interest representation and build long-term stability.

The party leadership may genuinely believe that it is doing what it takes to strengthen the party-state by broadening its social base. As the party metamorphosizes, there is still the nagging question of whether it is prepared to democratize itself. No precedent exists to guide the CCP through such unchartered waters and the risks of failure are enormous. If the party falters, the breakup of the world's most populous nation is a possibility. While Jiang may have taken a courageous step forward, the onus is on Hu Jintao and other leaders to see the democratization process through. The jury is still out on whether the CCP will succeed in this endeavour.

ENDNOTES

1   Jiang Zemin, 'Jiang Zemin zai qingzhu Zhongguo gongchandang chengli bashi zhounian dahui shang de jianghua' [Jiang Zemin's Speech at the Conference Celebrating the 80th Anniversary of the Chinese Communist Party, 1 July 2001), *Renmin ribao* [People's Daily], 2 July 2001. Also 'Entrepreneurs from Non-Public Sector Hail Jiang's Speech,' *Beijing Review*, 9 August 2001.

2   *Ming pao*, 23 July 2001.

3   Lin Yanzhi, 'Gongchandang yao lingdao he jiayu xin zichan jieji' [The CCP Must Lead and Control the New Bourgeoisie], *Zhengli de zhuiqiu* [The Seeking of Truth], no. 5, (2001), pp. 2-11.

4   Zhang Dejiang, 'Yao mingque siying qiyezhu buneng rudang' [To Make Clear that Private Entrepreneurs Cannot Join the Party], *Zhengli de zhuiqiu*, no. 5. (2001), p. 28. Zhang's original paper was published in *Dang de jianshe* [Party Constructing], no. 4, (2000).

5   'Showdown of Ideologies,' *South China Morning Post*, 15 August 2001; and 'Party Closes Leftist Journal that Opposed Jiang,' *South China Morning Post*, 14 August 2001.

6   'Dissenting Leftist Websites Taken off from Internet,' *South China Morning Post*, 3 September 2001).

7   'Jiang urged the armed forces to thoroughly understand the July 1 Speech,' *Ming pao*, 3 September 2001.

8   This paper focuses primarily on Hirschman's definition, see Albert O. Hirschman, *The Passions and the Interests: Political Arguments for Capitalism before its Triumph* (Princeton, NJ: Princeton University Press, 1977); and Albert O.Hirschman, 'The Concept of Interest: from Euphemism to Tautology' and 'Rival Views of Market Society,' in Albert O. Hirschman, *Rival Views of Market Society and Other Recent Essays* (Cambridge, MA: Harvard University Press, 1992), pp. 35-55, 105-41.

9   Hirschman, 'The Concept of Interest,' p. 35.

10   *Ibid.*, p. 43.

11   *Ibid.*, p. 36.

12   *Ibid.*, p. 42.

13   *Ibid.*, p. 43.

14   Cited in Hirschman, *Rival Views of Market Society and Other Recent Essays*, p. 107. For a discussion of Montesquieu's ideas, also see Stephen Rosow, 'Commerce, Power and Justice: Montesquieu on International Politics,' *Review of Politics*, vol. 46, no. 3, (1984), pp. 346-67.

15   Hirschman, *The Passions and the Interests*, p. 87.

16   *Ibid.*, pp. 89-93.

17   Adam Smith, *Wealth of Nations* (Oxford: Oxford University Press, 1976), pp. 443, 456.

18   Similar ideas are also expressed by Milton Friedman, *Capitalism and Freedom* (Chicago: University of Chicago Press, 1982).

19   Franz Schurmann, *Ideology and Organization in Communist China* (Berkeley, CA: University of California Press, 1968), p. 1.

20   For example, Tang Tsou, *The Cultural Revolution and Post-Mao Reforms: A Historical Perspective* (Chicago: The University of Chicago Press, 1986).

21   Tiejun Cheng and Mark Selden, 'The Construction of Spatial Hierarchies: China's Hukou and Danwei System,' in Timothy Cheek and Tony Saich (eds.), *New Perspectives on State Socialism in China* (Armonk, NY: M. E. Sharpe, 1977), pp. 23-50.

22   All organizations in urban China where people worked such as enterprises, retail shops, hospitals, schools, civil associations, government organs were called '*danwei.*' Roughly speaking, three types of *danwei* can be identified: 1) enterprise units, including all units engaged in making profit; 2) non-profit units, including scientific, educational, professional, cultural, athletic and healthcare organizations; and 3) administrative units or governmental organs. For a discussion of the *danwei* system, see Xiaobo Lü and Elizabeth J. Perry (eds.), *Danwei: The Changing Chinese Workplace in Historical and Comparative Perspective* (Armond, NY: M. E. Sharpe, 1997), pp. 3-7.

23   For a discussion of 'conscription society,' see Gregory J. Kasza, *The Conscription Society: Administered Mass Organization* (New Haven, CT: Yale University Press, 1995).

24   Vivienne Shue, 'State Power and Social Organization in China,' in Joel S. Migdal, Atul Kohli and Vivienne Shue (eds.), *State Power and Social Forces: Domination and Transformation in the Third World* (New York, NY: Cambridge University Press, 1994), pp. 65-88.

25   On 18 December 1978, the Chinese Communist Party held the historic Third Plenum of the 11th Party Congress in Beijing. The Third Plenum shifted the party's priority from Maoist class struggle to economic modernization. Officially, the Third Plenum marks the beginning of China's market-style economic reform and the open-door policy.

26   For a discussion of China's economic reform and development in the 1980s, see Barry Naughton, *Growing out of the Plan: Chinese Economic Reform 1978-1993* (New York: Cambridge University Press, 1996).

27   Wang Gungwu, *The Chinese Way: China's Position in International Relations* (Oslo: Scandinavian University Press, 1995).

28   For a discussion of different perceptions on socialism and capitalism, see Yan Sun, *The Chinese Reassessment of Socialism, 1976-1992* (Princeton, NJ: Princeton University Press, 1995).

29   Wang Gungwu discussed why the leadership used the term 'socialist market economy' rather than capitalism, see Wang, *The Chinese Way*, part one.

30   Yan Sun, *The Chinese Reassessment of Socialism, 1976-1992*.

31   Deng Xiaoping, 'Zai Wuchang, Shenzhen, Zhuhai, Shanghai dengdi de tanhua yaodian,' [Main Points in the Speeches Made in Wuchang, Shenzhen, Zhuhai, and Shanghai,' 18 January-21 February 1992], in Deng, *Deng Xiaoping wenxuan* [Selected Works of Deng Xiaoping], vol. 3 (Beijing: Renmin chubanshe, 1993), p. 379.

32   Hirschman, *Shifting Involvements: Private Interest and Public Action* (Princeton, NJ: Princeton University Press, 1982).

33   This is not the place for a full discussion of this rising interest-based social order. But it is worth noting that terms associated with economic interests such as 'interest' (or 'interests') and 'class' have been increasingly used by scholars in China to analyse the Chinese society since Deng's *Nanxun*. See, Zhu Guanglei et al. (eds.), *Dangdai Zhongguo shehui ge jieceng fenxi* [An Analysis of Social Strata in Contemporary China] (Tianjin: Tianjin renmin chubanshe, 1998); Liang Xiaosheng, *Zhongguo shehui ge jieceng fenxi* [An Analysis of Social Strata in China] (Beijing: Jingji ribao chubanshe, 1998); Lu Xueyi and Jing Tiankuai (eds.), *Zhuanxing zhong de Zhongguo shehui* [Chinese Society in Transition], (Ha'erbin: Heilongjiang renmin chubanshe, 1994); Qin Shaoxiang and Jia Ting, *Shehui xin qunti tanmi: Zhongguo siqing qiyezhu jieceng* [A Study of A New Social Group: China's Private Enterprise Class] (Beijing: Zhongguo fazhan chubanshe, 1993).

34   For discussions of increasing autonomy of social groups, see Wang Ying, et al. (eds.), *Shehui zhongjian ceng: gaige yu Zhongguo de shetuan zuzhi* [Intermediate Social Strata: the Reform and Social Groups in China] (Beijing: Zhongguo fazhan chubanshe, 1993); Deborah S. Davis et al. (eds.), *Urban Spaces in Contemporary China: the Potential for Autonomy and Community in post-Mao China* (Washington, DC: Woodrow Wilson Center Press /Cambridge and New York: Cambridge University Press, 1995); Timothy Brook and B. Michael Frolic (eds.), *Civil Society in China* (Armonk, NY: M. E. Sharpe, 1997); Gordon White, Jude Howell and Shang Xiaoyuan, *In Search of Civil Society: Market Reform and Social Change in Contemporary China* (Oxford: Oxford University Press, 1996).

35   Li Qiang, 'Guanyu siyingjingji de ruogan ziliao' [Data on the Private Economy], *Zhengli de zhuiqiu* no. 5 (2001), pp. 18-19.

36   *Ibid.*, p. 19.

37   Hu Angang (ed.), *Zhongguo tiaozhan fubai* [China: Fighting against Corruption], (Hangzhou: Zhejiang renmin chubanshe, 2001), p. 49.

38   Hein Mallee, 'China's Household Registration System under Reform,' in Alan Hunter and Kim-kwong Chan (eds.), *Protestantism in Contemporary China* (Cambridge: Cambridge University Press, 1993), pp. 10-16.

39   For a description, see John Wong, 'The *Xia Hai* Phenomenon in China,' *Ritsumeikan Journal of International Relations and Area Studies*, vol. 6 (March 1994), pp. 1-10.

40   Li Qiang, 'Guanyu siyingjingji de ruogan ziliao,' p. 23.

41   Cited in *ibid.*, pp. 23-24.

42   'Major Corruption Cases,' *Beijing Review*, 22 May 2000, p. 14.

43   *Renmin ribao*, 15 September 2000, p. 1.

44   Zou Keyuan, 'Why China's Rampant Corruption Cannot be Checked by Laws Alone,' *EAI Background Brief No. 74*, East Asian Institute, National University of Singapore, (2 November 2000).

45   *China Daily*, 6 March 2000.

46   Børge Bakken, 'State Control and Social Control in China,' in Kjeld Erik Brødsgaard and Susan Young (eds.), *State Capacity in Japan, Taiwan, China and Vietnam* (Oxford: Oxford University Press, 2000), pp. 185-202.

47   The annual survey reports are organized by the Institute of Sociology of the Chinese Academy of Social Sciences; see its annual report, Ru Xin et al. (eds.), *Shehui lanpishu: Zhongguo shehui xingshi fenxi yu yuce* [Social Bluebook: Analysis and Forecast of Social Situation in China], various issues. (Beijing: Shehui kexue wenxian chubanshe).

48   Wang Chunguang, '1997-1998 nian: Zhongguo shehui wending zhuangkuang de diaocha' [A Survey on Social Stability in 1997-1998], in Ru Xin et al. (eds.), *Shehui lanpishu 1998* [Social Bluebook 1998] (Beijing: Shehui kexue wenxian chubanshe, 1998), p. 127.

49   Cited in Li Qiang, 'Guanyu siyingjingji,' p. 27.

50   *Ibid.*, p. 26.

51   Jiang Nanyang, 'Lun siying qiyezhu de zhengzhi cenyu' [Political Participation by the Owners of Private Businesses], in Zhang Houyi and Ming Zhili (eds.), *Zhongguo siying qiye fazhan baogao 1978-1998* [A Report of the Development of Private Enterprises in China, 1978-1998] (Beijing: Shehui kexue wenxuan chubanshe, 1999), pp. 103-17.

52   Keyuan Zou and Yongnian Zheng, 'China's Third Constitutional Amendment: an Assessment,' in A. J. De Roo and R. W. Jagtenberg (eds.), *Yearbook Law and Legal Practice in East Asia*, vol. 4, 1999 (The Hague, London and Boston: Kluwer Law International, 2000), pp. 29-42.

53   John Pomfret, 'Why "Beijing Spring" Cooled: Dissidents Overstepped,' *International Herald Tribune*, 4 January 1999, pp. 1, 7.

54 For a discussion of this constitutional amendment, see Zou and Zheng, 'China's Third Constitutional Amendment: An Assessment.'

55 The Xinhua News Agency, 'Jiang Zemin tongzhi zai quanguo dangxiao gongzuo huiyi shang de jianghua,' 9 June 2000 [Comrade Jiang Zemin's Talk in National Party Schools Working Conference, 9 June 2000], *Renmin ribao*, 17 July 2000.

56 Lin Yanzhi, 'Gongchandang yao lingdao he jiayu xin zichan jieji.'

57 Ignatius Wibowo, 'Party Recruitment and the Future of the Chinese Communist Party,' *EAI Background Brief No. 101*, East Asian Institute, National University of Singapore, 7 September 2001.

58 Hong Yung Lee, *From Revolutionary Cadres to Party Technocrats in Socialist China* (Berkeley: University of California Press, 1991); and Cheng Li and David Bachman, 'Localism, Elitism, and Immobilism: Elite Formation and Social Change in Post-Mao China,' *World Politics*, vol. 42, no. 1, (October 1989), pp. 64-94.

59 Shaoguang Wang, 'The Social and Political Implications of China's WTO Membership,' *Journal of Contemporary China*, vol. 9, no. 25, (2000), p. 380.

60 John Pomfret, 'Why "Beijing Spring" Cooled.'

61 For some recent discussions of China's People's Congress system, see Kevin O'Brien, 'Chinese People's Congresses and Legislative Embeddedness: Understanding Early Organizational Development,' *Comparative Political Studies*, vol. 27, no. 4, (1994), pp. 80-107; O'Brien, 'Institutionalizing Chinese Legislatures: Trade-offs between Autonomy and Capacity,' *Legislative Studies Quarterly*, vol. 23, no. 1, (1998), pp. 91-108; and Murray Scot Tanner, *The Politics of Lawmaking in Post-Mao China: Institutions, Processes and Democratic Perspectives* (New York: Oxford University Press, 1998).

62 David Reeve, *GOLKAR of Indonesia: An Alternative to the Party System* (Singapore: Oxford University Press, 1985). It is worthwhile to note that the fall of the GOLKAR was not because of its institutional design, but because of the lack of internal democracy within the organization.

63 For example, Gordon White, Jude Howell and Shang Xiaoyuan, *In Search of Civil Society*.

Editors and Contributors

Editors

Kjeld Erik BRØDSGAARD, Professor of International Business in Asia/China and Director of the Asia Research Centre Copenhagen Business School

ZHENG Yongnian, Senior Research Fellow, East Asian Institute, National University of Singapore

Contributors

Børge BAKKEN, Fellow, Division of Pacific and Asian History, Research School of Pacific and Asian Studies, The Australian National University

CHAO Chien-min, Professor, The Sun Yat-sen Graduate Institute for Social Sciences and Humanities, National Chengchi University, Taiwan

Maria EDIN, Postdoctoral Fellow, Department of Political Science, Swedish School of Advanced Asia Pacific Studies (SSAAPS), Uppsala University

Heike HOLBIG, Research Fellow, Institute of Asian Affairs, Hamburg, Germany

Kazuko KOJIMA, Assistant Professor, College of International Studies, University of Tsukuba, Japan

Ryosei KOKUBUN, Director of Center for Area Studies and Professor of Political Science Department, Keio University, Tokyo, Japan

Pierre F. LANDRY, Assistant Professor of Political Science, Yale University and Research Fellow, Research Center for the Study of Contemporary China, Peking University

David SHAMBAUGH, Professor of Political Science and International Affairs and Director of the China Policy Program, George Washington University

Stig THØGERSEN, Associate Professor of Language and Society, East Asian Department, Institute of History and Area Studies, University of Aarhus

Index

Aabenhus, Ole, 216
Academy of Social Sciences, 33
ACFIC. *See* All-China Federation of
  Industry and Commerce
Adelman, Jonathan, 111
agriculture, cadres involvement in, 207–8, 210
Alagappa, Muthiah, 111, 114
Alexander, Norman C, 55
All-China Federation of Industry and
  Commerce, 248, 258, 265, 267
'Two think-ofs' *(liang si)* campaign, 255
All-China Federation of Trade Unions, 40
Almanac of Private Economy in China 2000, 248
Alpermann, Bjorn, 215–16
Anagnost, Ann, 215
Anhui province, 62, 155, 248, 250
Anti-Rightist Movement, 290
Asian civil-military relations, 109

Bachman, David, 91, 169, 301
Bakken, Børge, 6–8, 13, 51, 55, 215, 254–5,
  267–68, 300
Bangladesh, civil-military relations, 109
Banqiao township, 199
Barmé, Geremie, 55–56
Barnett, A Doak, 20, 87
Beijing city, 219, 222, 225, 236
Beijing province, 62, 67, 82–3, 87, 99, 119,
  155, 219, 222, 225, 236
Benxi, 220
Bernstein, Thomas P, 190
biaoyan, 46
Bickford, Thomas, 112–13
Blecher, M, 165, 168
Blum, Samantha, 113
Bo, Zhiyue, 142, 168, 186, 189, 191
Bo Xilai, 151
Bo Yibo, 42
Bramall, Chris, 53
Bringing the State Back In, 1
Brødsgaard, Kjeld Erik, 6, 8, 11, 21, 87–90,
  168, 179, 189, 265, 300
Brook, Timothy, 299
Bullard, Monte, 111
Burns, John P, 87, 89–90, 168, 188–89

Cabestan, Jean-Pierre, 90, 188
Canon, David T, 138
Cao Jinqing, 192–3, 197, 209, 213, 215–16
capitalism
  advocated by intellectuals, 275

Chinese culture and, 275
  de-ideologization of, 276
  entrepreneur members of
    People's Congress, 186
  entrepreneurs admitted to party,
    17, 34, 40, 196–7, 239–40,
    250–62, 269–70, 273, 287,
    291–3
  four little dragons, 274–5
  ideological safeguards against, 251
  justified by "Three
    Representations," 15–16
  "market socialism," 27
  Marxism-Leninism and, 251–2
  *minying keji qiye de chuangye
    renyuan he jishu renyuan*, 33
  PLA statement on western
    armies, 108
  selling of party membership, 36
  view of old cadres, 197, 291
Carothers, Thomas, 17–18, 21
CASS. *See* Chinese Academy of Social
  Sciences
CCP. *See* Chinese Communist Party
Central Committee
  banning of entrepreneurs, 249, 251
  educational level, 70, 89
  Organization Department, 74–7, 84–7
cadre development programme, 80–2
  department heads 1921-2002
    [table], 75
  nomenklatura system, 67, 73–4,
    81, 89, 142, 152, 177,
    179–80, 189
  zuzhibu, 180
  PLA reports to, 107
  technocracy, 58
Central School of Administration, 81
Chan, Anita, 53
Chan Che-Po, 177, 188
Chan Kim-kwong, 300
Chan Wai-Yin, 189
Chang Chun-hsiang, 138
Changchun, 165
Chao Chien-Min, 9, 138
charisma
  becoming nostalgia, 30–1
  leaders, 23
  rationalization of, 41
  routinization of, 30
  traditionalization of, 41

resumption of, 17, 57, 74, 86
place in China studies, 4–6
pressure from private sector,
    286–8
ranking of targets, 183–4
recruitment
intellectuals, 197
"outstanding elements" *(youxiu
    fenzi)*, 196, 200, 239, 249,
    257, 293
relations with People's Liberation
    Army, 9, 92–114
relations with the state, 9, 116, 125, 134
renmin minzhu zhuanzheng, 26
role in rural areas, 224
role in *shequ* construction, 224–35
seen as outdated, 5
'separating party from
    government,' 103
shequ party organizations, 225–34
education of members, 229
sixiang zhengzhi juewu, 37
social democratic elements, 291
socioeconomic transformation
    and party governance, 6–16
Stalinist tradition, 134
statute, 248–9
strategic guidance rather than
    direct involvement, 175
street party organizations, 225, 228
technocracy, 58, 177, 198
United Front Department, 265
'vanguard of the working class,'
    26, 196, 240, 254
zhongyang, 165
zuzhi bumen, 143
zuzhi renshi xitong, 143
See also Central Committee;
    Cultural Revolution; Deng
    Xiaoping; economic
    reforms; Great Leap
    Forward; Hu Jintao-Wen
    Jiabao; Hua Guofeng; Jiang
    Zemin; Mao Zedong; party
    cadres; Party Congresses;
    party ideology; party
    leaders; party membership;
    Politburo; propaganda;
    Qiushi; Zhao Ziyang
Chinese Federation of Unions, 123
Chinese Federation of Women, 123
Chinese People's Political Consultative
    Conference, 236
    ninth 1998, 287
Chinese Urban Development Research
    Council, 145, 166

Chinese Women's Federation, 119–20
Chongqing province, 124, 128, 137, 219
Chonqing, 165
Chonqing city, 219, 222
Christiansen, Flemming, 190
Chu Junhong, 168
cities. *See* municipalities
class differences, 35
CMC. *See* Central Military Commission
    under People's Republic of China
Cohen, Myron, 205, 215
collective enterprises, 198
    leasing of, 244
Colton, Timothy, 111–12, 138
communist parties
Chinese (*See* Chinese Communist Party)
    Eastern European, 5, 7, 110,
        197, 276, 280
    Soviet, 5, 7, 24, 110, 197, 257,
        276, 280
Communist Youth League, 250, 295
community development programme. *See
    shequ*
Company Law, 123
Confucian social order, 97
'conscription society,' 274, 298
Contract Law, 123
corruption
    accompanied by growth in
        crime, 284
    anti-corruption measures, 284
cadre tenure, 159–60
    during economic reforms, 115, 136
    gongzuo pingyi, 129
    Jiang Zemin's awareness of, 115
    'money politics,' 256
    party position, 49, 166
    private sector, 255–6, 283–4
    Qiushi articles, 49–50, 56
    research, 216
    statistics, 284
    "Three Representations," 32–3, 49
    township officials, 203
    widespread, 208
Corruption Perceptions Index of
    Transparency International 2000, 284
CPC. *See* Chinese Communist Party
CPPCC. *See* Chinese People's Political
    Consultative Conference
Crane, George, 168
cremation, 183
CUDRC. *See* Chinese Urban Development
    Research Council
Cui, Ruchun, 169
Cui, Shixin, 168
Cultural Revolution, 290

Liu Junde, 165, 169
Liu Shaoqi, 65
Liu Zheng, 138
Lo, Carlos Wing-Hung, 188
local government, 141–74, 245
Local People's Congress
    meetings, 127
    power of, 133–4
    power of directors, 126
Local People's Congress Standing
    Committees, 126
Loewenberg, Gerhard, 138
Long, J Scott, 169
Lowenthal, Abraham F, 111
LPC. *See* Local People's Congress
Lu Feng, 76
Lu-Hsun Hung, 112
Lu Xueyi, 52, 265–67, 299
Luo Suying, 56

Ma Shu-Yun, 189
MacFarquhar, Roderick, 188
Machiavelli, 46, 56
Mainwaring, Scott, 20
Mallee, Hein, 300
Manion, Melanie, 87, 169, 189
Manoharan, Thiagarajan, 91
Mansfeldova, Denka, 20
Mao Minghua, 236
Mao Zedong, 112
    charisma, 23
    communes, 203
    death, 290
    dependent upon class struggle, 292
    factions under, 295
    genuinely revolutionary party
    under, 293
    hall of fame, 7, 41
    headed Organization
    Department, 74
    Little Red Book, 41
    'Political power grows out of the
        barrel of a gun!', 99
    sixiang, 41
    stressed redness (ideology), 84
    "the party controls the gun," 92–3
    totalitarian state power, 273–4
    warnings against de-Maofication, 42
Mao Zedong Thought, 41
    party constitution, 15
    study of, 229
Markowski, Radoslaw, 20
Marx, Karl, 35, 51
Marxism-Leninism
    Deng Xiaoping, 251–2
    future for, 132

Jiang Zemin, 195
    party constitution, 15
    party-state dictatorship, 125
    revision of basic labour theory,
        33–4, 35–6
    role of army, 96
    spin-doctoring, 35
    still relevant to China, 7
    study of, 229
    theory of party building, 31–2
materialism, 7
mayors *(shizhang)*
    appointed by provinces, 142,
        144, 147, 152
    average tenure [table], 150
    career opportunities, 144–7
    control by party, 164–5, 166
    characteristics, 147–9, 151, 162–4
    [tables], 148–9
    education [table], 148
    female [table], 162
    minority [table], 163
    overwhelmingly *Han*, 147
    political fate
    appointment to concurrent
    posts, 185–6
    effect of municipal performance,
        143, 158–9, 185
    [table], 153, 160
    promotion, 150–64
    effect of age [table], 163
    effect of individual
    characteristics, 161–4
    effects of gender and ethnicity,
        161–2
    ordered probability estimates
    [table], 155–8
    by province [table], 154
    provincial differences, 154–5
    regional disparities, 163
McCormick, Barret L, 138
media
    Asiaweek, 197
    China aktuell, 91
    Fazhi gongzuo bao, 123
    leftist journals suspended, 42, 270
    People's Daily, 37, 40, 49
    Rongcheng gongzuo tongxun, 206,
        209–11, 215
    Zhenli de zhuiqiu [Seeking
        Truth], 42, 270
    Zhonggongdangshi yanjiu, 257, 260
    Zhongguo tongji nianjian, 265
    Zhongliu [The Central Pillar],
        42, 270
    See also Qiushi; Xinhua reports

Tong, James, 165, 170
tourism, 292
trade unions, 40, 259–60
Travers, Tony, 188
triads, 256
Tuanpai, 295
Tucker, Robert C, 140

unemployment, 35, 40, 225, 233, 270
Unger, Jonathan, 138, 215
United States
 Congress, 115, 118, 120
 as example of capitalism, 275
urban-rural differences, 35, 141–2, 224

Ven, Hans van de, 112
Vietnam, civil-military relations, 109
Vogel, Ezra F, 88
Volges, Ivan, 111

Wade, Robert, 3
Walder, Andrew, 50, 56, 87, 166, 170, 247,
 266–67
Wan Li, 42
Wang, Daohan, 171
Wang, Ling, 171
Wang, Shaoguang, 169–70, 301
Wang, Ting, 189
Wang Chunguang, 300
Wang Enmao, 42
Wang Gungwu, 91, 213, 299
Wang Hanbin, 42
Wang Ruilin, 94
Wang Sibin, 223–4, 237
Wang Xia, 167
Wang Ying, 299
Wang Yumei, 216
Watson, Andrew, 166, 170
Weber, Max, 6, 23, 30, 37, 41, 52
Wei, Y. Dennis, 170
Wei Jianxing, 83
Weiner, Myron, 19
Weng, Byron, 140
West depicted as hostile to China, 32
Whampoa Military Academy, 98
What is to Be Done, 58–9
White, Gordon, 21, 87, 299, 301
White, Lynn, 70, 88–89
Whiting, Susan, 166, 171, 189, 191, 213
Wibowo, Ignatius, 266–67
Winckler, Edwin A, 191
Wittgenstein, [Ludwig], 43
Won Wenzou, 138, 140
Wong, Christine P W, 166, 171
Wong, John, 91, 300

workers
 'basic labourers' *(jichu laodong)*,
 254
 dagong zhi, 34
 exploitation incongruent with
 Marxism, 35–6, 270
 managers *(jingli renyuan)*, 250
 private sector, 242–3
 rural migrants exploited in
 cities, 33–4
 traditional constituents of party,
 269
 vulnerability, 293
 zhigong zhi, 34
Workers' Federation, 119–20
World Trade Organization, 45, 229, 245
WTO. *See* World Trade Organization
Wu Bangguo, 166
Wu Guangzheng, 82
Wu Guoguang, 140
Wu Yi, 166
Wuhan, 165, 221–2
wuzhi wenming, 32

X. L. Ding, 53
Xiamen, 165
Xian, 165
Xi'an, 220, 222
xianshi biaoxian, 37, 43, 48
 situationalist behaviour, 45
Xiaobo Lü, 91, 190–91, 216
Xiaolin Guo, 216
Xiaowei Zang, 89
Xie, Qingkui, 166, 171
Xin Liu, 208–9, 216
Xinhua reports, 32, 52–53, 55–56, 253, 266
Xinjiang province, 154
Xu Jiangrui, 113
Xu Mingyang, 167
Xu Xiaoqing, 161
Xuanfei, 198–204

Yan Huai, 137, 140
Yan Shuhan, 197
Yan Sun, 299
Yang, Dali, 166, 171, 177, 188
Yang Baibing, 42
Yang Guangyu, 216
Yang Shangkun, 99
Yang Shengchun, 140
Yang Zhonghua, 56
Yasheng Huang, 90
Yichang, 229
Yin Fuying, 267–68
You Ji, 111

Other Titles on Politics and International Relations

Damage Control: The Chinese Communist Party in the Jiang Zemin Era
edited by Wang Gungwu and Zheng Yongnian
ISBN 981-210-259-0

Will China Become Democratic?
by Zheng Yongnian
ISBN 981-210-353-8

China and the ASEAN States
by Leo Suryadinata
ISBN 981-210-356-2